Facing An Unequal World

**SAGE STUDIES IN
INTERNATIONAL SOCIOLOGY**

Series Editor Chaime Marcuello Servós (2016– ongoing)
Editor, Departament of Psychology and Sociology,
Zaragoza University, Spain

Facing An Unequal World

Challenges for Global Sociology

Edited by **Raquel Sosa Elízaga**

SSIS SERIES   SAGE STUDIES IN INTERNATIONAL SOCIOLOGY: **64**

Los Angeles I London I New Delhi
Singapore I Washington DC I Melbourne

Los Angeles | London | New Delhi
Singapore | Washington DC | Melbourne

SAGE Publications Ltd
1 Oliver's Yard
55 City Road
London EC1Y 1SP

SAGE Publications Inc.
2455 Teller Road
Thousand Oaks, California 91320

SAGE Publications India Pvt Ltd
B 1/I 1 Mohan Cooperative Industrial Area
Mathura Road
New Delhi 110 044

SAGE Publications Asia-Pacific Pte Ltd
3 Church Street
#10-04 Samsung Hub
Singapore 049483

First published 2018

Library of Congress Control Number: 2017946093

British Library Cataloguing in Publication data

A catalogue record for this book is available from the
British Library

ISBN 978-1-5264-3556-9
ISBN 978-1-5264-3557-6 (pbk)

Editor: Robert Rojek
Editorial assistant: Catriona McMullen
Production editor: Katherine Haw
Copyeditor: Christine Bitten
Proofreader: Lynda Watson
Indexer: Charmian Parkin
Marketing manager: Susheel Gokarakonda
Cover design: Wendy Scott
Typeset by: C&M Digitals (P) Ltd, Chennai, India
Printed in the UK

Contents

About the Editor and Contributors

Raquel Sosa Elízaga, Editor. Born in Mexico City, on the 24th February 1955. Resident in Mexico City. Email: rsosa@unam.mx

Degrees in Sociology, Latin American Studies, and PhD in History, National Autonomous University of Mexico. Full Time Professor at the Center for Latin American Studies of the Faculty of Social and Political Sciences, since January, 1976. Vice President of Program of the International Sociological Association, from 2010 to 2014. Member of its Program Committee from 1998 to 2002; Member of its Executive Committee, from 2006 to 2010. President of the Asociación Latinoamericana de Sociología, from 1985 to 1987, and member of its Council of Ex Presidents, since 2013. Secretary of Social Development and of Culture in the Mexico City Government, from 2000 to 2005, and from 2005 to 2006. Published *Educación y exclusión,* Mexico, Facultad de Ciencias Políticas y Sociales, UNAM, 2017; "Reflexiones sobre la tradición sociológica, los dilemas de nuestro tiempo y el porvenir" en Castañeda, Dávila et al, *El futuro de las ciencias sociales en un entorno globalizado,* México, Facultad de Ciencias Políticas y Sociales, UNAM, 2017; *Hacia la recuperación de la soberanía educativa en América Latina: conciencia crítica y programa.* México, UNAM/CLACSO, 2012; *Pensar con cabeza propia. Educación y pensamiento crítico en América Latina.* Septiembre de 2011. CLACSO, *Cuadernos del pensamiento crítico latinoamericano.* Consejo Latinoamericano de Ciencias Sociales. Número 45, año 4, 10 de diciembre de 2011; Co-authored with Irene Sánchez, *América Latina: los desafíos del pensamiento crítico,* México, Siglo XXI, 2004.

Contributors

Peter Alexander, Professor of Sociology and Director of Centre for Social Change at the University of Johannesburg, South Africa. PhD. in History, London University. Member of the International Sociological Association. Author of *Racism, Resistance and Revolution*, 1987; *Workers, War and the Origins of Apartheid*, 2000; with Luke Sinwell, Thapelo Lekgowa, Botsang Mmope and Bongani Xezwi, *Marikana: A View from the Mountain and a Case to Answer*, 2012; and with Claire Ceruti, Keke Motseke, Mosa Phadi and Kim Wale, *Class in Soweto*, 2013. Editor of, with Rick Halpern, *Racializing Class, Classifying Race*, 2000; and with Marcelle C. Dawson and Meera Ichharam, *Globalisation and New Identities: A View from the Middle*, 2006.

Walden Bello, Professor of Sociology and Public Administration at the University of the Philippines Diliman, as well as Executive Director of Focus on the Global South. PhD in Princeton University. Author of *Dragons in Distress: Asia's Miracle Economies in Crisis*, with Stephanie Rosenfeld, 1990; with Cunningham, Shea and Li, Kheng Po, *A Siamese Tragedy: Development & Disintegration in Modern Thailand,* 1999; with Mittal, Anuradha, *The Future in the Balance: Essays on Globalization and Resistance*, 2001; *Deglobalization Ideas for a New World Economy*, 2001; *The Food Wars*, 2009; *Capitalism's Last Stand?: Deglobalization in the Age of Austerity*, 2013.

Jean-Michel Bonvin, Professor of Sociology at the University of Geneva, Switzerland. PhD in Sociology, La Sorbonne, Paris. Member of ISA. Author of *Investir dans la protection sociale – atouts et limites pour la Suisse / Reformieren durch Investieren? Chancen und Grenzen des Sozialinvestitionsstaats in der Schweiz*, with S. Dahmen, 2017; "Towards a Critical Sociology of Democracy: The Potential of the Capability Approach", in *Critical Sociology*, with F. Laruffa and E. Rosenstein (2017); "The Ambivalence of Social Policies and the Challenge of Human Development". In H.-U. Otto, S. Pantazis, H. Ziegler and A. Potsi (Eds.), *Human Development in Times of Crisis: Renegotiating Social Justice* (2017); "Children's Rights as Evolving Capabilities, Towards a Processual and Contextualised Conception of Social Justice". In *Ethical Perspectives*, with D. Stoecklin (2015); *Facing Trajectories from School to Work – Towards a Capability-Friendly Youth Policy in Europe*, with H.-U. Otto, R. Atzmüller, T. Berthet et al. (2015); Amartya Sen, *Une politique de la liberté*, with N. Farvaque (2008).

José Esteban Castro, Principal Researcher, National Technical and Scientific Council (CONICET), based at the Institute of the Conurbated Area (ICO), National University of General Sarmiento (UNGS), Argentina. Emeritus Professor of Sociology at Newcastle University, United Kingdom. DPhil in Politics, Oxford University. Member of the International Sociological Association. Corresponding Member of the Mexican Academy of Sciences. Author of *Water, Power, and Citizenship. Social Struggle in the Basin of Mexico*, Palgrave-Macmillan, 2006; editor, with L. Heller, of *Water and Sanitation Services: Public Policy and Management* (Spanish and Portuguese), Earthscan-Routledge, 2009; author of *Water and Democracy in Latin America*, State University of Paraiba Press (EDUEPB), Brazil, 2016; editor, with B. Fowler and L. Gomes, *Time, Science, and the Critique of Technological Reason. Essays in Honour of Hermínio Martins*, Palgrave, 2018. Co-ordinator of the WATERLAT-GOBACIT Network (www.waterlat.org).

Ana Esther Ceceña, Professor at the National Autonomous University of Mexico. PhD in International Economic Relations. Director of the Latinoamerican Geopolitical Observatory. Author of: *De los saberes de la emancipación y de la dominación; Derivas del mundo en el que caben todos los mundos; Los desafíos de las emancipaciones en un contexto militarizado; Hegemonías y emancipaciones en el Siglo XXI; Posneoliberalism and its bifurcations; On the Complex Relation Between Knowledges and Emancipations; Las corporaciones y el sistema-mundo; Chevron. Paradigma de la catástrofe civilizatoria.*

Sarah El Jamal, holds an MA in Middle Eastern Studies and BA in Economics from the American University of Beirut (AUB). Her research interests include poverty measurement and reduction, social protection and policy, labor justice, and taxation justice. She is currently a Program Coordinator and Researcher at the Issam Fares Institute for Public Policy and International Affairs at the AUB. Her most recent publication is *Poverty, Inequality, and Social Protection in Lebanon*, a research report written and published in partnership with Oxfam.

Sari Hanafi, Professor of Sociology at the American University of Beirut. PhD in Sociology from the Ecole des Hautes Etudes en Sciences

Sociales-Paris. Vice President for National Associations at the ISA Executive Committee. Author of: *The Power of Inclusive Exclusion: Anatomy of Israeli Rule in The Occupied Palestinian Territories*, 2009; *The Emergence of a Palestinian Globalized Elite: Donors, International Organizations and Local NGOs*, 2005; and *UNRWA and Palestinian Refugees: From Relief and Works to Human Development* (Edited with L. Takkenberg and L. Hilal), 2009. His last book is *Knowledge Production in the Arab World: The Impossible Promise* (with R. Arvanitis).

Paulo Henrique Martins, Professor at the Universidade Federal de Pernambuco, Brasil. PhD in Sociology, Université La Sorbonne. Former President of Asociación Latinoamericana de Sociología. Member of ISA. Co-author of *Sociologia da Dádiva. Sociologias* 2014; "Controversias y Concurrencias Latinoamericanas" – Revista da ALAS, 2014; "Bien Vivir, uma metáfora que libera a experiência sensível dos Direitos Coletivos na Saúde" en *Revista Latinoamericana de Estudios sobre Cuerpos, Emociones y Sociedad*, 2014; co-author of "Durkheim, Mauss e a atualidade da escola sociológica francesa" en *Sociologias*, 2013; "Revisitando os fundamentos das modernidades periféricas: dádiva, mercado e pacto" en *Revista Brasileira de Sociologia*, 2013.

Hsin-Huang Michael Hsiao, Distinguished Research Fellow at Institute of Sociology, Academia Sinica, Taiwan; Professor of Sociology in National Taiwan University and National Sun Yat-Sen University; and Chair Professor of Hakka Studies, National Central University. PhD Sociology, State University of New York at Buffalo. Member of International Sociological Association. Publications: *Urban Climate Issues and Governance in Taiwan* (in Chinese, co-editor, National Taiwan University Press, 2017); *Citizens, Civil Society and Heritage-Making in Asia* (in English, co-editor, ISEAS/ IOS, Academia Sinica/ IIAS, 2017); *The Lessons of Taiwan's Local Environment* (in Chinese, editor, Chu-Liu Publications, 2015); *Globalization and New Intra-Urban Dynamics in Asian Cities* (in English, co-editor, National Taiwan University Press, 2014).

Keng-Ming Hsu, Associate Professor at the department of Social and Public Affairs, University of Taipei, Taiwan. PhD in Public Administration, National Cheng Chi University. Publications: "The Preliminary Study of Constructing the Indicators of City Climate Risk Governance", *Thought and Words*, 52(4), 2014; with Hsin-Huang Michael Hsiao, "Social Indicators of Climate-Related Risk in Taiwan", *City and Planning*, 42(1), 2015; with Chi, Chun-Chieh, and Hsin-Huang Michael Hsiao, "Climate Change, Intergenerational Justice, and Sustainability: Concept, Indicators, and Policy, Taiwan Economic Forecast and Policy", *Taiwan Economic Forecast and Policy*, 46(2), 2016.

Chih-Jou Jay Chen, Research Fellow at the Institute of Sociology at Academia Sinica, a jointly appointed Professor at National Tsing-Hua University, and an adjunct Professor at National Taiwan University. PhD in Sociology from Duke University. President of Taiwanese Sociological Association (2018–19). Member of the International Sociological Association. Author of *Transforming Rural China: How Local Institutions Shape Property Rights in China* (Routledge, 2004), and the co-editor of *Social Capital and its Institutional Contingency: A Study of the United States, China and Taiwan* (Routledge, 2013).

Harold Kerbo, Professor of Sociology, Cal Poly University, Oklahoma. PhD Virginia Polytechnic Institute and State University (1975). Member of the American Sociological Association. Author of *Sociology: Social Structure and Social Conflict* (MacMillan, 1989); *Social Stratification and Inequality*, McGraw-Hill, now in its 7th edition; with John A. McKinstry, *Who Rules Japan?: The Inner-Circles of Economic and Political Power* (Greenwood/Praeger, 1995); *Social Problems* now in its 10th edition (first author James Coleman, Prentice-Hall, 2008); *World Poverty: Global Inequality and the Modern World System*, McGraw-Hill in 2006, with a second edition forthcoming (Oxford University Press).

Habibiul Haque Khondker, PhD (Pittsburgh) is Professor at the Department of Humanities and Social Sciences at Zayed University, Abu Dhabi, UAE and co-President of Research Committee 9 (Social Transformations and Sociology of Development) of the International Sociological Association. Khondker co-edited *Asia and Europe in Globalization: Continents, Regions, and Nations* (Brill, 2006) with Goran Therborn. He co-authored *Globalization: East/West.* (Sage, 2010) with Bryan Turner. He also co-edited *The Middle East and the 21st Century Globalization.* (Dubai and Abu Dhabi: Zayed University Press, 2010) with Jan Nederveen Pieterse. Khondker's recent publications incudes, among others, "Class, Identity, and Insecurity: Bangladeshi Temporary Migrants in the UAE", *Current Sociology* (forthcoming, 2018).

Grace Khunou, Professor in the Sociology Department at the University of Johannesburg. Active member of ISA. Author of "Men's health: an analysis of the representations of Men's health in the Sowetan Newspaper", *Comunicatio*: 32, 2013; editor of book *The Emergent Middle Class* 2015, Routledge; co-editor of Special Issues with Nduna M. on Father Absence in the *Open Family Studies Journal* 2015; with Nethononda A., and Pillay, R. "Social Work is Women's Work: An Analysis of Students' Perceptions as a Career Choice Determinant", *Social Work Practitioner Researcher*, 2(1), 2012.

Edgardo Lander, Professor of Social Sciences at the Universidad Central de Venezuela in Caracas. Fellow member of the Transnational Institute, Amsterdam. PhD in Sociology, Harvard University. Member of ISA. Editor, *La colonialidad del saber: Eurocentrismo y ciencias sociales. Perspectivas latinoamericanas.* UNESCO/CLACSO, Buenos Aires, 2000; *La democracia en las ciencias sociales latinoamericanas contemporáneas,* Caracas,1997; editor, *El límite de la civilización industrial. Perspectivas latinoamericanas en torno al postdesarrollo*, UCV, Caracas, 1995; *Neoliberalismo, sociedad civil y democracia. Ensayos sobre América Latina y Venezuela*, UCV, Caracas, 1995.

Susan McDaniel, Professor of Sociology and Canada Research Chair in Global Population and Life Course, Prentice Research Chair in Global Population and Economy, Director of the Prentice Institute, University of Lethbridge, Canada. PhD in Sociology, University of Alberta. Former Vice President for Publications in the ISA Executive Committee, Past Editor of *Current Sociology*, and of the *Canadian Journal of Sociology*. From 2018, she will be President of ISA RC06 Committee on Family Research. Author of: *Is the Math Sufficient? Aging Workforce and the Future Labour Market in Canada* (2014); *Global Ageing in the Twenty-First Century. Challenges, Opportunities and Implications* (2014); and many other books, book chapters and articles.

Saskia Sassen, is the Robert S. Lynd Professor of Sociology and Member, The Committee on Global Thought, Columbia University (www.saskiasas sen.com). Her books include *Expulsions: Brutality and Complexity in the Global Economy* (Harvard University Press/Belknap 2014) now out in 18 languages. Recent books are *Territory, Authority, Rights: From Medieval to Global Assemblages* (Princeton University Press 2008), *A Sociology of Globalization* (W.W. Norton 2007), and the 5th fully updated edition of *Cities in a World Economy* (Sage 2018). Among older books are *The Global City* (Princeton University Press 1991/2001), and *Guests and Aliens* (New Press 1999). Her books are translated into over 20 languages. She is the recipient of diverse awards and multiple doctor honoris causa. She was awarded the Principe de Asturias 2013 Prize in the Social Sciences, made a Chevalier de l'Ordre des Arts et Lettres by the French government, and made a Foreign Member of the Royal Academy of the Sciences of Netherland.

Ari Sitas, Professor of Sociology at Cape Town University, South Africa. PhD in Sociology. Former Vice President of Program in the ISA. Author of *Voices that Reason*, by Ari Sitas; *Black Mamba Rising: South African Worker Poets in Struggle*, with Alfred Temba Qabula, Mi S'dumo Hlatshwayo and Nise Malange; *William Zungu: A Xmas Story*; *Slave Trades*. (2009) The Mandela Decade 1990–2000 (forthcoming Spring) University of South Africa Press; *The Ethic of Reconciliation*, 2008; Editor and author of *Managing Change in 19 KwaZulu-Natal's Industries*, 1995, now *Critical Studies Series*, University of KwaZulu-Natal; with Dilek Latif, *Prospects of Reconciliation and Co-Existence on the Island of Cyprus*, 2007; *Theoretical Parables*, 2004.

Göran Therborn, Professor Emeritus of Sociology at Cambridge University, UK. PhD in Sociology, Lund University, Sweden. Former Member of the Executive and of the Program Committee in ISA. Author of *Science, Class & Society* (Verso, 1976); "The rule of capital and the rise of democracy" (*New Left Review*, no. 103, 1977); *What Does the Ruling Class do When it Rules?* (1978); *The Ideology of Power and the Power of Ideology* (1978); *Why Some Peoples are More Unemployed than Others* (1986); *European Modernity and Beyond: The Trajectory of European Societies, 1945–2000* (1995); *Between Sex and Power: Family in the World, 1900–2000* (2004); *From Marxism to Post-Marxism?* (2008); (co-editor) *Handbook of European Societies: Social Transformations in the 21st Century* (2010); *The World: Beginner's Guide* (2011); *The Killing Fields of Inequality* (2013); *Cities of Power* (2017).

Aylin Topal, Associate Professor of Political Science and Public Administration, Middle East Technical University. Chairperson of Latin and North American Studies, Middle East Technical University. Author of *Boosting Competitiveness by Decentralization: A Subnational Comparison of Local Development in Mexico* (Ashgate Publishing, 2012; Routledge, 2016). Author of several journal articles and chapters in edited volumes on regional, urban and rural development in Mexico and state-capital-labor relations under neoliberalism in Turkey.

Hiroyuki Torigoe, President of Otemae University. Professor Emeritus at the Waseda University, Japan. PhD in Japanese Culture. President of Japan Sociological Society (2012–15). Author of 'Life environmentalism: A model developed under environmental degradation', in the *International Journal of Japanese Sociology*, 2014; *Natural energy!* (Iwanami booklet) by the power of the region, 2010; 'Think from the standpoint of consumers', *Environmental Sociology*, 2004; *Visiting the Flower Yoshino – Ecology and its History* (Shueisha Shinsho), 2003.

Chizuko Ueno, Professor at the Kyoto University, Japan. PhD in Sociology. Member of ISA. Author of: *The Modern Family in Japan: Its Rise and Fall*. Victoria, Australia, 2009. "The Politics of Memory: Nation, Individual and Self" in *History & Memory*, 1999; *Nationalism and Gender*. Victoria, Australia, 2004; *Capitalist and Patriarchal – Horizon of Marxist Feminism*, Japan, 2009.

Carlos Walter Porto-Gonçalves, Professor at the Universidade Federal Fluminense, Brazil. PhD, Geography. Author of *Geo-grafias: movimientos sociales, nuevas territorialidades y 17 sustentabilidad*. México, 2001; *Geografando nos varadouros do mundo: da territorialidade seringalista (o seringal) à territorialidade seringueira (a Reserva Extrativista)*. Brasília, 2003; *A Globalização da Natureza e a Natureza da Globalização*. Rio de Janeiro, 2006; *Geografia da violência no campo brasileiro: o que dizem os dados de 2003*. in *Revista Crítica de Ciências Sociais*, 2006.

1

Introduction

Raquel Sosa Elízaga

In July 2014, more than 4000 sociologists met at Yokohama to exchange views and research findings on the crucial challenge of the 21st century – the confrontation and eventual elimination of the processes of structural inequality that affect millions of human beings today.

According to the proceedings of this Congress, we have been able to confirm that the instability and uncertainty that characterize the world today can be roughly explained by the existence of an immense and vertiginous accumulation of wealth by a few, which in turn has precipitated the dispossession, impoverishment and exclusion of millions of human beings in all latitudes of our planet.

Even though it is true that not a single society has ever been free of the burden of this ballast, vast evidence confirms that throughout the 20th century, particularly in its last three decades, as well as from the beginning of the 21st century, deterioration in life's conditions for nearly a third of the world's inhabitants has been aggravated by a tragic combination of new forms of accumulation and dispossession, war, all sorts of violence, massive population displacements and migration, socio/natural disasters associated to climatic change, and the neglect, relegation or even dismantling of models of social organization centered on the value and defence of common and public services and institutions. In this context, the accumulation and overlap of all types of injustice not only complicates or impedes the realization of legitimate aspirations and rights of the inhabitants of the earth to live in a dignified manner, but it also condemns thousands of defenceless human beings to death.

It thus becomes clear that these years' international scenario is an image of violence, power struggles, intolerance, unlimited greed and unimaginable lacks. And then, if we are aware of the destruction and devastation of natural resources, essential to life, by water contamination, wasteful use and confrontation over the control of oil and minerals, the overcrowding of urban settlements, massive migration, the destruction of important cultural resources and of the world's heritage, we cannot but be alarmed and feel obliged to contribute not only with explanations, but also with as much as we can to surmount a human crisis that threatens every living being on Earth.

The inequality in the recognition of ethnic or gender differences, preferences or orientations, access to indispensable goods and services for the existence of a dignified human life, as well as the constraints in the access to symbolic assets, generate violence and deepen social conflicts. At the same time, survival in extreme situations and war increases the exclusion of vulnerable groups and, consequently, adds to inequality. It also appears that the mechanisms used to apply new global designs, such as multilateral and bilateral agreements for free trade have greatly contributed to inequality, as they grant benefits to capital, but limit the rights of the people. When capital can move freely, while people are repressed if they attempt to do likewise, the correlation between forces is radically altered in favour of capital, and workers cease to be able to negotiate collectively; thus, greater inequality is generated.

To make an accurate diagnosis of the present phenomenon of inequality, as well as the oppression and the risks that contemporary societies face, is an urgent collective task, way beyond the scope of academic sociology. The contribution of experts, wherever they may be found (in academia, governments, civil and social organizations), is required, but above all, it is also equally urgent that we manage to listen to the voice of citizens and communities. In a certain sense, the knowledge of the difficulties being faced by millions of human beings today should lay the foundations of an ethical crusade, in order to reach a common understanding of the true, present and future meaning of sustainable life, with the restoration and prevention of further destruction of natural resources and common goods; equal distribution of wealth; respect, inclusion and tolerance for diversity; exercise of individual and collective basic rights; recognition of community and people's autonomy and rights; the respect for identity, liberty, creativity and the principle of solidarity as the basis of alternative forms of coexistence.

Aware of the risks produced by the destruction of the social fabric, the state of neglect suffered by millions of human beings that barely survive, and the magnitude of the deficiencies that prevent most of the human beings from realizing their imagination, intelligence and sensitivity potential in order to achieve an improvement in their living conditions, their families and their communities, the United Nations issued a statement in the year 2000. Supported by 147 governments, it established the Millennium Goals, which were meant to be fulfilled by the year 2015 (UN, 2000). Although this initiative has drawn criticism because it is considered to be the *minimal point* of departure for governments, since it only deals with the consequences – extreme poverty, childbirth mortality, the spread of HIV/AIDS, to mention but a few of its objectives – and not the deeper roots of inequality, it has really contributed to make a larger public aware of some of the more alarming aspects of this phenomenon. Specifically, the Millennium Goals have proved to be an inspiration for sectors that, one way or the other, have the power to determine the future of their countries through governing the processes of decision making and the design of public policies. Additionally, in recent years, we have witnessed important initiatives that share the concern about the need to transform and radically improve life on the planet. Among other valuable contributions to this debate, we must recognize that of the World Social Forum, which gathered nearly 60,000 people in 2011 in Dakar, in order to discuss and confront possibilities and alternatives for a better life on Earth (WSF, 2011). On the other side of the planet, the World People's Conference on Climatic Change and the Rights of Mother Earth, held in Cochabamba, Bolivia in early 2010 (Acuerdo de los Pueblos, 2010) also constituted a milestone in the promotion of alternatives that can guarantee both the continuity and dignity of human beings, and the respect and care of nature.

This is the context in which the latest International Sociological Association's contribution has taken place. An incredibly sensitive community of academics and professionals such as the International Sociological Association, aware of these social transformations in the world, could not be absent from this debate. The great tradition of multi, inter and transdisciplinary works in which the most complex problems of the present-day world are addressed; its unique condition of being academically, scientifically, regionally, institutionally and organically plural have made our Association ideally qualified to face the challenge of contributing to this international debate.

Out of the enormous effort made by the Program Committee during the years 2010 and 2014[1] both the plenaries and this book were originally organized in five major topics:

The dimensions of inequality: Configurations of structural inequalities and structures of power

Inequality in the world includes multiple dimensions and appears as an increasingly complex phenomenon, one which is difficult to unravel.

It can be measured in terms of gender, family, community or generation; distribution of income or human development; gender preferences or orientations, cultural diversity, ethnic origin, national or regional; migratory status, displacement or refuge; dispossession, deterritorialization or impoverishment; access to goods, services or resources; vulnerability due to situations of natural disaster, war or violence; the double pain suffered by women, indigenous people, the youth, migrants and displaced, among many others, caused by violence and exclusion; deprivation from the exercise of the rights of citizenship and sovereignty. It is a fact that inequalities overlap and aggravate in the world, while experts find it increasingly difficult to identify and name the links among its different dimensions and dynamics. In this sense, for example, we cannot obviate that racism has become a device for the naturalization of inequalities, as for the unequal, hierarchical construction of different forms of knowledge, so that knowledge proceeding from the more favoured members in today's unequal society is considered privileged or superior. Similarly, if we refer to *dispossession* to give but two examples, we cannot ignore the seriousness of the deeply unequal appropriation/use/exploitation of the natural resources of a planet with limited load capacity, where the abundance of some is only made possible by the deficiency of others.

Conceptions of justice in different historical and cultural traditions

We are at a stage of human history where the accumulation of knowledge on different expressions of social and institutional organization, the formulation of concepts, categories and models must face the great challenge of explaining and contributing to the solution of crises in practically all aspects of social life. The scopes and consequences of such crises are unpredictable, but they undoubtedly test our capacity to sustain, question, propose and imagine different paradigms of civilization.

These paradigms allow us to analyze the development of different ways of territorialization of social life, based on the recognition and inclusion of those who have been excluded from the main streams of development; as well as to set principles and values conducive to a more harmonious and sustainable reproduction of our communities. This is the direction in which the analysis and proposals formulated by a significant group of authors (Esping-Anderson, 1990; Quijano, 1990; Wallerstein, 1996; Bourdieu, 2003; De Souza Santos, 2006; Harvey, 2006; Therborn, 2006; Sen, 2010; Amin, 2011) have established strong bases for contemporary debates, and so illuminate our hopes of contributing to propose conditions for the survival in dignity and peace to the human beings who inhabit our planet.

But such paradigms must also cast a view on recent developments that may force us to reconsider concepts associated to an integrated society, social development, and a universal understanding of justice.

Conflicts on environmental justice and sustainable future

In a world where different perspectives of organization, the availability and distribution of the work force, ways and means of production, distribution and exchange of goods and services, ideologies and knowledge are articulated and/or confronted; where millions of human beings suffer from conflicts where their integrity is threatened, or are forced to abandon their homes in disaster zones; in which young people, women, migrants and members of originary peoples suffer a double pain caused by exclusion and violence; in a world where strategies for power, resistance and search for alternatives are formulated and practiced at all levels, the knowledge of the processes through which inequality is generated, reproduced or intensified is both complex and intriguing. It presupposes the identification of spatialities and temporalities in order to understand the scope of conflicts, confrontations, ruptures and discontinuities. The fields in which inequality is expressed are also meaningful, as they include science and law, as well as art and culture. Inequality also presupposes the organization of resistance, the formation and consolidation of social movements, the creation of languages and networks, building imaginary scenarios. True and deep knowledge of the processes of construction and possible deconstruction of inequalities, as well as of the individual and collective actors that produce or confront them, is urgent in order to prevent policies and practices that have either generated or aggravated them.

Social injuries of inequality

The fulfillment of the Millennium Goals – or at least some of them – has become a common interest shared by a great number of governments, academics and social organizations around the world. However, the repetition and aggravation of social crises, the renewal and creation of different forms of inequality and exclusion, out of the ones considered in the Goals, as well as in the traditional conceptual framework, force us to make the same and

other questions we might probably not have thought of to truly understand
the nature and scope of the human crisis we are living at present.

Overcoming inequalities: Actors and experiences

We must recognize that contemporary societies embrace important historical and contemporary struggles against inequality and in favour of the
recognition of individual and collective rights, the results of which are
stimulating, although they may not be considered definitive. The pressure
exerted by important mobilized sectors of society has allowed the opening
of a wide spectrum in which legality and legitimacy for the reversion of
inequality is based: from human rights to public policies for *equalization*.
Sociology is obliged to recognize the existing links among basic social
demands, the requirement for the establishment of human rights, the recognition of peoples', women's, youths' and others' rights, the enforce-
ability of these rights, social empowerment and the building of new forms
of citizenship. The guidelines for debate, proposed to the participants
in the semi plenaries, allowed both a fruitful debate and enlightening
contributions.

The active participation of the authors of each and every one of the
texts in this book has gone through deep reflections, revisions and reconstruction, with the contribution of our SSIS reviewers, coordinated by
Sujata Patel, and later, by Chaime Marcuello. After nearly two years of
very hard work, we have finally arrived at a point where the original
kaleidoscope we presented at the Yokohama Congress has taken its own
shape, been remodelled and come to be expressed, I believe, in its true
value and dimension: that of a synthetic view of contemporary inequality in the world, where all perspectives, all research experiences come
together as a clear, critical understanding of the way in which capitalism
has been reorganized to favour accumulation, luxury, excessive expenses
of a few, and poverty, lack of access to basic goods, services and rights,
frailty, dispossession and instability, of a growing and significant part of
the world's population.

Exclusion, the extreme to inequality or expulsion, as the strategic decision to expel/discard others from whatever circuits capital and market may
conduct, is achieved through a series of complex operations that include
physical segregation – to the point of seclusion or invisibilization –
appropriation of land, water, natural and strategic resources, like mining,
but also, making use of whatever instruments and mechanisms available
to ensure that those excluded/expelled will never stand in a position to

claim anything but what is conditionally offered to them at the acceptance of their inferiority, ignorance and deficiency. Discrimination, violence, war, and of course, economic and financial concentration and its social, cultural, symbolic and political consequences have become the living stamps of this era.

In Part One of our book, *Capitalism and Inequality: Globalized Economies and Fractured Societies,* the authors have achieved the very difficult task of presenting a general frame in which it is visible that capitalism has built deep polarizations, in which finance and extraction form the perfect combination for wild accumulation, while 'the poor, of the displaced in poor countries ... are warehoused in formal and informal refugee camps; minoritized and persecuted in rich countries, ... warehoused in prisons; workers whose bodies are destroyed on the job and rendered useless, ... warehoused in ghettoes and slums' (Sassen, in Chapter 2 of this book).

In this 'epochal transition on this shrinking planet', Ari Sitas, in Chapter 3, considers that it is nevertheless possible to identify the obsession of economic growth, though 'growth for growth's sake is the philosophy of cancer cells and mutinous viruses'. If thought about as a new phase of international division of labour, it seems to him that manufacturing has shifted South and East, while symbolic values remain in the North. Rather than a de-industrialization, we are thus witnessing a re-location of capital production of commodities, which has exerted an immense pressure on working class standards everywhere. Contrary to what Marx imagined for an advanced capitalist era, accumulation has not led to socialization of production and empowerment of workers, but the fragmentation, dispersal, insecurity, vulnerability, overwork and weakening of labourers and their unions. Explosive forms of resistance, disconnection and discontent have turned out to be the signs and symbols of struggles of the dispossessed.

Up to this second decade of our new century, sociological debate had focused on social differences as forms of social stratification. As Göran Therborn proposes in Chapter 4 of this book, this view has turned to be completely insufficient to understand what can only be called *vital inequalities*, that is, an 'historical social construction by which the possibilities of realizing human capability are allocated unequally'. Parental and social milieu, seen through intergenerational lenses, have an enormous importance in perpetuating the basic mechanisms of inequality (detachment, exclusion, hierarchization and exploitation). Once again, the content and scope of relations of power are determinant in the continuity or rupture of all social disadvantages.

In Part Two, *Economic, Territorial and Social Dimensions of Inequality,* the authors give us a broad panorama of the dimensions of inequality in our world today. First, they look upon diverse explanations of the relation between globalization, with periods of noticeable economic growth, and the increase of inequality. Harold Kerbo's case study of the differences between Thailand and Cambodia, finds that historical trends and contemporary government policies can account for differences in growth, poverty reduction and population wellbeing, though in an authoritarian State in Thailand; while corruption, unsupervised reception of international aid and general government disorder may broadly explain the increase of income inequality, unemployment and unrest, in Cambodia.

Habibul Khondker makes full use of Göran Therborn's conception on vital, income and resource inequality while analyzing the Middle Eastern and North African countries. He explains the reasons for paradoxical findings of poverty reduction and inequality increase in the experiences of political instability, wars, violence and economic crises due to variations in oil prices, which have caused, among other things, wide young unemployment, aggravated gender inequality and destabilized families and rural communities, many of whom have been forcefully displaced.

Carlos Walter Porto-Gonçalves in Chapter 7 of this book, portrays a critical understanding of the risks posed to the world's most biodiverse region, the Amazon, after the continuation of predatory, colonial and developmental plans to conquer and submit nature (forests, water, land), while ignoring or despising the peoples who have inhabited it for more than 17,000 years. He affirms that 'prevailing views are *about* the Amazon, and not visions *of* the Amazon'. 'To consider Amazon in an anthropocentric way, as in the Eurocentric tradition, authorizes "domination of nature" as it would supposedly exist for the service of men. And as we know, this means men, and to a lesser extent women, not in a generic way, but meaning white and bourgeois men.' Porto-Gonçalves explains the damages caused by recent huge investment projects launched by public and private alliances, in which transnational corporations disown and displace populations to freely destroy valuable resources, with the compliance of the governments of the region. He proposes a different integration of the Amazon, in which people and nature are included and considered as part of a human, cultural and live patrimony that cannot continue to be wildly, irrationally and with impunity exploited and vanished.

Keng-Ming Hsu and Hsin-Huang Michael Hsiao warn us in Chapter 8 of this book, of the prevailing views of natural disasters as a matter that has been dealt with by elaborating risk maps, organizing general prevention and intervention programmes after disasters and, mainly, considering only the so-called scientific perspective, which frequently ignores social vulnerabilities, crucial in truly facing the aggravation of inequalities and risks of death for millions of human beings. They quote the *2015 Global Assessment Report on Disaster Reduction* released by the United Nations to report that 'average annual losses worldwide resulting from disasters like earthquakes, tsunamis, tropical cyclones and floods are US $134 billion, and it is predicted that such disaster losses will increase year after year'. They also quote the United Nations Office for Disaster Risk Reduction (UNISDR), which calculates 165 million people were affected by flood in 2007, 74.8% of these being Asian inhabitants. Their research proves the high-risk potential suffered by high social vulnerable populations, and considers that their prolonged suffering is not limited to the immediate consequences of disasters, but to the aggravating and endangering inequalities they suffer due to their 'class, occupation, race, gender, disability status, health status, age, immigration status and social networks, as well as to the degree of impact on people's lives after a catastrophe'. It is particularly to these questions that governments should pay real attention in order to reduce risk and loss of lives.

One of the main characteristics of this book is that it recognizes particular expressions of inequality that must be attended, if we not only aim at understanding how capitalist trends determine new forms of work exploitation or obtaining more profits, but also seek an adequate inclusion of new needs in order to incorporate them into our general knowledge of social problems resulting in significant proposals of new social policies.

Chizuko Ueno in Chapter 9 of this book introduces the picture of a hurt and disintegrated Japanese society. For example, after the Fukushima disaster, the surrounding community were again victimized by evacuation, where youth and parents, 'especially mothers with young children', were likely to be evacuated, leaving husbands and old parents behind. In a time of low fertility in the country, with population decrease, the government has not ceased to deregulate employment, increasing irregular workers. Sixty per cent of women employed have irregular work, and this again impacts on fertility, as pregnant women can easily lose their jobs on giving birth. The most dramatic situation, though, is that of the new condition of women available for the reserve army of labour force after the absence of foreign workers: 'gender serves as a functional equivalent with race and ethnicity in other developed countries'.

In Chapter 10, Susan McDaniel analyzes the growth of paid caring, which has become part of the 'public sphere of paid work', creating a particular relationship (duel, she calls it) of production and reproduction spaces, 'in which labour relationships are taking place largely, but not exclusively, between women who are increasingly unequal. It is a gendered encounter intertwining production and reproduction. This is a space for construction and maintenance of social hierarchies/social inequalities that are widening within most countries and growing globally.'

In a brief essay, Hiroyuki Torigoe (Chapter 11 of this book) shows the experience of the Taketomi Island in Okinawa Prefecture, on the southwestern border of Japan, where the community has basically been saved by appealing to its historical and cultural traditions, resisting the pressures of developers with the premise that 'money is for one generation but land is for future generations', and recreating their economy according to their own rules, the *Taketomi Chapter*, which has allowed the very small population of the island to get rid of inequality.

Jean-Michel Bonvin, in Chapter 12, contributes to the discussion of what has been left behind in public policies with a reconstruction of Amartya Sen's thought by looking into the limits of plans and programmes intended to overcome inequalities. He emphasizes that equality cannot mean forceful unification of social needs, nor does equality of resources ensure equality of capabilities. He proposes that 'equalization of capabilities requires adjusting the scope of public intervention to the specific circumstances of people: the more they are deprived or negatively affected in their living conditions and capacity to act autonomously, ... the more they need to be provided with extensive resources and interventions ...'. 'Human rights', Bonvin concludes, 'should not be conceived in such a way to promote specific modes of being or doing over others, ... but they should be designed so as to open for all human beings opportunities of choosing life trajectories they have reason to value'. Complementing some of Yuval-Davis' ideas, Bonvin considers that 'the requirements of social justice do not derive from a "view from nowhere", but are to be situated and contextualized'.

Digging deep into the philosophical roots of social actions, Ana Esther Ceceña, in Chapter 13 of this book, deconstructs the Monsanto project of unifying and universalizing crops and the grain market all over the world. With its infrastructure in 66 countries and its 32,000 employees, this transnational corporation – just being sold to another giant, Bayer – has made the most dramatic effort to regularize, patent, objectify and transform genetically modified seeds into dependent seeds (*terminator seeds*).

By breaking up and preventing natural interaction in agriculture, Monsanto deconstructs social relationships and hierarchies, establishing them as simple subject–object relations. Ceceña stipulates, 'A voiding of concrete, distinct, inequiparable substance is operated, in order to place everything in conditions of comparison and exchangeability. Universal, abstract and epistemologically commited to the modern vision referents are built, and they prevent the recognition of diversity, while tending to displace it to the level of abnormality or insufficiency.' Dramatic image of what has been proposed as a universal, homogeneous, exchangeable world of human beings and commodities in a world increasingly dominated by the enterprise order.

Sarah El Jamal and Sari Hanafi, in Chapter 14, close this section by demonstrating that social studies in the Arab region have become unified and a closed circle, basically dominated by closed clusters in which very few authors are forced to consider and cite one another, and where almost every one of them has worked in the World Bank's research teams. Unfortunately, the lack of originality, of the opening of new trends is an extremely delicate question – overcoming inequality and reducing poverty has sometimes led to the aggravation of a problem that certainly needs more and critical views. In a way, these two papers that close our Part Two are extremely significant: they have dared to be critical about the way in which diversity has not been considered in certain social studies, giving way to a presumed, arbitrary, forced homogeneity, and not, to problematize and enrich, situate, contextualize and find alternatives to the most important social problems in our world.

Finally, Part Three of our book, *Reforms, Resistance and Alternatives: New Ways Towards Social Justice* begins by presenting the insightful works of the distinguished scholars and politically experienced Walden Bello and Edgardo Lander. Bello, in Chapter 15, explores the limits and possibilities of reforms within the neoliberal hegemony in Southeast Asia, particularly Thailand and the Philippines. He analyzes risks and alternatives in dealing with reforms such as health care, agriculture and the fight against corruption. All these involve the risk of intervention of manipulative threatened elites who will try to derail all progressive transformations. He values even the minimal steps forward in the worst scenarios, but puts forward the proposal of the combination of both representative and direct democracy, with a strong civil society, vigilance in parliament and constant participation as counterbalances to the intervention of conservative forces against all reforms.

Edgardo Lander begins reminding us in Chapter 16 that Latin America is 'by far, the most unequal continent' and further explaining that 'the current inequities in the continent are the result of five centuries of colonial racist history characterized by the systematic subjugation, extermination, exploitation and exclusion of indigenous peoples and Afro-descendants'. The combination of *exporters-of-nature* economies, the use of the *civilization and barbarism* logic and a monocultural conception that privileged conditioned cash transfers to any option of reform has led to perpetuate all sorts of colonial forms of integration within the international division of 'labor and nature'. As alternatives, Lander proposes that the dimension of 'intergenerational justice' be established through the recognition and reorganization of States and citizens through the inclusion of a multinational and pluricultural perspective: 'this implies the recognition of the multiplicity of languages, the diverse forms of property, juridical regimes, modalities of production, as well as the plurality of knowledges and forms of relating to the rest of the web of life.'

The South African experience has motivated Grace Khunou (in Chapter 17) to discuss the efficacity and depth of social reforms by arguing the need for a new conception of gender in order to guarantee true access to citizenship rights: 'the constitution that protects your right is insignificant if you are unable to access these rights through employment and access to social services like health'. Khunou considers that by forcing homogeneous and unilateral approaches to social justice, the State can only reinforce and aggravate inequality. She proposes the adoption of a multiple gender view (she refers in particular to masculinities) in order to prevent true exclusion.

In Chapter 18, Paulo Henrique Martins develops the notion of wellbeing proposed and enacted by the Bolivian Government after the proclamation of its new Constitution in 2009. Inspired by Cohen and Honnuth, Martins claims that a true democracy should be based on 'social liberty, mediated by mutual recognition inspiring intersubjectivity equality'. Nurtured by the *Pacha Mama* (Mother Earth) Aymara cosmovision, Martins rejects the modern colonial perspective, based exclusively on economic growth, and proposes a new ethical principle 'structuring another modernity that values the plurality, deepening the renewal of the economic, cultural and political thinking'.

Chih-Jou Jay Chen has made an intensive and extensive case study on the development of social protests during the past ten years in China. Although he recognizes different economic motivations both in urban and rural communities (wages, living conditions, resistance against land seizures, etc.), he opens the scope in Chapter 19 of this book to clearly perceive the way in which protests have more and more turned towards rights defence, struggles against governmental misdeeds (corruption) and critique of authoritarian rule. Violence has also been a significant component in these protests, particularly in small localities, either rural or urban. Chen concludes that 'China's current political system lacks effective channels for citizens to express genuine grievances, and to seek redress from the misdemeanors of local officials, and therefore social unrest is on the rise'.

In Chapter 20, Peter Alexander draws complex conclusions following the mining crisis in South Africa, after the Marikana Massacre. He proves with abundant documents and testimonies that the core of the conflict is not a mere labour case (although wages and working conditions were definitely part of the initial stages of the struggle), but one that involves the resistance against the interference of multinational corporations in the laws and practice of the democratic State. He underlines, arguing against Piketty's comments on the case, that academics should go beyond their scholar and theoretical views and seek to comprehend social reality in its multidimensional configurations.

Aylin Topal, in Chapter 21, refers to the broad consequences of the civil resistance initiated by the Tekel workers on strike in Turkey. The way they faced the State, the repression they were submitted to, but most of all, their clarity of objectives and understanding of what was at the bottom of a capital–labour contradiction, transformed their movement into a global social and civic resistance, in which different grievances were included, and a new rights movement emerged – 'There is a need for new, creative forms of organization with an ability to initiate collective action on a long-lasting basis.'

Finally, in Chapter 22, Esteban Castro strongly stands in favour of present and future international forms of organization and integration in order to regulate the production and exchange of goods and services needed by the population, and not only favouring the sole accumulation of wealth in the hands of very few. He uses Latin American experiences such as Mercosur, ALBA, CELAC and UNASUR and demands that these crucial organisms favour not only economic growth and increasing international exchange (in an extractivist view), but reorient their views to include ecological, as well as social justice and equality.

On behalf of my colleagues, to whom I wish to express my appreciation and admiration, I sincerely wish that the readers of this volume will keep a broader and more complex view of the inequalities our world suffers today, and also feel the urge to actively work on rethinking, proposing and, as much as they can, enact changes in their lives and lives of others to ensure a dignified life for everyone on earth.

Note

1   The committee was chaired by Raquel Sosa Elízaga, and its members were: Michael Burawoy, Margaret Abraham, Tina Uys, Koichi Hasegawa, Sari Hanafi, Chin Chun, Markus Schulz, Esteban Castro, Edgardo Lander, Göran Therborn, Kalpana Kannabiran and Benjamín Tejerina.

References

Acuerdo de los Pueblos (World People's Conference on Climatic Change and the Rights of Mother Earth) (2010). Cochabamba, Bolivia, April.

Amin, S. (2011). *Global history. A view from the South.* Cape Town: Pambazuka Press.

Bourdieu, P. (2003). *Counterfire: Against the tyranny of the market.* London: Verso.

De Souza Santos, B. (2007). *Another knowledge is possible: Beyond northern epistemologies.* London: Verso.

Esping-Anderson, G. (1990). *The three worlds of welfare capitalism.* London: Polity Press.

Harvey, D. (2006). *Spaces of global capitalism: A theory of uneven geographical development.* London: Verso.

Quijano, A. (1990). *Modernidad, identidad y utopía.* Lima: Colección 4 suyus.

Sen, A. (2010). *The idea of justice. In memory of John Rawls.* Cambridge, MA: Harvard University Press.

Therborn, G. (2006). *Inequalities of the world: New theoretical frameworks, multiple empirical approaches.* London: Verso.

United Nations Organization (2000). *The Declaration of the Millennium.* Geneva: UNO.

Wallerstein, I. (1996). *World inequality.* Montreal: Black Rose Books.

World Social Forum (2011). Declaration by the Assembly of Social Movements, Dakar. Available at: http://fsm2011.org/en/wsf2011.

Part One

Capitalism and Inequality: Globalized Economies and Fractured Societies

2

When Extractive Logics Rule: Proliferating Expulsions*

Saskia Sassen

The Keynesian period was one of mass production and mass construction of suburban space; this brought with it an economic logic that valued people as workers and *consumers*. The current phase of advanced capitalism is dominated by sectors, such as finance, far less geared towards mass consumption even if the latter still accounts for a vast share of the global economy. Elsewhere (Sassen, 2014) I have examined in what ways finance is actually radically different from traditional banking and is, rather, akin to an extractive sector – a term not usually applied to finance. Mining is extractive, as is plantation agriculture. But so is Google in many ways, as it thrives on the gathering of vast troves of existing information. And Facebook's share values depend on the continuous expansion of the numbers of its subscribers.

The fact that the last two decades have seen a sharp growth in the number of people 'expelled' from a middle class or prosperous working class life is not unconnected to this ascendant logic of extraction. This logic finds extreme forms in particular countries, notably the United States, but also several African countries that once had strong manufacturing economies but now have become mainly extractive economies to the benefit of small local elites and big foreign companies. It is the manufacturing and construction driven economies of China, and to a lesser extent India, that today are actively generating expanding middle classes. But also here declines are setting in. And it is not necessarily due to some evolution process that repeats the West's trajectory. It is because of a larger global economic logic that emerges in the 1980s and now is present in China as well. Most likely China will not replicate what were at the time strong and much admired economic trajectories in Japan, South Korea and Taiwan, with widely distributed economic and social benefits.

The logics of expulsion that mark the current post-1980s period tend to counter such distributive potentials. I use the term 'expelled' to mark the extreme moment in familiar processes – so extreme that our standard categories for measuring and analyzing such trends cannot capture them. They include the growing numbers of the abjectly poor, of the displaced in poor countries who are warehoused in formal and informal refugee camps, of the minoritized and persecuted in rich countries who are warehoused in prisons, of workers whose bodies are destroyed on the job and rendered useless at far too young an age, of able-bodied surplus populations stuck in ghettoes and slums. But I also use it to capture the destruction of land and water bodies, leaving behind dead land and water. My argument is that the expanding range of expulsions is actually signaling a deeper systemic transformation, one documented in bits and pieces in multiple specialized studies but not quite narrated as an overarching dynamic that is taking us into a new phase of global capitalism.

In this short chapter I confine myself to only two cases that make visible how some of today's much-admired growth innovations are actually highly destructive. One case is that of massive acquisitions of land by rich and powerful firms and governments in countries that are rather poor and powerless, and often run by unaccountable elites. The acquired land is for developing plantations, mines, and water supplies for bottling companies such as Nestlé and Coca Cola. Our standard measures of growth register this type of transformation – the corporatizing of what was once smallholder agriculture – as a growth in GDP and a sign of development/modernization. In fact, the smallholder agriculture they replace is a far better development mode, enabling land and water to have long lives, and more geared towards local populations rather than export. The second case I focus on is the so-called sub-prime mortgage that left 14 million households in the US without a home and impoverished. This so-called 'mortgage' was an instrument that had nothing to do with enabling low-income people to own a home. Rather, it used the fiction of a mortgage so that the financial system could access material goods to create so-called *asset*-backed securities which is what high-level investors wanted: they were asking for assets rather than yet another derivative based on an interest rate and in a dubious value-chain.

The larger condition behind these two cases I briefly examine in this chapter is that we confront a human and economic landscape marked by sharply dualizing dynamics, a subject I develop at length elsewhere (Sassen, 2014, 2017). On the one hand, we see the familiar reconditioning of terrain in the direction of growing organizational and technological complexity, epitomized by the state of the art space of global cities in the North and the South (a subject developed in Sassen, 2001; 2016), and on the other hand, a mix of conditions often coded with the seemingly neutral term of 'a growing surplus population'. A key underlying condition of this 'surplus' is the growing expanse of territory that is devastated by mining and plantations, poverty and disease, by various kinds of armed conflict, and by governments rendered dysfunctional by acute corruption and a crippling international debt-regime. Elsewhere (Sassen, 2016) I have documented how these diverse processes are generating a massive loss of habitat that is also partly feeding new kinds of migrant and refugee flows across several areas of the world.

The repositioning of territory in the global division of functions

The extent of land acquisitions in the global South by multinational corporations (MNCs) and governments of rich countries over the last few years marks a new phase. It is a new profit-producing mechanism that can thrive on the devastations produced by the dominant logic of the last two decades: the repositioning of national sovereign territory as *land* for sale on the global market. This is largely land in Sub-Saharan Africa, in Central Asia and in Latin America, with over 200 million hectares from 2006 to 2010 bought/leased by rich investors and rich governments to grow food, to access underground water tables, and to access minerals and metals.[1]

It is not the first time in modern times; this is a recurrent dynamic that tends to be part of imperial realignments. China's acquiring of mines in Africa is linked to its rise as a global power. Britain, France, the US, and others all did this in their early imperial phases, and in many cases have owned vast stretches of land in foreign countries for hundreds of years. But each phase has its particularities. One key feature of the current period is that unlike past empires, today's world consists largely of nation states recognized as sovereign, no matter how feeble this sovereign power is in many cases. Rather than imperial grab, the mechanism is foreign direct investment in its many instantiations, each presented as good for the economic development of host countries.

The contractual formats under which this land is acquired include direct acquisitions and leasing. A few examples signal the range of buyers and of locations (see Sassen, 2014 for sources). Africa is a major destination for land acquisitions. South Korea has signed deals for 690,000 hectares and the United Arab Emirates (UAE) for 400,000 hectares, both in Sudan. Saudi investors are spending $100 million to raise wheat, barley and rice on land leased to them by Ethiopia's government; they received tax exemptions and export the crop back to Saudi Arabia. China secured the right to grow palm oil for biofuels on 2.8 million hectares in Congo, which would be the world's largest palm-oil plantation. It is negotiating to grow biofuels on 2 million hectares in Zambia. Perhaps less known than the African case is the fact that privatized land in the territories of the former Soviet Union, especially in Russia and Ukraine, is also becoming the object of much foreign acquisition. Such acquisitions included the following: a Swedish company, Alpcot Agro, bought 128,000 hectares in Russia; South Korea's Hyundai Heavy Industries paid $6.5 million for a majority stake in Khorol Zerno, a company that owns 10,000 hectares in eastern Siberia; Morgan Stanley bought 40,000 hectares in Ukraine; Gulf investors are planning to acquire Pava, the first Russian grain processor to be floated on the financial markets to sell 40% of its landowning division, giving them access to 500,000 hectares.

These developments are part of a larger combination of trends. First, there is the immediate fact of how the global demand for food, partly fed by the half million strong new middle classes of Asia, has meant that there are profits to be had in food and land. We now have a global market for land and food controlled by large firms and some governments, and it has been a growth sector throughout the financial crisis. Under these conditions pricing is a controlled affair. Secondly, there is the ongoing demand for familiar metals and minerals but also a whole new need for metals and minerals hitherto not much exploited as their demand arises from the more recent developments in the electronics sector. Africa, much less densely populated and built up than other parts of the world, has become a key destination for investments in this new type of mining alongside the ongoing mining of more traditional components.

Thirdly, there is the growing demand for water and the exhaustion of underground water tables in several areas of the world. Fourth, and least noted perhaps, is the sharp decline in foreign direct investment (FDI) in manufacturing in Africa, also signaling the repositioning of African territory as a source of metals and minerals rather than a place for people oriented development. Manufacturing can contribute to the growth of a modest middle class in ways that extractive sectors cannot. South Africa and Nigeria, generally Africa's top two FDI recipients, have had a sharp rise in FDI in the primary sector and a sharp fall in the manufacturing sector. In Nigeria, where foreign investment in oil has long been a major factor: the share of the primary sector in inward FDI stock stood at 75% in 2015, up from 43% in 1990. Other African countries have seen similar shifts. Even in Madagascar, one of the few, mostly small, countries where manufacturing FDI inflows began to increase in the 1990s, this increase has remained well below that of the primary sector.

These developments had a massive shadow effect on the larger local populations.[2] Among these is the destruction of smallholder agriculture and the exhaustion of land and water bodies due to plantations, mines, and water grabs for the former as well as for the water bottlers such as Nestlé and Coca-Cola. One effect has been the sharp growth of survival economies where before there often was small-scale commercial agriculture and local manufacturing. Heavy government debt imposed by older IMF and World Bank programs on these countries have further expanded the need for survival alternatives, not only for ordinary people, but also for governments and traditional enterprises (small local factories and local commerce). It all has further accentuated some of the negative outcomes of the IMF and World Bank programs of the last 30 years, with their massive contribution to heavy debt burdens.

One outcome has been what I have elsewhere named (and described in detail) as the making of counter-geographies of survival, of profit-making, and of government revenue enhancement (see Sassen, 2014). Many of these counter-geographies are irregular and even criminal, as in the trafficking of people. Furthermore, economic globalization has provided an institutional infrastructure for cross-border flows and global markets, thereby facilitating the operation of these counter-geographies on a global scale.

The reinvented sub-prime mortgage: A new global frontier for finance

Very different yet, I would argue, structurally equivalent in its capacity to destroy mid-level modest survival capacities was the deployment of a financial instrument that ruined 14 million households in the US in just a few years. In what follows I argue that the specific way of using the sub-prime mortgage in the 2001–7 period makes it a dangerous instrument that is likely to be used worldwide over the next decade. It is a mistake to see this instrument as having to do with providing modest income households with housing. It has rather to do with a structural condition of high finance marked by the combination of a growing demand for asset-backed securities given extremely high levels of speculative investments. This structural condition is at the heart of the actual event that momentarily brought the system to a (partial) standstill – the credit-default swap crisis of September 2008 – which in turn suggests an even keener interest in asset-backed securities, and hence in the speculative use of sub-prime mortgages. I see this as one of the new global frontiers for finance, specifically, the billions of modest-income households worldwide. The effect could be yet another brutal sorting, with expulsions from more traditional economies, not unlike the consequences of the structural adjustment crises in the global South discussed in the first half of this paper.

Much has been made, especially in the US media, of the sub-prime mortgage crisis as a source of the larger 2008 crisis. Modest-income families unable to pay their mortgage were often represented as irresponsible for having taken on these mortgages. But the facts show another pattern. The overall value of the sub-prime mortgage losses was too small to bring this powerful financial system down.

What triggered the crisis was a far more complex financial innovation. The key was the growing demand for asset-backed securities by investors, in a market where the outstanding value of derivatives in 2007, right before the crisis, was $630 trillion, or 14 times the value of global GDP. The total value of financial assets (which is a form of debt) in the US stood at almost five times (450%) the value of its GDP in 2006, before the crisis was evident. The UK, Japan and the Netherlands, all had a similar ratio (McKinsey & Company, 2008, p. 11). From 2005 to 2006 the total value of the world's financial assets grew by 17% (in nominal terms, 13% at constant exchange rates) reaching $167 trillion. This is not only an all-time high value; it also reflects a higher growth rate in 2006 than the annual average of 9.1% since 1980. This points to growing financial deepening. The total value of financial assets stood at $12 trillion in 1980, $94 trillion in 2000, and $142 trillion in 2005. And by 2014 it stood at over a quadrillion while 14 million households had lost their homes in the US (for full sources please see Sassen, 2014, Chapter 3).

This was the context within which the demand for asset-backed securities became acute. To address this demand, even sub-prime mortgage debt could be used as an asset. Sellers of these mortgages needed vast quantities of them to make it work for high finance: 500 such sub-prime mortgages needed to be sold by each agent per week to make it all work. As the demand for asset-backed securities grew, so did the push by sub-prime mortgage sellers to have buyers sign on, regardless of capacity to pay the mortgage. This combination of demand and increasingly low-quality assets meant mixing slices of poor quality mortgages with high-grade debt. Out came an enormously complex instrument that was also enormously opaque; nobody could completely trace what was there. When the millions of foreclosures began in 2006 (see Table 2.1 below), investors had a crisis of confidence; it was impossible to tell what was the toxic component in their investments.

Table 2.1 US home foreclosures per year, 2006–14

New US home foreclosures per year, 2006–14

2006: 1.2 million
2007: 2.2 million
2008: 3.1 million
2009: 3.9 million
2010: 2.9 million
2011: 2,698,967
2012: 2,304,941
2013: foreclosure filed on 1,361,795 properties
2014: foreclosure filed on 1,117,426 properties

Source: Federal Reserve Bank data as organized by RealtyTrac

This so-called sub-prime mortgage had nothing to do with the original concept of the sub-prime mortgage, which was a valuable instrument to enable modest-income households to buy a house. It was simply a financial instrument that could make profits for investors even if those households in the end could not pay the mortgages and thereby lost both their home and whatever savings and future earnings they had put into it – a catastrophic and life-changing event for millions of these households. This becomes clear in the microcosm that is New York City. Whites in NYC, who have a far higher average income than all other groups in New York City, were far less likely to have sub-prime mortgages than all other groups. Thus 9.1% of all whites got sub-prime mortgages in 2006 compared with 13.6% of Asians, 28.6% of Hispanics, and 40.7% of blacks. If we consider the most acute period – 2003 to 2005 – it more than doubled for whites, but it basically tripled for Asians and Hispanics and quadrupled for blacks.

Table 2.2 Rate of sub-prime lending by race in New York City, 2002–6

	2002	**2003**	**2004**	**2005**	**2006**
White	4.6%	6.2%	7.2%	11.2%	9.1%
Black	13.4%	20.5%	35.2%	47.1%	40.7%
Hispanic	11.9%	18.1%	27.6%	39.3%	28.6%
Asian	4.2%	6.2%	9.4%	18.3%	13.6%

Source: Furman Center for Real Estate and Urban Policy, 2007.
[http://furmancenter.org/files/FurmanCenterHMDAAnalysis_000.pdf] Retrieved 26 July 2008

There were, then, two very separate crises: the crisis of the people who had been sold these mortgages and the crisis of confidence in the investor community. The millions of home foreclosures were a signal that something was wrong, but in itself, it could not have brought down the financial system. There is a profound irony in this crisis of confidence: the brilliance of those who make these financial instruments became the undoing of a large number of investors (besides the undoing of the modest-income families who had been sold these mortgages). The toxic link was that for these mortgages to work as assets for investors, vast numbers of mortgages were sold regardless of whether these homebuyers could pay their monthly fee. The faster these mortgages could be sold, the faster they could be bundled into investment instruments and sold off to investors. Overall, sub-prime mortgages more than tripled from 2000 to 2006, and accounted for 20% of all mortgages in the US in 2006. This premium on speed also secured the fees for the sub-prime mortgage sellers and reduced the effects of mortgage default on the profits of the sub-prime sellers. In fact, those sub-prime sellers that did not sell off these mortgages as part of investment instruments went bankrupt eventually, but not before having secured fees.

In brief, the financial sector invented some of its most complicated financial instruments to extract the meager savings of modest households in order to produce an 'asset' – the mortgage on a house.

An important question raised by these types of logics is the extent to which developed and developing countries will follow this troublesome path (Sassen, 2008). It has become another way of extracting value from individuals.[3] In this case, through home mortgages that even very poor households are invited to buy, partly because the sellers are merely after the contract that represents an asset, in order to bundle them up and sell the package to an investor, thereby passing on the risk and removing an incentive to care whether the home owner manages to pay the mortgage.

But unlike the clear realignments we see in vast stretches of the global South, it is not clear how these devastated urban spaces in the global North will be incorporated into the circuits of advanced capitalism. One possibility is signaled by the rapidly expanding acquisition of high-level investments in properties in more and more cities across the world.

Conclusion

The financial innovation that destroyed 14 million households in the US is the systemic equivalent, albeit on a much smaller scale, of the global

South countries devastated by an imposed debt-buying regime imposed by the international banking system which prioritized debt-repayment over all other state expenditures. These are two manifestations of the systemic deepening of advanced capitalism, one marked by its potential to spread globally and the other marked by its full enactment in the global South.

One way of conceiving of this systemic deepening is as an expansion of the operational space for advanced capitalism – it expels people both in the global South and in the North even as it incorporates terrain. The devastated economies of the global South subjected to several decades of debt servicing, are now being incorporated into the circuits of advanced capitalism, including the formation of Global South elites even as most of their populations get poorer. This incorporation is via several circuits, including rising imports of mass consumption goods that have contributed to devastate local factories and shops. Most recently, we see new types of mining and the accelerated acquisition of millions of hectares of land by foreign investors – to grow food and extract water and minerals, mostly to the benefit of the capital investing countries and, to a far lesser extent, local elites.

A second, very different extractive mode can be seen in such a radically different instance as the sub-prime mortgage crisis, a largely global North dynamic. I see the sub-prime mortgage as extending the domain for high finance by using 16 plus million households to construct asset-backed securities of interest to the high-level investors circuit. Over 14 million of these households ended losing their homes, often years after the financial sector had earned billions from those asset-backed securities. We can see in this 'brilliant' innovation the delinking of the financial circuit from the actual material entity that is the house, and hence from the neighborhood and from the people who got the mortgage. All of these materialities – the houses, the buyers – become irrelevant once the asset-backed securities have been developed and sold to the high-level investors circuit. It is akin to wanting only the horns of the rhino, and throwing away the rest of the animal, devaluing it, no matter its possible multiple utilities. Or using the human body to harvest some organs, and seeing no value in all the other organs, let alone the full human being, so it can all be discarded.

This systemic shift signals that the sharp increase in displaced peoples, in poverty, in deaths from curable illnesses, are part of this new phase, and have added to the concentration of wealth.

Notes

*   This text is based on the author's book *Expulsions: Brutality and Complexity in the Global Economy* (Harvard University Press/Belknap Book, 2014).

1   For a fully developed analysis and sources see Chapter 2 in Sassen, 2014.
2   For a full development of these issues see Chapter 1 in Sassen, 2014.
3   There is also the possibility that the acquiring of 'urban land' becomes of interest, certainly in many cities of the Global North, but also eventually beyond. Elsewhere I have examined the rapid growth in investment in properties in more and more cities and argue that to some extent this is about the buying of urban land, not simply properties, even if the latter are the medium (see www.theguardian.com/cities/2015/nov/24/who-owns-our-cities-and-why-this-urban-takeover-should-concern-us-all). See also Sassen, 2014.

References

Furman Center for Real Estate and Urban Policy (2007). 'New housing data continue to show signs of danger for New York City's homeowners, Furman Center Analysis concludes', 15 October. New York: Furman Center for Real Estate and Urban Policy. Available at: http://furmancenter.org/files/FurmanCenterHMDAAnalysis_000.pdf (accessed 26 July 2008).
Sassen, S. (2008). 'Two stops in today's new global geographies: Shaping novel labor supplies and employment regimes', *American Behavioral Scientist*, 52(3): 457–96.
Sassen, S. (2014). *Expulsions: Brutality and Complexity in the Global Economy.* Cambridge, MA: Belknap Press of Harvard University Press.
Sassen, S. (2016). 'A massive loss of habitat: New drivers for migration', *Sociology of Development*, 2: 204–33.
Sassen, S. (2017). 'Predatory formations dressed in Wall Street suits and algorithmic math', *Science, Technology & Society* 22(1): 6–20.
Sassen, S. (2018). *Cities in a World Economy*, 4th edn. Thousand Oaks: Sage.

3

Resilience, Resistance and Rewiring the World Economy: A View from the South

Ari Sitas

I

We are in the midst of an epochal transition on this shrinking planet. According to colleagues of the Braudellian School we are in the midst of a world-systemic change of profound proportions.[1] According to quite recent historical work of Sinologists, Indian Ocean researchers, Indian scholars and BRICS-related pilot studies, it is something that approximates the changes unleashed between the 14th and16th centuries in our recent history.[2]

These crucial centuries saw the involution of the non-West and the relational rise of the foraging states of Europe. The descriptor, 'the Great Divergence' has accompanied a number of debates in economic and social history, in historical sociology and in civilizational studies.[3] This more contemporary transition if it is to happen at all, will be made possible by emerging powers like BRICS and their regional cohorts.

If for a moment we stopped reading the news underneath a 'European street light' in the words of Andre Gunder Frank,[4] and tried to fathom how this looks from the mid-point of Doha or the extremities of Beijing, Delhi, Moscow, Johannesburg or Brasilia, it is obvious that the old centres of prestige and hegemony and their mutant offspring are fading and for reasons that are quite rational, they are defensively fanning out discord. There is a potential Syria in all of us.[5]

Our current research on economic transactions in the world shows this clearly as at the centre of the system are two energy points: the USA and China with the rest in peculiar orbits around them – the former in economic decline, the latter with energy points in the East and within the BRICS domain and with Europe receding into a peculiar introversion. Indeed, what sustains the USA in pole position is its China link. Within that constellation, Africa is emerging from the insignificance of the 1970s and 1980s to appear inside the picture. Yet, its energy points are not synergistic: there is little between Lagos, Kinshasa and Addis but all are emerging close to China, India and South Africa who act as important intermediaries. What is certain is that the old imperial patterning of the world economy is receding.[6]

It is ironic that the capitalist world economy is being powered up by China, India, Russia, Brazil, all of them in concert, and with South Africa in tow, they are powering up growth rates in Africa that keep the zero and minus growth rates of the old world ticking over.[7] The rising economic prowess of the BRICS partners is a significant driver of an African growth boom. BRICS trade with Africa has been estimated to have reached $340 bn in 2012, a tenfold increase over the course of a decade, according to South Africa's Minister of International Affairs, Maite Nkoana-Mashabane.[8]

But growth for growth's sake is the philosophy of cancer cells and mutinous viruses; the nature and quality of that growth is deeply at issue. (The cancer cells idea is pilfered from Berkeley University's John Wright.) We are not sure of the civilizational imprint the new emerging powers are bringing about as an alternative to the Bretton Woods framework. All we know is that neither neo-liberalism nor crass managerialism have been the elixir for success. They have been what Virodene was to the fight against HIV – a self-interested quackery. This transition has not been pretty: inequalities are becoming indefensible and proliferating in new ways, authoritarian and quasi-fascist restoration movements are everywhere and the old conceptual canopies are torn up. It is a moment of opportunity and danger.[9]

There is a real tension emerging in this reconfiguration of the world: in the late 19th century Britain and France managed to combine power and value. The former was the obvious capacity to impose a political hegemony and a world market that prioritized its welfare in competition and in concert with other European powers. But it also managed to couple the prestige and hegemony of its symbolic and material goods. Paris was always in contention for the *aesthetic* aspect of the symbolic but as far as educational and cultural capital, London was the brand of prestige and the arch-signifier for mimicry the world over.[10]

On the other hand, it also prevailed (although catch up was on its way) in the world of manufacture and trade. The USA was to climb on the back of all this in the post-second world war period. Here is the tension: the hub of manufacture and material goods has shifted South and predominantly East whilst the hub of symbolic value remains North.[11]

Within this context, the BRICS effort to rebalance the global financial architecture, to find a cooperative way of enhancing growth, to create a New Development Bank and a Contingent Reserve Arrangement in 2016 and to use the 4 trillion dollars of foreign reserve that they hold to do so, has profound implications but it may not succeed to redress the damages of two decades of market fundamentalism and reckless financialization.[12]

The power-elites in the governments of China, India, Brazil and South Africa understand that they chose policies that opened them to the world market, inter alia, the Four Modernizations policy[13], the post-Nehru liberalizing trajectory[14], the Cardoso-led reforms[15] and the GEAR policy in South Africa[16] were the peculiar way each one of them took. The reasons were obvious. The difference between them and governments in the north was that they understood neo-liberal reforms as tools for maximizing their 'development' within the world economy and not as a philosophical principle. They chose export-led growth. Yet, their ideologies took them away from the 'tool' and within the range of 'principle'. Even the harshest and most authoritative one of them, China, had to backtrack to their growth for growth's sake scenario, after a phase of rural and small-town insurrection spread throughout the society three years ago.[17]

Let us spell it out: in all of these societies, the Down phase of 2008 and their chosen reforms have generated a serious crisis. The crisis involved the inability of their working classes to reproduce themselves at appropriate levels to survive. By working class I mean all those people who do not own means of production and who are compelled to work for a wage to reproduce themselves (many of them don't) and whose households, whether in the city or in the countryside depend primarily on working people to survive. Viewed in the broadest sense the main struggle has been (apart from China) about access to livelihoods as such in the formal and informal economies of mainly their cities – about their rights at worst to remain in the street.[18]

It has also been a struggle in the organized sectors, the ones that belong to trade unions (even in China), to keep a sense of material decency and most of their earnings are a further means of reproduction for many who depend on them. By implication their struggles have shifted to a whole range of other issues that affect their reproduction: over local authorities – against rates, provision of water and electricity and issues that have spawned social movements over rents, housing, land, squatting rights, energy costs and environmental issues. Also about money-lenders and financial services for the poor, about policing of their neighbourhoods and all in all, about forcing the state to transform their redistributive principles – to spend on all of that, but also on transport, education and the community.[19]

The power elites in all four societies are in a quandary – the ANC is in serious re-think mode having re-emerged from a crisis, the PT is in crisis, Congress Party and the Communist Party India Marxist are in crisis with the ascendance of the BJP and so is the Communist Party of China. Unlike other political parties their history traps them in their founding principles to a promise of redistribution and any failure to do so, constitutes a crisis of legitimacy.[20]

If they ignore that, then the new reconfigured world order would create power elites that act as intermediaries for the global redistribution of this capitalist growth upwards. Their distance between their aspirations and their mass base will become unbridgeable.

II

If Marx was right that capitalism appeared as a vast accumulation of commodities, the production of them is at a historic premium. In the West, Marx's 'productivism' has been rubbished – at least for social theory it has been passé for a while. The production of use and exchange values has become irrelevant to the analysis of modern or post-modern societies, to theories about them and to the praxis necessary to deal with forms of social injustice: farewell to the working class! What we are left with are capitalists, identities and consumption. Capitalists remain necessary because the system is still about dividends and investments. Identities are more important explananda of agency and choice. Consumption, yes, because that is the ultimate target of desire/choice.[21] Well, I don't think so – it is an important and partial angle on the world.

Most certainly there is a new geography of production. Conceptually we cannot understand this as a 'de-industrialization' and a 'relocation' of industry from the West to the South (this has occurred and continues to do so in all directions) but as industrialization proper, industrialization period, at growth rates in terms of tonnage that make the Fordist period of the 1960s–1970s look rather paltry. It is enough to make ecologists shudder.

Take steel: the world produced a record 1.24 billion tons of crude steel in 2006, and close to 1.6 billion tons last year. The world production of steel stood at 700 million tons in 1980; this means that it has doubled and within that China produces more than the entire world did in 1980 and now produces more than 53% of the world's output by the beginning of 2014. This is a lot of steel.[22]

And by implication the mining of iron ore and the energy needed has grown exponentially. This is not only related to ferrous metals like iron but also to non-ferrous metals as well, where China is leading the way. Indian interests in the meantime have acquired the majority shareholding of South Africa's para-statal giant, Iscor (now Mittal Steel), whilst South Africa's other giant, Highveld Steel, has been taken over by Russian interests.[23]

Steel-making in its crude form is a primary process and would not immediately indicate whether manufacturing as a whole is on the 'up'. Well it is; checking on all finished product areas of the metalworking industry in the world, including ship-building, automobile and transport-related vehicle manufacture, machinery and wire, construction steel and transport equipment are all up. The most volatile is the automobile industry which, in the main, is controlled by a small number of Western multinationals and suffers from seasonal ups and downs, but it has also been on the 'up' and each of the big ones are gearing up major capital-intensive investments, expecting high rates of growth. But a staggering increase of the share of the automobile market involved Chinese, Indian and Korean firms. So it was until the crash up. It was on the way up.[24]

Granted, in terms of economic growth measured in GDP terms, the world growth rate was a modest 4.4% and it was yanked up by a few economies (again China and India are clear examples in a way that the US at a 0% growth and Europe at a −0.9% are not) but it was up from the global high of the 1970s or the Imperial 1900s. It has crashed ... but there is no up-path of whatever kind which will not be driven by growth within these emerging powers.[25]

My first point is that we are not in a post-industrial world. This is the partial view inculcated by thinkers who have been accustomed to view their slice of the planet as instantly generalizable as the new socio-human destiny. We are living through a fascinating phase where there are a number of post-industrial countries or regions but whose reproduction would collapse if *other* countries or regions stopped doing the earth-shovelling and the blue-collar stuff. The illusion is compounded because of issues of 'scale'. It was because Manufacturing or Industry was so concentrated in such a small portion of the planet since the 19th century that when it did spread out over such a large land-mass and populations, it appeared to be diminutive, a diffusion, a shrinking.

And given the countries or regions that it can be found in (which were not non-industrial by the way to start with), with their large agrarian populations and complex urban–rural transactional economies, what is more than ever before can disappear from the scholarly radar. What finally compounds the illusion is that in value or price terms, the share of production has been diminishing vis-à-vis services and knowledge goods as a percentage of global and national GDPs. This is more than an accurate phenomenon but it spells out the following: so much labour and effort in exchange for so little! All factors of production, save energy that remains volatile, have plummeted in value terms.[26]

The second point then is that this reconfiguration, starting with the market fundamentalism of the 1980s, has meant a downward pressure on working-class standards everywhere. True, Marx was prescient that capitalist accumulation had to involve the growing concentration and centralization of wealth in fewer and private hands. Yet its corollary has not occurred: the conflict between such a private appropriation of people's energy with the increasing socialization of production. The socialized and waged factory-based proletariat, conscious of what it wants and wanting what it knows, coordinated through a Party, the Modern Prince, has not emerged in dominance anywhere in the recent period. The concentration and centralization of wealth and its increasing independence from political constraints and regulation can be demonstrated amply. The power and sway of a number of multinationals/transnationals (TNCs) is staggering.[27]

Furthermore, the shift of the total share of economic activity to a service sector and the decline of blue-collar work has had enormous implications for trade unions and the power-base of most trade union formations in the industrial and industrializing countries of the South from Brazil to India: instead of these patterns socializing the world of work, *they have led to fragmentation and dispersal*; instead of leading to job security, they have achieved the opposite, insecurity; instead of revolutionizing the consumption norms of the working population they have led to a persistent and pervasive inequality in life-chances within regions, between regions, within and between countries and so on.[28]

By implication, economic growth has meant vulnerability, overwork, flexible and non-standard work with its concommitant weakening of trade unions. Such shifts have also affected the divisions between mental and manual distinctions on the shop floor. If the drive for worker participation was to have won inroads into the conception, decision and strategizing centres of the world of work, such victories are in crisis as this function is increasingly being outsourced.

Thirdly, on the African continent, social processes, accommodation and conflict need an understanding of this epochal transition, the prior structural adjustment period but most importantly how the African landscape is responding to the new waves of accumulation, together with the location of the continent in these networks of livelihoods-creation and strife. This growth of an average of 7.7% is powered by two energy grids: the need for oil, raw materials, minerals, flora, fauna and agro-inputs and by the entry of BRICS-linked capital with China, South Africa and India forming an avant-garde on the continent and large scale remittances from a third African diaspora, a new migrant proletariat, the largest ever, a movement from below that is highly diverse and intterconnected.[29]

There are another two processes. A move of micro-entrepreneurs from China, India, Pakistan, Bangladesh, Ethiopia, Somalia and increasingly the Levant into small-town economies, dragging behind them commodities from the East and micro-entrepreneurs from most of Africa to the East and dragging back with them a similar array of goods. Finally, there is the world of the illicit, controlled by large-scale syndicates that are shaping, through gangs and networks, life on the ground and new patterns of unregulated production.[30]

In short, the structural adjustment programmes of the 1980s and the 1990s, including the violence and strife of those years have started an enormous process of de-peasantization which does not translate into de-ruralization, as remittances and oscillations from country to town and town to country leave the villages intact.[31]

This shift has fed into some of the fastest urban growth phenomena in the world: Lagos, Khartum and Kinshasa are three of the five fastest growing cities in the world.[32] They are enclaves of improvisation and survivalist strategy capturing the majority of migrants and the city's chronically unemployed. Then there are those who fled crossing borders who exist and subsist in large UN encampments or cities of adjacent countries; then, fanning out they will be found in three main destinations – Europe (many caught in the camps in Europe's margins), the Middle East and South Africa. In South Africa's case it is guesstimated that 10% of its working population is made up of such migrants from, in the main, 19 African countries. A final growing tendency is heading Eastwards.[33]

All these energies are below the elite's radar: there has been explosive urban resistance in most mega-cities which needs its own sociology. That there has been and that there persists a popular discontent and disconnect from power elites in Africa and the Middle East is not enough. Such a 'disconnect' has not been new. With rare exceptions both dispositions have been an underlying feature of post-colonial urban life.[34] After the enthusiasms of independence and the shock of the new, people learnt to shrug their shoulders, got used to speak under their breath and tended to worry about the local landlords, shack-lords and their goons rather than the emerging post-colonial overlords.

As in Ben Okri's fiction, political formations would sometimes arrive as the Party of the Rich or the Party of the Poor, beat up a few locals and make sure that they got another mandate on election day from the fewer and fewer that turned up to cast their ballots in usually to be discarded boxes.[35] Such contrary dispositions have been the stuff of literature and of popular song and the kind of stuff that subsisted from the bazaar and marketplace to the worker quarters. You did not need to be a sociologist to sense this recalcitrant popular culture, its grotesque and humorous realism from Kinshasa, Lagos to Cairo.[36]

In rare moments of genius such dispositions were captured in novels like the *Beautyful Ones are not yet Born* or in the vivid descriptions of the 'harafish' in Mahfouz's prose. The deep disappointment about promises promised and never kept, about the bureaucratic hell of post-colonial states, about the death of dreams turned to stoicism and perseverance. Otherwise, you needed to sense the murmurs in the stadia where men acted out their passions, in the stalls where women more than sold and bartered wares, in the street, by the mosque or at the drinking dens and palm-wine joints.

Whereas the discontent would be submerged, the disconnect in particular did guarantee some predictability and stability in daily life – the big men and their wives were over there, or on TV, or in the infuriating cavalcades that jammed the streets ... but, as long as they were there and the taxman remained invisible, life went on. It was only when this distance was breached or the predictability shattered that discontent turned to protest. But then, protest leaders would quickly be 'sorted out' so well that most chose to leave the country rather than get used to the constant beatings.

The state was supposed to worry about models of development, its comprador cold war arrangements, look after the military and parades, cry about the national debt, re-borrow to keep its standards of life, filch some money off to Switzerland. That much, people could tolerate. What was and remained 'not proper' was to impose livelihoods hardship on its subjects or mess with people's daily dignity and such breaches did start with Structural Adjustment Programmes and their 'conditionalities'.

Of course, countries like Egypt could use their proximity to Israel to get some unconditional treatment for a while but most, remote from Jerusalem or oil rigs had to make do with the conditions.

In popular cultures furthermore, the way leaderships 'played' the cold war was less of an immediate concern than the fact that they were all seen to have been corrupted.[37] The perception that this was so was enforced by the rise of Political Islam since the Iranian Revolution. That most elites were deemed parasitic was a statement of fact rather than a debating question.[38]

But when Structural Adjustment Programmes bit, despite some riots here and there, those that had the means and networks to help them move, started out the diaspora that we have just described – this was a globalization from below and despite fences. It was a politics of flight rather than resistance where the new economic fugitives met prior communities of their own, made up of prior migrations, internment camps and prior refugees.[39]

And there, thanks to the new media of communication, new connections, communities and meanings were deepening the 'disconnect' from the elites they had left behind. The ructions that shook North Africa and the Middle East starting from Tunis this time were not about 'immiseration'. No, they occurred at a moment of an unacceptable breach: Africa was growing at an unprecedented level as we had described – with Tunisia, Libya, Ethiopia and Egypt growing at more than 10% per annum for five years when the crisis struck.[40] It was the way the regimes responded to look after themselves and their immediate supplicants, passing all the strain onto their urban and rural harafish that cracked the truce. In most cities in Africa – Lagos, Accra, Addis, Nairobi, Luanda, Maputo to name but a few – people have been actively protesting and challenging dispensations.[41]

Workers, Precarious Jobbers, Students, Informal and Formal Bazaar Traders, the Middle Classes and most noticeably Women, many, many women across classes responded to the young man setting himself alight. The whole region responded in profound ways and Tahrir Square, with its stones raining and its fierce resistance, became an icon of social dignity and social being everywhere. It was not merely an explosion limited to the Arab world.

Fourthly, the 'disconnect' and 'discontent' has found at least four important outlets: in the growth of socio-political Islam and evangelical Christianity[42]; in ethnic and village-based associations[43]; in a populism that demands authoritative 'others' to intervene and sort out local politics of authority; and in secularist, work, craft, student, social welfare or trade-based associations. The mistake left movements make is to celebrate all manifestations of resistance without understanding their nature, patterns and quality. Yes, students and workers were the epicenter of the beginning of the Arab spring, but not the sole force of its maturing.[44]

It is a complex politics – defined at its diasporic end with the experience of racism and derogation, especially in Europe and the Gulf, finding support networks across their ethnic niches, being defined and being in similar spaces as other 'troublesome' people, being identified as serious border-breechers, moving through no-go areas controlled by armed insurgents, facing vigilantisms in every possible poorer area, being drawn into and out of campaigns of moral restoration: re-assertions of patriarchy and hetero-normativity, in and through that, establishing communities of trust, practice and survival has been an enormous task.

All such traditions and psychic commitments are to be found among the millions of foreign migrants in South Africa.[45] South Africa like all other BRICS countries has a mining and industrial base that has been shrinking somewhat and declining in value-terms vis-à-vis services but whose working processes and the fragmentation outlined above, the casualization and outsourcing of its non-core activities and the informalization of many tasks that constitute any of its value-chains, opened up the space for the absorption of foreign migrants.

Furthermore, the casual nature of some farming, domestic and hospitality services have done something similar. Additionally, vending and informal trading conducted by migrants has penetrated the core of black working-class life. Given South Africa's unemployment problem this has turned often into violent confrontations, but also, it has gone the other way, through growing networks of solidarity.[46]

Furthermore, South Africa has been a higher education destination for the African continent with more than 10% of its undergraduate and more than 20% of its post-graduate education. Whereas at least half of such students are from the continent's economic, professional and political elites, the rest are the children of these migrating networks who subsist economically, culturally and socially within them. Associations and networks that have been spawned in this process are in good formal relationships with South Africa's two largest trade union federations: COSATU and NACTU. Many of their affiliates have sister industrial trade unions in most of the SADC areas; informal traders are linked across the continent and the linkages back to the villages and broadly the countryside remain active.[47]

It is within this new and complex reconfiguration 'from below' – linking villages, home country mega-cities and the diaspora that pressure will emerge to shape a pro-poor BRICS agenda, if at all. Whereas existing power blocs will strive to articulate the regions through their development bank, infrastructurally creating common renewable energy sources (hydro), integrated railway and transport systems, telecommunications and informational pathways systems, it is within these new emerging energies that the relaxation of the impediments for the movement of people and goods within regions; a strong drive towards nutritional democracy will be found; a move in the customary areas and villages from subsistence to sustenance and an increase of the non-commodified social asset base of communities and strong redistributive policies at a regional level.

In South Africa, Brazil, India and China the class tensions and conflicts are intensifying.[48] There is no space here to describe the forms of polarization that are proliferating. Similarly extensive horizontal networks of trade unions, civic associations, landless movements, women's networks and political formations are proliferating between these countries. All one can say is that unless these energies imprint themselves on the epochal and systemic change the inequalities and forms of dispossession may increase exponentially.

If such movements and energies do not come to shape the priorities of what BRICS countries understand as their 'development', we may be in the throes of a horrendous new phase of surplus and resource extraction. It will be a phase beyond the Washington consensus and beyond simplistic assertions of the Polanyian counter-movement, as if that ever happened without people.

The late Giovanni Arrighi concluded his *Adam Smith in Beijing* as follows, in the hope that China and India would be at the heart of the emergence of a new more inclusive Bandung:

> For a new Bandung can do what the old could not: it can mobilize and use the global market as an instrument of equalization of South-North power relations. The foundations of the old Bandung were strictly political-ideological and as such, were easily destroyed by the monetarist counterrevolution. The foundations of the Bandung that may be emerging now, in contrast, are primarily economic and as such, far more solid.[49]

To that effect he quotes the past Minister of Foreign Relations of India: '(it) was built on an idealistic conception of Asian brotherhood, based on shared experiences of colonialism and of cultural ties ... The rhythm of the region today is determined, however, as much by trade, investment and production as by history and culture.'[50]

It is precisely the tensions over the 'rhythm' and character of this change in the division of labour that sociology has to pay attention to. Unlike the 14–16th centuries where the emergence of Europe from forager to hegemon was predicated on another's involution, the interconnected nature of economic life makes involution a complex process: Europe will not decline but large swathes of it will as the recent German-led structural adjustment of its territory implied; Brazil might emerge in Mercosur in a peculiar marriage between Bolivarian ideas and resource piracy; in short, an involution of the US might end the Chinese and Indian miracles. As long as growth and accumulation are at the core of any world system, another world will be hardly possible.

Notes

1   Chase-Dunn, C.K. (1991) *Global Formation: Structures of the World Economy*. London, Oxford and New York: Basil Blackwell; Wallerstein, I. (2000) *The Wallerstein Reader*. Yale: Yale University Press.

2   Sherratt, A. (2000) 'Envisioning global change: A long-term perspective', in R.A. Denemark, J. Friedman, B.K. Gills and J. Modelski (eds), *World System History: The Social Science of Long-term Change*. London/New York: Routledge. pp. 115–32; Sherratt, A. (2004) *Trade Routes: The Growth of Global Trade*, ArchAtlas, Version 4.1. Available at: www.archatlas.org/Trade/Trade.php (accessed 28 March 2014); Curtin, P.D. (1984) *Cross-cultural Trade in World History*. Cambridge: Cambridge University Press; Andrews, K.R. (1985) *Trade, Plunder, and Settlement: Maritime Enterprise and the Genesis of the British Empire, 1480–1630*. Cambridge: Cambridge University Press; Inikori, J.E (1992a) 'Africa in world history' in B.A. Ogot (ed.), *General History of Africa*, Vol. V, 16th–18th Century. Berkeley: Heineman and California: Unesco; Inikori, J.E (1992) *The Chaining of a Continent: Export Demand for Captives and the History of Africa South of the Sahara, 1450–1870*. Kingston, Jamaica: Mona; Inikori, J.E (2002) *Africans and the Industrial Revolution*. Cambridge: Cambridge University Press; Hall, R. (1998) *Empires of the Monsoon: A History of the Indian Ocean and its Invaders*. London: Harper Collins; Habib, I. (1995) *Essays in Indian History – Towards a Marxist Perception*. Delhi: Tulika Books; Eaton, R. (2013) 'Revisiting the Persian cosmopolis', *Asia Times*, 19 July. Available at: www.atimes.com/atimes/South_Asia/SOU-01-190713.html.; Frank, A.G. and Gills, B.K. (1993) *The World System: Five Hundred Years or Five Thousand?* London: Routledge; Pomeranz, K. and Topik, S. (2012) *The World that Trade Created: Society, Culture and the World Economy, 1400 to the Present*, 3rd edn. London: Routledge.

3   Lach, D. and van Kley, E. (1993) *Asia in the Making of Europe*. Chicago: Chicago University Press; Wong, R.B. (1997) *China Transformed: Historical Change and the Limits of European Experience*. Cornell: Cornell University Press; Pomeranz, K. (2000) *The Great Divergence: China, Europe and the Making of the Modern World Economy*. Princeton: Princeton University Press; Buck, D.D. (1999) 'Was it pluck or luck that made the west grow rich?', *Journal of World History*, 10(2): 413–30; Brook, T. (1998) *The Confusions of*

Pleasure: Commerce and Culture in Ming China. Berkeley: University of California Press; Brook, T. (2010) *Troubled Empire: China in the Yuan and the Ming Dynasties*. Cambridge, MA: Harvard University Press; Bhambra, G. (2007) *Rethinking Modernity*. London: Palgrave; Hung, H. (2008) 'Agricultural revolution and elite reproduction in Qing China: The transition to capitalism debate revisited', *American Sociological Review*, 73(4).

    4   Frank, A.G. (1998) *Reorient: Global Economy in the Asian Age*. Berkeley: University of California Press; Chase-Dunn, C. (2000) 'Review of Andre Gunder Frank's "Reorient: Global Economy in the Asian Age"', *American Journal of Sociology*, 105(4).

    5   Arrighi, G. (2005) 'Hegemony unraveling – I', *New Left Review*, II/32; Arrighi, G. (2005) 'Hegemony unraveling – II', *New Left Review*, II/33.

    6   Tables by Kershan Parcham in Sitas, A. et al. (2014) *Reconfiguring the World System: BRICS and the Challenges of Historical Change-A Preliminary Research Report*. Johannesburg: National Institute for the Humanities and the Social Sciences.

    7   Observer Foundation (2013) *A Long Term Vision for BRICS*, Draft Document, Observer Research, New Delhi. Also materials and data in preparation of *BRICS Long Term Vision*, BRICS Think Tanks Council.

    8   Department of Foreign Affairs/International Cooperation, Ministerial Speeches, 11 July 2014.

    9   Sitas, A., Keim, N., Damodaran, S., Trimikliniotis, N. and Garba, F. (2014) *Gauging and Engaging Deviance, 1600–2000*. Delhi: Tulika Press.

    10   Hobsbawm, E.J. (1989) *The Age of Empire, 1875–1914*. London: Abacus. For the downside, see: Davis, M. (2001) *Late Victorian Holocausts, El Nino Famines and the Making of the Third World*. London: Verso.

    11   Sitas et al., *Reconfiguring the World System*.

    12   Harvey, D. (2007) *A Brief History of Neoliberalism*. Oxford: Oxford University Press.

    13   Betlleheim, C. (1978) *The Great Leap Backward*. New York: Monthly Review Press; Selden, M. (2003) 'Rethinking China's socialist economic development', *Political Economy of Chinese Development*, 3–38.

    14   Jalan, B. (1971) 'Review: '*The Story of Industrialization*', *Economic and Political Weekly*, 6(10); Rudolph, L. and Hoeber Rudolph, S. (1987) *In Pursuit of Lakshmi*. Delhi: Orient Longman; Das, A.N. (1994) 'Brazil or India: Comparing notes on industrialization', *Economic and Political Weekly*, 19 February; Ghosh, J. and Chandekar, C.P. (eds) (2010) *After Crisis*. Delhi: Tulika Press.

    15   Baer, W. (1980) 'Evaluating the impasse of Brazil's industrialization', *Luso-Brazilian Review*, 10(3); Furtado, C. (1984) 'Researching Brazil's recession', *Third World Quarterly*, 6(3).

    16   Marais, H. (2001) *South Africa: Limits to Change*. London: Palgrave Macmillan.

    17   Whyte, M.K. (ed.) (2010) *One Country, Two Societies: Rural-Urban Inequality in Contemporary China*. Boston, MA: Harvard University Press.

    18   Webster, E. and Von Holdt, K. (eds) (2005) *Beyond the Apartheid Workplace. Studies in Transition*. Scottsville: University of KwaZulu-Natal Press; Breman, J. (2008) *Jan Breman Omnibus: Comprising of Peasants, Migrants and Paupers; Wage Hunters and Gatherers and the Labouring Poor in India*. Oxford: University Press; Sitas, A. (2010) *The Mandela Decade – Labour, Culture and Politics in Post-Apartheid South Africa*. Pretoria: University of South Africa Press; Standing, G. (2011) *The Precariat: The New Dangerous Class*. London: Bloomsbury.

19   Ibid.

20   Sader, E. (2005) 'Taking Lula's measure', *New Left Review,* 33; De Oliveira, F. (2006) 'Lula in the labyrinth', *New Left Review,* 42.

21   Whether it is from the work of Jean Baudrillard in the 70s, Andre Gorz in the 80s, Ulrich Beck in the 80s and 90s and/or Manuel Castells in the 90s and the 2000s, the shift away from 'productivism' to identities and consumption has been persistent.

22   International Iron and Steel Institute data base, accessed 2012.

23   *World Steel Organisation: World Steel in Figures.* Available at: www.worldsteel.org.

24   UNIDO (2009) *World Industrialization Report.* Vienna: UNIDO.

25   Figures from UNCTAD (United Nations Conference on Trade and Development) (2014) *Economic Development in Africa.* New York: UNCTAD. According to the World Bank (available at: data.worldbank.org) in 2016, global growth has slumped to 3% with UK and the USA improving somewhat at 2.9 and 1.5% respectively. Russia, Brazil and South Africa have also slumped below but China and India are still far ahead at 7.8% growth per annum.

26   See Sitas et al. (2014), *Reconfiguring the World System.*

27   Fonseca, J. (2014) 'Large enterprises and corporate power', in I. Wallerstein, *The World is Out of Joint.* New York: Paradigm.

28   Korzeniewicz, R.P. and Moran, T.P. (2010) *Unveiling Inequality.* New York: Russell Sage Foundation.

29   Boardman, H.G. (2007) *Africa's Silk Road: China's and India's New Economic Frontier.* Washington DC: The International Bank for Reconstruction and Development/ The World Bank; Alden, C., Large, D. and de Oliveira, R.S. (2008) *China Returns to Africa: A Superpower and a Continent Embrace.* London: C Hurst; Miller, D., Saunders, R. and Oloyede, O. (2008) 'South African corporations and post-apartheid expansion in Africa', *African Sociological Review*, 12(1); Simpfendorfer, B. (2011) *The New Silk Road: How a Rising Arab World is Turning Away from the West and Rediscovering China*, revised edn. London: Palgrave Macmillan.

30   See Castells, M. (2002) *End of Millennium.* Oxford: Blackwells.

31   From Third African Diaspora data base (600 qualitative interviews), Sociology Department, University of Cape Town.

32   Taylor, P.J., Firth, A., Hoyler, M. and Smith, D. (2010) 'Explosive city growth in the modern world-system: An initial inventory derived from urban demographic changes', *Urban Geography*, 31(7): 865–84; Taylor, P. et al. (2014) 'Cities', in I. Wallerstein, *Time is Out of Joint: World Polarizations.* New York: Paradigm Books; Chandler, T. (1987) *Four Thousand Years of Urban Growth: An Historical Census.* Queenston: St. David's University Press.

33   Landau, L.B. (ed.) (2012) *Exorcising the Devil Within – Xenophobia, Violence and Statecraft in Contemporary South Africa.* Johannesburg: Witwatersrand University Press.

34   Bayat, A. (2013) *Life as Politics – How Ordinary People Change the Middle East.* Palo Alto: Stanford University Press.

35   Okri, B. (1993) *The Famished Road.* London: Anchor.

36   African Centre for the Cities; El Azzazi et al. (2011) 'The Egyptian Revolution – a participant's account from Tahrir Square', *Anthropology Today,* 27(2); El-Afidi, A. (2011) 'Constituting liberty…', *Third World Quarterly,* 32(7); Abdelhalim, J. (2015) 'Can subjects become citizens?', *Transience,* 6(1).

37   Sitas, A. (2011) 'Unassimilable otherness: The reworking of traumas by refugees in contemporary South Africa', in R. Eyerman et al. (eds), *Narrating Trauma: On the Impact of Collective Suffering*. New York: Paradigm Publishers.

38   Ibid.

39   Sitas, A. and Lorgat, A. (2011) *The Human Social Dynamics in Development Grand Challenge Proposal: Mapping the Third African Diaspora*. Cape Town; Patterson, T.R. and Kelley, R.D.G. (2000) 'Unfinished migrations: Reflections on the African diaspora and the making of the modern world', *African Studies Review*, 43(1): 11–45.

40   See *The Plan of Action for the Strategy of Africa's Accelerated Industrialization*, CAMI (Conference of African Ministers of Industry) Bureau, Addis Ababa, 2008.

41   See Omege, K. (ed.) (2015) *The Crisis of Postcoloniality in Africa*. Dakar: CODESRIA Publications.

42   See for example, Dijhorn, E. et al. (eds) (2013) *Militancy and Violence in West Africa*. Abingdon, Oxon: Routledge; and Englund, H. (ed.) (2011) *Christianity and Public Culture in Africa*. Athens: Ohio University Press.

43   Sitas et al., *Gauging and Engaging*.

44   Bayat, A. (2006) *Middle East and its Subaltern Politics and Movements*. Istanbul: Iletisin; Bayat, *Life as Politics*.

45   Cohen, R. (2006) *Migration and its Enemies: Global Capital, Migrant Labour and the Nation-state*. London: Ashgate Publishing; Castles, S. and Miller, M.J. (2009) *The Age of Migration: International Population Movements in the Modern World*. New York: The Guilford Press.

46   Nyamnjoh, F.B. (2006) *Insiders and Outsiders: Citizenship and Xenophobia in Contemporary Southern Africa*. London: Zed Books; Garba, F. (2012) '"Amakwerekwere" and "Burger" – of livelihood and belonging: African diasporas in Germany and South Africa', Masters Thesis, Global Studies, Freiburg University.

47   Deumert, A. and Mabandla, N. (2013) 'Every day a new shop pops up: South Africa's "new" Chinese diaspora and the multilingual transformation of rural towns', *English Today*, 29(1): 44–52; Ighobor, K. (2013) 'China in the heart of Africa', *Africa Renewal online*, January.

48   Martin, W. (2008) 'Washington consensus, Bandung consensus or People's consensus?', *African Sociological Review*, 12(1); Singer, A. (2014) 'Rebellion in Brazil', *New Left Review*, 85.

49   Arrighi, G. (2007) *Adam Smith in Beijing: Lineages of the twenty-first century*. London: Verso; Arrighi, G. and Zhang, L. (2009) 'Beyond the Washington consensus: A new Bandung', in J. Shefner and P. Fernandez-Kelly (eds), *Globalization and Beyond*. University Park, PA: Pennsylvania State University Press.

50   Arrighi, *Adam Smith*, pp. 384–5.

4

Stratification *Requiescat in Pace**: Paradigm Shift from 'Stratification' and Mobility to Inequality

Göran Therborn

Hopefully the 2014 Yokohama Congress of the ISA will generate a paradigm shift within sociology. Isn't it odd, that among the fifty-plus Research Committees of the ISA, there is not one focusing explicitly on inequality? Instead, we have RC28 on 'Social Stratification', a venerable club of technically very sophisticated members mainly interested in 'social mobility', a notion the undertext of which has always been that inequality does not really matter. What matters are people's chances of moving up the ladder of inequality, within a generation or over two generations. As two representative figures, writing about 'four generations' of stratification research have put it, 'The core questions of our field, regarding to what extent, in what ways, and under what conditions processes of social mobility and status attainment vary in different social contexts ...' (Treiman and Ganzeboom 2000: 140). Now, currently actually active members of RC28 are most likely to be concerned with inequality, but their, so far, accepted historical legacy is a hindrance.

'Stratification' derives from geology, and was imported into sociology by the great Russian-turned-American conservative Pitirim Sorokin, who was interested in social mobility – the research of which he was one of the pioneers – but hardly in inequality. The concept was further theorized by Talcott Parsons and included in 'structural-functionalism' as a hierarchy of evaluations of social positions by a presumed social consensus.

The theoretical world of stratification and the actual one of inequality seem to exist on different planets. Stratification does not stunt children and cut the lifespan of the disadvantaged, inequality does. Higher strata do not stigmatize and humiliate lower ones, as existential inequality means. Higher strata do not exclude, subordinate, and exploit other strata, as happens in the actual world of inequality (see further Therborn 2013). Sociologists of social mobility have often seen themselves as scientific flag captains of the discipline, as a vanguard of methodological sophistication. Without delving into any serious intra-disciplinary comparison, I am more inclined to accept than to dispute this claim. However, I also have the impression that after the landmark contributions of Eriksson and Goldthorpe (1992) and of Shavit and Blossfeld (1993) the paradigm has lost its dynamism of originality and creativity. Within the mobility framework itself, it can be argued that the two most creative later developments have come from outside sociology altogether, from John Roemer (1998) and from Gregory Clark (2014). Both authors (economists) take mobility studies onto a new methodological level, with direct relevance to issues of inequality. '... [T]he time has come ...', Immanuel Wallerstein (1979: 133) wrote in his obituary of modernization, 'to look reality in its face.' Saying goodbye to stratificationism means the same thing.

A sociological turn to concerns of inequality had better start from Amartya Sen's (1992; 2009) mind-opening question – 'Inequality of what?' – and his agenda-setting answer: inequality of capability to function fully as a human being.

Human inequality is a historical social construction by which the possibilities of realizing human capability are allocated unequally. Human beings differ, but inequality is not difference. Differences are given – by God or by nature – or chosen, e.g. a style of life or an opinion. That, for instance, some individuals draw a better lot out of the genetic lottery is a difference, and not inequality. But that many children are barred from developing fully, cognitively and socially, by their parental and societal milieu, is inequality.

Conventional sociological wisdom on the topic, especially in the US and the UK, has tried to grasp complexities of inequality by highlighting descriptive categories of its manifestations, such as the trinity of class, gender, and race, and their 'intersectionality'. It is high time to go beyond that, into theorizations of the meaning of human inequality, its analytical dimensions, its processes and mechanisms.

Human beings, and their functioning, can be understood from three fundamental angles, first as living organisms, susceptible to pain and pleasure, health and illness, and with a definite, though variable, life span. Inequality in this respect we may term *vital inequality*, and we can measure it most conveniently as health or life expectancy, but also by looking at other indicators of socially induced organismic growth, such as early child development. Secondly, human beings are also seen as persons, or subjects, with a will, a mind, a psyche, and as such endowed with an intrinsic autonomy, which can be constricted and contested by others, for various reasons and in various ways. As persons, humans are receptive to treatments with recognition and respect, or their opposites of ignorance, contempt, and humiliation. This is the *existential* dimension of inequality. Racism, sexism, and patriarchy are the most notorious, but far from the only examples. Thirdly, humans are social actors, in need of resources to act effectively. The unequal distribution of resources among human actors, *resource inequality*, is an ostentatious third aspect of inequality, and income (with monetary wealth) is the most convertible resource currency. Social contacts and power are other relevant resources, though much more difficult to measure and compare. By the way, talent is another actor's resource, but a given endowment and not an expression of inequality.

The production of inequality

The production process had better be seen at two levels, one systemic, which has been the predominant, implicit sociological conception, and one inter-generational and inter-personal, highlighted by psychologists and (some exceptional) economists (Cunha and Heckman 2009; Heckman and Mosso 2014). Both should be brought into focus. The four basic mechanisms of inequality (Therborn 2013: 54ff) – distanciation, exclusion, hierarchization and exploitation – apply to both.

The systemic production of inequality

At the macro level, vital inequality is shaped by population ecology, i.e., how the population is distributed, with respect to the food supply, among safe or disease-prone, polluting, or hazardous environments, in relation to medical-hygienic knowledge, and in terms of access to a health care system. Existential inequality is rooted in socio-cultural systems of inferiority and superiority, buttressed and protected by polities, and fitted into economic systems, from macho nomad pastoralism to plantation slavery and capitalism, and into political boundaries between citizens and others. Modern states have a decisive capacity to make or break institutionalized existential inequality, establishing, maintaining or abolishing institutions like slavery, apartheid, and segregation, patriarchal or sexist rules and laws.

Resource inequality is governed by the political economy of a mode of production, and by political rule and policies. In the contemporary world, the economic system is capitalism and its drive of capital accumulation.

But the political dimension should not be relegated to secondary significance. Once established, the state has been crucial to the allocation of
human capability. State power has historically produced the most colos-
sal manifestations of resource inequality, still to be seen in the enormous
monuments of rulers to themselves, such as the Giza pyramids or the
underground imperial city in Chang'an. Modern state spaces largely shape
the life expectancy, the existential conditions, as well as the income of
the human population (Milanovic 2011: 112ff). In our time states have a
great redistributive capacity, taking out a third of market income inequality in Germany, around 18% in USA, and 40% in Sweden (OECD 2011:
Table 7.3). In the rest of the world, there is much less state redistribution.
Even at the height of the recent Latin American moment of equality, maximum income distribution was less than in USA, 15% in Uruguay, 12%
in Argentina and Brazil, 7% in Mexico, 2% per cent in Colombia (Hanni
et al. 2015: Table 1).

The family systems are imbricated with the other inequality-producing
systems and have powerful effects on all three dimensions of inequality.
The sternly patriarchal family systems of South and East Asia have until
rather recently cut the lives of girls by infanticide (common in pre-modern
China) and/or by under-nutrition and medical non- or under-treatment
(frequent in most of South Asia). Currently, misogynist vital inequality
is mainly produced by sex-selective abortions (Therborn 2004: 110–21),
a practice recently spread to post-Communist Caucasus (Michael et al.
2013). Patriarchy, a major manifestation of existential inequality, is, of
course, one aspect of family systems. The preservation and accumulation
of property, status, and other resources, were what the aristocratic and the
bourgeois family were primarily about, in their marriage strategies and
their generation of heirs. Inheritance rules are part of all family systems,
and as such crucial allocators of resources in all economic systems of
private property.

The interpersonal, intergenerational generation of unequal individuals

The micro perspective focuses on the generation of unequal individuals
through inter-individual inter-generational interaction. This means paying attention to two processes necessary for the making of functioning
humans: *capability formation* and *self formation*, the former a focus of
the new economics of inequality (Heckman and Mosso 2014), the latter a
classical concern of social psychology.

Capability may be seen as skills, motoric, cognitive, and social. They have a potential provided by an inherited genetic program, but the extent of the latter's actualization and development is determined by interaction with mother, father, and/or other proximate individuals. It has been known for some time to be affected also by foetal experiences *in utero*, such as mother's malnutrition, resulting in underweight babies, tending to slower and truncated capability development, and more proneness to heart disease and diabetes later in life (Risnes 2011).

Recent biological research is now beginning to unravel mechanisms of this kind of foetus–mother interaction, as *epigenetic* processes. They refer to changes in the expression of the child's genetic program which do not derive from its DNA. Maternal nutrition, pollution exposure, drug abuse, and social trauma during pregnancy are external social factors discovered to be internalizeable by the foetus and capable of altering the child's genetic course (Kaur et al. 2013; Resendiz et al. 2013).

Humans are not born equal. Socially created inequality starts before birth, spawning unequal health and life expectancy. After birth, capability formation proceeds very fast, and its foundations are mostly established by the age of three. While capability, of course, increases well after that, early underdevelopment creates a handicap which rapidly becomes increasingly difficult, and by adolescence almost impossible, to repair (Cunha and Heckman 2009: 327ff). Unequal capability predisposes adult actors to unequal resources, even before unequal inheritance of property and contacts.

Self formation is the second fundamental aspect of child development, unfolding in interaction with social others, producing personal selves, reflective personalities, aware of who they are and of their place in their social environment. From a perspective of existential (in)equality, the two most significant aspects are the development or not of self-esteem and of self-confidence. The very meaning of racism and of patriarchy is to deny self-esteem and self-confidence to Black (or any other racial target) and girl children, and to install shame, self-contempt, fear instead. Such punitive processes are, of course, far from always successful, but they usually inflict lasting wounds on your self and your self-conception.

Prejudice and stigma impact as stressors on the victims, and have as such both somatic and psychological effects (for an overview, see, e.g., Williams and Mohammed 2009). They also by themselves cause underperformance by the targets. Experimental psychology has shown that groups, for example of girls and boys, Blacks and Whites, members of different castes, experimentally told they are inferior, perform badly on given tasks, and vice versa better if told they are expected to be superior (Mass and Cadinu 2003; Hoff and Pandey 2006).

Children of poor, oppressed and/or discriminated populations are loaded with two sets of heavy burdens, which cause many or most of them to under-perform. One is the burden of social determinants of ill-health, stunted development, and deficient emotional security and cognitive stimulation, all bearing upon capability formation. The other operates through the negative impacts on self-development of esteem, confidence, and ambition by existential processes of stigmatization, humiliation, and frightening. Both these childhood experiences tend to have life-long effects, beginning life-curves of cumulated disadvantages (see further Therborn 2016; cf. Schafer et al. 2011).

These cumulated disadvantages are 'effects of race' and/or gender, not out of any genetic determination but effects of experiences of racist/sexist social constructions. What the American writer Ta-Nehisi Coates (2015: 7) has said about race may be generalized to gender: race and gender are the children of racism and sexism, not their father and mother.

The systemic production of inequality operates through the inter-individual inter-generational processes of capability and self formation. But the latter can also function *sub rosa* beneath, before or after systemic institutions, as, for example, racist or sexist everyday practices. European anti-Semitism before Nazism, US police and judicial racism under a Black Presidency, and sexism after public patriarchy, and, of course, class relations or class-ism after proclamations of equal opportunity are bitter manifestations. The very early handicaps of capability and self forma-tion among oppressed or discriminated groups are crucial to egalitarian attention and policy practice, not only for their enduring effects on the victims, for generations. Systemic inequalities tend to leave a structural legacy of advantages and disadvantages for a long time after the system itself has been dismantled institutionally, and disadvantages tend to feed and reinforce stereotypical prejudice that any disadvantaged population is inherently inferior – Blacks, Indians, women, 'Gypsies', workers, poor people in general.

The family: Producing the capabilities and the selves of the rulers and the ruled

The family is the pivot between the systemic and the individual, the most pertinent social environment of self and capability formation, and parental–child relations are central to their development. Connecting this to the social systems of political economy means looking into how differentiated families at the same time produced ruling class selves and capabilities, and the selves and capabilities of peasants, slaves, and workers. To my knowledge, the family formation of the children of different classes is not yet a systematic topic of family sociology, and my own work (Therborn 2004) was focused on patriarchy and fertility. While this obviously is not the place to remedy that lacuna, two sets of observation pertaining to the generation of unequal individuals may be squeezed in. One refers to the middle and upper middle class of capitalist societies of today. The other to the working classes of contemporary developed capitalism.

Middle class families of North Atlantic capitalism have become more educationally homogamous (Hou and Myles 2007), more stable, and more actively involved in the capability and self making of their children (Murray 2012: Ch. 8; Putnam 2015: 62ff). This may partly derive from cultural change – the '1968' movement of Feminism and of personal development – but also from the marketization and globalization of society where competitive capabilities and selves have become much more important. The classical bourgeois family in its production of a new bourgeois generation could largely rely on property inheritance and social contacts vouching for 'good family', and focused on a cultured, rather than a competitive, education.

At the opposite end of contemporary capitalism, in the world of the precariat (Standing 2011), the opposite is happening (Statistics Sweden 2013; Murray 2012; Cherlin 2014; Putnam 2015). Sexual partnerships are becoming more unstable, with the economic situation and prospects of the partners, resulting in an increasing proportion of children growing up with single mothers, which nearly always means in relative poverty and with little 'cultural capital' bequeathed.

We have seen this dual family and individual development pattern before. One was Euro-American plantation slavery, and its Creole family system of strong White patriarchy with male sexual predation, on one side, and the denial of slave family formation on the other, creating a macho sexist, matrifocal kin pattern among Blacks (Therborn 2004: 155ff). Something similar, though not as sinister, happened in rapidly urbanizing and industrializing 19th century Europe, and probably in equivalent cities of the Americas, with a huge increase of births outside marriage (Therborn 2004: 148ff). Industrial development and the stabilization of an industrial working class, largely adopting the bourgeois family as a model, changed these precarious and informal partnerships into white gown and veil marriages with respectable stability (Gillis 1985: 232ff), spawning disciplined working-class selves capable of working industrial capitalism.

The neoliberal financial capitalist destruction of the industrial working class, creating the precariat, has pulled the carpet under the industrial working-class family. While driving children and adult individuals apart, the new duality of the North Atlantic family pattern has a systemic rationale similar to that of the Creole duality of slaveowners' patriarchal family and slaves' non-family. The current duality is geared to producing, on the one hand, competitive middle-class children for a competitive middle-class society, and on the other, insecure, low-skilled, non-attached children for the precarious, albeit always necessary, jobs servicing the 'creative' classes (cf. Cherlin 2014: 172ff).

Life courses of inequality

As an inter-generational inter-personal process, inequality is best understood from the perspective of the human life course. Social inequality means life courses of cumulated advantages or disadvantages (cf. DiPrete and Eirich 2006), with some, usually minority, stations of possible redress or reversal. It operates remarkably similarly all over the planet, albeit at very different levels of absolute deprivation or privilege. In a recent work (Therborn 2016) I have tried to outline life curves of inequality, of cumulative advantages and disadvantages, from the epigenetics of socially induced unequal foetal developments to the socially unequal health and life prospects of old age.

Profiles of human trajectories may be illustrated by a free-hand sketch, without proper metrics, of two life curves of capability realization possibilities (see Figure 4.1). The curves should be seen as referring primarily to large social groups, such as the middle and the working classes, rather than to the poles of luxury and misery. For simplicity, pre-old age mortality is not taken into account in the picture (but in the above-mentioned text).

The moral basis of egalitarianism

There is a frequent cheap resentment against the rich, which serious citizens, not to speak of serious scholars, should be wary of. It is often without any ethical consideration, sometimes simply egotistically expressing a desire for oneself to be richer than others. Alternatively, it is thoughtlessly inconsistent, riling against bonuses of bankers and business executives,

Göran Therborn

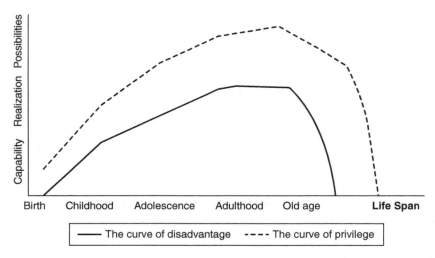

Figure 4.1 Life curves of inequality

while devotionally devouring the sports and entertainment pages about the emoluments and the luxury life of the highest paid stars.

While there is no, and never will be, exact measure of generally desirable equality and of unacceptable inequality, a moral person recognizes an outrage when she sees one. Moral persons have two fundamental reasons to be egalitarian, and both refer to the consequences of inequality, not to the rewards per se. One is individualist, the other social, and they are supplementary to each other, not contradictory. Both start from the post-Auschwitz, post-colonial assumption, that all human beings are, from a moral point of view, essentially equal, and the possibilities of each are of equal moral concern.

From an individualist perspective, inequality is an evil as a violation of a human right to develop into and to be able to function in full human capability. This violation is not only an effect of traumatic motherhood, birth, and early childhood – and the systemic generation of such conditions – but also of public remedial interventions being starved of resources by appropriations by the rich, or of social conditions being ignored by politicians looking at the world from the lap of the privileged. Competitive self and capability formation has an intrinsic, potentially anti-human drive: the only thing that matters is success. 'Losers' have no rights, becoming sub-human.

From a social angle, a stunting of human capability is a waste of social talent and capacity, and the social division into privileged and others comes at a high cost, abolishing common vision, social trust, and hindering collective action for common goods. Like in 'a prisoner's dilemma', both the excluded poor of the slums and the privileged in their walled-off, razor-wired, privately guarded mansions would be better off in a more egalitarian, trustful society.

When does inequality change?

Brief answer: When the relations of power between the privileged and the disadvantaged change, in terms of economic, political, and socio-cultural – of commitment and cohesion – resources. Moral critiques are part of popular commitment and cohesion, and as such important to popular mobilization and struggles. More resources than moral will be required for social change, but once instituted with the power of other popular resources, moral norms of equality and decency can have a considerable impact. The forces of privilege have good reasons to be afraid of a moral economy.

Note

* In global sociology, knowledge of Latin, the classical language of one of the world's five largest civilizations, should not be assumed to be universal. The gravestone phrase means, 'rest in peace'.

References

Cherlin, A. (2014). *Labour's Love Lost. The Rise and Fall of the Working-Class Family in America*. New York, Russell Sage Foundation.

Coates, T-N. (2015). *Between the World and Me*. New York, Speigel and Grau.

Clark, G. (2014). *The Son Also Rises*. Princeton, Princeton University Press.

Cunha, F., and Heckman, J. (2009). 'The Economics and Psychology of Inequality and Human Development', *Journal of the European Economic Association* 7(2–3), 320–64.

DiPrete, T., and Eirich, G. (2006). 'Cumulative Advantage as a Mechanism for Inequality: A Review of Theoretical and Empirical Developments', *Annual Review of Sociology* 32, 271–97.

Eriksson, R., and Goldthorpe, J. (1992). *The Constant Flux*. Oxford, Clarendon Press.

Gillis, J. (1985). *For Better, For Worse. British Marriages, 1600 to the Present*. Oxford, Oxford University Press.

Hanni, M., Martner, R., and Podestá, A. (2015). 'El potencial redistributivo de la fiscalidad en América Latina', *Revista CEPAL* (Augusto), 11–24.

Heckman, J., and Mosso, S. (2014). 'The Economics of Human Development and Social Mobility', *American Review of Economics* 6: 689–733.

Hoff, K., and Pandey, P. (2006). 'Discrimination, Social Inequality, and Durable Inequalities', *American Economic Review* 96(2), 206–11.

Hou F., and Myles, J. (2007). 'The Changing Role of Education in the Marriage Market: Assortative Marriage in Canada and the United States since the 1970s', *Statistics Canada Research Paper.*

Kaur, P., Shorey, L.E., Ho, E., Dashwood, R.H., and Williams, D.E. (2013). 'The Epigenome as a Potential Mediator of Cancer Prevention by Dietary Psychochemicals: The Fetus as Target', *Nutrition Review* 71(7), 441–47.

Mass, A., and Cadinu, M., (2003). 'Stereotype Threat: When Minorities Underperform', *European Review of Social Psychology* 14(1), 243–75.

Michael, M., King, L., Guo, L., McKee, M., Richardson, E., and Stuckler, D. (2013). 'The Mystery of Missing Female Children in the Caucasus: An Analysis of Sex Ratios by Birth-Order', *International Perspectives on Sexual and Reproductive Health* 39(2), 97–102.

Milanovic, B. (2011). *The Haves and the Have-Nots*. New York, Basic Books.

Murray, C. (2012). *Coming Apart*. New York, Crown Forum.

OECD (2011). *Divided We Stand*. Available at: www.oecd.org.

Putnam, R. (2015). *Our Kids*. New York, Simon & Schuster.

Resendiz, M., Chen, Y., Oztürk, N.C., and Zhou, F.C. (2013). 'Epigenetic Medicine and Fetal Alcohol Spectrum Disorders', *Epigenomics* 5(1), 73–86.

Risnes, K. (2011). 'Birthweight and Mortality in Adulthood: A Systematic Review and Meta-Analysis', *International Journal of Epidemiology* 40, 647–61.

Roemer, J. (1998). *Equality of Opportunity*. Cambridge MA, Harvard University Press.

Schafer, M., Ferraro, K., and Mostillo, S. (2011). 'Children of Misfortune: Early Adversity and Cumulative Inequality in Perceived Life Trajectories', *American Journal of Sociology* 116(4), 1053–91.

Sen, A. (1992). *Inequality Reexamined*. Cambridge MA, Harvard University Press.

Sen, A. (2009). *The Idea of Justice*. London, Allen Lane.

Shavit, Y., and Blossfeld, H-P. (1993). *Persistent Inequality*. Boulder CO, Westview Press.

Standing, G. (2011). *The Precariat*. London, Bloomsbury.

Statistics Sweden (2013). *Barn, förälrdrar, separationer*. Stockholm, Statistics Sweden.

Therborn, G. (2004). *Between Sex and Power. Family in the World, 1900–2000*. London, Routledge.

Therborn, G. (2013). *The Killing Fields of Inequality*. Cambridge, Polity.

Therborn, G. (2016). 'Life-curves of Inequality', *Korean Journal of Sociology* 49(6), 47–61.

Treiman, D., and Ganzeboom, H. (2000). 'The Fourth Generation of Comparative Stratification Research', pp. 122–50 in S. Quah and A. Sales (eds), *The International Handbook of Sociology*, London, Sage.

Wallerstein, I. (1979). 'Modernization. Requiescat in Pace', pp. 132–37 in L. Coser and O. Larsen, (eds), *The Uses of Controversy in Sociology*. New York: Free Press.

Williams, D., and Mohammed, S. (2009). 'Discrimination and Racial Disparities in Health: Evidence and Needed Research', *Journal of Behavioral Medicine* 32(1), 1–20.

Part Two

Economic, Territorial and Social Dimensions of Inequality

5

Globalization, Uneven Economic Development, Inequality and Poverty: The Interactive Effects Between Position in the Modern World System and Domestic Stratification Systems*

Harold Kerbo

Various data sources indicate that in the last decade or two, world poverty has decreased and global inequality between nations has gone down. However, within many less developed countries and even among some of the rich countries, primarily in the United States, inequality has increased rather dramatically while poverty has not gone down, or at times increased. From the 1970s, research that focused on less developed nations, following the modern world system perspective, has shown that globalization (measured by indicators such as foreign direct investment), had mostly lead to increasing inequality and less long term economic development in many if not most nations (and in some cases even higher poverty). And there is increasing evidence that a large part of the increasing inequality in the United States, in contrast to many EU countries, is related to economic globalization.

More recent evidence, however, has suggested that the impact of economic globalization has contradictory effects in both highly developed and less developed nations around the world.

Other data show that less developed countries in Asia, in contrast to Africa and Latin America, are more likely to have more evenly spread economic development and less poverty from increasing ties to the global economy.

The present paper focuses on data and several years of fieldwork in four Buddhist countries in Southeast Asia (Thailand, Vietnam, Laos, and Cambodia) to identify some of the causes of the impact of ties to the global economy which vary even *within* Asian countries, showing some Southeast Asian countries (such as Cambodia) share more characteristics with African or Latin American countries that are related to very uneven economic development, rapidly increasing inequality, and no or little poverty reduction.

This paper suggests how differences in domestic stratification systems (or different forms of political economy) are the key to understanding the varied impacts of economic globalization in both rich and less developed nations around the world.

In recent decades, there have been dozens of books about the negative or positive outcomes of economic globalization for both rich and poor countries (for example, see Mander and Goldsmith, 1996; Stiglitz, 2002; Rudra, 2008). The first wave of empirical research on the negative effects of globalization came in the 1970s with research on less developed countries from the modern world system perspective, following the long-standing assertions from the older dependence theories. Several research articles with data from the 1960s and 1970s did in fact show that more economic penetration from rich nations into less developed nations had negative effects such as greater inequality, more poverty, and less long-term economic development (for a summary, see Kerbo, 2005; Kerbo, 2006: Chapter 4).

The second wave of concern about the negative effects of globalization has come more recently with growing inequality and lower wages and benefits in some advanced post-industrial countries. This outcome for the working and middle classes in richer countries was first noticed in the US; the 'great U-turn' was a term from the 1980s to describe this growing inequality in the United States after several decades of reduced inequality (Harrison and Bluestone, 1988).

This U-turn has since been found in a number of other advanced industrial nations, with concern increasing since the 'great recession' from 2008, and now with Thomas Piketty's new book *Capital in the Twenty-First Century* (2014). What is termed 'the shrinking middle class,' particularly in the United States, has also been partly attributed to the effects of globalization and the loss of good paying middle-income jobs (see Kerbo, 2012).

The negative impact of economic globalization on both rich and less developed countries, however, is by no means universal, at least in significant levels. By the 1990s research on globalization and less developed countries was no longer showing significant correlations with respect to levels of FDI and less long-term economic development or growing poverty (Kerbo, 2006; 2011; 2012: Chapter 16). More qualitative comparative studies (some of which I have done) have shown that some less developed countries, with obvious examples being China, Taiwan, South Korea, Thailand, and now Vietnam, are benefitting from globalization and FDI with strong economic development and poverty reduction, though income inequality has increased moderately. Many other less developed countries, however, continue following the trends of growing inequality, more poverty, and less long-term economic development, with obvious cases being most Sub Saharan African countries, many Latin American countries, and some in Asia such as Cambodia, Laos, the Philippines, and Bangladesh (Kerbo, 2011).

With respect to rich nations today, however, the new concern about growing income and wealth inequality has not sufficiently considered there are wide differences between nations. As Piketty (2014) shows, there are trends toward greater inequality of income and wealth around the globe, but there are wide differences in the degrees of this growing inequality which Piketty has overlooked.

As the greatly expanded global economy developed in the last decades of the 20th century, both rich and less developed nations found it difficult to isolate themselves from the global economy. But as I will describe below, a key difference has been that *the state in some of these countries has been willing and able to protect the long-term interests of their nation and citizens from many of the negative effects of this expanded global economy.* Thus, the nagging question becomes *why some less developed countries are harmed by growing globalization and others have been able to benefit, or at least have minimal harm.* And in the same frame, the question becomes *why has inequality been rising sharply, with wages, jobs, and benefits for workers falling in some richer countries and only slightly if at all in other rich countries.* The thesis of this chapter is that the answers lay in differences in the stratifications systems, or broadly speaking the political economies, among both rich and less developed countries.

Not all Asian nations have states willing or able to protect the long-term national interests and those of their citizens in the face of greater ties to the global economy. Two countries in Southeast Asia are strong representatives of these contrasting types of countries, Thailand (though Vietnam can now be included) compared to Cambodia. Thus, we can focus on contrasting conditions in Thailand and Cambodia, and why and how one country has had some success in protecting long-term national interests while the other has not.

Economic Conditions in Southeast Asia[1]

We turn now to a brief overview of economic conditions in Southeast Asian countries, with a focus on comparative conditions in Thailand and Cambodia. Much of the information below comes from years of teaching and research in Southeast Asia, and more recently two years of sustained fieldwork in Thailand, Cambodia, Laos, and Vietnam which was funded by a generous grant from the Japan Foundation's Abe Fellowship Program 1.

Compared to earlier decades, the first years of the 21st century have been much better for a few Cambodians. Annual GNP growth has hovered around the 8 to 10 percent range (World Bank, 2006a, 2006b, 2007a, 2007b, 2009, 2014). Every year there are more and more new hotels, casinos, and shopping malls in the capital, Phnom Penh. In Siem Reap, gateway city to the almost 1000-year-old Angkor Wat, there is a massive building boom now that it is safe for tourists. Natural resources and textiles, however, are the only major exports. Cambodia's economic development of recent years has left 90 percent of the people untouched, or in many cases worse off (Kerbo, 2011). As I have documented in my fieldwork, this economic development has severely harmed tens of thousands of poor Cambodians who have been rounded up like prisoners in the middle of the night and dumped into resettlement camps in the countryside where most have no homes, no jobs, nor agricultural land. The vast majority of Cambodians continue to live in villages with no fresh water or electricity (90 percent), and insufficient land to adequately feed their families (World Bank, 2009). Thousands are losing their small plots of land to land grabs by the Cambodian elite and foreign business partners (mostly South Korean and Chinese). (For example, see Cambodian Human Rights Action Committee, 2009.) As local World Bank reports suggested (World Bank, 2006b, 2007a), we found in almost every village where interviews were conducted that others have been forced to sell their land to pay hospital bills to save the lives of their children. The 2014 World Bank development report estimated that almost 50 percent of Cambodians live on less than $2 per day. Historians tell us the majority of Cambodians today live pretty much as they did 1000 years ago (for example, see Chandler, 1996; Tully, 2006).

As I will describe below, much, but not all, of the continuing tragedy for Cambodians is related to the government in place since the mid-1980s (Kerbo, 2011). For 2014 the annual corruption report from Transparency International ranks Cambodia among the most corrupt countries in the world (Transparency International, 2015), with many other reports concurring (World Bank, 2006a, 2007b).

Table 5.1 GNP per Capita, Economic Development, and Poverty Rates*

	GNI per Capita (PPP, 2012)	Annual percent Growth in GNP (2011–12)	National Poverty Line (2007–10)**	Percent below	
				$1.25 per day	$2 per day
Cambodia	$2,330	7.3	30.1%	18.6% (2008)	49.5%
Thailand	9,280	6.5	8.1	<2 (2010)	4.1
Malaysia	16,270	5.6	3.8	<2 (2009)	2.3
Indonesia	4,730	4.9	13.3	16.2 (2011)	43.3
Philippines	4,380	6.8	26.5	18.4 (2009)	41.5
Vietnam	3,620	5.2	14.5	16.9 (2008)	43.4
Laos	2,690	8.2	27.6	33.9 (2008)	66.0

	Gini Coefficients for Inequalities	
	income inequality	land inequality
Cambodia	.42	.69
Thailand	.42	.47
Malaysia	.49	—
Indonesia	.34	.46
Philippines	.44	.57
Vietnam	.34	.50
Laos	.35	.41

Sources: World Bank *World Development Report, 2008*, and World Bank *World Development Indicators, Poverty Data Supplement, 2008*; *World Development Indicators, 2014*; *World Bank Development Report 2012*; United Nations *Human Development Report, 2008/ 2009*.

**Includes estimates of value of income from family production such as family's own production agriculture, which is not the case with the World Bank $1.25 per day or $2 per day estimates.

Table 5.2 Comparative Conditions for Agriculture and Rural
Infrastructure*

	Health care	fresh water % of pop(2008)	Improved Sanitation(2008)	Irrigation % farm land(2008)
Cambodia	almost none	41	17	7
Thailand	basic health care free	99	99	31
Vietnam	basic health care free++	85	61	45
Laos		51	30	19

	Paved Roads %	Fertilizer kg per hector(2008)	Electric power kwh per capita(2008)	Electricity % of pop with(2008)
Cambodia	6.3	5	164 (2011)	9
Thailand	98.0	133	2,316 (2011)	99
Vietnam	25	324	1,073 (2011)	84
Laos	14.4		179 (2007)	

Sources: World Bank, *World Development Report, 2008*; *World Development Indicators, 2014*; United Nations, *Human Development Report, 2008*; *Sustaining Growth in a Challenging Environment, Cambodian Country Economic Memorandum*, 2009.

+ Foreign NGOs have experimental programs health care in a few regions of Cambodia. They are testing policies of funding local government clinics or funding clinic run completely by the NGO.

++ Outpatient clinic visits for minor injuries or illness costs around $3, though hospital stays can cost around $700. There is low cost annual health insurance for about $70 per year which cuts hospital costs in half.

As can be seen from Tables 5.1 and 5.2, while Cambodia has had a relatively high GNP growth in recent years, the country lags behind almost all of its neighbors with respect to GNP per capita and poverty reduction. The World Bank's $1.25 per day extreme poverty measure (World Bank, 2014) puts Cambodia only above that of Laos (though my fieldwork indicates these figures are misleading for Laos because 40 percent of the population are hill tribe peoples in remote mountain areas – Kerbo, 2011). But when we consider the national poverty lines for each country, a poverty line which gives a better measure of actual consumption (e.g., including the value of family production food), Cambodia has the highest poverty rate. Particularly troubling for Cambodia, however, is the rapid rise in land inequality, which now shows a Gini coefficient of .69, putting Cambodia ahead of all other Southeast Asian nations and close to most Latin American countries. In 1993, only 3 percent of rural Cambodians were estimated to be landless, whereas by 2004 it was over 20 percent (World Bank, 2006a: 85). Amnesty International in Cambodia has estimated that this landless figure had increased substantially by 2008, with some 150,000 former urban slum people evicted between 2005 and 2008 (Amnesty International, 2008). Since 2008, and especially in 2014, these land grabs have been estimated to increase by more than 200 percent by the NGO Licadho (*Phnom Penh Post*, 31 March 2015).

After the first couple of months doing fieldwork in Cambodia from 2006, I returned to Thailand. I had been in every region of Thailand over the last 25 years, including most of the provincial cities in northeastern Thailand. In one sense, this is an unfair comparison. As shown in Table 5.1, Thailand is way ahead of Cambodia in economic development and poverty reduction.

But the key point is that poverty reduction in Thailand has been falling rapidly in recent decades, while that of Cambodia has not. The World Bank's *World Development Report, 1990* provided us with poverty estimates for Thailand using the national poverty line estimate for 1962 and 1986 (there were no $1 per day estimates back then). While the measures may be a little different for these early years, we get a rough idea of the changes: in 1962 Thailand's poverty rate was 59 percent of the population, and by 1986 it had come down to 26 percent of the population. Currently Thailand's poverty rate is about 8 percent of the population (World Bank, 2014). There were some early attempts at economic development in the second half of the 19th century, but it was not until the 1950s that the Thai government began to think seriously about economic development, with more development plans coming in the 1960s and 1970s.

Comparative analysis of the state in Thailand and Cambodia

The new 'buzz words' coming out of the World Bank these days are 'good governance' and 'state capacity' or 'institutional capacity.' By good governance they mean government efficiency and low corruption. By state capacity they mean the ability and even the existence of government institutions to do the normal things governments are supposed to do all over the world. Many social scientists have shown that various measures of

government efficiency are strongly related to poverty reduction and economic development in less developed countries all over the world. One
research team of UC Berkeley sociologists created a 'Weberianness scale'
named after the famous German sociologist, Max Weber, who about
100 years ago wrote the definitive work on the nature of bureaucracies and
how they should function. Using this scale to measure efficient government in developing countries, this Berkeley team and others have shown
such scales to be strongly related to GNP growth in less developed countries (Evans and Rauch, 1999; Henderson et al., 2007; Kerbo and Ziltener,
2015). A key reason economic development and poverty reduction is higher
in Asia than Latin America and Africa today is that many Asian countries
have some of the highest scores on measures of government efficiency.
Thailand is one of those Asian countries rated fairly high (though below
countries such as South Korea and Taiwan) on the various 'Weberianness
scales.' As a consequence, Thailand has been able to establish and carry
out development policies with some success. Even by the early 1990s one
could see most rural areas of Thailand were far more developed than what
is found in Cambodia today. Back then there were some Thai villages with
no running water, but very few without electricity. Most villages already
had good roads to take their produce to market, government projects to aid
the expansion of water control and irrigation, as well as schools and clinics near every village. And since 1990 one could see the slow transition
of a key indicator of rural economic development in the region – the shift
to 'iron buffalos.' There are still live water buffalos in Thailand, but not
so many, and few being used as draft animals. (The situation is in striking
contrast to what one finds in Cambodia today.) The versatile 'iron buffalos' now serve as a handheld plow or, with a change of tires and a trailer
hitched to the back, a motorized cart taking people and goods to fields or
market. By the 1990s, however, most rural people in Thailand already had
pickup trucks for the second job.

From the beginning of their development push the Thai development
policies put their small farmers on a relatively equal priority with urban
industry. Much of this was on the insistence of the highly revered and
recently deceased Thai King, Rama IX, though political activism among
Thai small farmers helped push these rural development policies (see
Kerbo, 2011; Walker, 2012).

Rural development projects helped small Thai farmers with irrigation,
electricity, and good roads which increased production and their standards of living. While rural–urban income differences remain in Thailand,
and in recent years have increased somewhat, they are less than in most

developing countries. With a stronger economic base in the countryside, Thailand began the usual policies of 'import substitution.' Using high tariffs and import quotes, the country tried to minimize the amount of manufactured goods they must buy from other countries. When achieved relatively well this means sending less money to these other countries to pay for their imports. The money was then saved for investment in Thailand to produce goods that would otherwise be imported, and now exported, most importantly, producing jobs and profits for Thai corporations and their employees.

From 2001 Thailand began another set of policies to further reduce rural poverty and inequality, particularly in the north, northeast, and the south of Thailand where rural poverty rates have always been higher. In large part, these policies were to build a voting base for Prime Minister Thaksin's new political party elected to office that year. The policies worked quite well in building that voter base among small farmers *and* to further improve the economic standing of small farmers. (A key reason Thai politics remain volatile today is that Thaksin and his banned political party enjoys continuing strong support among Thai farmers since his government was overthrown in a military coup in 2006 and another coup in 2014 after the political parties supported by Thaksin received a majority of votes again and again since 2001.) The most important poverty reduction programs since 2001 include the '30 Baht Health Care System' (about $0.75 at the time), a 'People's Bank' with micro loans to the urban poor and small farmers, and the promotion of small factories with lower skilled jobs in the rural rather than only urban areas.

Few of these scales measuring 'Weberianness' of governmental institutions or government efficiency have information from Cambodia. The disruption of civil war and continuing Khmer Rouge attacks until well into the 1990s prevented data collection. Earlier studies show Thailand, Vietnam, and even Laos, score fairly high, and jive with what I saw during my fieldwork and interviews with NGOs and government officials in these countries. A 2006 World Bank report was finally able to measure government efficiency in Cambodia. The country ranked among the bottom 10 percent of countries all over the world, with only Burma and North Korea ranking lower in East and Southeast Asia. This report also jives with my interviews and observations around Cambodia (again, see Kerbo, 2011 for a summary of these reports).

One of my first interviews in Cambodia was with a high government official in a ministry dealing with economic development and poverty reduction. Our discussion of what ails Cambodia was amazingly frank, with government inefficiency and corruption placed on center stage. This official was kind enough to give me several documents containing government development plans and his ministry's recent data on poverty conditions. Most valuable, however, was the inside information about problems within government agencies such as his. This neatly dressed man with a rather pleasant smile and quiet voice spoke impeccable English though his college education was in Belgium.

In his somewhat academic looking office in the ministry we began with small talk which eventually, as usual, got around to the Khmer Rouge years. He was in his early 20s when the Khmer Rouge took over in 1975, and like all others living in Phnom Penh, he and his family were captured by young boys wearing black 'pajamas' and carrying big AK-47s, then marched for days into the countryside before they reached an empty field where he would spend his next 4 years growing rice. Like others, he told stories of eating lizards and all sorts of bugs when he could find them, drinking water from muddy ponds, and being watched constantly by those young Khmer Rouge boys carrying big AK-47s. Many people were killed before his eyes, mostly those who did not work as hard as these boys with the big guns thought they should, or showed disrespect in any form. And like others, he told of the attempts by the Khmer Rouge to determine his background and education. He survived by convincing the Khmer Rouge he was from a family of unskilled laborers with no education. His father disappeared during the Khmer Rouge years, and after the Vietnamese invasion in 1979 he returned to Phnom Penh with his mother, homeless and looking for some way to make a living. He was lucky to hear that the new government backed by the Vietnamese was looking for anyone with a college education for new government positions. With approximately 300 people left in the country with a college education the new government was desperate to find people to help run the government, or what was emerging as such in those early years in Cambodia without the Khmer Rouge.

As we moved into my primary questions, he pulled out more government documents showing me what his agency had determined must be done to improve economic development in the countryside and reduce poverty. Given what I knew on the subject, and Cambodia's situation at the time, these plans appeared quite sound and logical. He knew that economic development in Phnom Penh must go along with development and poverty reduction in the countryside, and knew all too well what people in the countryside needed.

Toward the end of our meeting he turned to me with a sad and frustrated look on his face and asked that I not quote him. He told me something like, 'I feel like I am wasting my time. We develop these plans, get some foreign donor to help with money, and then nothing happens. The plans never get implemented and the money disappears.' He added, 'and government claims of poverty reduction in Phnom Penh are not to be trusted' (they don't really include all the homeless migrants in the city, for example), 'though their figures of high poverty with almost no change in the countryside since the early 1990s are more accurate.' His agency was told a couple of years ago that 65 percent of development aid should be spent in the rural areas and the rest in urban areas. In reality, he told me, what little aid money is actually spent rather than stolen goes for urban projects. I was to see for myself all too clearly what he said over the next two years of fieldwork.

During my first interviews in Phnom Penh I also had a meeting with a well educated and intelligent lady with a relatively high government ministry position who told me she seldom actually works for the government. My interview was in her office at a branch of one of the biggest international aid agencies known, I am sure, to all of my readers. Many government officials like herself, she told me, work in their official ministry offices only when foreign donors come up with money for some project. The specific project which she currently headed for the international NGO was focused on training local government officials to better understand their duties, perform their jobs more efficiently, and with less corruption. In short, they were trying to build what the World Bank and UN call 'government capacity' among local government officials in Cambodia. After I was able to interview 'commune' and 'tonbom' (a local government district covering about 10 villages) officials in Vietnam and Thailand in later stages of my fieldwork, I could easily see the contrast of professionalism and efficiency compared to their counterparts in Cambodia. When asked if her work with local government officials was doing any good she told me sadly, 'probably not.' With very little education and almost no experience among these rural officials her agency was making little progress. Their NGO funding was about to run out and the training program was to conclude after covering a very small part of Cambodia.

My years of travels through northeastern Thailand, and more recent two years of fieldwork, have led to similar insights into Cambodia's problems. Clearly, the Cambodian government is corrupt, dysfunctional, and simply lacks what development experts call 'institutional capacity.' The problem, however, is not restricted to Cambodia's central government. Visiting village after village in Thailand one cannot help but became more and more impressed with the elected headmen and their advisory councils. While reviewing photos and field notes it became obvious: A person can go into a Thai village unannounced and ask to talk with the headman, and when they are suddenly confronted with detailed questions about the village, such as how many families there are, how much land do they have, what is the rice yield and income from other sources, exactly how they are using money from the 'One Million Baht' program, etc., etc., these headmen had quick, detailed answers. They were asked many other questions about government aid programs, which ones were in their village, and how they get this aid. In every case these headmen, despite the unannounced visit and without notes or record books, could recite impressive amounts of precise figures. In short, it became clear that these guys are professionals. These village headmen are on the ground level of what is relatively good governance in Thailand. Most headmen in Cambodian villages know very little about such things and have very little training, and they were quite often put in place simply to make sure that village people do not rebel against Hun Sen's Cambodian Peoples Party.

The nature of the state and the impact of globalization: A conclusion

Next to follow was Thailand and a few other Southeast Asian countries. Since the 1932 military coup that overthrew the absolute monarchy, the Thai government has mostly been headed by the military. There was some democracy in the 1970s, only to be overturned in another military coup. Then again from the 1990s there was more democracy until another military coup ended that in 2006. One September morning in 2006, and again in May 2014, Thai and foreign business people in the country woke up with a shock to see the tanks and soldiers had taken over the streets of Bangkok. After breakfast, these business people went to work as usual with little concern for the Thai economy. The Thai stock market showed its agreement; there was only a little downward blip before the market returned to its usual upward trend. These people knew who would continue to run the vital functions of government. Even by the late 1800s, and especially after 1932, Thailand had established an unelected and well-educated government ministry which could run governmental institutions even when elected politicians were overly corrupt or thrown out of power by a military coup.

After the complete collapse of governmental institutions after the Khmer Rouge took power in 1975, Vietnam tried to establish some functioning government institutions after they invaded Cambodia in 1979. After the Khmer Rouge become an insignificant threat in Cambodia the

United Nations began its first serious attempt at nation building from 1992 (Kerbo, 2011). By most indicators, however, this attempt at rebuilding governmental institutions has failed. Unlike most other East and Southeast Asian nations, Cambodia continues to have weak and inadequate governmental institutions, especially outside of Phnom Penh. What Cambodia has is a political elite that is highly corrupt, unable to implement sound development policies, and with this corruption is allowing foreign companies (especially from China and South Korea) to exploit Cambodian resources and labor. Unlike most of East and Southeast Asia, in other words, Cambodia does not have a political economy that is able to deal with the wider global economy in ways that can protect Cambodian people and maintain a sustainable economy that can significantly raise living standards and significantly reduce poverty.

It is important to restate that *some form of democracy is preferable to human rights and dignity*. But unfortunately, in today's global economy with powerful multinational corporations able to exploit weak, less developed nations, a rather strong, rather undemocratic state, is sometimes necessary to protect national interests (Kerbo, 2005, 2011, forthcoming). In less developed countries it is economic development which eventually brings some form of democracy, not the other way around. South Korea and Taiwan have gone through the process of economic development producing more democracy and human rights. Other less developed countries have repressive states unable to produce economic development, and therefore remain repressive, predator states. Elsewhere I have tried to explain the reasons why some corrupt, predator states remain so, while others are able to protect national interests and achieve economic development and then some form of democracy (Kerbo and Ziltener, 2015; Kerbo, forthcoming). Thailand is going through that transition period. Two military coups in the past 10 years (2006 and 2014) have been attempts by the old elites to prevent this transition. But the lessons of history suggest these old Thai elites will eventually fail to block some form of democracy.

Notes

* The author's original version included a comparison between less developed (Thailand, Cambodia, Laos, Vietnam) and more developed countries (USA and Germany). For reasons of space, we have only included the first part of his study, that is, the arguments and conclusions on his East Asian case studies. The complete text is yet to be published.

1 The main sources of information were interviews with more than 200 poor families in 20 villages from each region of Cambodia, as well as slum areas in the capital and provincial cities (United Nations, 2013). In Vietnam, we interviewed dozens of families in ten

villages in central and southern Vietnam, as well as in urban slum areas. In Thailand, the focus was only upon northeastern Thailand, Issan, the poorest region of the country, where we interviewed dozens of families in eight villages. In Laos, we first encountered obstacles when trying to obtain government permission and local academic support to conduct research, but were finally able to do so by the spring of 2008. We conducted interviews in Laos with several families in only three villages, but traveled through villages in three major low land areas of Laos up and down the Mekong River to assess economic conditions and infrastructure development. (See Appendix 1 in Kerbo, 2011, for the locations in each country.) In all four countries, we had dozens of interviews with government officials and foreign NGO personnel, as well as academics who had some knowledge of poverty conditions in these countries.

We should note again that the research focus was on 'low land' people who are the majority in these countries (though only a slight majority in Laos – Chamberlain, 2006), rather than hill tribe peoples. In every Southeast Asian country, these hill tribe people experience more poverty and are certainly worthy of much more attention. But because of many different issues relating to their poverty compared to low land people, hill tribe people were mostly ignored in this research.

References

Amnesty International (2008). *Rights Razed: Forced Evictions in Cambodia.* Available at: www.amnesty.org.

Cambodian Human Rights Action Committee (2009). *Losing Ground: Forced Evictions and Intimidation in Cambodia.* Available at: www.chrac.org/eng/.

Chamberlain, James (2006). *Participatory Lao Poverty Assessment.* National Statistics Center: Asian Development Bank.

Chandler, David (1996). *A History of Cambodia.* Boulder, CO: Westview Press.

Evans, Peter and James Rauch (1999). 'Bureaucracy and growth', *American Sociology Review,* 64: 748–65.

Harrison, Bennett and Barry, Bluestone (1988). *The Great U-Turn.* New York: Basic Books.

Henderson, Jeffrey, David Hulme, Hossein Jalilian and Richard Phillips (2007). 'Bureaucratic Effects: "Weberian" State Agencies and Poverty Reduction.' *Sociology* 41: 515–32.

Kerbo, Harold (2005). 'Foreign Investment and Disparities in Economic Development and Poverty Reduction: An Historical Comparative Analysis of the Buddhist Countries of Southeast Asia.' *International Journal of Comparative Sociology* 46: 425–60.

Kerbo, Harold (2006). *World Poverty: Global Inequality and the Modern World System.* New York: McGraw-Hill.

Kerbo, Harold (2011). *The Persistence of Poverty in Cambodia: From the Killing Fields to Today.* Jefferson, NC and London: McFarland Press.

Kerbo, Harold (2012). *Social Stratification and Inequality: Class Conflict in Historical, Comparative, and Global Perspective,* 8th edn. New York: McGraw-Hill.

Kerbo, Harold (Forthcoming). 'The State and Economic Development in East and Southeast Asia: The Advantage of an Ancient Civilization', in Samuel Cohen and Rae Blumburg (eds), *Development in Crisis.* London: Routledge.

Kerbo, Harold and Patrick Ziltener (2015). 'Sustainable Development and Poverty Reduction in the Modern World System: Southeast Asia and the Negative Case of Cambodia', pp. 201–20 in Immanuel Wallerstein, Chris Chase-Dunn, and Christian Suter (eds), *Overcoming Global Inequalities*. Boulder, CO: Paradigm Publishers.

Kerbo, Harold and Patrick Ziltener (2015). 'Sustainable development and poverty', *Journal of World System Research*, 15: 223–2213.

Mander, Jerry and Edward Goldsmith (eds) (1996). *The Case Against the Global Economy*. San Francisco: Sierra Books.

Piketty, Thomas (2014). *Capital in the Twenty-First Century*. Cambridge, MA: Harvard University Press.

Rudra, Nita (2008). *Globalization and the Race to the Bottom in Developing Countries: Who Really Gets Hurt?* Cambridge: Cambridge University Press.

Stiglitz, Joseph (2002). *Globalization and its Discontents*. New York: Norton.

Transparency International (2015). *Corruption Perceptions Index, 2015*. Available at: www.transparency.org.

Tully, John (2006). *A Short History of Cambodia: From Empire to Survival*. Sydney: Allen and Unwin.

United Nations (2008). *Human Development Report, 2008*. New York: Palgrave Macmillan.

United Nations (2013). *Human Development Report, 2013*. New York: Palgrave Macmillan.

Walker, Andrew (2012). *Thailand's Political Peasants: Power in the Modern Rural Economy*. Madison: University of Wisconsin Press.

World Bank (2006a). *World Development Report, 2006: Equity and Development in Cambodia*. Available at: www.worldbank.org.

World Bank (2006b). *Cambodian Poverty Assessment, 2006*. Phnom Penh.

World Bank (2007a). *Cambodia: Sharing Growth Equity and Development Report, 2007*. Phnom Penh.

World Bank (2007b). *A Decade of Measuring the Quality of Governance*. Available at: www.worldbank.org.

World Bank (2008a). *World Development Report, 2008*. New York: Oxford University Press.

World Bank (2008b). *World Development Indicators, Poverty Data, A Supplement to World Development Indicators*. New York: Oxford University Press.

World Bank (2009). *Sustaining Growth in a Challenging Environment*, Cambodian Country Economic Memorandum, Phnom Penh.

World Bank (2012). *World Development Report*. New York: Oxford University Press.

World Bank (2014). *World Development Indicators*. New York: Oxford University Press.

6

Poverty and Inequality in the Arab World

Habibul Haque Khondker*

Introduction

Social inequality and poverty are persistent in the world we live in. Inequalities persist both between and within countries. The severity of the problem is illustrated in a report by Oxfam which shows that the top 1 per cent of income earners owns roughly 50 per cent of global income, and the 80 richest individuals in the world own as much wealth as the bottom 3.5 billion (Oxfam, 2014, in *The Guardian*, 2015). Since Arab World does not claim any privilege of exceptionality, it has its share of inequality and poverty. While the point about social inequality is easy to make, the issue of poverty is mired in debates and technical controversies. The definitions of poverty vary. According to the conventional definition of poverty, the number of poor in the world is one billion. However, according to the Oxford Poverty and Human Development Initiative, which uses a multidimensional poverty index, more than 1.6 billion people are living in poverty around the world (www.ophi.org.uk/multidimensional-poverty-index/). Different criteria of measuring poverty yield different results and numbers. Arab World is generally comprised of nearly two-dozen states. For the purpose of this paper, we focus on the Middle East and North Africa (MENA) as a region. The Middle East is saturated with various images of prosperity, wealth, shining towers and sometimes exploitation of labor, especially temporary migrant laborers, and, in recent years, terrorism, endless civil wars and the rise of dreadful ISIL (aka, ISIS or Daesh). Yet beneath the multiple images, the issues of poverty and inequality remain hidden. The exploited foreign workers in the rich Gulf States or the victims of civil war, or the economic refugees risking their lives to cross into the fabled prosperity and security of Europe provide piecemeal images of the region. Poverty and inequality are not always the first impression of the region. And for valid reasons, for poverty and inequality in the region are not as stark as they are in, say, South Asia or Sub-Saharan Africa. Yet, if one looks hard the intra-regional inequality is quite obvious with far-reaching implications. What is striking in the MENA region is its diversity reflected in the mapping of inequality and poverty. Broadly, the MENA countries can be classified on the basis of unequal natural endowments: as hydrocarbon-rich wealthy countries and hydrocarbon-deficient poor countries. Both groups of countries were experiencing economic growth in the first decade of the twenty-first century.

According to the World Bank, Egypt, Tunisia, Iran, Lebanon, Jordan, Yemen and Libya experienced rapid economic growth between 2000 and 2010, and suffered economic decline following the dramatic changes of 2011 (World Bank, 2014). In 2011, at the onset of the 'Arab Spring', a series of social uprisings starting from Tunisia, Egypt and Bahrain led to some positive but mostly disastrous consequences in the region. In January 2011, unemployment in Saudi Arabia reached 10.5 per cent; UN official estimates were even higher, triggering strikes by unemployed teachers. In Tunisia, Muhammad Bu Azizi, a fruit salesman, set himself on fire triggering mass unrest and the eventual downfall of the longstanding authoritarian government. The poor unauthorized salesman was driven by poverty and had no other alternative means to feed his family. A price hike of basic food prices in Algeria in January 2011 led to food riots, police intervention and death of the demonstrators. It would be one-sided to attribute unrest in the Middle East to poverty and inequality, for there were other factors behind the momentous changes, both local and external, but the role played by scarcity and demographic bulge cannot be denied. Yet one should not exaggerate the unemployment factor alone. Months after the 'Arab Spring', in June 2011 at the International Conference on Middle East Economic Association at Barcelona's Graduate School of Economics, speakers deliberated on the possible links between poverty and unemployment in the Arab Spring countries and the social uprisings. While in 2011 the unemployment rate in North African countries ranged between 9 per cent and 14 per cent, Spain at that time had an unemployment rate of 20 per cent. Even in youth unemployment, which varied between 17 and 31 per cent in the Arab Spring countries, Spain had youth unemployment of 43.6 per cent (Montalvo, 2012).

Both structural and situational factors help explain social inequality in the Middle East and North Africa. Geography, especially, climatic condition, quality of polity or governance, historically structured poverty and inequality and durable unemployment are important components of the structural factors. In some parts, for example, Palestine–Israel, violence is structured to creating conditions of durable inequality and poverty. At the same time, under situational factors one has to take into account that the region is embroiled in war and mayhem produced by external interventions as well as local conditions intensifying poverty and deprivation resulting in a massive humanitarian crisis. The situational factors are not ephemeral or less important; for example, the killing of 38 foreign tourists in Tunisia in late June 2015 by the so-called 'Islamic State' or Daesh operatives is an example of a situational factor, which had adverse consequences on the tourism industry, a major source of revenue, and thus on Tunisian economy. Egypt too has been affected by declining tourism revenue and struggling (in the middle of 2015) to regain the pre-2011 figure of US$12.5 billion a year achieved in 2010 (Bayoumy, 2015). The global political economy bridges the structural and the situational factors. For example, a decline in petroleum prices intensifies political instability or economic sanctions imposed to 'punish' recalcitrant leaders take a heavy toll on the poor and vulnerable.

The level of immiserization, poverty and vulnerability that can be noticed in the war zones and in the refugee camps are visceral. But the poverty and inequality that we discuss here are somewhat abstract, yet durable and institutional. The functioning of society not only sustains structures of poverty but also reproduces them. The normalization of poverty and inequality is part of the intractableness of these issues. The main objective of the paper is not to examine the relationship between poverty and inequality in the MENA region with the Arab Spring, but to argue that a clearer mapping of the conditions of poverty and inequality will be a necessary condition to ensure sustainability and envision a future of social justice in this region. The paper seeks to identify some of the challenges the existing poverty and inequality create and the responses that may be considered. Here the role of the state is crucial.

The literature on the role of inequalities as a barrier for socio-economic growth is rich, which goes back to Simon Kuznets's hypothesis of inverse U curve. Kuznets argued that in the short term, economic growth may cause social inequality hence it is like taking a bitter pill for long-term economic prosperity, hence, social stability and peace (and social justice). The view of Kuznets was initially presented as a hypothesis – not a theory. Kuznets, according to Thomas Piketty, noted a sharp decrease in income inequality in the United States between 1913 and 1948 (Piketty, 2014). But that was not the result of normal progression of economy as indicated by Kuznets's inverted U curve; the external factors such as the two world wars, progressive taxation, the New Deal in the United States all aided the so-called 'normal progression' of the economy. The hypothesis of Kuznets, evident in the question mark of his famous 1953 essay, gained a theoretical status in the interpretations of his protagonists as well as his critics. A number of researchers have challenged the Kuznets proposition (for example, Bourguignon, 2004; Palma, 2011; Piketty, 2014). Armed with the East Asian development experience, a number of social scientists also questioned the wisdom of Kuznets and the mainstream economic thinking and signaled the possibility of equitable growth.

Globally, the zones that are experiencing economic growth, for example, East Asia are more equitable than Latin America. At the same time, some of the fastest growing economies in Africa are also known to be extremely unequal. The jury is still out on the question. Income inequality increased, globally, in the 1980s and 1990s and declined in 2000s. There was also a remarkable decline in income poverty since the early 1980s and an improvement in living standards in 2000s in the developing countries is noticed (Alvaredo and Gasparini, 2015). One of the reasons for the decline of global poverty is due to massive poverty reduction in China. However, as Chen and Ravallion (2008) have indicated that even when China is omitted, global poverty reduction is still considerable. Even in China, there are regional variations in the reduction of poverty. Globally too, there are considerable unevenness. While some countries have experienced little poverty reduction, there are cases where poverty has increased. While some economists are convinced that the income inequality is declining under the global economic integration (Dollar and Kraay, 2002), others present an opposite view (Wade, 2004). Fifteen of the nineteen countries in the Middle East region have met the MDG's hunger target. It is only due to the recent protracted conflicts that the trend is being reversed.

Definition of social inequality remains imprecise. Therborn uses the definition of equality developed by economist Amartya Sen for whom equality is, 'equality of capability to function fully as a human being. Such a capability clearly entails survival, health (and aids for disability), freedom and knowledge (education) to choose one's life-path, and resources to pursue it' (Sen, 1992, quoted in Therborn, 2013: 41). In discussing poverty and inequality in the MENA region, we draw upon Göran Therborn's multi-dimensional, sociological framework of social inequality, which broadens the traditional income-based understanding of inequality. Therborn has conceptualized three types of inequality that can have a deleterious influence on the health and wellbeing of an individual, and deny them their ability to fully function as a human being. First, *vital inequality* – socially constructed means of inequality such as mortality rates, life expectancy, etc. Next is *existential inequality,* which constitutes denial of personhood, rights, dignity, respect, degrees of freedom and self-development. Finally, *resource inequality* – the inability of human actors to act to their full capability (Therborn, 2013: 48 [emphasis added]). Perpetuating these fields of inequality are four mechanisms, which work to polarize different groups of people in society; *distanciation* (a systemic process designed to discern 'winners and losers'); *exclusion* (the division of in-groups and out-groups); *hierarchization* (formal organizations of inequality) and *exploitation* (unfairly capitalizing on the often physical labor of others) (Therborn, 2013: 62 [emphasis in the original]). However, the author argues that these mechanisms are not entirely exclusive of each other despite a belief that all four can account for the generation of most kinds of inequality.

Rather than looking at income or resource inequality as the only form of social inequality in the MENA, we consider exclusion and hierarchization as well. Due to space limitation, we examine the conditions of social inequalities in key countries, such as Egypt with only an overview of the MENA region. In light of the post-Millennium Development Goals agenda of the United Nations the focus has been placed on a sustainable development agenda which includes: (a) dignity: to end poverty and fight inequality; (b) people: to ensure healthy lives, knowledge and the inclusion of women and children; (c) prosperity: to grow a strong, inclusive and transformative economy; (d) planet: to protect our ecosystems for all societies and our children; (e) justice: to promote safe and peaceful societies and strong institutions; and (f) partnership: to catalyze global solidarity for sustainable development (UN General Assembly, 2014).

Table 6.1　Arab region

Proportion of people living under $1.25 a day	HDI	GDP (PPP) (2005$)	GNI	Life Expectancy	Maternal Mortality Ratio	Years of Schooling
7.4 %	65.2%	8104	8317	71	176.07	6

Source: UNDP (2014)

Arab states have made steady progress over 40 years in income, education and health care as measured by the Human Development Index (HDI). Oman, Saudi Arabia, Tunisia, Algeria and Morocco are all among the top 10 HDI performers, while Libya was among the leading 10 countries in non-income HDI achievement since 1970. This is predictable, given the extremely low starting values for all three components of HDI and the large investments in social services undertaken by many Arab governments since the 1970s. However, the rate of progress on human development slowed down noticeably since 1990. Moreover, the overall HDI shows marked divergence in patterns of human development among Arab countries, with the United Arab Emirates, Qatar, and Bahrain all ranking in the top quarter of countries while Sudan, Djibouti and Yemen are among the lowest. Compared to other developing regions of the world, the Arab region does not stand out for poverty as much as for inequality. In poverty counts, the Arab region scores lower than South Asia and Sub-Saharan Africa. However, considerable intra-regional differences exist. Both Djibouti and Yemen have a high poverty rate compared to the rest.

Table 6.2 shows the Arab region's Human Development Index in comparison with the other regions of the world. The Arab states, in terms of human development indicators, are not in a dire situation compared to the rest of the world.

The MENA countries span all the four categories in the UN Human Development Report from Very High to Low HDI. The variation in human development indicators in the region is presented in Table 6.3.

Table 6.2   Human Development Index by world regions

REGION	HDI	Life Expectancy	Years of Schooling	GNI per capita
Latin America and the Caribbean	0.740	74.9	7.9	13,767
Europe and Central Asia	0.738	71.3	9.6	12,415
East Asia and the Pacific	0.703	74.0	7.4	10,499
Arab States	0.682	70.2	6.3	15,817
South Asia	0.588	67.2	4.7	5,195
Sub-Saharan Region	0.502	56.8	4.8	3,152

Source: UNDP (2014)

Table 6.3   Human Development ranking of the MENA States in 2014

HDI Rank	Country	Human Development Index (HDI) Value, 2013	Life expectancy at birth (years), 2013	Mean years of schooling (years), 2012	Gross national income (GNI) per capita (2011 PPP $), 2013
17	Israel	0.888	81.8	12.5	29,966
31	Qatar	0.851	78.4	9.1	119,029
34	Saudi Arabia	0.830	75.5	8.7	52,109
39	Malta	0.829	79.8	9.9	27,022
40	UAE	0.827	76.8	9.1	58,068
44	Bahrain	0.815	76.6	9.4	32,072
46	Kuwait	0.814	74.3	7.2	85,820
55	Libya	0.784	75.3	7.5	21,666
56	Oman	0.783	76.6	6.8	42,191
65	Lebanon	0.765	80	7.9	16,263
75	Iran	0.749	74	7.8	13,451
77	Jordan	0.745	73.9	9.9	11,137
90	Tunisia	0.721	75.9	6.5	10,440
93	Algeria	0.717	71	7.6	12,555
107	Palestine	0.686	73.2	6.9	5,168
110	Egypt	0.682	71.2	6.4	10,400
118	Syria	0.658	74.6	6.6	5,771
120	Iraq	0.642	69.4	5.6	14,007
129	Morocco	0.617	70.9	4.4	6,905
154	Yemen	0.506	63.1	2.5	3,945
159	Comoros	0.488	60.87	2.85	1,505
170	Djibouti	0.467	61.8	3.8	3,109

Very High Human Development: Israel to Kuwait (7)
High Human Development: Libya to Algeria (7)
Medium Human Development: Palestine to Morocco (5)
Low Human Development: Yemen, Comoros and Djibouti (3)

Source: The Human Development Report (UNDP, 2014) pp. 160–2

Let us look at the poverty level via the Multidimensional Poverty Index in the Arab Spring countries at the onset of social uprisings in 2011 (see Table 6.4).

Table 6.4 MPI in the Arab Spring countries

Income level	Tunisia Survey: MICS Year: 2011–12	Syria Survey: MICS Year: 2006	Egypt Survey: DHS Year: 2008	Iraq Survey: MICS Year: 2011	Yemen Survey: MICS Year: 2006
	Upper middle income	Lower middle income	Lower middle income	Upper middle income	Lower middle income
(GNI)* per capita	4,360	1,850	3,160	6,710	1,330
(HDI)**	0.721	0.658	0.682	0.642	0.500
MPI Value	0.004	0.021	0.024	0.045	0.283
MPI Poor	1.16%	5.53%	5.96%	11.64%	52.51%
MPI Poor and Destitute	0.26%	----	----	1.39%	----
$1.25/day Poor	0.74%	1.71%	1.68%	3.91%	9.78%
Inequality (Gini Index)	0.358	0.358	0.308	0.295	0.359

*Gross National Income
**Human Development Index

Source: Multidimensional Poverty Index is a composite of http://hdr.undp.org/en/content/table-6-multidimensional-poverty-index-mpi

Taking Egypt as a case in point, it has been shown that despite the attention given to the issue of 'inequality' both within and outside Egypt as the source of discontent and uprisings, the Gini coefficient declined in the decade prior to the Arab Spring. It declined from 36.1 per cent in 2000 to 30.7 per cent in 2009. Between 1996 and 2010 the Egyptian economy grew above 5 per cent, and between 2006 and 2008, 7 per cent. Yet people's perception – as shown in the World Values survey conducted in 2000 and 2008 – revealed that people became more averse to poverty and inequality. Studies on household income, expenditure and consumption survey also revealed a mismatch between GDP growth and the growth in household income (Verme et al., 2014).

So it can be surmised that income inequality might not have been the heart of the reason for discontent that led to the Egyptian uprising but the perception of inequality and unfulfilled expectations did play a role among other factors. The data published in the middle of 2015, in fact, shows improvement in the Egyptian economy with economic growth reaching 5.6 per cent in the first half of the financial year of 2015 compared to 1.2 per cent in the same period in 2014. Unemployment was also found to be moving downward at 13 per cent, which was still higher than the pre-Arab Spring level (World Bank, 2015).

Table 6.5 Global Hunger Index Report: Selected Countries

Country	Rank	1990	1995	2000	2005	2014
Syria	8	7.8	6.1	<5	5.1	5.9
Iraq	27	8.6	11.9	12.8	11.6	12.7
Djibouti	59	34.1	29.4	28.5	25.6	19.5
Yemen	69	30.1	27.8	27.8	28	23.4
Indonesia	22	20.5	17.8	16.1	15.2	10.3
Philippines	29	20.1	17.5	17.9	14.7	13.1
India	55	31.2	26.9	25.5	24.2	17.8
Bangladesh	57	36.6	34.4	24.0	19.8	19.1
Pakistan	57	26.7	23.3	22.1	21.0	19.1

There are five other countries from the MENA region mentioned in the Global Hunger Report that all had less than (<5) percentage of people considered as hungry in the criteria of GHI. These countries are Algeria, Egypt, Iran, Jordan and Kuwait.

Data source: von Grebmer et al, IFPRI (2014). Reproduced with permission from the International Food Policy Research Institute www.ifpri.org. The original table is available online at http://dx.doi.org/10.2499/9780896299580.

In order to examine the situation of poverty and inequality, it may be also useful to look at data on hunger and lack of nutrition on the world level as indicators. Table 6.5 shows that some of the countries in turmoil today (2015) in the Middle East were not known for hunger and deprivation compared to the relatively stable countries in South Asia that featured prominently in the Global Hunger Index Report, which present data from 76 countries. The lower the rank, the least hunger there is.

Challenges

While Arab countries have made significant progress on several development indicators over the past four decades, such as improving life expectancy and school enrolment, the region could have been more effective in translating its considerable wealth and potential into commensurate development gains. The Arab region faces various sociopolitical, gender, economic and environmental challenges. In terms of gender inequality, according to the Global Gender Gap Index (World Economic Forum, 2014), UAE is ranked 115 of 142 countries scoring the highest in the MENA with 0.6457, while Saudi Arabia is ranked 130. Bangladesh with a much lower per capita income was ranked 68 scoring 0.6973.

The proportion of people living on less than $1.25 a day fell from 6 per cent in the 1990s to 4 per cent in the 2000s, remarkably lower than other developing regions (with an average of 24 per cent). GDP per capita varies from a high of 77,987 in Qatar to 980 in Comoros. However, the magnitude of poverty and the ranking of the Arab region change considerably with higher poverty lines. In 2008, based on the $1.25 line, the region has almost the same headcount poverty rate of the far richer Latin America and Caribbean region, yet based on the $2.75 line its poverty rate is double that of Latin America and the Caribbean. According to the IFAD report of 2011, some mixed pictures emerge. The incidence of extreme rural poverty fell from nearly 10 to 4 per cent over the preceding two decades, at the same time because of the food price hike of 2008 there was an increase of 14 per cent in the numbers of hungry people from 2008 to 2009 in the MENA region (Ifad.org). It was not only a situational crisis; there was an underlying food insecurity in the region linked to heavy dependency on food imports, severe water scarcity and demographic pressures (IFAD, 2011). Food security also remains a challenge. After the food crises of 2007–8 and 2009–10 food security became a concern for MENA. Yet, with innovative approaches to resource management and organization, Arab states can combine their financial, technical and environmental assets to devise effective solutions. Policymakers have discussed the possibility of establishing a regional funding mechanism for such purposes. Sudan for example, is a country that could be invested in to grow large amounts of food because of its wealth in water and land resources. Several countries have been able to bring down poverty levels over the past 15 to 20 years; however they remain high in Yemen, Algeria, Egypt, Morocco and Tunisia (Azour, 2014).

Based on the available data it is difficult to attribute lack of economic growth as a major factor that caused the 'Arab Spring'. Despite the overall economic growth, unemployment, especially high youth unemployment might have been a factor. The situation of high youth unemployment remains a major challenge in the region. The economic growth being uneven was not able to absorb the rising number of youth in the labor force. Youth unemployment rates range from 39 per cent in Saudi Arabia, to 34 per cent in Egypt and 31 per cent in Tunisia (Azour, 2014); these figures are higher than in the rest of the world with few exceptions. The brewing political unrest caused by the growing demands of the unemployed youth in Tunisia in early 2016 threatens its political stability.

Population growth rate in the MENA region is still high. There also remains intra-regional variation. Fertility in MENA declined from 7 children per woman around 1960 to 3.6 children in 2001. The total fertility rate was less than 3 in Bahrain, Iran, Lebanon, Tunisia, and Turkey, and was more than 5 in Iraq, Oman, Palestinian Territory, Saudi Arabia, and Yemen (Roudi, 2001). The fertility rate in Egypt fell to 2.1 under active birth control plans of Hosni Mubarak but now has reverted to 3.5, a rate higher than Iran and Saudi Arabia (*Economist*, 6 June 2015). In 2015, of the region's population of nearly 380 million, more than 50% are under the age of 25.

Human and income poverty reflect the convergence of social, economic and political exclusion. While 50 per cent of the Arab population is rural, agriculture, the primary occupation in rural settings, accounts for only 15 per cent of the Arab GDP. High unemployment rates prevail. Despite the region's oil wealth, states have not succeeded in increasing human wellbeing. Agriculture, the primary occupation in rural inhabitants (40 per cent of the Arab population) accounts for only 7 per cent of the Arab GDP and employs only 26 per cent of its work force. Weak social, political and administrative accountability mechanisms and politically oriented socioeconomic planning models have resulted in the neglect of large parts of the population. These nations face the challenge of forming new, accountable governments that reflect popular aspirations. Despite economic growth recorded in mid-2015, according to the latest data of 2013, 26 per cent of Egypt's population lived below the poverty line (World Bank, 2015). In Egypt where only about 3 per cent of its land area is cultivated, but desertification, and construction work fuelled by economic activity and a rapidly growing population, are eating into this resource, posing a significant threat to domestic food production. Egypt loses an estimated 11,736 hectares of agricultural land every year, making the nation's 3.1 million hectares of agricultural land prone 'to total destruction in the foreseeable future', according to one expert. Rising ground water, poor drainage practices and encroaching sand dunes as well as rising sea levels causing seawater to infiltrate into groundwater, also pose a threat to agricultural land and lowers land productivity (see www.irinnews.org/report/93193/egypt-desertification-threat-to-local-food-production).

What is to be done?

The performance of the MENA region has been impressive in reducing the hunger situation until 2011, yet income inequality and various existential inequalities hamstring the region. In other words, MENA has done well in reducing vital inequality up to a point, and poorly in both resource inequality and existential inequality. Gender inequality remains a major challenge. Effective social policies of the developmental states can enhance existential equality. On resource inequality, the results are mixed. The declining trend of poverty in the non-hydrocarbon rich countries has been in reversal due to escalating wars and conflicts.

The Arab Spring brought to surface the growing tension between authoritarian regimes and the aspirations of their citizens, and the uprisings were a call for political openings and a new social contract. In order to achieve sustainable development and social justice, the MENA region is in need of developmental states with accountability and institutional efficiency. The weak civil society organizations in the region lack resources, if not capability, to act as champions for social justice. The continued foreign incursions of the superpowers both in the form of military and political interventions as well as the infiltration of foreign fighters fighting to establish a quasi-theocratic state continue to exacerbate the problems of the region. The region needs a functional and effective structure of sustainable governance that can meet the challenge of growing population, poverty, environmental degradation, unemployment and the failing education. The role of international cooperation remains vital, but the governments of the region also need to cooperate. The precondition for a fully functioning and effective government is the condition of peace. The challenge at the moment (in early 2016) is cessation of conflict and to bring about conditions of peace before long-standing structural changes can be implemented. A regional approach towards fighting poverty and unemployment and environmental sustainability will ensure social justice.

Note

* What we call Arab World in this discussion is also known as Middle East and North Africa (MENA) in the terminology of the United Nations and other international and regional institutions. The 22 countries that comprise MENA stretch from the Levant and the Arabian Peninsula extending from the Atlantic to the Indian Ocean. With isolated exceptions, the region's principal language is Arabic and Islam is the predominant religion. Six hydrocarbon rich nations in the Arabian Gulf: Saudi Arabia, Kuwait, Bahrain, the United Arab Emirates and Qatar make up the Gulf Cooperation Council (GCC).

References

Alvaredo, F. and Gasparini, L. (2015) 'Recent Trends in Inequality and Poverty in Developing Countries', in *Handbook of Income Distribution*, Vol. 2: 697–705.

Azour, J. (2014) *Social Justice in the Arab World*. New York: The United Nations.

Bayoumy, Y. (2015) 'Year into Sisi's Power, Egyptians Iament Persistent Hardships', July 1 http://i929fm.com/news/articles/2015/jul/01/year-into-sisis-power-egyptians-lament-persistent-hardships/ (accessed on July 12, 2016).

Bourguignon, F. (2004) *The Poverty–Growth–Inequality Triangle*. New Delhi: Indian Council for Research on International Economic Relations.

Chen, S. and Ravallion, M. (2008) 'The Developing World is Poorer than we Thought, but No Less Successful in the Fight against Poverty', Poverty Research Paper 4703. Washington, DC: World Bank.

Dollar, D. and Kraay, A. (2002) 'Spreading the wealth', *Foreign Affairs*. 81(1): 120–33.

Economist, The (2015) 'Egypt's demography! The too fertile cresecent', 6 June p. 40.

Guardian, The (2015) 'New Oxfam Report says Half of the Global Wealth held by 1%', 19 January.

IFAD (2011) *Rural Poverty Report*, 2011 Rome: IFAD.

Montalvo, J.G. (2012) 'The Arab Spring in the Middle East and North African Region: It is not the Economy!', *Topics in MENA Economies,* 14. Available at: www.luc.orgs/meea/.

Palma, J.G. (2011) 'Homogeneous Middles vs. Heterogeneous Tails, and the End of the "Inverted-U": The Share of the Rich is What it's all About', *Development and Change*, 42(1).

Piketty, T. (2014) *Capital in the Twenty-First Century*. Cambridge, MA: Harvard University Press.

Roudi, F. (2001) *Population Trends and Challenges in the Middle East and North Africa*, Population Reference Bureau. Available at: www.prb.org/Publications/Reports/2001/PopulationTrendsandChallengesintheMiddleEastandNorthAfrica.aspx.

Sen, A.K. (1992) *Inequality Reexamined*. Cambridge, MA: Harvard University Press.

Therborn, G. (2013) *The Killing Fields of Inequality*. Cambridge: Polity.

United Nations Development Programme (2014) *The Human Development Report, Sustaining Human Progress: Reducing Vulnerabilities and Building Resilience*. All material reproduced under the Creative Commons Attribution 3.0 IGO Licence. Available at: https://creativecommons.org/licenses/by/3.0/igo/legalcode.

United Nations General Assembly (2014) *The Road to Dignity by 2030: Ending Poverty, Transforming All Lives and Protecting the Planet*, A/69/700. New York: United Nations.

Verme, P., Milanovic, B., Al-Shawarby, S., El Tawila, S., Gadallah, M. and El-Majeed, E.A.A. (2014) *Inside Inequality in the Arab Republic of Egypt: Facts and Perceptions*. Washington, DC: The World Bank.

von Grebmer, K., Saltzman, A., Birol, E., Wiesmann, D., Prasai, N., Yin, S., Yohannes, Y., Menon, P., Thompson, J., and Sonntag, A. (2014) *2014 Global Hunger Index: The Challenge of Hidden Hunger*. Bonn, Washington, DC, and Dublin: Welthungerhilfe, International Food Policy Research Institute, and Concern Worldwide. http://dx.doi.org/10.2499/9780896299580.

Wade, R. H. (2004) 'Is globalization reducing poverty and inequality?', *World Development* 32(4): 567–89.

World Bank, The (2014) *World Development Report 2014, Risk and Opportunity: Managing Risk for Development*. Washington, DC: The World Bank.

World Bank, The (2015) *World Development Report 2015: Mind, Society, and Behavior*. Washington, DC: The World Bank.

World Economic Forum (2014) *The Global Gender Gap Report 2014*. Available at: http://reports.weforum.org/global-gender-gap-report-2014/?doing_wp_cron=1499959931.3050560951232910156250.

7

Amazonia: Territorial Tensions in Progress

Carlos Walter Porto-Gonçalves *

This essay analyzes the complex and contradictory Amazon sociogeo-graphical dynamics, by highlighting the many existing territorialities there from which different possibilities for the future of the region emanate. The distinct geographic scales involved (local, regional, national and interna-tional/global) and tensions/contradictions/conflicts that are being taken up by the social groups are considered. Those that derive from the new phase of regional reconfiguration through infrastructure megaprojects are emphasized.

Introduction: Of power relations and views on Amazon

The Amazon being a region located in a peripheral position within periph-eral countries in the modern colonial capitalist world system, it seems out of the question that it has the power to speak about itself. Thus, prevailing views are *about* the Amazon and not visions *of the* Amazon. And even when talking about the Amazon, visions are not the views of Amazonians, its people/ethnicities/nationalities and social groups/classes in subaltern situation/oppression/exploitation. The best-known image of the Amazon is a huge river basin, the largest in the world, covering an extensive rain-forest, an area of 8 million square kilometers, covering 'demographic gaps'. This is strictly a colonial image that marks the geohistorical forma-tion of the region from the arrival of the self-styled 'colonizer–invader', for the peoples of the region, and which ignores that the region has been inhabited for at least 17,000 years. In the Amazon of Brazil today, the ear-liest record known is 11,200 years at the Old Stone site in the municipality of Monte Alegre, Pará.

This colonial vision takes as natural the fact that there are five predomi-nant languages – Spanish, Portuguese, English, French and Dutch – and little is known about the 385 indigenous peoples who live there, and the more than 200 other languages that are spoken. And little has been said about the fact that its five colonial languages already indicate that the region was globalized five centuries ago and that the people who live there have experienced this colonial invasion since then, despite nationalist discourses that ignore this long history of existence. These views subsidize policies that silence/invisibilize these peoples/ethnic groups/nations, as well as the quilombo/pallenqueras peasant and black communities (ribeirinhos, seringueiros, castanheiros, etc.), together with the broad trajectory of occupation of the region and its body of knowledges produced during more than 17,000 years. Some of these ideas have been central in policy-making on and to (not with) the region, namely: I – Amazon as pristine nature; II – Amazon as demographic void; III – Amazon as 'reserve' and inexhaustible source of resources and: IV – Amazon as the region of the future. Let's highlight that to deal with the separate nature of life/of culture of the peoples is a meaning ignored by most peoples/cultures that live there. In technical and cultural practices of Andean–Amazonian soils peoples, forest, rivers, lakes and lagoons are living conditions with which they have to deal and with which they have developed doings/knowledges, positive conditions of production/life creation. Thus, the idea of an intangible nature, recently invoked by the sociologist Alvaro Garcia Linera, Vice-President of Bolivia, against the Andean–Amazonian peoples of TIPNIS, does not consider the practices of the peoples that live there. Contrary to what he states, these peoples have always appropriated the life conditions that the region offers them. To consider Amazon in an anthropocentric way, as in the eurocentric tradition, authorizes 'domination of nature' as it would supposedly exist for the service of men. And as we know, this means men, and to a lesser extent women, not in a generic way, but meaning white and bourgeois men.

Thus, that region, if seen as Nature, would be supposedly set to be dominated by man, and by culture, as we have seen, not any man or any culture. After all, we live under the paradigm that separates Nature, on the one hand, and man/culture on the other. In this view, one side is active-man, and the other, passive-nature. The second dominates the first, and thus, nature, the *other*, is subdued. We are properly prepared to accept that provision of entities as if it were natural. Here is the coloniality of knowledge and power (Lander, 2006; Anibal Quijano). The idea of a 'demographic vacuum', present today in the official documents of the IIRSA/ COSIPLAN[1], actually authorizes its occupation by non-Amazonians, as it is declared empty. Empty of people, the Amazon is the force of nature, an inexhaustible source of resources that would be reserved for another time, when others would fulfill the role of redeeming our societies of 'backwardness' and underdevelopment. Anyway, being future means it is not present and thus, the cycle is closed, because the demographic void tells us that there is no one present and the area is reserved for those who come from outside. The concepts of Reserve and the idea of demographic void show themselves as colonial.

As to the 'magma of imaginary meanings' (Castoriadis, 1982) that founds modern (and colonial) society, the Amazon fits in to be subjected to capital accumulation plans and/or development of productive forces, with the supplier role of 'natural resources', as in other societies/continents/countries/regions/colonies. This is the backdrop against which a new (new?) reading key is imposed, again from outside, from the late 1960s and especially the 1970s: the ecological key. This new (?) reading key approaches old conservationist outlooks, with strong roots in the US (Sierra Club), which seek that the creation of protected areas depends on their scientific or aesthetic value (national parks, biological reserves, etc.), and has the IUCN – International Union for Conservation of Nature – as its main international institution. This new (?) reading key has the industry linked to genetic engineering and new materials as one of its supports. In a way, these sectors have a different relationship with the sources of materials in its appreciation of genetic material (biodiversity, germplasm), unlike traditional sectors that put the forest below for the advancement of livestock, or to any monoculture[2].

This distinct relationship between sectors of the capitalist class in relation to the work object – for some, what matters is the naked land and in big extensions, while for others, earth means germplasm and biological diversity – paved the way for social groups hitherto invisibilized to enter the political scene: indigenous peoples, maroon/pallenqueros/cimarrones and peasants/ribeirinhos (and others), and so gave birth to the 'ecologism of the poor' or 'popular ecology' (Martinez Allier), 'socioenvironmentalism' or 'ecosocialism'. There emerges a political ecology with a strong relationship with popular movements in Latin America. In the Amazon, the rubber tapper (*seringueiros*) movement broke the paradigm that separates man and nature when it established an approach to indigenous peoples as the Alliance of Forest Peoples (Allianca dos Povos da Floresta).

Of power relations, of internal political geography

The vast basin covered by extensive tropical rainforest covers an area of 8 million square kilometers, including the 'territorial funds' (Robert Moraes) of eight sovereign countries and also a political colony of France. It must be taken into account that the various territorial states are made up of 'historical blocs' (Gramsci, 1985), shaped by its different regions and their relations/internal alliances. These 'territorial funds' are regions whose 'historical blocs' of power are situated in a subordinate relationship within the social and power relations that make up the internal political geography of the Amazon countries. We cannot fail to consider that these regional 'historical blocs' are shaped by social and power relations and thus we can identify groups/classes located in different positions, either as hegemonic classes or groups or those in a subordinated situation, including Amazon itself. This is the case of afro–indo–amazonid peasants, ethnic groups/people/indigenous nations and poor urban neighborhoods.

It is under this power complex game that we analyze the region. These social and power relations have become even more complex in the last 40 years with the political and geographical reconfiguration of the modern colonial capitalist world system. In this context, new possibilities for social and power relations between places, between regions and between countries have been opened. The modern capitalist colonial world system has, since 1960, a crisis of its patterns of power (and knowledge). One of its pillars – the idea of domination of nature that founds all its technical-scientific rationality – is beginning to be questioned. Since the late 1960s new values emanate from the streets, among them, the ecological ones. We have seen that there is a reframing of the Amazon, now for its role in planetary ecological dynamics. However, the region also undergoes a radical change in its forms of sociogeographical organization, still based on the old paradigm with the construction of major roads, expansion of mining, oil and gas, and export agriculture.

Until 1960, the region was sociogeographically organized around the paddy fields and forests, following the course of rivers and the surrounding lakes and lagoons. The new sociogeographical pattern after the 1960s comes with its highways and railways by land and barring its rivers (Porto-Gonçalves, 2001). According to Paul Little, during the last two decades, 'the magnitude of the environmental impacts of megaprojects is of a qualitatively higher order than in previous waves of expansion of borders due to the size and geographical scope of the projects, the number of projects being built simultaneously and the huge amount of capital injected into them' (Little, 2013). A new sociogeographical pattern has been established with a different socio-metabolical dynamic – 'the industrialization of the jungle'.

Understanding the complexity of Amazonian social metabolism

Many peoples have inhabited the Amazon for over 17,000 years, in a complex process of co-evolution with an extremely complex and highly biologically diversified ecosystem, that gave rise to a huge cultural diversity. We are facing what Willam Ballee and Darell Posey called a 'cultural, humid, tropical forest'.

The enormous primary biological productivity (40 to 70 tons of biomass per hectare/year) helps to understand why so many small human groups have managed to survive in the region. Jose Verissimo (1857–1916), one of the most lucid intellectuals of the Brazilian Amazon, born in Obidos in Pará, had stressed that the primary biological richness managed by the cultural practices of these populations has achieved the possibility of re-existing in capitalism, because it provided the material conditions for its self-reproduction (Veríssimo, 1970). We are therefore facing a huge ethical and political challenge with explicit ecological implications. After all, there are many people/ethnicities/nationalities who find themselves in a diluted concept of citizenship based on the idea that individuals lead democracies that do not respect the differences. There is thus an internal colonialism (Casanova, 2007) which ignores the multiple nationalities/peoples/ethnic groups that inhabit the same territory of different states/societies that see themselves as uni-national and, therefore, promote a huge waste of human experience, as the happy characterization of Boaventura de Sousa Santos, because of their 'internal colonialism' (Casanova, 2007).

The enormous 'primary biological productivity' (Leff, 2004) we have referred to, was formed with the predominant lateritic soils of the region, which according to the prevailing view in the conventional science, would be low fertility soils. This is a paradox: the greatest volume of biomass per area of the world – between 500 and 700 tons per hectare – was formed in what are considered low fertility soils, because they are processed by leaching, which dissolves their calcium, potassium and sodium. However, the annual yield from 8 to 10% of the biomass stock implies an average of 40 to 70 tons of biomass per hectare/year! There is nowhere in the world that has a biomass yield per hectare of this magnitude! Here again, it is essential to see connections between conventional scientific knowledge and ancestral–historical knowledge. That is because these soils are poor due to the accentuation of the leaching process[3] that occurs when you remove the forest that provides them with organic matter, which in turn gives rise to humus and which then supports this huge biomass. Thus, the Amazonian soils are poor only in the disjunctive analytical perspective that drives science to separate the organic from the inorganic, chemical biological, climatic biological and finally, the forest floor. A holistic view is needed to show that the soil-water-climate (Sun) - forest- climate forms a complex metabolism in which the forest provides organic matter to form the humus that sustains the forest. So Amazonian soils are rich because they live with the forest. The practices/knowledges of those who have just arrived in the area are unaware of this dynamic and, due to their colonial mentality, refuse to recognize that there are peoples/cultures that live with and by it. So with their preconceptions, more precisely by their prejudices, they promote an (epistemological?) deforestation in advance, as they see the forest as an obstacle, because they want the bare land to serve their monocultures or their pastures for cattle. They do not advocate an occupation *with* the forest, they destroy the forest. If the forest is taken as a source of life, ancestral, millenary knowledge, it should be at least a source of inspiration.

And more, this huge geographical extent of the Amazon, from immemorial times, was connected to the Pacific coast and the Andean highlands through what John Murra (2002) designated 'maximum control of ecological levels' that prevailed until the early days of the invasion/conquest of modern colonial capitalism. Thus, as 'cold lands', 'mild lands' and 'hot lands', they would be enshrined in the language of geographers and the people, provided that they offer conditions of possibility of raw energy for life that would be managed based on the principles of complementarity and reciprocity through cosmogonies/practices of different peoples/ cultures that lived or inhabited them (Josef Estermann). So the indigenous- peasant traditions of the Amazon would at least be recognized as a source of inspiration and challenge us to a dialogue with the conventional scientific tradition, while inviting us to live *with* and not *against* the forest, in a dialogue of knowledges, in interculturalism. However, the dialogue between peoples/cultures does not happen in a vacuum of social and power relations and if it is meant to happen, it needs to establish social and power relations based on *isonomy,* political equity. For that, it is essential to overcome the coloniality of knowledge (and power) which by degrading other human beings sets the conditions to colonize them (after all, no one colonizes an equal), ultimately promotes a huge 'waste of human experience' (Santos, 2001).

The complex Amazonian metabolism is based on an equilibrium of climate/water/vegetation/soil, which is extremely delicate, while the Eurocentric matrix of knowledge that colonizes our universities and our thinking, does not have appropriate technologies to deal with it.

The enormous richness of knowledge and technological complex of the peoples/cultures that inhabit the region must not be forgotten.

Amazon, the great sociometabolic transformation:
Sociogeographic standards in tension

Until the 1960s, all modern colonial capitalist incursions into the Amazon were discontinuous in space and time, while configuring expansion fronts/ located invasions. Until then, multiple cultural practices prevailed, as they had been conformed 17,000 years ago, and were based on the high biological productivity metabolism noted above, where 'the river commands life', conforming an occupation around the 'river-floodplain-forest'. Since the 1960s, a new sociogeographical configuration was imposed and countered this pattern of ancestor–historical occupation.

The national/global geopolitical context of the post-war nationalism was imposed in various forms, as national developmentalism, as revolutionary nationalism, both developmental and therefore colonial[4]. In Latin America, either to the right or the left, the twin themes of development and national (and even continental) integration came to occupy the political and ideological scenario. Soon after the Cuban Revolution in 1960, the United States put in place a new strategy for Latin America with the 'Alliance for Progress'. This mechanism offered credits to build up the integration infrastructure. The Amazon was the 'Achilles heel' of integration; the whole physical integration of the region and of every country that claimed rights of sovereignty was fragile. These 'territorial funds' and sociogeographical dynamics around the rivers, did not connect to the most dynamic geo-economic and political centers, capitalistically speaking, of their respective countries. Instead, the rivers ran in the opposite direction to their capitals and their more dynamic geographical centers of capitalist development. Thus, the integration of the Amazon was configured as both an internal and external geopolitical challenge at the same time. After all, the logistics of integration needed availability of capital, but not only that. It also lacked a political project of national integration in the strong sense, that is, to integrate not only the geographical space, but also to integrate socially and culturally the nation, which was not on the political horizon of traditional oligarchies. The issue of land reform, for example, was a real wall separating the classes even before the Berlin Wall. In the case of the Amazon, social integration necessarily implied the question of 'internal colonialism' in view that it is a region inhabited by hundreds of ethnic groups/peoples/indigenous nationalities and

African liberated slaves that exerted their freedom in their quilombos, pallenques and cumbes.

The State, as it could not stop doing – especially after the war – assumed the prerogative of a territorial authorising office to physically integrate the Amazon. On this issue, the left and right of the political and ideological spectrum maintained colonial perspectives and ignored the great multitude of peoples/ethnicities/nationalities and the complex social and power relations that make up the Amazon. Perhaps this happened less in the Peruvian case where, in a way, the predictions of Jose Carlos Mariategui on the necessary indigenous revolutionary role in the Andean world were confirmed; where a radical agrarian reform was undertaken by the government of General Velasco Alvarado, who incorporated the collective rights of peoples and indigenous nationalities to their territories (Varese, 2013). In Bolivia, by contrast, the revolutionary nationalist government emanated from the Revolution of 1952, not only disowned the communal territories of the ayllus of the Aymaran and Quechuan peoples, dividing them into small peasant properties, but it also encouraged the occupation of the valleys of the rivers coming down from the Andes, some of them in the Amazon direction, promoting integration with 'colonization' of the Andean peasants. In the struggle for land and agrarian reform, they thought of the region in the perspective of small private property, ignoring the multiple territorialities ancestors–historically conformed, where frequently community practices of production/reproduction conditions for life predominated. The different land reforms, with the exception of Peru, were carried out under the sign of colonization, disqualifying the Amazonian inhabitants to whom, often, the practice of clearing involves killing, as theirs are not uninhabited lands. Brazil was the country in which the State developed the broadest actions against the standard-ancestral history of sociogeographical occupation around the rivers, wetlands, forests, especially after 1964 with the civil–military dictatorial government. The new pattern of invasion[5]/occupation built roads on land and paved the way for an expanded reproduction of capital and deforestation, the expansion of logging, extensive livestock and various monocultures in large estates, energy exploration (hydropower, oil and gas) and mining on a large scale, and also stimulating the colonization by migrants from all Brazilian regions.

Anyway, especially after the 1960s, the Amazon began to experience territorial tensions derived from two sociogeographic patterns in conflict, namely, the pattern ancestor–historically organized around the river-flood-plain-forest, and the pattern that would be organized around the firm-land road/soil/subsoil. In Brazil, particularly, this tension strictly confronted the multiple territorialities, not only because it stopped the flow of water with the dams, but also because it assumed the geopolitical logic of linking both East–West and the Northeast to the Amazon and thus, transecting the watershed, as well as integrating the Amazon to the South–Center of the country and thus, creating roads advancing by interfluves, that is, by watershed. In this case, deforestation was made from interfluves that should be protected. Finally, a pattern of occupation based on coloniality disregarded and, more than that, ignored the region in its geography and culture of their peoples/cultures – based on a geopolitical view that sees space but does not see the people – produced road designs and dams that would bring both devastating and perverse effects.

Violence, as we know, modernly grows stronger when it comes in the name of the 'Manifest Destiny', as in the US, or of the heroes of the country, such as in Brazil's dictatorship – 'Brazil, love it or leave it' – or in the name (and the order) of progress and civilization against the world, as one day was used against the infidels, the non-Christians[6]. And in the Amazon as a region of jungle and wildlife, violence is even more cruel when the colonial imaginary, this territorial expansion of capital, is made against the *other*, the different, and is legitimized and activated by rage accumulation and profit. To kill and deforest becomes a common practice. 'Scurry[7]' everywhere. 'There was once a forest' and the 'Saga of the Amazon', song-poem by Vital Faria.

Since then, the pattern of adaptation of ancestral–historically human settlements conformed to the rivers and the forest was difficult to reproduce due to the penetration of the new patterns and their voracious dynamics of consumption of matter and energy. Each new road in the Amazon stimulates forest invasions and accelerates precarious urbanization processes; both phenomena serve to increase the demand for the construction of roads, requires more water for human consumption in concentrated spaces, more energy in the form of kilowatts and in the form of food. The new spatio-temporal dynamics of matter and energy is now controlled by the global time of oligopolic competition of capital in the international market, which requires a lot of energy. The time of competitiveness produces a spatio-temporal disconnection of raw power by setting a subordinate space (and all its biogeophysical cycles) to the time of capital. This new dynamic of matter and energy in the Amazon space-time, which began in 1960/70, will intensify and become more complex in the 1990s by the most direct interests of capital and its neoliberal policies ('open regionalism'), whose productive dynamic will travel to Asia especially to China, with the unimaginable alliance of the Chinese Communist Party to large transnational corporations, whose headquarters are in the central countries, now known as the imperialist left[8]. Since the beginning of the modern colonial capitalist world system to our days, we have witnessed the gradual shift of the geographical center of the dynamics of capitalist production to Asia, leaving the background of the North Atlantic. The effects on the Amazon, especially for ethnic groups/peoples/nationalities and other groups/classes of Amazonians in subaltern situations will be huge!

The Amazon and its (dis)integration in dispute

Already during the 1990s, multilateral organizations (IDB and IBRD) in association with governments of different countries of the Americas had been urging a new level in their relations. Since 1994, negotiations were being made to establish a new 'system of norms' as Milton Santos (2004) would say; a Freedom Trade Agreement, which would be the support base for what later would be configured as a new 'system of objects' (Santos, 2004), namely the PPP (Plan Puebla-Panama) and IIRSA (Initiative for the Integration of South American Regional Infrastructure). Vicente Fox, from Mexico, and Fernando Henrique Cardoso, from Brazil, appeared in 2000 as protagonists of this geographical and political reconfiguration of the PPP and IIRSA. Both the IIRSA and PPP gave material form (roads, dams, power plants, ports, airports and communications) to create the 'general conditions of production' necessary for the capitalists to operate and conduct their private goals of profit.

At the same time, there were many social movements' resistance struggles against neoliberalism in progress on the continent, which would allow other political forces, that some intellectuals called post-neoliberal (Emir Sader), to reach the governments of various countries, starting with the election (1998) and inauguration (1999) of Hugo Chávez in Venezuela. This Bolivarian tradition in Venezuela would be the basis of an update of the historical divide in the US relations with/against Latin America. Negotiations seeking Interamericanism, a key expression of US diplomacy towards other American countries, with the FTAA – Alliance of Free Trade of the Americas – would, from the beginning of the new century (2000), be openly challenged as an update of the Monroe Doctrine and its ambiguous expression 'America is for Americans.'[9] With the election (2002) and inauguration (2003) of Lula da Silva, what had seemed difficult for governments sympathetic to neoliberalism, would become viable, that is, the resumption of the State role. This is the case of BNDES, which financed big Brazilian corporations in order to build great public works, and IIRSA's 'system of objects' (Santos, 2004)[10]. Thus, a project was born from the bowels of neoliberalism aimed at generating financial conditions to be materialized in a government formed out of their direct control. The growing importance of China in the global economy would serve as a justification for the geopolitical affirmation of Brazil in the South American subcontinent as a protagonist of regional integration (IIRSA/COSIPLAN, UNASUR). Business opportunities with Asia, particularly with China, which is the largest *commodities* importer in the world, would open space for the expansion of agribusiness capital (soy, corn, meat, eucalyptus), mineral exploration and large companies in engineering and construction (roads, dams, ports, etc.), fundamental for the creation of infrastructure for those sectors.[11]

We face, therefore, a regional/continental global deep geographical reconfiguration that opens a new phase of capital accumulation and a new and unimaginable alliance between classes and sectors (managers of the syndicalism of pension funds,[12] financial capital, military officers and diplomacy, engineering and construction companies, big capitalist corporations, agrobusiness and mining, and managers of the Chinese Communist Party).

It is worth mentioning, for its implications to areas/regions that were affected by the works of IIRSA, some concepts that underlie this new land management, conceived as Axes of Integration and Development – EID – which were thought to facilitate the flow of goods through 'corridors'. It is no longer the region as the structuring concept, but the *axes* and their *corridors*. Finally, the flow is more important than what is fixed. For this, they proposed ten Axes of Integration, five of which directly affect the Amazon. There are huge implications to this new theoretical and conceptual scope, especially the change of scale. The Ten Axes of Development of IIRS were thought as means of physical integration to markets on a global scale and were not aimed at the local scale, regional or even national. Local, regional and even national scales are considered as passage, flux, corridor. It is no longer the region which is taken as a reference for integration, whether the Amazon or any other. Access to land, water in the subsoil and its minerals, oil and gas are disputed by sectors with unequal power in the Axes of Development and their corridors attract large capitals to appropriate the land for rent, impose their spatiotemporal dynamics and their production volumes, attract local sectors linked to small business and real estate speculation and other (drugs, prostitution).

Thus, in this new reconfiguration, the Amazon will be involved, or rather dis-engaged in dynamics to integrate the sub-continent to the global market through a geographical reconfiguration of great magnitude. Since then, Amazon will be seen as an insert, no longer discontinuous in space and time, but of a strategic political action of another magnitude, due to the volume of financial resources involved, and in another pan-Amazon/ South American scale of global integration with IIRSA and the five Integration and Development Axes that cross the region.

If, from the years 1960/1970, we could talk about the early phase of megaprojects in the Amazon, now we are facing a Megaproject that structures several Megaprojects. A new geographical pattern that Paul Little called 'jungle industrialization' and that will bring enormous ecological, cultural and political consequences not only for the region but for the entire planet. These interventions on the region have a degree of pan-Amazonian coordination never shown before. An inter-State performance level properly pan-Amazonian emerges. The magnitude of the social and environmental impacts of megaprojects is a qualitatively higher order due to the size and geographic scope of projects, the number of projects being built simultaneously and the huge amount of capital injected into them (Little, 2013).

In 2010, UNASUR took control of the IIRSA project portfolio with COSIPLAN – South American Council of Infrastructure and Planning. There are 544 projects with an estimated amount of investment in the order of 130 billion dollars. Of its 31 priority projects, 14 concern the Amazon. In all cases, transport and communications projects. The financing of infrastructure megaprojects comes mainly from public sources, either through national development banks, or through multilateral banks. These loans therefore fall into public debt.

Several of these Megaprojects involve binational agreements, such as the one between Ecuador and China, in order to finance and construct the Coca Coda Sinclair Dam; or the one involving Venezuela and the Chinese company Citic Group to make the mining map of the country; and, the ambitious Peru–Brazil Energy Agreement, that covers the financing of a body of works and not a particular work in the Andean Amazon.

Thus, conflicting interests, crossed by several geopolitical strategies, determine the future of the Amazon and its peoples, namely: 1) US imperialism, with its proposal for the Pacific Alliance and the Free Trade Agreements that, in many cases, seeks to derail South American integration[13]; 2) Latin American unity, especially South America, driven by Brazil (UNASUR) which, according to some authors has a sub-imperialist component; 3) integration driven by Venezuela/Bolivia/ Ecuador (ALBA); 4) the increasing presence of China in the region and

(5) indigenous and peasant territoriality that find themselves as objects of an intense violence, the one coming from this integration that integrates the 'top' and disintegrates 'los de abajo' (those below)!

Thus, the Amazonian populations are facing new challenges in their emancipatory struggles, like the degree of pan-Amazonian coordination, in a way that had never been shown before. One cannot understand the fate of the Amazon, especially the Amazonians in subaltern situations, ignoring these territorial tensions that run through the region.

And in the presence of the meaning that the Amazon has on the environmental collapse caused by the capitalist civilizational dynamics of eurocentrical matrix, new and old paradigms and practices come into conflict: the old paradigm of 'destructive extraction', plunder, rapine and devastation; the ecological paradigm of 'standing forest' which, in turn, puts tension on the one hand on the capitalist side of the 'green economy' and its 'genetic latifundia' (which unites the financial capital and related industries of biotechnology and genetic engineering, where big international NGOs dispute spaces to other social movements), and on the other hand, movements fighting 'for life, dignity and the territory', as the slogan of the massive demonstrations that in 1990 started in the Bolivian and Ecuadorian Amazon, or the slogan 'there is no forest protection without the people of the forest' that will affirm another perspective of 'standing forest' to consider 'extractive reserves' as 'the agrarian reform of the tappers (seringueiros)' as Chico Mendes proposed.

Conflicts and resistances

Conflict, it is important to stress, always extends the knowledge that society has about its problems by introducing, in practice and publicly, the contradictory, that is, to bring other views to the public. In short, more of one analytical perspective on a given question (Tapia, 2012).

Since 2006, in Brazil, there are records confirming that traditional populations are the main victims of the agrarian/agricultural advance, according to CPT, with over 60% involved in conflicts. According to CIMI, more than 560 indigenous leaders were murdered between 2005 and 2015 in Brazil. Indeed, conflicts over land and territory have increased in Brazil since 2003.

There are at least six major miners' *fronts* that are generating strong local impact, occasioning conflicts, namely: (1) the gold mining region of Madre de Dios in Peru; (2) Ecuador's Andean-Amazonian southeast in the provinces of Morona Santiago and Zamora Chinchipe with the projects Fruta del Norte and Mirador; (3) a bauxite exploration area oper-ated by the Chinese company Bosai in Guyana; and in Brazil, still other fronts: (4) the Carajás project in Marabá/Parauapebas, in Pará, where pig iron and other minerals are produced, operated by the Vale company; (5) the Pitinga Mine in Presidente Figueiredo, at the Amazonas state, where Taboca Company extracts tin and tantalum (raw material for cell battery) and (6) the Juruti project in the municipality of the same name, in Pará, where Alcoa Company exploits bauxite. Water, so abundant in the largest river basin of the world, has become the subject of intense wrangling, both by the high volumes demanded by mining, and because of pollution or increased turbidity that decrease the amount of fish.

Often, the State acts on its own initiative, either under the influence or in collusion with the big companies in the agro, oil and mining busi-nesses, and it has been reversing the environmental legislation restricting the rights of ethnic groups/peoples/nationalities, provoking severe con-flicts with the peasants with its non-compliance of ILO Convention 169 and of land reform, supporting or accepting financing from the companies in the creation of units of 'environmental protection' as in the Trombetas river region, in Pará, where the Rio do Norte mining operates; or accept-ing the ideology of 'rational use of the forest' when reduced to the logic of technoscience proposed by conventional engineering, as has been imposed in Acre, Brazil, against the proposed popular environmentalism defended by Chico Mendes; or accepting the financialization of nature, as with the Global NGO-enterprise called Global Canopy Programme, via large NGOs (WWF, EDF, CI, UICN), with the carbon market. Often these initiatives imply restrictions on ancestral cultural–historically molded practices. This is one of the most perverse effects of the so-called green economy, i.e., green capitalism.

Against the construction of the hydroelectric companies in Inambari, Peru, one of the most intense environmental conflicts in the Amazon, and probably throughout Latin America, was settled. The Peruvian government was forced to take a step back and canceled the license of works at Inambari. The uprising against this project is part of a long process of growth of resist-ance against mining in the country and the region. There were:

45-days of strike in which there were six dead and 30 wounded. Twice the protesters tried to take the Juliaca airport in the main city of the state (Puno), with 300 thousand inhabitants (...) Repression made five dead. In response, the crowds blocked the city, burned the Azángaro village police station and destroyed sites of several transnational enterprises in Juliaca. (Zibechi, 2012)

In the case conflict of Juliaca, in Puno department, one needs to register, again, that it is a conflict involving communities in a struggle for water. Juliaca, for example, is located near the Laguna Arapa, which is part of the Titicaca Lake complex. This movement coalesced (1) the struggle for life against the hydroelectric project Inambari, (2) and the struggle against the mineral exploitation at Santa Ana, by the Canadian company Bear Creek Mining; (3), the communities in struggle for cleaning the Ramis River, contaminated by formal and informal mining; and (4) all those who reject other mining projects in one of the poorest states in the country (Zibechi, 2012). Aymara and Quechua communities, peasants, urban workers, traders, students and professionals participated, with the support of local authorities, forming a vast social front. The Front in Defense of the Natural Resources at Southern Puno was one of the main references, though not the only, since it made part of a broad convergence, with the participation of local and grassroots organizations and others that are part of the Conacami (National Confederation of Communities Affected by Mining).

It is interesting to note that since the late 1980s, and specially since 1990, a particular power bloc has been constituted from the social groups/ classes in subaltern situations, in which the Amazon has been highlighted. We refer, in particular, to the Alliance of Forest Peoples (Alianca dos Povos da Floresta) that articulated forest farmers, such as rubber tappers (seringueiros) (Chico Mendes, Osmarino Amancio Rodrigues de Barros Raimundo, Dercy Telles) and indigenous peoples (David Kopenawa Yanomami and Krenak) in Brazil, and two large public demonstrations that in 1990, started in the Amazon, Ecuador and Bolivia, and were directed towards the capitals of Quito and La Paz, with the slogan of struggle for life, for dignity and for territory.

These Amazonian movements articulate urban and non-urban worlds and mark a new cycle of struggles in Latin America. These struggles were reinforced from the year 2000 with the Water War (Guerra da Agua) in Cochabamba, Bolivia, which is a city located in the high Andean-Amazonian valleys; and today, these struggles are being updated in Juliaca (Puno), Conga (Cajamarca), Bagua, Peru, TIPNIS, Bolivia, Yasuny National Park, in Ecuador, in Belo Monte and Jirau and Santo Antônio, Brazil, in the struggles of the Munduruku people against the dams in Rio Tapajós.

Given the magnitude scale of megaprojects involving the various Axes of Development of IIRSA/COSIPLAN, many of these conflicts have transfrontier implications. This is the case of the hydroelectric plants of

Santo Antônio and Jirau on the Madeira River, which had no cross-border environmental assessment and the first major flood that hit the region occurred after the closing of the dams, which hit the populations of the two countries.

Finally, the future has arrived and gives us a great past ahead

Countries having sovereignty over the Amazon have been, in the last 40 years, the subject of strong pressure by capitals of the central countries because of their ecological function to the dynamic balance of the planet's climate, its enormous biological diversity and the enormous wealth of water it houses. It should be emphasized that these capitals, which have been worldly consolidated, exert a certain cultural hegemony that is based on a way of life increasingly under the aegis of the 'American way of life'. This subjective dimension of *way of life* is anchored in a particular mode of production which implies profound metabolic changes, although with uneven effects in its various geographies. Thus, geographically uneven dynamics of income and of capitalist development waste continue to demand agricultural and mineral raw materials, oil and gas and thus stimulates the increase of deforestation, exploitation of fossils, which increase greenhouse gases in the planet as a whole and, in a proportion, increasingly intense in the Amazon itself.

In the midst of these contradictions, the Amazonian populations have suffered the effects of policies of both 'protection' of the forest, and of agriculture, mining, fossil fuels, damming of rivers for hydroelectrics, pressing them by giving other uses to their water or polluting them, either by mercury, by turbidity or pesticides. Social movements, in particular, see themselves facing enormous challenges to overcome these contradictions, including the divisions that the expansion/capital invasion places within the movements themselves. NGOs which were initially, in the 1970s and 1980s, very close to social movements fighting for the right to invent rights, for social justice and to 'democratize democracy' (Santos, 2001), began to see growing among them, little by little, those who seek to approach the business world and no longer position themselves with those who protagonize struggle and engage themselves in conflicts, thus becoming part of the 'new governance', where conflict gives way to consensus in a context of neoliberal hegemony which increases the criminalization of those who participate in conflicts. This sets up a 'perverse confluence' (Evelina Dagnino), where discourses of popular participation lose substance and there are no further talks about land reform, territorial and environmental justice; these are substituted by poverty alleviation programs, and the promise of mitigating the adverse environmental effects with discourses of 'social and environmental responsibility', as stated in the enterprises' portfolios, and those of their business NGOs partners.

The richness of the forest, its biodiversity, the large ancestral–historical knowledge, its immense hydric wealth, make the region a major asset for social movements in their struggles involved in multiple geographical scales. Thus, the dialogue of the Amazon/the Amazonians with the world has gained strength and meaning to the exact extent that these conditions of production/reproduction of life – the hydrological cycles, their role in the climate balance, biological diversity and its high primary biological productivity – remain with the knowledge produced by multiple people/ethnicities/nationalities and social groups/classes in subaltern situations that inhabit the region. It is therefore an epistemic and political struggle, according to the happy expression by Catherine Walsh and Luis Macas.

Let us not forget that one of the main sources of inspiration that emanates from this ancient and historical co-evolution is shaped in multiple ways of eating, healing and living creatively, woven upon a 'productive extractivism' (hunting, gathering, fishing, agroforestry) that knew/knows how to value the extremely high primary biological productivity offered by the region, and which serves as a support for a strong sense of freedom and autonomy of its people, as noted by one of the most brilliant intellectuals of the Pará region, José Verissimo (1857–1916). This is why so many people, so many ethnicities, many nationalities could break free and create spaces for life in freedom. The African slaves were able to take advantage of this enormous primary biological productivity to free themselves (*cimarron/quilombar*) to, finally, make their *pallenques*, their *cumbes*, their *quilombos*.

It is necessary to overcome the coloniality of knowledge and power in order to open an intercultural dialogue of knowledge. 'There is no forest protection without the people of the forest', said Chico Mendes. Infrastructural megaprojects and the regulation of land use and subsoil in the liberal–colonial perspective is occasioning the expansion of large capitalist projects in the Amazon that are endangering the entire patrimony of knowledge, established there for 17,000 years by multiple peoples/ethnicities/nationalities and social groups/classes, and not only by the forest.

The Indians, the *cimarrones/maroon/pallenqueros* or the Indians, in voluntary isolation or in search of the Loma Santa, are inspiring experiences of other horizons of meaning that at least deserve to be heard at this time of crisis of the power (and knowledge) pattern of modern coloniality (Quijano), in which European civilization threatens humanity in its diversity and the planet, with the environmental crisis that involves a metabolic rupture, which has been promoted especially after the industrial revolution (in social and power relations), and fossilism.

The expansion of the current pattern of capital accumulation with its five Axes of Development crossing the Amazon in its voracious demand for energy and matter, integrates more effectively the Amazon to the international division of labor in the old colonial condition, as a supply area of agricultural raw materials and minerals. And we insist it does so to feed a lifestyle and a socio-cultural-political regime subordinated to the logic of capital accumulation based on the exploitation of labor/nature of the periphery of the world system, particularly aggravated in peripheric regions of peripheric countries, such as the Amazon. Several researchers have been calling attention to this corporate model, which is exceeding the carrying capacity of the planet with an ecological footprint that even if it threatens us all, it is made through a colonial way, with an uneven geography of income and waste. Mahatma Ghandi had alerted us when he said that 'to develop England the entire planet was necessary', and asked: 'what will be needed to develop India?' Replace India with the ecological footprint of China, the United States, Western Europe and Japan and we will understand why we have to overcome capitalism and colonialism.

Given the pan-Amazon magnitude and the new range of megaprojects power constituted by IIRSA, it becomes necessary to make a strategic environmental assessment, and no longer an isolated one-by-one project. There is a perverse synergy going on between roads, dams, ports, oil and gas exploration, widespread mineral exploration, advancement of transnational power of complex agrobusiness, that completely changes the scale of what is involved for the Amazon and the planet.

When we look at the rapid growth of mining in the last decade; the increasing number of lots recently requested, either for mineral exploration, or for oil and gas exploration; when we observe the vertiginous increase in the number of conflicts and the dizzying expansion of deforested areas with its hot spots we see that the future has arrived and, it seems, modern colonial past is updated!

Perhaps the Amazon offers us another horizon of meaning for life for being a region, given the strength of what European civilization conceived as nature, and for being seen as 'the last frontier', which puts this civilizational model in front of itself: after all, this civilization affirms the primacy of the domination of nature, and what is this civilization when it no longer finds any nature to dominate? Maybe the Amazon is filling that void with its strength. Let us listen to what their peoples in their struggle for life, dignity and territory have to say. What they are offering us is another theoretical-political lexicon where the State is not only national, but plurinational; where the State recognizes that within the same territory multiple territorialities inhabit; where more than a struggle for land, the struggle is for land and territory; no more alternatives of development, but alternatives to development; where nature is the bearer of rights, as enshrined in the new Magna Cartas of Bolivia and Ecuador.

Finally, the future of the Amazon is inextricably linked to the future of humanity and the planet, such as the expansion/forest retreat was/is related to the advance/retreat of glaciations. The dynamic equilibrium of the planet means warm and cold weather, rain and drought, high and low lands, in complementariness and reciprocity, as suggested by several cosmogonies of the ancestors. Different peoples and cultures have developed/ differentiated making use of these different conditions of possibilities for life. Thus, as the planet, humanity must be seen in its difference, in its diversity. The dignity of each people/culture, is a condition for true equality. The Amazon offers these sources of inspiration because of its metabolic strength and its richness of knowledge. The current capitalist expansion puts all that at risk. Thus, to overcome capitalism it means, at the same time, to overcome the colonialism that has always accompanied it. Let us not forget that the primitive accumulation was always part of civilized accumulation!

Notes

* This article is a result of the research, Geography of Social Conflicts in Latin America, made with the support of CNPQ. It was written in dialogue with Dr Luiz Fernando Scheibe, in his position of Tutor of the Post Doctorate Program of the Interdisciplinary Program Society and Nature, at UFSC. It was presented before the Cátedra Amazonia, at the Institute of High Studies of the National Ecuador State, coordinated by Francois Houtart. This edited version was translated to English by Raquel Sosa Elízaga.

1   COSIPLAN (Consejo Interamericano de Infraestructura y Planeamiento), the Inter American Council of Infrastructure and Planning, was established in 2009 with IDB funds, within UNASUR (Unión de Naciones Sudamericanas), the Union of South American Nations, integrated by Uruguay, Argentina, Chile, Peru, Venezuela, Ecuador, Guyana, Surinam and Bolivia. IIRSA (Integración de Infraestructura Regional Sudamericana), the South American Integration of Regional Infrastructure, was put to work as a Technical Forum of COSIPLAN in 2011.

2   Further on, there will be a pact among these sectors about an economic–ecological zoning to territorially divide the area of each of them. This is the situation we find ourselves at this time.

3   Extraction process in which a powerful solvent is used.

4   Let us not forget that, until the 1930s, Europeans talked about civilizing/colonizing Africa, and after the Second World War and the national and/or revolutionary struggles, they no longer talked about civilizing/colonizing, but about developing Africa and 'the rest of the world' (Escobar, 1996).

5   The expression *invasion* is rigorous if we take into consideration the peoples of the region that were not even consulted. The colonial idea of 'demographic vacuum' shows itself at the service of whom it is.

6   Spaniards constituted the first territorially unified states, this is the geographical form of modern (and colonial, as we know) power organization. And they did so expelling not only the Moors, but also the Jews. Ethnical cleaning, we would call it today.

7   Comic in which mice fight with all their strength in order to defeat a beast.

8   According to Anthony Bebbington (2007), during the period 1990–2007, mining investments increased 90% worldwide. During that same period, those in Latin America increased 400%.

9   The consolidation of US hegemony finds resistance of different orders in Latin America, and not only from the left of the political-ideological spectre. The civil military dictatorship, which overcame the national-popular government of Jango Goulart in Brazil, in 1964, while apprehending communists, would denounce the military agreement between Brazil and the US in 1976. Records prove that General Ernesto Geisel, then dictator-President, denounced the Agreement because the US refused to give access to nuclear technology, according to what had been signed. Afterwards, the dictatorial Brazilian government established a Nuclear Agreement with Germany to build the Nuclear Factory of Angra dos Reis. As can be seen, the territorial logic is not resumed within the logic of capital, even though both rule as institutions of the capitalist world system. In some countries, as in Brazil, an industrial–financial bourgeoisie kept, even through neoliberalism, its control over important enterprises, basically in the field of civil engineering, and institutions like the BNDDEs, Petrobrás and the Banco do Brasil. That implies that the dynamics of accumulation must be, at least, negotiated by them with great corporations and global institutions. For example, the haste with which ex-President Fernando Collor de Mello pretended to open Brazilian markets to international concurrence, helps to explain their permanence. Even at FIESP, a powerful and conservative entrepreneur entity of Sao Paulo, that supported him, retired its support after this posture.

10   Since 1952, when it was created, BNDES was not authorized to finance enterprises out of national territory. A decree by Lula da Silva, in 2003, guaranteed that those investments would even use resources from the Fundo de Amparo ao Trabalhador (workers' pensions). Hardly a government attuned with neoliberalism would have conditions to do that.

11   Particularly because of its alliance with entrepreneur sectors of the area of engineering and civil construction (Oderbrecht, OAS, Camargo Correia, among others), whose interests are strongly linked to the ideology of Brasil Grande (Big Brazil), the geopolitics of Brasil Potencia (Brazil Power), which are part of the power nucleus of the country,

especially after the founding of Brasilia, in 1960, and that of the great public works of the era of the dictatorship (1964–85).

12   In Brazil, the biggest pension funds (Petrobrás, Banco do Brasil, Caixa Económica Federal) are being managed, from 2003, by sectors of syndicalism linked to the CUT (Unified Central of Workers) and to the PT (Government's party at the time), and will play a protagonist role in the political Alliance with sectors of the grand capital. The pension funds control close to 7% of the Brazilian GNP.

13   US support of the attempted coup in Venezuela in 2002 was explicit, and so it was in the attempted move of separatism in the so-called Media Luna (Half Moon) in Bolivia, in 2010, to give only two mainly publicized examples.

References

Casanova, P.G. (2004) *Las nuevas ciencias y las humanidades. De la academia a la política*. Barcelona: Anthropos.

Casanova, P.G. (2007) 'Colonialismo interno (una redefinición)'. In A. Boron, J. Amadeo and S. Gonzalez (eds), *A teoria marxista hoje. Problemas e perspectivas*. Buenos Aires, Clacso.

Castoriadis, C. (1982) *A instituição imaginária da sociedade*. Rio de Janeiro, Paz e Terra.

Escobar, A. (1996) *Pacífico ¿Desarrollo o diversidad? Estado, capital y movimientos sociales en el pacífico colombiano*. Bogotá, CEREC-ECOFONDO.

Gramsci, A. (1974) *A questão meridional*. São Paulo, Revista TEMAS.

Gramsci, A. (1987) 'La Nueva Dimensión del Trabajo', *Jornal El País*. Madrid, Espanha.

Lander, E. (2006) *A colonialidade do saber: eurocentrismo e ciências sociais. Perspectivas Latino-americanas*. Buenos Aires/São Paulo, Clacso.

Leff, E. (2004) *Racionalidad ambiental. La reapropiación social de la naturaleza*. México, Siglo XIX.

Murra, J. (2002) 'El Mundo Andino: población, medio ambiente y economia', *Fondo Editorial PUC*, Lima, Peru.

Porto-Gonçalves, C.W. (2001) *Geo-grafías. Movimientos sociales, nuevas territoriali-dades y sustentabilidades*. México, SIGLO XXI.

Posey, D. (2002) *Kayapó ethnoecology and culture* (K. Plederleith, ed.). London, Routledge.

Santos, B. de Sousa (ed.) (2001) *A crítica da razão indolente: contra o desperdício da experiência humana*. São Paulo, Cortez.

Santos, M. (2004) *A Natureza do Espaço: Técnica e Tempo*, 4th edn. São Paulo, Edusp.

Varese, S. (2013) 'La ética cosmocéntrica de los pueblos indígenas de la Amazonia: Elementos para una crítica de la civilización', in S. Varese, F. Apffel-Marglin, R. Rumrrill and V. Selva, *De la destrucción de la Amazonia al paradigma de la regeneración*. Lima, IWGIA.

Veríssimo, J. (1970) *Estudos Amazônicos*. Belém, UFPA.

Walsh, C., Schwy, F. and Castro-Gómez, S. (eds) (2002) *Indisciplinar las ciencias sociales. Geopolíticas del conocimiento y colonialidad del poder. Perspectivas desde lo Andino*. Quito, UASB/Abya Yala.

Zibechi, R. (2012) *Brasil potencia. Entre la integración regional y un nuevo imperialismo*. México, DF, Bajo Tierra Ediciones.

8

Climate Change and Vulnerable Urban Groups: Comparative Analysis of Taipei and Kaohsiung*

Keng-Ming Hsu and
Hsin-Huang Michael Hsiao

In the trend of global climate change, the frequency and patterns of disasters have no longer been included in the concept of traditional governance. Instead, less predictable, extreme environmental disasters have replaced them. Many urban climate governance issues have mushroomed, and have gradually changed the vulnerability of Taipei City and Kaohsiung City.

It is noteworthy that vulnerable groups like the common poor, old, young, weak, and sick in society have less abundant resources, and encounter limitations and problems compared to the middle class in the context of city climate governance. The aforementioned various social problems are all included in the concept of 'shared risk', which means that everyone in the community is affected by similar risk impacts, but climate change actually has different influences on different groups.

Therefore, we plan to use GIS (Geographic Information System) to create 'local indicators of spatial association' of potential flood regions to try to understand and compare the distribution of vulnerable groups living in flood-prone areas of Taipei City and Kaohsiung City to see whether there exists a significant clustering phenomenon. We hope to reflect the relationship between vulnerability to natural disasters and social vulnerability through the calculations and graphic results in GIS and then help clarify the current status of various groups' ability to face climate change, and examine the basis for future disaster prevention policies of Taipei City and Kaohsiung City.

Preface

When investigating vulnerability to natural disasters or climate change in the past, scholars have neglected influences resulting from the social dimension, such as social factors involved in the vulnerability of populations by region, including industry characteristics, demographic composition, health care, race and class composition, poverty, social injustice, environmental policy quality, the power of supervision held by civil society, and so on. In recent years, social aspects of vulnerability and resilience affecting such disasters have gradually garnered attention, such as Cutter (1996) discussing social factors causing vulnerability to disasters in a region. Building on that, Cutter (2003) constructed a social vulnerability index (SOVI) and incorporated concepts for assessing 'socio-economic vulnerability' using counties' population, social and economic data in the US.

After Hurricane Katrina caused serious disasters, all social circles in the US placed great emphasis on direct and indirect emerging social problems related to abnormal climate change, the lack of a sustainable urban environment, and the resultant unprecedented pressures and crises. It is necessary to clearly record detailed data on every clear and observable risk such as climate change or extreme weather or disaster events such as floods, droughts, loss of biodiversity, or accidental damage to public facilities, on the one hand, and new and urgent urban social problems which result, such as new social injustices, class antagonisms and deterioration, emerging environmental victims, accidental death, and pandemics, in order to assess patterns of causality, measure correlations, and analyze a variety of coping strategies in a systematic way.

In other words, the relationship between social dimensions or factors and climate change is a dialectical relationship with reciprocal causation. Cities with different degrees of social vulnerability have varying social consequences after climate change and disasters; likewise, cities with varying degrees of social resilience also presumably produce different countermeasures and behaviors in response to climate change. Moreover, urban space development often tends to establish a homogenized urban space. That is, government departments intentionally or unintentionally take the differences of citizens and urban society into consideration, but many urban space users cannot express their needs and opinion (Rahder and Milgrom, 2004). In particular, the needs of fringe populations are often ignored or suppressed, including different races or ethnic groups, classes, genders, and handicapped people.

In recent years, urban social problems and the countermeasures related to climate change and even the countermeasures related to relevant social movements have gradually been given more attention by government departments (Thomas, 2000). Internationally, in urban research, scholars have also begun to pay attention to the needs for space of specific vulnerable groups, and the degree to which such groups lack the resources and ability to withstand climate change disasters. Taiwan's cities, which are a type of ecological island, will encounter new social problems when facing the impacts and challenges of climate change, and western countries will need to respond to their own similar challenges through various strategies. Therefore, we hope our government will study the impact on society of climate change, and clarify the existing situation in terms of flooding and different categories of vulnerable groups in Taipei City and Kaohsiung City. Then, the above information should be used as the basis for further elaborating Taiwan's city-level disaster prevention policies.

Literature review

The primary task of the Copenhagen Climate Conference was to determine sustainable development planning for coping with global warming from 2012 to 2020. However, a new draft of the climate protocol was expected to have been passed by this conference, but instead, the *Copenhagen Accord* was merely 'taken note of' rather than passed. As such, it lacks legally binding carbon reduction targets for individual countries, and also has no detailed descriptions of how the funds are to be raised and allocated, due to different views of each participating country.

Internationally, there have been limited achievements on reducing greenhouse gas emissions by governments, so extreme weather events are frequently seen around the world, including hurricanes, flooding, droughts, blizzards, heat waves, cold waves, and earthquakes, all against the backdrop of global warming. However, although cities take up less than 1% of the Earth's surface area, they account for about 75% of the global population, 75% of energy consumption, and 80% of greenhouse gas emissions (ICLEI, 2009). Because of urban agglomeration, cities are major contributors to greenhouse gases, and thus to the greenhouse effect. Therefore, the International Council for Local Environmental Initiatives (ICLEI) proposed that government departments should make cities priority areas for carbon reduction.

The above discussion makes us realize the importance of coping with climate change for cities. In order to effectively respond to widespread and complex issues corresponding to climate change, it is truly necessary to adopt new urban governance measures.

Climate change

The recent Climate Change Science Report published by the Inter-governmental Panel on Climate Change (IPCC) estimated that before the end of this century the global average temperature will rise 1.8 to 4 degrees Celsius, and even as high as 6.4 degrees compared to the average from 1980 to 1999. With the intensification of the effects of warming, the frequency and the intensity of extreme weather events has already been observed, and it is estimated that this will only increase (IPCC, 2007).

In view of rising temperatures, melting polar icebergs, sea level rise, and shoreline retreat, the frequency, wind power and rainfall distribution of tropical cyclones, typhoons and hurricanes will lead to other unusual problems including floods, cloudbursts, and droughts in the future. In the context of these extreme events, sea level rise is expected to lead to risks like flooding, droughts and water shortages, storm surges, coastal flood overflows, and coastal erosion, and will even affect other areas of human society (such as water resources, agriculture, public health, etc.) (IPCC, 2012).

Overall flooding review

The *2015 Global Assessment Report on Disaster Reduction* released by the United Nations Office for Disaster Risk Reduction (UNISDR) pointed out that climate change is undoubtedly increasing the risk of disasters and the cost of disaster management in many countries. Average annual losses worldwide resulting from disasters like earthquakes, tsunamis, tropical cyclones and floods are US$314 billion, and it is predicted that such disaster losses will increase year after year. Furthermore, if we cannot mitigate this disaster risk, we will not truly achieve sustainable development. In recent years, in the context of abnormal weather and rapid environmental changes, the number of natural disasters around the globe has been increasing, and is much higher than in the 1980s and 1990s (UNISDR, 2015).

In a statistical report on past climate change based on data from Taiwanese meteorology stations including Keelung, Taipei, Taichung, Tainan and Kaohsiung by the Ministry of Science and Technology enti-tled *Taiwan Climate Change Prediction and Information Platform*, the interannual variability of average rainfall is calculated for metropolitan areas and compared to the period of 1980 to 1999. Observing the interan-nual variability of total rainfall from 1897 to 2009, we can find that the

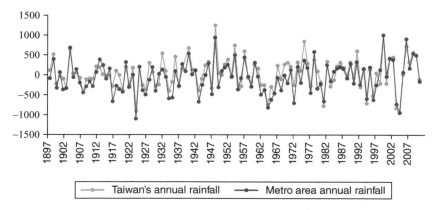

Figure 8.1   Total interannual variability of rainfall, 1897 to 2007

Source: Ministry of Science and Technology, 2015

magnitude of change has gradually increased (see Figure 8.1) (Ministry of Science and Technology, 2015).

Impact of flooding

International status

According to a statistical analysis of various disasters since 1994 by the United Nations (UNISDR, 2002), in natural or technological disasters, the impact of hydro-meteorological hazards accounted for 97% of affected people, and 60% of all property losses. However, floods and earthquakes have been the most serious natural disasters, accounting for 50% of all disaster-related deaths over the past decades. As such, hydro-climatic hazards have become critical issues for all people in the world in the 21st century.

Moreover, UNISDR (2008) counted a total of 399 national-level natural disasters throughout the world in 2007 (about the same as the annual average of 394 from 2000 to 2006), about half of which (206) were floods (the annual average was 172 from 2000 to 2006); flood-affected people numbered almost 165 million (up drastically from the annual average of 95 million from 2000 to 2006), and human flood deaths were 8,382 (higher than the previous annual average of 5,407 from 2000 to 2006); 74.8% of these natural disasters took place in Asia (the annual average was 78.8% from 2000 to 2006). These figures fully reveal the extent of environmental damage and influence on people due to flooding.

In the period of 2000 to 2008, the average number of floods per year was 176, while there were 147 floods in 2009. Both figures account for 45% of global natural disasters, making flooding the most frequently occurring type of disaster, with maximum effects on people (UNISDR, 2014).

Domestic status

In recent years, floods in Taiwan have emerged almost endlessly, such as after the moderate Typhoon Morakot in the southwestern part of Taiwan on 8 August 2009. Rainfall within a 24-hour and 48-hour period during Typhoon Morakot approached the world rainfall extreme. In addition, among the top 10 heaviest previous rainfalls in a single day over the years, all were surpassed by Typhoon Morakot except for the fifth, showing the amazing volume of rainfall produced by Typhoon Morakot.

The Water Resources Agency has conducted an analysis based on historical records of rainfall for periods of 24 hours, 48 hours, and 72 hours and a fixed number of years, to examine the 'return period', which is a hydrological term for the time lapse before reoccurence of a certain size of peak, for the sake of watershed management planning. The results show that for river basins including the Jhuoshuei River, Beigang River, Puzi River, Bazhang River, Jishui River, Zenguan River, Yanshui River, Erren River, Gaoping River, Donggang River, and Sihjhongsi River, there are many stations where the return period is more than 200 years and even more than 2000 years (Water Resources Agency, 2009: 3–4). In accordance with statistical results provided by the Central Emergency Operation Center on 30 August 2009, Typhoon Morakot caused a total of about 571 deaths, 106 missing, and 33 injured.

Taiwan is located at the boundary between the Philippine Sea Plate to the East and the Eurasian Plate to the West, and there are many disasters because of its geological fragility and steep terrain, and also because it is in 'Typhoon Alley', the part of the Northwestern Pacific particularly prone to such storms. Especially in recent years, the degree of harm caused by disasters has gradually become more severe due to growing populations and socio-economic development. In the international disaster database provided by the Centre for Research on the Epidemiology of Disasters (CRED), disasters are divided into seven categories (CRED, 2015). Some of the disaster categories, including those related to hydrology, meteorology, and climate, are directly related to climate change and are associated with threats to people's lives and properties in Taiwan (Chen et al., 2011). Because of the above adverse geographical factors, if the prediction provided by IPCC is true, then hydro-climatic disasters will have a lot of impact on Taiwan.

Therefore, it is important to develop not only a feasible method to assess the relative degree of vulnerability to flooding in each township and urban area so as to know what areas need more attention, time and efforts, but also ways to cope with flooding. Then, based on the assessment of flood vulnerability, governments can implement countermeasures against flooding (Hsiao, 2008). This is the motivation for this study.

Flood potential

Definition

According to the *Regulations for Publication of Flood Potential*, flood potential is assessed based on 'rainfall conditions, specific topography data, and water management methods'. Moreover, historical flooding data is used to create flood potential maps, prevent disaster and formulate relief plans in each municipality and county/city. Therefore, flood potential maps reflect possible flooding situations under certain circumstances, depending on hydrological events in a certain region.

In addition, we stimulate possible flooding situations in the process of normal operation of flood control facilities. Flood potential maps show possible flood depth and scope in the context of various rainfall conditions. According to the *Regulations for Publication of Flood Potential*, flood inundation probability maps are maps created for testing by the Ministry of Economic Affairs. After discussion and approval, the flood inundation probability maps are sent from the Ministry of Economic Affairs to every county and city government and provided to applicants.

Categories of flood potential map

The most important function of flood potential data is related to preparatory work to prevent flooding before typhoons and flooding occur. By strengthening the maintenance of flood-prevention measures in high flood potential areas by making good use of flood potential maps, potential impact and losses are hoped to be reduced. Specific and feasible actions include the following (National Applied Research Laboratories, 2012):

1. Studying flood prevention plans, and planning flood prevention areas;
2. On the basis of potential disasters, planning evacuation shelters and evacuation maps;
3. Flood control device with plans for supporting material;
4. Pre-deploying pump and flood control equipment;
5. Checking flood prevention gaps to increase resilience;

6. Strengthening security patrols and dredging in bottleneck segments of rivers in precautionary areas;
7. Strengthening drainage and rainwater sewer facilities;
8. Preparations for disaster prevention (watergate pumping station testing, sandbags, communications systems);
9. According to data provided by social welfare institutions, we have to preliminarily control disadvantaged groups, announce evacuation preparation, and solve any possible difficulties suffered by the public;
10. Reinforcing material preparation and delivery route planning to avoid dangerous sections in line with important monitoring of roads and bridges;
11. On the basis of disaster potential areas, promoting disaster prevention education advocacy and establishing an independent disaster prevention community;
12. Promoting long-term land-use plans to reduce exposure and risk of disasters.

Currently, common flood potential maps can generally be divided into two categories:

i. Return period: flood potential maps showing 10-year, 25-year, 50-year, 100-year, and 200-year return periods indicate the probability of occurrence of a storm of this size once in that number of years in a region. However, this is a simple probability and typically used for setting river protection standards (based on a certain magnitude of flooding). Thus, a common approach for estimation of return periods is frequency analysis (Yu and Hong, 2010: 39).

ii. Intensity of rainfall: precipitation per unit of time, such as mm/hour or mm/day, indicates the magnitude of rainfall; one method of calculation is viewing cumulative rainfall in 24 hours. According to the definition of precipitation intensity by the Central Weather Bureau, accumulated precipitation in 24 hours which is greater than 350mm is extremely torrential rain. Thus, most flood potential maps show the maximum flood depth which could occur in every region based on simulations in the event of cumulative rainfall up to 300mm (350mm), 450mm, and 600mm in 24 hours, taking into account the distribution of rainfall in space, normal operation of both reservoirs and flood control facilities, without overflows from dikes, and at high tide.

Vulnerable urban groups

Since Taiwan is in a special geographical location, located in a subtropical and tropical monsoon area, with rainstorms frequently caused by typhoons in July to October each year, it is subject to repeated flood disasters, often leading to many people suffering from flooding, with serious impact on life and property. In particular, for the vulnerable groups surviving at the bottom of society, the degree of suffering will probably be worse than that of many in the middle class in society, who have adequate and extensive resources. Thus, the uneven distribution of resources in society leads to uneven distribution of risk as well.

The Earth Summit first held in 1992 highlighted the importance of local governments in sustainable development. At the conference, Agenda 21 was passed, which proposed the concept of thinking globally, planning nationally and acting locally, as a result of calling on all countries in pursuit of sustainable development. Since then, because local government is the first line for promoting sustainable development and ecological protection, sustainable policies based on the core concept of cities (Huang et al., 2005) have sprung up like mushrooms. Urban Sustainability has recently become one of the key issues of environmental protection, and how social and economic development can be pursued without conflict with environmental protection is the primary consideration when formulating sustainable development policies.

In the 1950s, the world's urban population accounted for about 30% of its total population, and it has since grown to about 75%. In advanced countries, about three-quarters of the population live in cities. In the world's five largest metropolitan areas, the population of each is more than 20 million people, while there are 24 cities with at least 10 million people, 60 metropolitan areas where 5 million people live, and 150 cities with 2.5 million people. The more population is concentrated in a city, the greater the impact from climate change will be.

In fact, the most serious flood disaster areas are often located on downstream river plains. The reason is not only conditions of natural environment like climate and topography which could easily lead to a higher potential risk, but also due to the tendency of humans to live by rivers, which facilitate economic development and residence in the area, in turn resulting in cities there having a high density of population and greater economic development. But, if flooding occurs, it is particularly likely to cause significant losses due to increased exposure of life and property to risk. From this perspective, the concentration of population and economic development is likely to increase the vulnerability of cities to flooding, and deepen the resultant suffering.

In the international community, there is no lack of research on factors relevant to disasters and vulnerability. Wolf (2012: 1099) believes that so-called vulnerability is an assertion or a description of the future calamity due to natural disasters, and the disasters can be regarded as a stimulus. Yet, the view of Andrachuk and Smit (2012: 868) is that vulnerability is often regarded as the stress (exposure and sensitivity) caused by facing climate, and is inversely related to the ability (adaptive capability) to deal with climate pressures.

Currently, the concept of vulnerability is widely used in research on disaster risk, food security, and climate change. The so-called urban vulnerability means that the potential for suffering from losses due to the environmental hazards faced by cities includes three elements, which consist of exposure, sensitivity and adaptive capability. The concept of exposure refers to the approximate distance between the human community or the system and a specific pressure, disturbance, or disaster. The concept of sensitivity refers to the degree to which the population is affected by certain pressures, disturbances or hazards. The concept of adaptive capability refers to the resistance or the resilience in the face of hazards (Kienberger et al., 2009: 767).

Categories of vulnerable groups

The study illustrates the vulnerability caused by global climate change. Various researchers have considered what elements should be included within the dimensions of 'vulnerability', such as (in chronological order):

> Cutter (1996): socio-economic status, education, gender and family structure, race, age, employment, medical services, social dependence and special care population.

> Morrow (1999: 1–12): (1) household resources and vulnerability: gender, age, status, race, family structure; (2) limited resources and economics: low-income households; (3) personal resources: education level, experience, health, psychological qualities and family and social resources; (4) policy resources; (5) the vulnerable and women.

> Dilley and Boudreau (2001: 231): socio-economic status.

> Cutter et al. (2003: 242–58): divide it into potential damage and coping capacity. Economic status, age, health/disability status, residential patterns, risk perception, mitigation goals, psychological vulnerability, household structure, house ownership and insurance are potential damage factors which affect socio-economic status at the individual level. In addition, factors which could affect the ability of the individual to properly handle risk are economic capability, community status, occupation/unemployment, age, personal health/disability, gender, risk perception, mitigation goals, psychological vulnerability, household structure, and house ownership.

Schneiderbauer and Ehrlich (2004: 13): political system, economic and social culture.

Dwyer et al. (2004: 16): age, household type, income, car, gender, housing type, ownership, language ability, impairment in mobility, work, housing insurance, medical insurance, debts and deposits.

Chambers (2006): resource acquisition, and health.

Kuo et al. (2008): (1) individual: economic capacity, age, gender; (2) community: population density, disaster recovery consensus; (3) the government and society: urban development, infrastructure, resources and efficiency.

Wu and Chiang (2008): (1) disaster records: the frequency of disasters; (2) socio-economic factors: population ratio of solitary/disability/low-income households; (3) living environment: flood potential area scale.

Lee and Lu (2010): food, health, disaster preparedness of the poor, water resources, economic losses.

Li et al. (2010): the maximum possible loss (exposure), self-protection capability, restoration adaptability.

Lin et al. (2012): (1) individual: living conditions; (2) society: financial ability and social interaction; (3) environment: potential geological disasters; (4) policy: warning information, government organizations.

Yap (2013): occupation, class and socio-economic status, education, family structure and gender, race, unemployment, city and countryside.

In recent years, we have gradually come to fully realize the enormous impacts on human life caused by climate change. Because urban populations and economic activities are concentrated, urban climate governance will be a key factor in coping with the social vulnerabilities resulting from climate change.

'Vulnerability' refers to characteristics affecting the probability of disaster for individuals or groups, and their post-disaster resilience. These are often divided into physical vulnerability, economic vulnerability, and social vulnerability (Wisner et al., 2004). Social vulnerability is considered from the perspective of human systems to determine the characteristics of the degree of vulnerability; however, it is considered to also be determined by biological vulnerability, physical vulnerability, and the intensity and the frequency of the disaster itself (Adger et al., 2004: 29–30). The government often relies on analyzing vulnerability in a rational and objective way. The earlier surveys are carried out by hydrology and climate experts for disaster prevention in the field of natural vulnerability.

Yet, the scale and severity of disasters we currently face have already been surpassed. We have thus gradually become more focused on the status of the object attacked by disasters (referring to human social systems) before disaster strikes – in short, social vulnerability.

To assist disadvantaged groups, we further analyze the causes and effects of vulnerability. The concept of social vulnerability emphasizes that some social groups are always more vulnerable when disaster comes, and factors which affect vulnerability to disaster include class, occupation, race, gender, disability status, health status, age, immigration status and social networks. In addition to the probability of disaster, vulnerability also refers to the degree of impact on people's lives after a catastrophe (Cutter, 1996). From this disaster research view of vulnerability, it can be seen that scholars put much emphasis on issues involving structures, training courses for government staff, how to properly take care of social injustice, the distribution of power, and other issues.

Recently, there has been an increasing amount of domestic and international research on social vulnerability, and much has integrated the study of social resilience with it, which includes excessive reactions resulting from external pressures, behavior modification, recovery and other changes. For instance, Timmerman (1981) discussed resilience to climate change in societies. He wrote that resilience is the ability to recover from it as a social system withstanding the impact of disasters, and linked resilience to vulnerability. Although in studies on social resilience, some scholars may not take NGOs into consideration, we often see organizations and efforts help people recover from disasters, and these should be considered elements of the resilience of our society in the existing environmental network of Taiwan.

In the field of practice, work on vulnerability and resilience is often simultaneously carried out in current disaster risk management. But, in view of the importance of resilience, some scholars have gradually made the concept of resilience independent of the concept of vulnerability in their research (Perrings, 2000; Bruneau et al., 2003; Rose and Liao, 2005).

It can be seen that social vulnerability is closely associated with natural disasters, but scholars tend to analyze the degree of impact on residents in view of social vulnerability in most studies. However, in this series of related studies, those combining GIS with social vulnerability are few in number, and their contents mostly overlap with potential disaster.

Flooding and urban vulnerable groups

Many large cities around the world have attempted to use the concept of vulnerability to carry out disaster management. The majority of studies mention the results, policy thinking, and execution of disaster prevention could be used as a reference for Taiwan. In recent years, there have been many large, extreme environmental disasters in Taiwan like typhoon Kalmaegi (2008), typhoon Morakot (2009), typhoon Fanapi (2008), typhoon Nanmadol (2011), the southern plum rains of 2012, and typhoon Soulik (2013). On one hand, an increased probability of extreme rainfall events leads to frequent disasters; on the other hand, after the 921 earthquakes and typhoon Morakot, the original and fragile geological conditions were severely affected, making changes in disaster patterns and the scale of disasters likely going forward. At the same time, there are ongoing anthropogenic and social environment changes, including an aging population and the trend towards fewer children, urbanization, and land subsidence (Chen et al., 2011: 313). Due to all these changes, it is vital that our government pay attention to the related issues, actively deliberate, and take appropriate actions.

We find that there has been much research and discussion in the international academic community on social issues relevant to the concepts of vulnerability and disaster. After sorting out the domestic literature on climate risks, only a few studies are found to be involved in conducting national spatial planning for potential disasters, and there are few studies on issues discussing vulnerability.

In consideration of the above discussion on climate change and vulnerable groups in society, the problems of climate change issues are divided into climate variability (changes in climate-related factors over a long period of time) and extreme climate events. Because extreme weather events are usually rare, their intensity exceeds the threshold resulting in disaster. Therefore, extreme weather events should be addressed together with both climate change and disasters.

On the relevance of disasters and vulnerability, we adopt the view of scholars including Rygel et al. (2006: 743) in this study. They claim that we can analyze potential disaster areas, as well as potentially affected population, and assess the degree of losses expected in a particular type of event, and exposure to a potential disaster under certain conditions.

The foregoing interpretation of vulnerability is more in line with the viewpoint of the main victims in this article. We have done a thorough inquiry taking into account the influence of environmental variables, and categories of vulnerable groups. Our approach is different from the structural approach to disaster prevention by natural scientists in the past including coping actions, and engineering and technology like heightening dikes and building piers. Rather, many social factors like network relations, and political power and economics should be taken into consideration.

With the frequent occurrences of extreme weather events, a number of researchers have conducted many studies on the impact to the economy and society caused by natural disasters (Ward and Shively, 2011: 5). They try to change this data into a framework of analyzable data in the hope of preventing and reducing the impacts.

When disasters caused by climate change come, people whose lives and property are damaged are mostly those who are part of vulnerable social groups. Because vulnerable social groups often lack resources like health care, repairs to building structures, communications, water, and food, they can only sacrifice health care or food in order to meet their most basic needs, obtain social capital in their life history, etc. if they lack appropriate assistance to achieve social resilience after disasters. There is a vicious circle in which the marginalized, vulnerable social groups are bound to take more risks. Once they take excessive risks, it is difficult to help them move out of poverty, and so they continue to be a disaster-prone population, facing natural disasters in the future (Hsiao, 2007).

Furthermore, due to the impact of natural disasters, their intensity and the duration of their effect on cities may be increased. And this will cause more severe impacts for those residents with high social vulnerability (UN-Habitat, 2011).

Research design

In today's many disasters, flooding, especially in low-lying areas, is common in Taiwan. However, if the relevant information like accurate figures cannot be shown in a quantified manner in disaster research, then we cannot actually understand the relationship between the numbers and other factors. We are hoping to understand the distribution of both flooding and social vulnerability in Taipei City and Kaohsiung City in this study, so we focus on applying calculations of GIS, mapping and spatial analysis to determine the composition of vulnerable groups and flooding in these two cities so as to assist in the analysis of social property information on urban groups vulnerable to flooding, in order to provide our government with some policy proposals for issues of flooding governance of Taipei City and Kaohsiung City.

Social vulnerability

As discussed in the literature, there's a wide spectrum of opinions on problems of categories of vulnerable groups. But, because of the limited existing data from our government, we only find corresponding data including gender, age, disadvantaged groups, and socio-economic status and so on from the above social vulnerability factors.

First of all, generally speaking, economic conditions of women are universally lower than men. Secondly, in terms of age, infants and the elderly are subject to greater psychological impact and have a higher mortality rate when facing hazards. Furthermore, disadvantaged groups such as the handicapped are in need of care and protection by others. In addition, the socio-economic status of people will affect their ability to access social resources, responses for disaster warning and the length of time needed for recovery.

As mentioned above, we have collected data on the above vulnerable groups from the websites and annual bulletins of the Department of Social Welfare, Taipei City Government (Department of Social Welfare of Taipei City Government, 2015) and Social Affairs Bureau of Kaohsiung City Government (Social Affairs Bureau of Kaohsiung City Government, 2015), 'National Statistics' built by the Directorate-General of Budget, Accounting and Statistics, Executive Yuan (Directorate-General of Budget, Accounting and Statistics, 2015). After collecting the basic and statistical data, we first use a variety of statistics on vulnerable groups, divided by the population of each administrative area, use this proportion to convert to Z-scores, and then make subsequent calculations.

		Flood Potential	
		low	high
Social Vulnerability	low		
	high		

Figure 8.2 The interaction between the depth of flooding and social vulnerability

Source: Author's own. Adapted from data found at: DofSWTCG (2015); Executive Yuan (2015); SABofKCG (2015)

Relationship between the depth of flooding and social vulnerability

After assessing the distribution of the flood potential and vulnerable groups in Taipei City and Kaohsiung City, we created a 2*2 risk matrix (shown in Figures 8.2 and 8.3) which contains attributes of natural disasters and social vulnerability on the basis of the above data. Using this classification, we analyze the clustering status of vulnerable groups in Taipei City and Kaohsiung City.

In the risk matrix of Taipei City, there is only one region belonging to high natural vulnerability–low social vulnerability (Daan District, Zhongshan District, Zhongzheng District). This shows that there are fewer vulnerable groups in Taipei than in Kaohsiung City. In Kaohsiung City, the regions of high natural vulnerability are in coastal areas (such as Cieding District, Yungan District, Mituo District, Cijin District, and

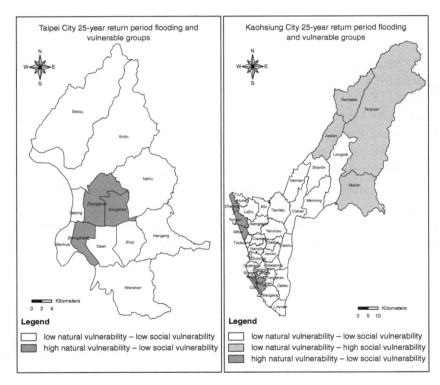

Figure 8.3   Taipei City and Kaohsiung City: 25-year return period flooding and vulnerable groups

Source: Author's own. Adapted from data found at: DofSWTCG (2015); Executive Yuan (2015); SABofKCG (2015)

Cianjhen District), and the regions of higher social vulnerability are in Jiashan District, Namasia District, Tauyuan District, and Maolin District.

A possible reason for this distribution in Taipei City and Kaohsiung City is a presumably lower proportion of vulnerable groups in the total population in Taipei City. Also, higher social vulnerability in Kaohsiung City is roughly in line with previous reports about clustering in the remote regions of mountainous areas. In order to further understand the actual disaster propensity of vulnerable groups, field research will be necessary.

Conclusion

For a long time, our government has planned a lot of flood control measures. In addition to the 'Special Act for Flood Management' approved by the Executive Yuan of the Republic of China in 2005, the Legislative Yuan of the Republic of China amended this regulation to the 'Regulation Project for Flood-Prone Areas' in 2006, and related departments prepared NT$80 billion over the course of eight years for flood-prevention programs (subsequently increased to 116 billion) (Ministry of Economic Affairs: 80 billion NT dollars, Ministry of Interior: 6 billion NT dollars, and Council of Agriculture: 30 billion NT dollars), and then proposed a subsequent treatment and maintenance management plan for flood-prone areas of NT$60 billion over six years, in order to effectively reduce the flooding problems in land subsidence areas, low-lying areas, and urban planning areas.

However, there are still some limits to good flood control projects, and disaster losses are inevitable when rainfall exceeds the design limit. Although the above situation highlights the significance of physical flood control projects, they are not the only steps which need to be taken. On account of the limits of hardware measures, our government should make a comprehensive disaster prevention strategy, create facilities to implement the project, and promulgate flexible policies which facilitate coordination between governments and their agencies to effectively reduce disaster losses (Li et al., 2010).

We can illustrate the concept of vulnerability and natural disasters in Taipei City and Kaohsiung City more specifically through collecting attribute data of categories of flood potential and vulnerable social groups, and using GIS to draw maps of Local Indicator of Spatial Association, the depth of flooding, and social vulnerabilities. Actually, our government can elastically set the standards for those certain areas on the basis of conditions in various administrative areas to be more in line with the actual situation and standards in that area. In this study, we use the concept of one standard deviation above the mean in the process of analysis through review of past academic research. If Taipei City Government and Kaohsiung City Government are very concerned about the problems of vulnerable groups in flood potential areas, relevant government officials in the local government can, when needed, also adjust the level of the standard deviation used.

In addition, if our government wants to enhance the capacity for disaster relief, government officials should not only rely on structural disaster relief work based on natural science, but also must combine it with academic disaster prevention research on social vulnerability caused by disasters and production of related flood-potential maps. We expect to clarify city climate risk by the perspective of social science research in Taiwan through this study.

The immediate purpose of this study is to preliminarily clarify social vulnerability related issues relevant to vulnerable groups in Taipei City and Kaohsiung City and how they overlap with flood maps. In the long term, we also hope to understand the social implications in light of the above information, and expect to explore the actual relationship between flooding and vulnerable groups of various categories in Taipei City and Kaohsiung City, to be used for developing and reviewing the actual disaster prevention policies so as to better cope with city climate risk in Taiwan going forward. Therefore, how to further strengthen related policies and supplement their deficiencies so as to create flexibility in coping with climate change in cities is an essential issue for both academia and government.

Note

* The authors would like to thank Academia Sinica for supporting the integrative project on 'Urban Response to Global Climate Change – Human Dimensions' in which the subproject on 'Urban Social Problems and Coping Strategies to Climate Change: Social Vulnerability and Resilience' has provided the third-year findings for our paper.

References

Adger W.N., Brooks, N., Kelly, M., Bentham, S., and Eriksen, S. (2004). *New Indicators of Vulnerability and Adaptive Capacity*. Norwich: Tyndall Centre for Climate Change Research.

Andrachuk, M., and Smit, B. (2012). Community-based vulnerability assessment of Tuktoyaktuk, NWT, Canada to environmental and socio-economic changes. *Regional Environmental Change*, 12 (4), 867–85.

Bruneau, M., Chang, S.E., Eguchi, R.T., Lee, G.C., O'Rourke, T.D., Reinhorn, A.M., Shinozuka, M., Tierney, K., Wallace, W.A., and von Winterfeldt, D. (2003). A framework to quantitatively assess and enhance seismic resilience of communities. *Earthquake Spectra*, 19 (4), 733–52.

Chambers, R. (2006). Vulnerability, coping and policy. *IDS Bulletin*, 37 (4), 33–40.

Chen, L.-C. et al. (2011). *Taiwan Climate Change Science Report* (Chapter VI Climate Change and Disaster Impact). Taipei: National Science Council.

CRED (The Centre for Research on the Epidemiology of Disasters) (2015). *EM-DAT Database*. Available at: www.emdat.be/database (accessed 17 July 2014).

Cutter, S.L. (1996). Vulnerability to environmental hazards. *Progress in Human Geography*, 20 (4), 529–39.

Cutter, S.L. (2003). The vulnerability of science and the science of vulnerability. *Annals of the Association of American Geographers*, 93 (1), 1–12.

Cutter, S.L., Boruff, B.J., and Shirley, W.L. (2003). Social vulnerability to environmental hazards. *Social Science Quarterly,* 84 (2), 242–60.

Department of Social Welfare of Taipei City Government (2015). Statistics. Available at: http://english.dosw.gov.taipei/lp.asp?ctNode=15826&CtUnit=5606&BaseDSD=7&mp=107002 (accessed 17 July 2015).

Dilley, M., and Boudreau, T.E. (2001). Coming to terms with vulnerability: A critique of the food security definition. *Food Policy*, 26 (3), 229–47.

Directorate-General of Budget, Accounting and Statistics (Executive Yuan, Taiwan) (2015). Statistics. Available at: www.dgbas.gov.tw/mp.asp?mp=1 (accessed 11 July 2015).

Dwyer, A., Zoppou, C., Nielsen, O., Day, S., and Roberts, S. (2004). *Quantifying Social Vulnerability: A Methodology for Identifying those at Risk to Natural Hazards*. Canberra: Geoscience Australia.

Hsiao, H.-C. (2008). A study of townships' flood hazard vulnerability assessment model. *Haw Kang Geographical Journal*, 21, 1–18.

Hsiao, H.-H. M. (2007). Reflection on income inequality problem and the middle classes issue in Taiwan. *Taiwan Journal of Democracy*, 4 (4), 143–50.

Huang, S.-L., Yeh, C.-T., and Chen, L.-L. (2005). A review of urban sustainability indicators: Systems framework and policy evaluation. *City and Planning,* 32 (2), 227–51.

Hung, H.-C., and Chen, L.-Y. (2012). An integrated assessment of vulnerability to typhoon and flood hazard in the Ta-Chia River basin. *Journal of Geographical Science*, 65, 79–96.

ICLEI (2009). *Local Solutions to Global Challenges*. Available at: http://incheon2010.iclei.org/fileadmin/templates/incheon2010/Download/Media_and_Press_Downloads/ICLEI_info-brochure09_singlepages-LR.pdf (accessed 15 July 2013).

IPCC (2007). *The Fourth Assessment Report*. Geneva: IPCC.

IPCC (2012). Managing the risks of extreme events and disasters to advance climate change adaptation: summary for policymakers. In C.B. Field et al. (eds), *A Special Report of Working Groups I and II of the Intergovernmental Panel on Climate Change* (pp. 1–19). Cambridge: Cambridge University Press.

Kienberger, S., Lang, S., and Zeil, P. (2009). Spatial vulnerability units-experts-based spatial modeling of socio-economic vulnerability in the salzach catchment. *Natural Hazards and Earth System Sciences*, 9, 767–78.

Kuo, Y.-L., Hsieh, W.-H., Shaw, D.-G., and Liao, K.-M. (2008). *Social Vulnerability Factor Analysis of Earthquakes in Metropolitan Area.* 2008 Conference and Members Assembly of Disaster Management Society of Taiwan, Taipei.

Lee, H.-C., and Lu, J.-C. (2010). Possible developments and application of social vulnerability in climate change. *NARL Quarterly*, 25, 53–61.

Li, H.-C., and Yang, H.-H. (2012). Assessing and applying social vulnerability index of slope-land disasters (SVIoL). *Urban and planning*, 39 (4), 375–40.

Li, H.-C., Yang, H.-H., Liao, K.-M., and Shaw, D.-G. (2010). Constructing social vulnerability index of flood disaster. *Journal of Architecture and Planning*, 10 (3), 163–82.

Lin, W.-Y., Hung, C.-T., and Tung, C.-M. (2012). *Study of Industrial Recovery and Adjustments of Disasters in Kaohsiung City – A Case Study of Liouguei District.* Taipei: National Science Council.

Ministry of Economic Affairs (2013). *Implementation of the Third Stage of Water-Disaster Prevention and Control Plan for Flood-Prone Area (2011–2013) (1st Amendment).* Taipei: Ministry of Economic Affairs.

Ministry of Science and Technology (2015). *Taiwan Statistics of Past Climate Change, Build of Taiwan Climate Change Prediction and Information Platform.* Available at: http://tccip.ncdr.nat.gov.tw/NCDR/forms/AreaVariation.aspx?p=rain. (accessed 20 April 2015).

Morrow, V. (1999). Conceptualizing social capital in relation to the well-being of children and young people: A critical review. *The Sociological Review,* 47 (4), 744–65.

National Applied Research Laboratories (2012). *Flooding and Landslides: How Much do you Know? This 'Hazard Potential Map' is a Guide to Safety in Disasters.* Available at: www.narlabs.org.tw/tw/epaper/section_1/information.php?SECTION_1_ID=59. (accessed 2 May 2015).

Perrings, C. (2000). Modeling loss of resilience in Agroecosystems: Rangelands in Botswana. *Environmental and Resource Economics*, 16, 185–210.

Rahder, B., and Milgrom, R. (2004). The uncertain city: Making space for difference. *Canadian Journal of Urban Research*, 13 (1), 27–45.

Rose, A., and Liao, S. (2005). Modeling regional economic resilience to disasters: A computable general equilibrium analysis of water service disruptions. *Journal of Regional Science*, 45 (1), 75–112.

Rygel, L., O'Sullivan, D., and Yarnal, B. (2006). A method for constructing a social vulnerability index: An application to hurricane storm surges in a developed country. *Mitigation and Adaptation Strategies for Global Change*, 11, 741–64.

Schneiderbauer, S., and Ehrlich, D. (2004). *Risk, Hazard and People's Vulnerability to Natural Hazards: A Review of Definitions, Concepts and Data.* Brussels: European Commission-Joint Research Centre Press.

Social Affairs Bureau of Kaohsiung City Government (2015). Statistics. Available at: http://socbu.kcg.gov.tw/ (accessed 14 July 2015).

Thomas, H. (2000). *Race and Planning: The UK Experience.* London: UCL Press.

Timmerman, P. (1981). *Vulnerability, Resilience and the Collapse of Society: A Review of Models and Possible Climatic Applications.* Toronto: Institute of Environmental Studies, University of Toronto.

UN-Habitat (2011). *Cities and Climate Change: Global Report on Human Settlements.* London; Washington, DC: Earthscan.

UNISDR (2002). *Socio-Economic Aspects of Water-Related Disaster Response*. Geneva: UNISDR.

UNISDR (2008). *Disasters in Numbers*. Available at: www.unisdr.org (accessed 18 June 2014).

UNISDR (2014). *Global Assessment Report on Disaster Risk Reduction 2014*. Geneva: UNISDR.

UNISDR (2015). *Global Assessment Report on Disaster Risk Reduction 2015*. Geneva: UNISDR.

Ward, P.S., and Shively, G.E. (2011). Disaster risk, social vulnerability and economic development. *Agricultural and Applied Economics Association*, 102984, 1–42.

Water Resources Agency (2009). *Analysis of Storm and Flood Flow in Typhoon Morakot*. Taipei: Water Resources Agency.

Water Resources Agency (2011). *Flood Potential Map*. Available at: http://fhy.wra.gov. tw/PUB_WEB_2011/Page/Frame_MenuLeft.aspx?sid=27 (accessed 22 April 2015).

Wisner, B., Blaikie, P., Cannon, T., and Davis, I. (2004). *At Risk: Natural Hazards, People's Vulnerability and Disasters*. New York: Routledge.

Wolf, S. (2012). Vulnerability and risk: Comparing assessment approaches. *Natural Hazards*, 61 (3), 1099–113.

Wu, J.-Y., and Chiang, Y.-J. (2008). The development and analysis on natural disaster statistics index system in Taiwan. *Journal of Geographical Science*, 51, 65–84.

Yap, K.-H. (2013). Can social vulnerability explain the distribution of mortality in the 921 earthquake? *Thought and Words*, 51 (1), 135–53.

Yu, J., and Hong, C.-H. (2010). Discussion of the estimation of rainfall return periods: A case study of Jiasian Rainfall Stations in Typhoon Morakot. *Taiwan Association of Hydraulic Engineering Science*, 13, 34–43.

9

The Coming of the New Class Society: Gender Matters

Chizuko Ueno

Introduction: After Fukushima

As a woman, and a specialist of gender studies, I may not necessarily represent Japanese sociologists, because gender studies still remain marginalized in many academic communities, with the sociologists' community as no exception. Nevertheless, it may be an appropriate choice for this panel, because gender is the main variable for inequality.

I must begin my speech by referring to the tragic disaster which Japan experienced on 11 March 2011. A big earthquake attacked the wide area of north-east coast of the Japanese main island, followed by the gigantic wave, called tsunami. More than 15,000 people were dead and missing as a result of this natural disaster, leaving survivors with traumatic experiences. Worse than that was an explosion of the nuclear power plants in Fukushima, caused by human error. There is no excuse because such an accident had been warned about, and even predicted by scientists for many years, and the electric company had a chance to prevent it. Now the Japanese territory has been exposed to the nuclear radiation three times in its history – Hiroshima, Nagasaki, and then Fukushima. In the last case, there is no one else to blame other than ourselves, which has brought a serious depression among intellectuals and citizens. Many thought, 'Japan must change.'

The victimized regions were depicted as a symbol of the local communities, with ageing population and declining industry. The earthquake and tsunami have accelerated the speed of disintegration of these communities, that were already cornered. Particularly in Fukushima, with the fear of nuclear radiation, youth and parents, especially mothers with young children, are more likely to be evacuated from their home towns, leaving their husbands and old parents behind. The disaster divided families and communities by age and gender. Those disintegrated communities were seen as a future vision of a Japanese society.

Neo-liberalist reform and gender

Japanese society has entered into a phase of population decrease, with rapid ageing and extremely low fertility – at its lowest in 2005 it was 1.26. This must be the time to downshift the gear towards a matured society. However, the current political administration with the prime minister, Abe Shinzo, still seeks for the fantasy of economic growth, called Abe-nomics, based on the success experience of the past.[1] They took advantage of the damage of the disaster as an excuse for generous public investment for construction business in the name of restoration, only to increase financial debt. The Japanese government is now indebted at the scale three times as much as the State budget. Japan now suffers from the twin debts both in finance and in trade, while it used to be the US who suffered from the twin debts 30 years ago, when Japan was flattered for 'Japan as Number One' (Vogel, 1980).

Who is responsible for this miserable result today? And who pays the price? In order to answer these questions, let me go back to the history some decades ago.

The year of 1991 was noted for the collapse of the Bubble economy. It was also noted as the year of the end of the cold war with the dis-integration of the Soviet Union, followed by a rapid globalization with severe international competition. Japan was thrown into the globalization in the midst of the economic recession. Up until then, Japan had enjoyed economic prosperity, boasting of the Japanese style management and the traditional Japanese family system, whereas the other advanced industrial societies struggled for structural changes.

In order to survive in the global competition, the Japanese government, together with employers' associations, decided to victimize women and youth by loosening labor regulations one after another under the neo-liberalist reform. The labor unionists gave agreement to the reform, as far as it protected their status quo, that is to say, full-time work with job security.

The deregulation of employment has been promoted in the past three decades, which has resulted in the increase of irregular workers, such as part-time, dispatch, contract, and temporary workers. Today, nearly 40% of the entire labor force are irregular workers, 22% among men, 57% among women (Labor Statistics, Ministry of Internal Affairs and Communications, 2015). Among youth in the age group between 15 and 24, 48.6% are irregular, which means that nearly half of new school leavers are thrown into the irregular labor market from the beginning of their career. From the gender perspective, nearly 70% of irregular workers are women, and among all women workers 60% are irregular workers.

The problem of irregular employment in Japan is special: first there is a huge wage gap between regular and irregular employment (about 60% of the wage of full-time workers); secondly, there is no job security for irregular workers, where they have no vision for career development; thirdly the medical insurance and unemployment security is not applied to most irregular workers. The income level of irregular employment is often lower than the social security level – they are known as the 'working poor' even though they work standard working hours (40 hours/week).

In the early stage of the depression, irregular employment was considered as a temporary transition to regular employment, especially for youth. They were expected to be involved in the regular labor market once the economy improved. But as the recession lasted longer than everyone expected, their poor labor condition tends to be fixed at the bottom of the labor market, where they will remain for the lifetime.

This neo-liberalist reform caused the negative impact on women in particular. Today, nearly 70% of women quit their jobs on giving birth, not by choice, but by force. As they are mostly irregular workers with no job security, once they inform their bosses of their pregnancy, it is easy for employers to terminate their employment by contract. Accordingly, they can nicely exercise gender discrimination not in the name of gender. It has kept Japanese women's labor force participation by age in M shape making the bottom during the reproductive age for the last couple of decades without change.

A new class society

Japan is now a class society with a widening class gap. The title of this presentation – The Coming of the New Class Society – is derived from Daniel Bell's book, *The Coming of the Post-Industrial Society* (Bell, 1973). In his book, he made a prediction of a rise of new ruling class, or a new class society. His prediction turned out to be true, with gender inequality restructured.[2]

In the 1970s after the rapid economic growth, the Japanese society was called a middle-class society with the second lowest income gap between the top and the bottom next to Sweden among the OECD countries, where more than 80% of the nation answered yes to the question whether they belong to the middle class. This thick stratum of the middle class served as the stabilizer of the Japanese system. In 30 years, this middle class became bi-polarized between the elite and the lower class, with the second biggest income gap between the top and the bottom next to the US among the OECD countries.

What has made this change? Who is responsible for this human made disaster?

My answer is that it was the male alliance among politicians, bureaucrats, employers, and labor unionists who are responsible for this outcome, because they made an agreement to promote the class gap. It was also an alliance between neo-liberalism and neo-conservatism, which is common with other countries. The current ABE administration is typical in the combination of neo-liberalist reform and the aggressive neo-nationalism, easy to understand. The conservative LDP (the Liberal Democratic Party) politicians mobilize hostile neo-nationalist feeling against China and Korea, especially North Korea, which is the last 'outlaw state' after Iraq.

Women and youth, especially young women, have been victimized. They are the ones who are forced to pay the price of the neo-liberalist reform. The price is also high for society because it has resulted in extreme low fertility, which leads to a shrinking labor market as well as consumer market. An interesting survey conducted by a governmental research institute shows that women with secure regular jobs are more likely to get married and give birth, compared with those with irregular employment (Higuchi and Ohta, 2004). This finding tells us if the government wishes to increase fertility, they'd better provide young women with secure jobs. Despite the lesson, the current neo-liberalist reform goes in the opposite direction to promote deregulation of employment much further.

Gender gap in Japan

Today, we have a class gap among men, as well as among women. Gender gap is worse. I have struggled as a feminist activist scholar for past 40 years, for most of my lifetime since the 70s, when we experienced the global simultaneity of second wave feminism. Such a question as whether Japanese women's status has been improved in the past 40 years, would be embarrassing to me as it is difficult to answer. If you take a look at the global ranking, Japan is ranked third in GDP, next to the US and China; 17th in HDI (Human Development Index, UNDP, Human Development Report 2015). But once gender is introduced, it goes down to 58th in GEM (Gender Empowerment Measure), and lower down to 111th in GGI (Gender Gap Index) among 144 countries (World Economic Forum, *The Global Gender Gap Report*, 2016), due mainly to the fact that women's representation in decision-making positions is very poor. Since the ratification of the UN Treaty of Elimination of All Forms of Women's Discrimination, women's status in most developed countries have been improved, leaving Japan as exceptional.

What explains this 'uniqueness' of Japanese women's low status? Is it a Japanese cultural tradition of the family system or the obedient nature of Japanese women? Culture does not serve as a sociological variable, as it is a black box with no definition.

My analysis is simple, but hopefully persuasive. Unlike other developed countries, where migrant labor is available for the reserve army of labor force, Japan lacks the substantial presence of foreign workers under strict immigration control. In this context, Japanese women substitute migrant workers as the disposable workers at the bottom of the labor force; in other words, gender serves as a functional equivalent with race and ethnicity in other developed countries. This explains fittingly why the Japanese women's status is so low among other developed countries.

This lack of migrant workers in unskilled jobs caused various problems for Japanese society: the lack of care workers for frail elderly people; the lack of caregivers for children of working mothers. Outsourcing the care burden, or reproductive labor, can be a solution for working mothers in south-east Asia such as Singapore and Hong Kong. This solution is not available for Japanese women. In Europe and the US as well, it is racial and ethnic minorities who serve as care workers. Though the government, together with some elite women, insist on introducing domestic workers from abroad, since there are other Asian countries such as the Philippines and Indonesia with a strong population pressure to export workers, I do not think it is appropriate to solve the care issue at the price of other minority women.

The population decrease can be replaced with population transfer instead of natural birth. However, the Japanese government would not apply a tolerant migration policy because of the exclusionist neo-nationalism. Conservative politicians are afraid of paying the high social cost for introduction of migrant workers, learning from the historical lessons that European countries have experienced. If Japan maintains this strict migrant control, the Japanese society must endure the population decrease, as there is no symptom to increase fertility.

Though care is always considered a woman's issue, in fact, it is a social and political issue so as to mobilize women for work. Historically speaking, child-care policy has not been a family friendly policy, nor women's policy but merely a labor policy like in most socialist countries. It aimed at the mobilization of women as a labor force by making them care-free (free from care burden, considered as a woman's special condition).

The combination of work and care between the heterosexual couples can be classified as the following four types.

A: Double earners + Public care service

B: Double earners + Commodification of care service

C: Male breadwinner + Female care giver

D: Double earners + Double care givers (egalitarian family)

The first two, A and B, are categorized as an outsourcing of care, which is divided into two options, one, the socialization in the public sector (A), the other, commodification in the market (B). The latter two, C and D, leave care as a family responsibility, which is divided into the two options, one by gender division (C), the other by gender equality (D). Type A is applied by advance welfare societies such as Scandinavian countries, at the price of heavy tax burden. Type B is allied by the Anglo-Saxon countries such as UK and US, as well as Singapore and Hong Kong in Asia, with the help of migrant care workers, at the cost of class gap. In both cases, care work is heavily gendered and racialized.[3] Type C is applied by Italy and Spain in European countries to be called a conservative welfare regime by Esping-Andersen (1990), as well as Japan and Korea in Asia, maintaining the modern division of labor between the sexes. Type D is theoretically possible, but least likely to take place where the wage gap by gender still exist (Fineman, 1995, 2004).[4]

With the type D as an exception, the types A, B, and C are ranked with the order of fertility rate with type A at the top, and type C at the bottom. If we consider fertility is a sign of the hope for the future society by individuals, we can understand the conservative gender division, or gender injustice I would say, would not give a positive vision for women. In Esping-Andersen's term (2009), gender inequality is less efficient for the future of the society. At the same time, we must remember that the seeming gender equality, or gender justice in redistribution of reproductive cost, in the same class group is only achieved at the price of other less privileged groups of people.

The reason why the type D is least likely is because men tend to transfer their care burden to the third party as they have a better opportunity cost in the labor market. It is simply because care work is placed at the bottom of the labor market as cheap labor in most societies. Then a question arises: why is care work low priced? It can be only explained with the fact that it is a woman's unpaid work.

At the end of my academic pursuit in my old book, *Patriarchy and Capitalism* (Ueno, 1990), I reached the following conclusion.

> Regardless of any variables, the issue of disparity inherent in the composition of labor will remain unsolved at the end: It is the fundamental question why the labor to give a birth, nurture and nurse until death for human beings (repro-duction labor) are regarded as ranked at the lowest among any other forms of labor. Until this problem is solved, challenges for feminism will remain forever. (Ueno, 1990: 308–9).

Territory and population are the two most important wealth areas for the modern nation state. Now the Japanese government is headed towards the population policy, which was once tabooed. It also tries to reform Article 9 of the Japanese Constitution so as to send Japanese military beyond the territory to compete with superpowers. However, what is wrong with the population decrease? This is the time to wake up from the illusive fantasy of growth both in population and power; instead, what we learned from 11 March is 'Japan must change.' The scenario has been already made towards the redistribution of social risks, namely, social solidarity, where women can take a great part. Anti-nuclear power and anti-militarism is the presumed condition.

In the end, let me close my speech with a hope that it would not be too late.

Notes

1   Unfortunately, Abe still keeps his office after three years since this presentation at the ISA, so that I have no reason to revise and update my paper.

2   About the impact of neo-liberalist reform on women, see Ueno, 2010, in English. Ueno (2013) also argues about 30 years of women's experience after the legislation of the Equal Employment Opportunity Law.

3   It is known in the Scandinavian countries that care workers employed in the public sector are much gendered (mostly women), and that there are migrant workers from neigh-boring countries such as Finland and Ukraine with a favorable foreign exchange rate for them.

4   This is why Martha Fineman (1995, 2004), a feminist legal theorist, argues about the post-egalitarian family theory, because egalitarian family in the feminist idealism is only possible with the exceptional condition where both a husband and a wife can enjoy a relatively autonomous control of time resource.

References

Bell, Daniel (1973) *The Coming of Post-Industrial Society: A Venture in Social Forecasting*. New York: Basic Books.

Esping-Andersen, Gøsta (1990) *The Three Worlds of Welfare Capitalism*. London: Polity Press.

Esping-Andersen, Gøsta (2009) *The Incomplete Revolution: Adapting to Women's New Roles*. Cambridge, UK; Malden, MA: Polity Press.

Fineman, Martha A. (1995) *The Neutered Mother, the Sexual Family and other Twentieth Century Tragedies*. New York: Taylor and Francis Books Inc.

Fineman, Martha, A. (2004) *The Autonomy Myth: A Theory of Dependency*. New York: The New Press.

Higuchi, Yoshio, and Ohta, Kiyoshi/Research Institute of Domestic Economy (2004) *Onna-tachi no Heisei Fukyo (Women in the Heisei Depression)*. Tokyo: Nihon Keizai Shinbunsha.

Human Development Index (2015) UNDP, *Human Development Report 2015*. Available at: http://hdr.undp.org/sites/default/files/2015_human_development_report.pdf.

Labor Statistics (2015) Ministry of Internal Affairs and Communications. Available at: www.stat.go.jp/data/roudou/index.htm.

Ueno, Chizuko (1990) *Kafuchosei to Shihonsei (Patriarchy and Capitalism)*. Tokyo: Iwanami Publishers.

Ueno, Chizuko (2010) 'Gender Equality and Multi-Culturalism under Japanese neo-Liberalist Reform in the Era of Globalization', in Miyoko Tsuimura and Mari Osawa (eds), *Gender Equality in Multi-Cultural Societies: Gender Diversity and the Conviviality in the Age of Globalization*. Sendai: Tohoku University Press, pp. 25–42.

Ueno, Chizuko (2013) *Onna-tachi no Sabaibaru Sakusen (The Survival Strategy for Women)*. Tokyo: Bungei Shunju Publishers.

Vogel, Ezra F. (1980) *Japan as Number One*. New York: Harper Collins.

World Economic Forum (2016) *The Global Gender Gap Report*. Available at: http://reports.weforum.org/global-gender-gap-report-2016/.

10

Duel of the Dualisms: Production and Reproduction Reconfiguring

*Susan A. McDaniel**

The processes and mechanisms by which inequalities are produced and reproduced globally are serpentine and rapidly changing. The standard historical narrative that economic life left the household, leaving caring behind in a separate sphere of family, has moved to another stage. Thought to be separate spheres of work and family, of paid and unpaid work, a significant blurring is occurring. Work is more often unpaid. Caring is more often paid. Economic inequalities leak into and out of care inequalities. Relying on two of the author's current research programs, on care migration and on the life course effects of the Great Recession of 2008, the duel and dance of the dualisms of production and reproduction in comparative contexts are explored through the prism of the work of care.

The theme of the 28th ISA World Congress of Sociology, 'Facing an Unequal World: Challenges for Global Sociology,' held in Yokohama, Japan in summer 2014, is apt and timely. Inequalities, always of paramount sociological interest, but seldom mentioned by popular media, are now on everyone's lips. Headline after headline expresses worry about growing inequalities and what they mean to societies, economies, well-being, life chances, dreams and ideologies, and even to democracy and political stability (see Banting and Myles, 2013; Burawoy, 2015; Corak, 2013; Stiglitz, 2012; Therborn, 2014). Even Pope Francis offered commentary on the perils of inequality (see Burawoy, 2015: 10–11). The subtitle of Nobel Laureate Joseph Stiglitz's 2012 book, reprinted in 2013, is *How Today's Divided Society Endangers our Future* – not a phrase one would readily attribute to an economist.

Topping the bestseller list and media interview circuit in 2014 is Thomas Piketty's *Capital in the Twenty-First Century* (2014). One may not think a lengthy economic treatise focussed on inequalities, one heavy with data and graphics, would be a popular bestseller. As an OECD report (2014: 1) suggests, 'Inequalities and policies to restore equal opportunities have moved to the forefront of the political debate in many countries.' Clearly, as the proliferation of news articles and editorials attest, inequalities are on the minds of the public, as well as the Occupy Movement.

The focus here is the reconfiguring of the processes and mechanisms by which inequalities are produced and reproduced within countries and globally, thus illuminating the duel of the dualisms of production and reproduction and the implications for a global sociology. The paper takes a multi-disciplinary perspective. Some suggest economists have outrun sociologists on the inequality file: 'Inequality was once the preserve of sociology, but the Pope and the new economists have stolen our thunder, up-staging us on our own terrain' (Burawoy, 2015: 11–12). This observation should not be overlooked. Sociologists well know the power of something repeated and its self-fulfilling consequences. This up-staging could have implications for the future development of a global sociology, and prompt us to be more interdisciplinary going forward.

We are coming to recognize that global political economies are increasingly serpentine and rapidly changing. The historical 'Just So' story of economic life migrating out of the nurturing, separate sphere of the household into the public sphere has moved sharply to another phase. The separate spheres concept, exemplified by the abundant work–family balance, public and policy discussions and studies, may be becoming decidedly archaic, perhaps along with its gendered script. Work in the public sphere is often done for no pay, or pay too low to qualify as 'making a living' and often taken for lack of other options, or supposedly love in the case of the feminized caring professions and occupations. Domestic care or nurturance is often done for pay, in the home but, wherever the locale, care is increasingly in the public sphere of paid work. What this paper does is contemplate the duel of the dualisms of production and reproduction through the *prism* of care work, relying on two of the author's ongoing research programs: one project on gender, migration and the work of care, and another on the life course effects of the Great Recession of 2008.

The latter part of the 2014 World Congress thematic question is 'Challenges for Global Sociology', which deserves some attention before returning to the question of an unequal world. We then weave the two threads of global sociology and inequality together to consider the duel of the dualisms of production and reproduction.

The project of global sociology can be seen through the lens of unequal relations of various sorts. An abundant, growing corpus of literature shows how what is known is structured fundamentally by inequality.

Sociologists may have been a little slow in taking up this flag; inequality determines what we know and how we know it. The challenge tends to be more structural than agentic, however. Sociologists at the World Congress of Sociology, with our gaze more fully on global challenges, may be leading the way in distancing ourselves at least a little from the hegemonic structures of Sociology of the North, or what some call the Atlantic perspective (Mignolo, 2002). These structures shuttle us into doing the kinds of research using methods and theoretical stances with a global North focus acceptable to highly ranked journals of the North (Connell, 2007; McDaniel, 2012).

Feminists initially focussed the attention of sociology on the obvious truth that what we know and how we know it is embedded in inequalities, which then determine who is given voice and what we take for granted. Dorothy Smith, a fellow Canadian, gifted us with the ingenious and highly applicable concept, 'relations of ruling' which encapsulates the notion that the ideas and ideologies of the dominant class rule us all, and any alternative truths we may have are suppressed even in our own consciousness as 'inferior' (Smith, 1987). She and others building on her 'institutional ethnography' have shown that women and others not in the dominant groups, develop a bifurcated consciousness wherein we simultaneously internalize the ideas of the ruling class while we maintain our own (see Smith, 2014).

Raewyn Connell at an ISA Sociology Forum soon after the publication of her pathbreaking book on *Southern Theory* (Connell, 2007), made this point eloquently:

> Open any introductory sociology textbook and you will probably find, in the first few pages, a discussion of founding fathers focused on Marx, Durkheim and Weber. The first chapter may also cite Comte, Spencer, Tönnies and Simmel, and perhaps a few others. In the view normally presented to students, these men created sociology in response to dramatic changes in European society.

Southern Theory is a book we in so-called global sociology very much need to experience. The origin story of sociology is a male, European creation. From them, descended to us, are wisdoms and theories on which we are to build, the story tells us.

Connell explains how this origin story engages in 'omission neglect' (my term, not hers). Omission neglect is borrowed from Arthur Conan Doyle's Sherlock Holmes, *The Dog that Didn't Bark in the Night*. That the dog did NOT bark is notable, but was overlooked searching for the usual barks. The origin story of sociology is similar, Connell teaches us in *Southern Theory* (2007); that sociology was happening outside the metropole of Europe, but it was not heard in the sociology origin narrative of Comte, Weber, Durkheim and Marx. There were no barks heard in the metropole, and those silences caused no concern. This is still happening, abetted and exacerbated by new forms of disciplinary practices and globality in academic accounting policies (McDaniel, 2012).

Relations of ruling are actively at work in contemporary neo-liberal agendas that have seeped into our universities' policies and beliefs. They are, after all, seeking the pats on the head and the funding treats that go with that approval, from neo-liberal states demanding accounting and rankings. Dorothy Smith (2014) pulls back the curtains in her piece in *Global Dialogue* on 'Sociology as a Vocation...' to tell us how it came to her that relations of ruling worked through coloniality in 1970s Canada: 'My Berkeley training had prepared me for operating like a legate of the Roman Empire, reproducing the order of Rome in a provincial region.' Despite Smith's subsequent optimism that Sociology no longer has that degree of 'imposed coherence' (2014), well warranted perhaps in some areas of sociological enterprise, neo-liberal hegemonic agendas are still structuring what we know in sociology and how we know it. As Connell unequivocally states:

> ... currently deepening extraversion [being oriented to external sources of intellectual authority] by locking the universities at the periphery into market competition and global ranking systems – in which the elite universities of the United States and Europe always appear on top, defining the 'excellence' others must strive for. Scholars in the periphery are now *under heavier pressure than ever* to publish in metropolitan journals, gain recognition in the metropole and form partnerships with prestigious centres. (Connell, 2014: 554; emphasis added)

It is important to note that the term 'extraversion' is not Connell's but, as she notes, is that of African philosopher, Hountondji (1997).

Based on analyses of the top ranked (Global North) sociology journals, despite a move toward internationalization, sociological work focussed on the Global South is far less likely to be accepted in these journals. Global rankings and practices of faculty evaluation via ranking of journals might be workable for sciences that are not situated in geographical specificities. For sociology, however, there is a homogenization consequence that blocks knowledge from the periphery from being read, heard, seen or built upon. If it does not become text, the knowledge does not exist. Being participant in the texts, technologies and disciplinary practices, to borrow and build upon Baudrillard's (1994) concept of 'hyper-reality,' scholars from the periphery are increasingly required, empirical research has found, by the accountability policies of their home universities in a strenuous quest for global rankings, to use the methods, geographic specificities (either actual or comparatively), as well as the theories and ideologies of the metropole journals (McDaniel, 2012).

Facing an unequal world and the duel of the dualisms

A long-standing fundamental dualism in sociology is production and reproduction. Interest has not been lost in this dualistic thinking, despite our eschewing of Talcott Parsons and significant theoretical advances made. Preoccupation has been on the massive influx of women in the global north into the so-called productive sector and what implications that has for social reproduction, particularly for care. A second major preoccupation has been demographic aging and the so-called 'care deficit.' Both of those literatures intersect with caring and inequalities.

Our interest here is on the reconfiguring of the processes and mechanisms by which inequalities are produced and reproduced globally through the duel of this dualism. We seek to explore the reconfiguring of production and reproduction through the prism of care work. Why care work? It is a prism, more than a lens, by which shifting relations of ruling by gender, class, global and national inequalities, as well as economic and social welfare institutions can be observed. Insights not only emerge but are refracted in multiple enticing ways.

Care is a universal human need. Infants and young children cannot survive without it and everyone needs it at some point in their lives; injury, physical or mental illness, or just for emotional support. Women, for most of history and societies, have been thought those best designed to serve the needs of others. This is particularly evident when thinking about mothering, but the intertwining of women with caring moves into the workplace, particularly in so-called caring occupations such as nursing, social work, day care, and teaching, and is generalized to many other work situations. Care thus represents as Folbre (2012) argues, a distinctive form of work, done for both love and money. Care has important implications for the quality of life in societies and yet is often taken for granted as occurring naturally as routine social reproduction or, when in demand, seen as a crisis needing immediate policy intervention.

But the work of care may be more than this at the macro-level. Here we extend and build on Fiona Williams' 'transnational care economy' (2011) where she conceptualizes three levels of analysis: micro-level everyday care practices, meso-level of national and international institutions, and macro-level of globalization. Our focus is on the macro-level, but the three levels are not fully separable, as pointed out by Vaittinen (2014). Care work may be, we speculate, an elastic cuff, extending and shrinking with inequalities, connecting production and reproduction in a transforming global political economy.

In the increasingly monetized caring relations, whether care workers are national or transnational migrants, we witness the quintessential paradigmatic meeting of unequals (Gorbán and Tizziani, 2014; Romero, 2011). Further, the encounter occurs either in a social reproduction or a semi-domestic space such as a day care, crèche, or elder care facility. These are spaces of reproduction not production *per se*, in which labour relationships are taking place largely, but not exclusively, between women who are increasingly unequal. It is a gendered encounter intertwining production and reproduction. This is a space for construction and maintenance of social hierarchies/social inequalities that are widening within most countries and growing globally.

We focus not on the micro-level encounter, but on macro-level inequalities that create the conditions for increasing opportunities for such encounters (Huber and Simpson, 2014; Sassen, 2014). The effect is to change the processes and mechanisms by which inequalities are exploited, sustained and possibly exacerbated, described by Sassen (2014) as brutal expulsions. Patel makes the point that 'Coloniality ... asserts that the uniqueness of European modernity was moored in the way race, gender and sexuality were used to control labour' (2014: 604). My argument is that the same conjunction of forces, knitted together by vast inequalities, is playing out in post-modernity on the terrain of care work.

As marital homogamy accelerates in the Global North adding to inequalities, with the opportunity costs for highly educated women to leave the realm of production also increasing, the need for productive labour in social reproductive care increases in parallel. This may not be linearly causal however. The 'baby penalty' women in the productive sector endure is largely a manifestation of relations of ruling, the prevalent belief among captains of industry, that women are natural carers, prioritizes reproduction over production (Couturier, 2014 among others). This becomes part of bifurcated consciousness both for women employing paid carers or utilizing daycare carers, and for those who are paid to do the caring.

Inequalities sustain them both, and at the same time reconfigure both production and reproduction and their relationship.

In effect, both supply and demand of productive social reproduction workers are sustained and connected by inequalities. The supply side entices us in the Care Migration research sub-project I am leading. In our study, we are casting a wide net to include in-home care workers for both children and elders, as well as those in agencies or institutional facilities. Like care workers themselves, our sense is that these various venues of care work are permeable with workers at times moving among them.

Prevailing widening inequalities can be used to explain the puzzlingly larger family sizes among better educated women in the United States, in the absence of the welfare state maternity or parental leaves available in most other countries of the Global North (Hazan and Zoabi, 2011). For most countries family size decreases as women become more educated. This is not the case in the US. In essence, the availability of a large pool of cheap, partially undocumented, labour resulting from very large income inequalities, who are willing (or needing) to work in domestic care work enables highly educated, high earning, mainly married women, to achieve the family sizes they wish without significant costs. It is inequalities, we speculate, that contribute to a supply of potential care workers, not necessarily demand for care, as the linear script repeatedly tells us (McDaniel and Um, 2015).

Our multi-method research on the life course effects of the Great Recession of 2008 has several findings that connect to the supply of potential care workers. First, we found those in mid-life, particularly women, have been increasing the care they provide intergenerationally (see McDaniel et al., 2013). While most of this care is informal/unpaid, some slip into formal care as stresses accumulate and incomes are needed, increasing both demand for, and supply of, paid care workers. Second, job losses among those of all generations has meant, over life courses, more 'huddling together' of generations in households and pooling of incomes. Third, and importantly, it is clear over time that low income risks have shifted from older people to youth. This shift increases the potential care worker supply among younger workers who need paid employment, and simultaneously, the possibility for older people to pay for care. This is consistent with the individualization of the risk and responsibility (see McDaniel and Um, 2015; McDaniel, 2015; Phillipson, 2015).

There is little doubt that reproductive labour has become both increasingly productive and global. This is where the prism of care work is particularly revelatory. The primary, although not the only, theoretical framework for looking at global care is the global care chain approach. Global care chains, the term used by Hochschild (2000: 131) to describe 'a series of personal links between people across the globe based on the paid or unpaid work of caring,' is derived from an earlier concept called the international division of reproductive labour or the international transfer of caretaking (Parreñas, 2000). Parreñas, in her initial conceptualization of the concept (2000: 561) sees inequalities as inherent to the formation of care chains:

> ... the migration and entrance into domestic work of Filipino women constitutes an international division of reproductive labor. This division of labor, which I name the international transfer of caretaking, refers to the three-tier transfer of reproductive labor among women in sending and receiving countries of migration. While class-privileged women purchase the low-wage services of migrant Filipina domestic workers, migrant Filipina domestic workers simultaneously purchase the even lower-wage services of poorer women left behind in the Philippines. In other words, migrant Filipina domestic workers hire poorer women in the Philippines to perform the reproductive labor that they are performing for wealthier women in receiving nations.

Twenty-first century global care chains are not only lengthened and multilateralized (Yeates, 2009; 2012) but are increasingly linked to national and international income inequality patterns. Hypothesized here, among the structural underpinnings of international care migration and domestic patterns of care, is that income inequalities contribute to an increased pool of potential careworkers. This was a crucial but largely overlooked factor in the changing political economy of care work and care migration. We ask whether growing income inequalities contribute to creating a ready supply of potential care providers that affects the degree to which families can rely on paid care workers. Or, does *supply* of potential care workers contribute to, or determine to some degree, demand for care or use of care services?

Weaving together the duel of production/reproduction dualisms and global sociology

What are the connections of this duel of the dualisms of production and reproduction with global sociology going forward? Deep inequalities are reconfiguring social institutions on multiple terrains. Looking at the reconfiguring of production and reproduction through the prism of care work leads to questioning the grand narrative of the dualisms. No longer aligned with the historic narrative of migrating from home to production, we find economic activity is bleeding more into the realm of social reproduction, contoured by global inequalities.

Transnational migration, motivated by global inequality, provides an abundance of low wage productive care labour. Temporary and permanent migrants, as well as recent refugees, are evidence of populations searching for opportunities. Many who enter care work arrive as accompanying family members with unrecognized credentials, or are displaced industrial workers, or mail-order brides or sex workers. The lines among these various groups are blurry, as the work of Constable (2007) and others has found.

As Vaittinen (2014: 1) suggests, '... the movement of care influences the making of structures. Thus, when the global care economy changes, it is obvious that so do the wider structures of the global political economy that *depend* on care' (2014: 2, emphasis in original). The suggestion is clear that the work of care is less linear, i.e. demand creates migratory streams that then become global care chains, than has previously been thought. Care seen in this context becomes a prism by which to glimpse shifting global relations of ruling. The plentiful potential supply of care workers thus creates the demand; it is not demand creating the need for a supply and the wider structures of political economy therefore transform in response.

One last but fundamentally important insight that seeing the work of care as a prism permits is a point that connects directly with the forward development of global sociology. In the *British Journal of Sociology*'s Annual Public Lecture 2013, Bev Skeggs (2014: 2) notes '... the "domestic labour debate" is to me still one of the most important debates in sociology ...'. If the debate is widened to include the new blurring of reproduction and production through care work, this view fits perfectly with my argument here. Skeggs (2014) adds a further point, which accentuates our prismatic look at the duel of the dualism of production and reproduction as examined through the work of care. She asks temptingly, 'Is domestic labour just a cost to capitalism rather than a form of surplus value, as Marx suggested, or is it the motor of capitalism? (Without biological reproduction, there would be no workers.)' (Skeggs, 2014: 2). We are suggesting through the prism of care work the role of social reproduction, contoured deeply by global and national inequalities, can be observed as linked to capitalism and its twenty-first century dynamics. That is why we call for a global sociology that connects with the new economics on inequality in a fully infused interdisciplinary way and widens its scope to see how the work of care links with a transforming global capitalism.

Note

* *Acknowledgements*: This is a revised version of a Plenary presentation at the World Congress of Sociology in Yokohama. Thank you to Raquel Sosa for the invitation to speak in Plenary Session II.1, Practice and Production of Inequality, *World Congress of Sociology*, Yokohama, and to Chin-Chun Yi for organizing and chairing the session. The research here is supported in part by a Social Sciences and Humanities Research Council (SSHRC) of Canada Partnership Grant: *Gender, Migration and the Work of Care* (Grant no. 895-2012-1021) on which the author was Co-Investigator; and by another SSHRC grant on which the author is Principal Investigator, *Income Inequality in Mid-Life, Looking Toward the Later Years: A Canada/U.S. Comparison* (Grant no. 410-2010-0814).

References

Banting, K. and Myles, J. (2013). 'Canadian Social Futures: Concluding Reflections,' pp. 413–27 in K. Banting and J. Myles (eds), *Inequality and the Fading of Redistributive Politics*. Vancouver: University of British Columbia Press.

Baudrillard, J. (1994). *Simulation and Simulacra*. Ann Arbor, MI: University of Michigan Press.

Burawoy, M. (2015). 'Facing an Unequal World,' *Current Sociology* 63(1): 5–34.

Connell, R. (2007). *Southern Theory: The Global Dynamics of Knowledge in Social Science*. Cambridge: Polity.

Connell, R. (2014). 'The Sociology of Gender in Southern Perspective,' *Current Sociology* 62(4): 550–67.

Constable, N. (2007). *Maid to Order in Hong Kong: Stories of Migrant Workers* (2nd edition). Ithaca, New York: Cornell University Press.

Corak, M. (2013). 'Income Inequality, Equality of Opportunity, and Intergenerational Mobility,' *The Journal of Economic Perspectives* 27(3): 79–102.

Couturier, L.K. (2014). 'Plus Ça Change: On Girls and Women in College,' *Change: The Magazine of Higher Learning* 46(2): 62.

Folbre, N. (ed.) (2012). *For Love and Money: Care Provision in the United States*. New York: Russell Sage Foundation.

Gorbán, D. and Tizziani, A. (2014). 'Inferiorization and Deference: The Construction of Social Hierarchies in the Context of Paid Domestic Labor,' *Women's Studies International Forum*. Available at: http://dx.doi.org/10.1016/j.wsif.2014.01.001 (accessed 4 July 2014).

Hazan, M. and Zoabi, H. (2011). 'Do Highly Educated Women Choose Smaller Families?' Discussion Paper no. 8590, Centre for Economic Policy Research, London, UK. Available at: www.cepr.org/pubs/dps/DP8590.asp (accessed 30 June 2012).

Hochschild, A. (2000). 'Global Care Chains and Emotional Surplus Value,' p. 131 in W. Hutton and A. Giddens (eds), *On the Edge: Living with Global Capitalism*. London: Jonathan Cape.

Hountondji, P.J. (1997). 'Introduction: Recentring Africa,' pp. 1–39 in P.J. Hountondji (ed.), *Endogenous Knowledge: Research Trails*. Dakar: LCODESRIE.

Huber, E. and Simpson, J.D. (2014). 'Income Inequality and Redistribution in Post-Industrial Democracies: Demographic, Economic and Political Determinants,' *Socio-Economic Review* 12(2): 245–67.

McDaniel, S.A. (2012). 'Precarious Disciplinary Intersections and Inconvenient Truths: Sociology in Search,' in D. Kalekin and A. Denis (eds), *Tradition and Renewal: The Shape of Sociology for the Twenty-First Century*. London, UK: Sage.

McDaniel, S.A. (2015). 'Global Ageing in Precarious Times,' *International Journal of Contemporary Sociology* 52(1), April.

McDaniel, S.A. and Um, S. (2015). 'More than Demand and Demographic Ageing: Transnational Ageing, Care and Care Migration,' in V. Horn and C. Schweppe (eds), *Transnational Aging: Current Insights and Future Perspectives*. New York and London: Routledge.

McDaniel, S.A., Gazso, A. and Um, S. (2013). 'Generationing Relations in Challenging Times: Americans and Canadians in Mid-Life in the Great Recession,' *Current Sociology* 61(3): 301–21. Available at: http://csi.sagepub.com/content/61/3/301.full. pdf+html.

Mignolo, W. (2002). 'The Geopolitics of Knowledge and the Colonial Difference,' *South Atlantic Quarterly* 101(1): 57–96.

OECD (2014). *Top Incomes and Taxation in OECD Countries: Was the Crisis a Game Changer?* Paris: OECD. Available at: www.oecd.org/social/OECD2014-FocusOnTopIncomes.pdf (accessed 20 May 2015).

Parreñas, R. (2000). 'Migrant Filipina Domestic Workers and the International Division of Reproductive Labor', *Gender and Society* 14(4): 560–80.

Patel, S. (2014). 'Afterward: Doing Global Sociology: Issues, Problems and Challenges,' *Current Sociology* 62(4): 603–13.

Phillipson, C. (2015). 'The Political Economy of Longevity: Developing New Forms of Solidarity for Later Life,' *The Sociological Quarterly* 56: 80–100.

Piketty, T. (2014). *Capital in the Twenty-First Century*. Cambridge, MA: Harvard University Press.

Romero, M. (2011). *The Maid's Daughter: Living Inside and Outside the American Dream*. New York, NY: New York University Press.

Sassen, S. (2014). *Expulsions: Brutality and Complexity in the Global Economy*. Cambridge, MA: The Belknap Press of Harvard University Press.

Skeggs, B. (2014). 'Values Beyond Value? Is Anything Beyond the Logic of Capital?', British Journal of Sociology Annual Public Lecture. *The British Journal of Sociology* 65(1): 1–20.

Smith, D.E. (1987). *The Everyday World as Problematic: A Feminist Sociology*. Toronto: University of Toronto Press.

Smith, D.E. (2014). 'Sociology as a Vocation: Lineages of Institutional Ethnography,' *Global Dialogue* 4(2): 4–5.

Stiglitz, J.E. (2012). *The Price of Inequality: How Today's Divided Society Endangers Our Future*. New York: W. W. Norton.

Therborn, G. (2014). *The Killing Fields of Inequality*. Cambridge, UK: Polity Press.

Vaittinen, T. (2014). 'Reading Global Care Chains as Migrant Trajectories: A Theoretical Framework for the Understanding of Structural Change,' *Women's Studies International Forum*. Available at: http://dx.doi.org/10.1016/j.wsif.2014.01.009 (accessed 4 July 2014).

Williams, F. (2011). 'Towards a Transnational Analysis of the Political Economy of Care,' pp. 21–38 in R. Mahon and F. Robinson (eds), *Feminist Ethics and Social Policy: Toward a New Global Political Economy of Care.* Vancouver: University of British Columbia Press.

Yeates, N. (2009). *Globalizing Care Economies and Migrant Workers: Explorations in Global Care Chains.* New York: Palgrave Macmillan.

Yeates, N. (2012). 'Global Care Chains: A State-of-the-Art Review and Future Directions in Care Transnationalization Research,' *Global Networks* 12(2): 135–54.

11

The Historic Environment in Opposition to Social Inequalities

Hiroyuki Torigoe

This article discusses the root causes of social inequalities experienced by a small island community in Japan and how these problems were eliminated. Aspects of this community's experience using its indigenous resources to bring about changes to prejudicial attitudes can be instructive for other communities struggling with misunderstandings, prejudices, discrimination, and social inequality.

Introduction

Environmental sociology has consistently maintained a strong interest in nature by focusing on the relationships between human activities and natural environments. One of the essential topics of environmental sociology centers on ways to preserve natural environments from the degradations of human activities.[1] Several countries have historic environments that are

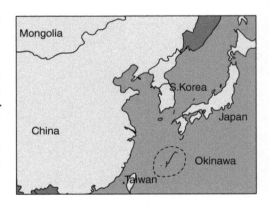

Figure 11.1 Location of Okinawa

indispensable fields for environmental sociology; Japan is one of those countries. In Japan, each local community maintains its long history and local historic sites, such as traditional buildings, bridges, and cultures. Thus, the historic environment creates landscapes and lifestyles. Human activities are important parts of the construction of picturesque landscapes because these settings often are the result of merged natural and historic settings.[2] The broad theme of this book is inequalities. Therefore, this article focuses on activities intended to preserve the historic environment in a community dedicated to reducing social inequalities.

The community under observation is Taketomi Island in Okinawa Prefecture, which is one of the outer islands near the southwestern border of Japan, with a subtropical climate (see Figure 11.1). Its islanders have historically suffered from two inequalities. First, until 1879, the Okinawa Prefecture area was a small independent nation named Ryukyu Kingdom. This nation was defeated and subsequently annexed by Japan, after which many mainland Japanese, particularly uneducated people, began to regard these islanders with contempt as defeated people. This situation made it difficult for islanders to find good jobs on the mainland and they also sometimes faced marriage partner problems.[3] The second source of inequality relates to the location of Taketomi Island, which was peripheral to Ryukyu Kingdom during its existence. The people of the kingdom considered Taketomi Islanders as non-cultured people living on a remote and isolated island. This cultural bias continued after Taketomi's incorporation into Japan.

Historical background of Taketomi Island

The small nation of Ryukyu Kingdom to which Taketomi Island belonged was established in about 1430 and, as mentioned, was taken by Japan in 1879. During its approximate 450-year history, the major industry was the so-called 'transit trade' between Japan and China and some Southeast Asian countries, such as Siam (Thailand), with large seagoing vessels. The Kingdom filled the need for transportation, but it did not have its own excess resources for trade. However, Taketomi Island was far from the Kingdom's capital, and the people subsisted on agriculture and fishery and did not benefit from the shipping industry. This coral island of $6.32m^2$ and a population of 385 in 2015 (1,061 known residents in 1737) provided poor soil for cultivation and limited fisheries inside the reefs.

After the annexation to Japan, the islanders' lifestyle did not change very much. In 1964, several artists from mainland Japan recognized the endemic beauty of their dwellings, coral walls, and everyday pottery (bowls and dishes). Despite the assessments of the beauty of their lifestyles, the praise had little influence among outsiders. Still there persisted prejudice which lead to inequalities.

In Japan, the 1970s was a period of economic growth and obsessive regional development. Developers from the mainland visited Taketomi Island to expand marine activities and purchased about 30 percent of the land from the islanders at bargain prices, which they could accomplish because of the islanders' extremity in the face of two severe droughts. Usually, people are happy to get money in situations like that when poverty is looming, but the Island's leaders were concerned that the indigenous culture, which the famous artists had appreciated, would disappear in response to the modernized marine facilities and influx of visitors from mainland Japan who had no interest in the local culture. The Island's community organized an anti-development movement named Preservation of Taketomi, which was supported by some mainlanders, such as artists' groups and indigenous islanders who had emigrated to the mainland for work. The movement's slogan was 'money is for one generation but land is for future generations.' Facing strong and persistent resistance, the developers were forced to abandon their plans.[4]

Findings of its own culture

One outcome of the anti-development movement was the islanders' realization of the value of their lifestyle and the culture that had been passed down from their ancestors. Initially, success against the development plan was contested among the islanders; not a few community members favored development. Therefore, when the anti-development movement had achieved its goals, the leaders believed it was necessary to develop a common philosophy in the community. Based on discussions in community meetings, they drew up a simple and understandable document, entitled *The Taketomi Island Chapter*, which comprised five directives: (1) don't sell land, (2) maintain a clean island, (3) maintain

Figure 11.2 Tourists enjoying public paths with white sand, coral rock walls, and flowers

the dwellings, (4) preserve the traditions, and (5) promote the lifestyle. The implementation of the activities set forth in the *Chapter* made the Taketomi Island residential areas more attractive spaces than before with respect to visual attractiveness (scenery). The beauty attracted tourists who enjoy the atmosphere of remote islands. The numbers of small restaurants and shops increased and some private homes transformed into inns. A local tourist company offered eco-tourism. Those changes meant that local people began to generate incomes from tourism in addition to income from their farming and fishing activities as the field and fishing harvests began to find a tourist market on the Island (see Figure 11.2).

In 1987, the Agency for Cultural Affairs in the central government selected the Taketomi Island community as the Preservation District for Groups of Historic Buildings (PDGHP). The PDGHP is a highly prestigious honor that brought the Island into the group of PDGHP areas already designated as famous historic sites known nationwide.

Today, Taketomi Island enjoys a healthy tourist industry (519,641 in 2014)[5], and it is known for its preservation of historic sites and for revitalization of the indigenous lifestyle. Although the number of tourists is large, tourism does not threaten the Island's culture because the tourists respect the lifestyle, the small houses with red tile roofs, and the white sand paths. Thus, the community members need not change their lifestyles to accommodate the tourist trade. Most importantly, the two types of inequality, which clearly existed before, have totally disappeared.

What is the secret of the disappearing inequality?

The reasons that inequality disappeared are complex and several factors contribute to pushing the inequalities aside. These factors become effective when they accumulate, and, therefore, I use the term 'tier' instead of 'factor' to indicate a bundle of factors. The first tier is the Basic Tier, which indicates a sense of confidence within the community that, despite inequalities imposed from the outside, they were worthy and appreciated by several prestigious artists and essayists who had visited the island (mostly in the 1960s). Importantly, there were some key persons among the islanders, such as a Buddhist priest, teachers, and a semi-professional cameraman who loved the Island's scenery and atmosphere and married a local woman. These individuals facilitated confidence and determination in the community, which led to the anti-development movement in the 1970s.

The Second Tier is the confirmation of the islanders' 'satisfactory lifestyle,' which was clarified and matured through the process of creating the *Taketomi Island Charter* (1986) after the anti-development movement. A satisfactory lifestyle in this community is not the same as mainland Japan's, where modern facilities are built one after another and people value independence and freedom. On Taketomi Island, the traditional dwellings, open to soft breezes and neighbors alike, are cherished, although some utilities, such as running water, and kitchens, were modernized. Islanders attend rituals, are encouraged to participate in the religious dancing festivals, and are expected to maintain the cleanliness of public paths. Islanders prefer strong human relationships to individualism. Their activities were rewarded with the nomination to the PDGHP with the financial support of the central government.[6] Here, I particularly point out that the islanders' annual festivals and rituals with dances and music are only for their own exaltation, and they are not intended for the tourists. In many places, indigenous cultural festivals and rituals gradually change to attract and entertain tourists, which has sometimes been blamed on anthropologists; but, at this point, the islanders' festivals are not commercialized.

The Third Tier is 'creation of tradition.' In a context where tourist trade is very active, the phrase 'creation of tradition' could suggest reforms, but in Taketomi Island, creation of tradition refers to the directives of the *Taketomi Island Chapter* that is meant to support the islanders. Therefore, creative changes were implemented on behalf of the islanders. Many of these changes were harmonious with the tourists' expectations of the island. A good example of the Third Tier is red-tiled roofs. Red-roofed houses were previously found throughout the Ryukyu Kingdom area, although they were restricted to the relatively higher-class dwellings. As recently as 1972, red-roofed houses comprised only 46 percent

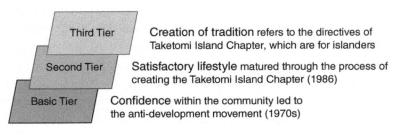

Figure 11.3 Three tiers of disappearing inequalities

of the dwellings, and the others were thatched or another style of roof.[7] This was historically the case because red tiles were expensive and thatch is free. However, there are no longer any thatched roofs; all of them have been replaced by red tiles, mostly because of increased incomes. Making that change gave the islanders a sense of satisfaction and a feeling of upward social mobility. The views of this community now are of traditional houses with red roofs, coral rock walls, and white sand paths, without exception.

Certainly, the three tiers have eliminated the inequalities that existed, but no one can put their finger on exactly when or how that change occurred. The change occurred without anyone noticing it.

Notes

1   Catton and Dunlap (1978) provided fresh insight in a New Environmental paradigm for environmental sociologists analyzing the relationships between humans and nature.

2   A typical idea that sometimes includes human elements is 'picturesque landscape'; found in England, it is particularly around the Lake District, where reputations have been influenced by traditional French and Italian landscape paintings (Gell, 1797; Martineau, 1854).

3   There are so many documents discussing their inequalities in their minority experiences. Books by Weiner (1997) and Robson (2012) are written in English. Especially see 'Troubled national identity: Ryukyuans/Okinawans' by Koji Taira in Weiner's book.

4   See Yanaka (2009).

5   From the statistics of Taketomi Town Office (2015).

6   See Fujioka (2001).

7   Fukuda (2005), a geographer, researched the red roofs in Taketomi Island and concluded that the recent increase in red-roofed houses is the result of new traditions.

References

Catton, W.R. and Dunlap, R.E. (1978). 'Paradigms, Theories and the Primacy of the HEP-NEP Distinction.' *The American Sociologist* 13.

Fujioka, W. (2001). 'Preservation of the Historic Landscape of a Village.' *Journal of Rural Studies*, 14.

Fukuda, T. (2005). 'The Movement of the MACHINAMI Conservation in Taketomi,' in A. Hiraoka (ed.), *Research into People, Life and Industry of the Japanese Islands*, Ohtsu, Kaiseisya Press.

Gell, W. (1797). *A Tour in the Lakes* (republished by William Rollinson (ed.) (2000), Smith Settle Ltd.).

Martineau, H. (1854). *Guide to Winderemere* (republished by W.R. Mitchell (1995), Castlerg Books).

Robson, S. (2012). *The Okinawan Diaspora in Japan: Crossing the Borders Within*, University of Hawaii Press.

Taketomi Town Office (2015). *The 2015 Vital Statistics.*

Yanaka, S. (2009). 'Community and Scenery, a Case of Taketomi,' in Y.F. Torigoe, *The Creation of Scenery and Regional Community*, Nobunkyou Press.

Weiner, M. (ed.) (1997). *Japan's Minorities: The Illusion of Homogeneity*, Routledge.

12

The Capability Approach, Social Development and Human Rights

Jean-Michel Bonvin

This chapter offers a synthetic view of how the capability approach allows grasping more adequately the multiple dimensions of inequality in the contemporary world and designing more appropriate interventions to tackle them. It first presents the main components of the capability approach and then shows the implications in the field of human rights and the struggle against inequalities. Section 1 focuses on the crucial issue of 'what should be equalized?', and what it entails. Section 2 emphasizes the relevance of processual dimensions to social justice and insists on the necessity of taking people's preferences and aspirations seriously. Section 3 draws some implications of the capabilities approach for the effective implementation of human rights. Section 4 briefly concludes.

'Equality of what?' – the original contribution of the capability approach

Inequalities are omnipresent in the contemporary world and it seems quite unrealistic to seek to suppress them altogether. Thus, a key issue is to identify what should be equalized, in other words on what kind of inequalities public and collective action should focus. In Amartya Sen's words, this relates to the selection of the informational basis of justice, i.e. the factual territory on which social justice interventions ought to be deployed.

In 'Equality of What?' (1980), Sen distinguishes between many approaches to equality and social justice against their answer to the question 'what should be equalized?'. He insists that capabilities are the right *equalizandum*, by contrast with resources or functionings. In Sen's words, capabilities are defined as the 'real freedom to lead the life one has reason to value' (e.g. Sen, 1999). Thus, Sen positions his conception within the 'equality of opportunities' approaches; for him, the pursuit of equality is not only a matter of financial redistribution, but also of providing equal chances or opportunities to lead a valuable life. This entails a more encompassing view of equality, which also includes equal respect and equal dignity for all human beings (Anderson, 1999).

Sen repeatedly emphasizes the difference between his conception and what he calls resourcist approaches focusing on the provision of equal resources to all members of society (Sen, 1990). Be it in Rawls' (primary goods – Rawls, 1971) or Dworkin's (extended resources – Dworkin, 1981) formula, equality of resources does not allow reaching equality of capabilities. This is mainly due to the fact that the mere possession of resources does not automatically translate into the full exercise of capabilities or real freedoms to lead a valuable life. There is a conversion process between the two, where parameters other than resources intervene. Sen often takes the following example to illustrate this point (e.g. Sen, 1983): the possession of a bike (a resource) does not provide any capability to the owner if she is not able to make use of it or if the context does not allow her to do so (due e.g. to the absence of proper roads or to discriminating social norms). In the same way, a disabled human being provided with the same amount of resources as an able-bodied person, will not enjoy the same capabilities. Therefore, the equalization of capabilities requires adjusting the scope of public intervention to the specific circumstances of people: the more they are deprived or negatively affected in their living conditions and capacity to act autonomously (because of poverty, disability, etc.), the more they need to be provided with extensive resources and interventions. This unequal treatment is perfectly congruent with the overall equality purpose of the capability approach. In Sen's view, focusing on resources only is not sufficient and is exposed to the Marxian critic of formalism: in other words, redistributing resources without taking into account the individual and contextual conversion factors may boil down to providing formal and not real rights to the holders of the redistributed resources. Sen claims that the equalization of resources is a necessary but not sufficient condition for implementing social justice and reducing inequalities. Further steps are needed to take into account the plurality of individual situations and social contexts and aim at real, rather than formal, equality of opportunities.

In Sen's words, equality of outcomes is defined in terms of functionings, i.e. what a person is or does, by contrast with what she can be or do. Sen's claim is that social justice should not focus on functionings, or actual ways of being and doing, but on capabilities, i.e. real opportunities to be and do what one has reason to value. By this token, Sen insists on a non-paternalistic view of social justice: specific functionings should not be imposed on people, who should rather be provided with real possibilities to access such functionings if they choose to do so. This implies, for instance, that human rights should not be conceived in such a way to promote specific modes of being or doing over others (which would expose them to the culturalist objection), but they should be designed so as to open for all human beings, opportunities of choosing life trajectories they have reason to value.

To sum up, a twofold distinction is at the core of the capability approach: on the one hand between resources and capabilities, claiming that a focus on resources risks resulting in formal equality, thus tolerating the existence of real and possibly significant inequalities; on the other hand, between capabilities and functionings, claiming that the latter, i.e. the actual way of behaving and making life choices, lies within the freedom and responsibility of individuals.

In this perspective, public action is called to encompass all dimensions that may contribute to the translation or conversion of formal rights or resources into concrete and real capabilities. This includes individual factors as well as the way they are valued or recognized in a specific society: hence not only individual competencies or qualifications or merit, but also the way these features and other ascribed characteristics such as gender, nationality, age, etc. are taken into account. Development of competences or empowerment is thus needed together with anti-discrimination policies ensuring that people are not penalized due to their sex, nationality, religion, age, social class, etc. Besides, social conversion factors such as the existence of valuable opportunities are also to be considered. As a matter of fact, competent and not-discriminated people may still be deprived of capabilities if valuable opportunities are not available. Indeed, the capability approach entails a relational view of equality and social justice, based on a conception of the human being as vulnerable and interdependent: the point is not to create a fully autonomous human being (in line with the *homo oeconomicus*), which would marginalize all those who are unable to meet these expectations; rather, the objective is to recognize the vulnerability of all human beings, their interdependence on each other and on collective resources in order to flourish. In this perspective, human frailty and vulnerability are not incompatible with the objective of developing the capabilities of all human beings, quite the contrary.

These remarks allow specifying the conception of equality of opportunities defended by Sen. His focus is on making opportunities real and effective, thus tackling as much as possible the Marxian criticism vis-à-vis the formalism of rights. Sen is well aware of the risk that equality of chances or opportunities remains purely formal and coexists with extensive real inequalities; he therefore insists on identifying what can make these opportunities effectively accessible to all human beings. This goes beyond formalistic views of equality of opportunities, but refrains from equality of outcomes and its possible paternalistic drifts.

Sen also distinguishes between transcendental and comparative views on social justice (Sen, 2006), the former defining an ideal yardstick from behind a veil of ignorance (Rawls) while the latter insists on departing from the actual situation of deprived people and on identifying what should be done to improve this situation and reduce the inequalities affecting them. Sen's comparative view suggests a dynamic stance on social justice, both identifying basic capabilities that can be considered as the minimal threshold to be granted to all human beings and insisting on the necessity to permanently strive for a further reduction of inequalities. Thus, the capability approach cannot be interpreted as a strictly sufficientist view on equality and social justice, insofar as the threshold of basic capabilities is not defined in a static and definitive way, but rather as a provisional target that, once reached, is to be substituted by other, more ambitious, objectives.

Individual preferences and social justice

The equalization of capabilities requires taking seriously people's reasons to value. This implies that the struggle against inequalities ought to be based on the aspirations of the people concerned and not on an abstract vision of equality or social justice imposed from above. Indeed, the life people have reason to value cannot be defined by third parties, independently of their voice. The requirements of social justice do not derive from 'a view from nowhere' (Nagel, 1989), but are to be situated and contextualised. In other words, the content of public action aiming at social justice and the reduction of inequalities ought to take account of individual preferences and aspirations, as well as social opportunities and circumstances.

However, this does not mean that all individual preferences should be supported via public action: some of them can be interpreted as expensive tastes (e.g. I would like to spend my holiday in Hawaii, to buy a luxury car, to be an opera singer, etc.) and should not open the door to rights or entitlements; others are adaptive (Elster, 1985) insofar as their content is adjusted to the concrete circumstances of people or results from a specific socialization process (e.g. battered women in India who resign themselves to their situation as it seems unavoidable in their context – Nussbaum, 2000). In both such cases, expensive tastes and adaptive preferences, Sen claims that individual preferences should not be supported as they cannot be envisaged as something people have reason to value. This is why Sen strongly opposes utilitarian conceptions of social justice focused on the subjective utility or pleasure that people draw from their lives. The objective of equalizing utility would indeed imply that individual preferences and their satisfaction are always to be considered as the adequate yardstick in matters of social justice. This is not the case in the capability approach, as it does not insist on what people value, but more specifically on what they *have reason to* value. The issue of rationality is then key in this perspective: not all preferences, but those which are reasonable, are to be supported.

What, then, does this notion of 'reason to value' mean within the capability approach? Sen's view on rationality clearly departs from the dominant conception of economic rationality focused on a calculus of costs and benefits. In this latter perspective, when someone wants to cut her finger but does not have a sharp knife to do it, the solution is to provide her with such a tool without questioning the reasonableness of her objective. The partisans of such a conception are defined by Sen as 'rational fools' (Sen, 1977). The value of objectives is not questioned; the only issue is to design efficient tools or instruments to reach them. Rationality, then, boils down to a matter of efficiency. In Sen's view, by contrast, it also includes intricate issues of appropriateness and reasonableness: in other words, are the ends that I pursue reasonable? If not, I should revise them to make them more appropriate. Rationality, then, is a complex question and its content and criteria cannot be decided beforehand (Sen, 2002), i.e. there are no universal criteria or principles that define, at all times and for all people, what should qualify as rational or, more adequately, as reasonable. A transcendental agreement on social justice and on rationality is impossible.

In this regard, Sen's position is close to conceptions like Walzer's spheres of justice (Walzer, 1983) or the French economy of conventions' focus on the diversity of principles of justification (Boltanski and Thévenot, 2006). Indeed, Sen admits that there is an inescapable plurality of legitimate reasons to value something and considers the recognition of this plurality as the necessary foundation for the non-paternalistic development of capabilities. Therefore, Sen advises taking seriously into account all reasons to value that are expressed by people. This implies that no person or no civilization (Western or other) can be *a priori* considered as the sole depository of the right conception of rationality or social justice. There is no one-size-fits-all solution to injustice and inequality; a plurality of interventions should be allowed to be deployed at local level, in order to take account of the diversity of individual aspirations and social circumstances. In other words, laws or any kind of central prescriptions (declarations of human rights, public policies, etc.) should allow for some contextualization, in order for local and individual specificities to be tackled adequately.

In Sen's view, such recognition of plurality does not lead to a relativistic conception of social justice, insofar as it is combined with a focus on public reasoning and democratic deliberation. Not all preferences, but only those that pass the test of public debate are considered as rational or reasonable and, therefore, can legitimately claim to be supported by public action. Democracy and public reasoning are envisaged as the adequate way to tackle the pluralism of values and preferences. In other words, the criterion that allows assessing the reasonableness of a preference is its ability to sustain a public debate.

However, not all public debates can be considered as guided by a concern for rational deliberation. That's why Sen insists on a requiring conception identified as 'unobstructed public reasoning' (Sen, 2009), where all viewpoints of all stakeholders can be expressed and confronted. The purpose of such a public debate, then, is to gather all relevant forms of 'positional objectivity' as Sen calls them (Sen, 1993). This complex notion implies that, when describing or assessing a social phenomenon, a person does it from a specific position in society, deriving from her past experience, her education, her social status, etc. For instance, youth violence will not be described or assessed in the same way by teachers, parents, bureaucrats or youth themselves. However, all these persons have something relevant to say about youth violence. This is what Sen calls 'positional objectivity', emphasizing that all these observations 'have some claim to being objective within their own terms' (Sen, 2002: 471). Social justice requires that all relevant positional objectivities be taken into account when defining the content of public action; otherwise, the risk exists that one specific view or positional objectivity is unduly imposed onto the other stakeholders. In order to avoid such biases, Sen advocates the extension of the public debate beyond local communities and national frontiers in order to include what he calls 'non-parochial views' (Sen, 2009) of impartial spectators not influenced by local interests. By this token, Sen does not seek to give priority to a 'view from nowhere', but to integrate in the public debate views from somewhere else, outside the local context, in order to allow public discussion to deconstruct local conceptions of rationality and social justice.

Seen from the capability perspective, public reasoning is a key component of the struggle against social inequalities: on the one hand, it allows questioning the reasonableness of individual preferences and identifying those deserving public support; on the other hand, it serves to challenge social norms and their discriminatory potential against the background of other positional objectivities. Thanks to this double contribution, public debate allows getting closer to a conception of social justice equalizing all people's capabilities, i.e. enhancing their real freedom to live a life they have reason to value.

Human rights and global justice in a capability perspective

In Sen's view, the viability of human rights requires that they survive such an 'unobstructed public reasoning'. Therefore, the foundation of human rights should not be an expert discourse or a majoritarian ballot, but an ongoing public discussion. Three aspects of human rights are especially emphasized in Sen's approach (Sen, 2004).

First, the capability perspective calls for a combination of encompassing interventions in terms of individual and social conversion factors and of refraining from paternalistic modes of action, in order to avoid imposing specific functionings that people might have no reason to value. This notably translates into Sen's insistence to consider people both as receivers in need of protection and as actors participating to society. In his words, people are not only 'passive receivers', they are also 'doers' (Sen, 1985). This conception entails a wide-ranging notion of human rights that includes and holds together both rights to well-being and rights to agency. Indeed, well-being and agency are complementary dimensions within the capability approach: people need to be both empowered to reach opportunities they have reason to value and left spaces for the deployment of their freedom of choice, i.e. for them to be the actors of their lives, and not only the passive receivers of collective benefits and services. This supports the indivisibility of human rights: civil rights, political rights and socio-economic rights are all prerequisites to an implementation of human rights promoting equal respect and equal dignity. Human beings enjoying civil and political rights, but deprived from socio-economic rights do not reach the full development of their capabilities; all the same, individuals receiving generous benefits and having access to high-quality services, but not allowed to exercise their civil and political freedoms, are not able to enhance their capabilities up to their full potential. A capability perspective to human rights therefore requires that they encompass all three generations of human rights: civil and political rights that consider the individuals as actors in the democratic process, which extends far beyond the political arenas to include all spaces where collective decision-making takes place (e.g. the firm, the economic sector, the school, the family, associations, etc.); and socioeconomic and cultural rights that guarantee that all members of society enjoy the same access to valuable opportunities through redistribution of resources and provision of universal services.

Second, Sen always refrains from defining a precise list of human rights, even though he sometimes gives some hints as to what should be considered as important for the development of capabilities. In *Development as Freedom* (1999) he identifies five categories of instrumental freedoms, i.e. freedoms that are necessary to enhance the capabilities of all people: a) political freedoms, e.g. democratic processes, freedom to criticize and scrutinize authorities, free media, etc.; b) economic facilities, i.e. freedom to access and use resources freely; c) social opportunities, i.e. access to health care and education for all; d) transparency guarantees, which he considers as the foundation of trust, e.g. by ensuring that the information given is clear and fully disclosed; e) protective security, i.e. social protection or benefits in favor of the most vulnerable. Although these give clear indications about what should be considered as a human right, Sen never goes on developing a full list of central capabilities that would hold independently of the context.[1] He insists that the only criterion to decide about what should be considered as a human right is public reasoning. In his words, the viability of human rights depends on their ability to 'survive unobstructed public reasoning' at global level. He indeed considers global dialogue as the way to question and deconstruct local biases and prejudices: if submitted to the scrutiny of outside actors, such parochial conceptions of human rights will not resist this test. Hence public reasoning, in the encompassing notion given above, is the key to identifying human rights. This is a never-ending task, as conceptions that seem to be consensual at one point of time, may well appear as prejudiced or biased if new actors are integrated in the public debate. Thus, what is pursued in the capability perspective is not a definitive list of human rights, but a provisional agreement on some human rights that can be amended or completed according to future public discussions. Such provisional solutions are not interpreted as problematic, as they can be revised and improved in the future.

Incompleteness is also necessary in order to take account of the diversity of social situations and arrangements throughout the world. If human rights are too precisely defined, they run the risk of imposing a paternalistic conception of what is a valuable life to people who hold another view about such issues. In Sen's view, the way out of such a paternalistic drift is not relativism, or the unconditional recognition of human and cultural diversity, rather it is to submit all such conceptions to the test of public reasoning. The result will certainly be more vague and indefinite (e.g. a declaration of ethical principles), but it will be more adjustable to the plurality of existing circumstances. Hence, incompleteness and vagueness are the conditions for the implementation of a variety of acceptable solutions at local level; while democracy and public reasoning allow rejecting those local conceptions that can be deemed as unreasonable.

Third, human rights are ethical claims. As such they are not perfect obligations or coercive rules; rather they are imperfect obligations insofar as they do not impose strict and clear legal duties, but a moral duty to do something in order to implement them. The performance of such a duty can be achieved via legislative provisions, but this task goes far beyond legislative arenas to encompass a plurality of economic, social, civil society, etc. actors. In this perspective, public agitation, media mobilization, benevolent action, etc. are all means to reach the implementation of human rights and the enhancement of human capabilities. In Sen's perspective, these tasks do not lie in the sole responsibility of the State; therefore, the present impossibility to set up a global democratic government does by no means imply that no steps can be taken toward a better recognition of the dignity of all human beings.

Conclusion

The capability approach suggests a specific way to tackle the issue of social justice and equality in contemporary societies. It paves the way toward equality of real and valuable opportunities, promoting equal respect and equal dignity for all human beings. This chapter has identified the prerequisites for the implementation of such a conception, in the form of individual and socio-structural conversion factors and recognition of the individual freedom of choice. It has also shown what conception of human rights as encompassing, though incomplete, and imperfect obligations this entails. As such, the capability approach is one of the most promising avenues in terms of normative theory, empirical research and policy-making, for tackling the issue of contemporary inequalities.

Note

1   By contrast, Nussbaum (2000) proposes such a list, but at the same time submits it to permanent revision. She thus identifies clear yardsticks for public action in the field of human rights.

References

Anderson, E. (1999) 'What is the Point of Equality?', *Ethics*, 109(2), 287–337.
Boltanski, L. and Thévenot, L. (2006) *On Justification, Economies of Worth*, Princeton and Oxford: Princeton University Press.
Dworkin, R. (1981) 'What is Equality? Part 2: Equality of Resources', *Philosophy & Public Affairs*, 10(4), 283–345.
Elster, J. (1985) *Sour Grapes, Studies in the Subversion of Rationality*, Cambridge: Cambridge University Press.
Nagel, T. (1989) *The View from Nowhere*, Oxford: Oxford University Press.
Nussbaum, M. (2000) *Women and Human Development, The Capabilities Approach*, Cambridge: Cambridge University Press.
Rawls, J. (1971) *A Theory of Justice*, Cambridge, MA: Harvard University Press.
Sen, A. (1977) 'Rational Fools: A Critique of the Behavioral Foundations of Economic Theory', *Philosophy & Public Affairs*, 6(4), 317–44.
Sen, A. (1980) 'Equality of What?', in *The Tanner Lecture on Human Values, I*, Cambridge: Cambridge University Press, pp. 197–220.
Sen, A. (1983) 'Development: Which Way Now', *The Economic Journal*, 93(372), 745–62.
Sen, A. (1985) 'Well-Being, Agency and Freedom. The Dewey Lectures 1984', *The Journal of Philosophy*, 82(4), 169–221.
Sen, A. (1990) 'Justice: Means versus Freedoms', *Philosophy & Public Affairs*, 19(2), 111–21.
Sen, A. (1993) 'Positional Objectivity', *Philosophy & Public Affairs*, 22(2), 126–45.
Sen, A. (1999) *Development as Freedom*, New York: Alfred Knopf.
Sen, A. (2002) *Rationality and Freedom*, London and Cambridge: Harvard University Press.
Sen, A. (2004) 'Elements of a Human Rights Theory', *Philosophy & Public Affairs*, 32(4), 315–56.
Sen, A. (2006) 'What Do We Want from a Theory of Justice', *Journal of Philosophy*, 103(5): 215–38.
Sen, A. (2009) *The Idea of Justice*. London and Cambridge: Harvard University Press.
Walzer, M. (1983) *Spheres of Justice, A Defence of Pluralism and Equality*, New York: Basic Books.

13

Two Dissident Ways of Reading on Inequality

Ana Esther Ceceña*

> In 1492, natives discovered that they were Indians, they discovered that they lived in America; they discovered that they were naked; they discovered that sin existed; they discovered that they owed obedience to another world's king and queen, and to a god from another sky, and that this god had invented guilt, and clothes, and that he had ordered that whoever worshipped the sun and the moon and the earth and the rain that wets it, should be burned alive.
>
> Eduardo Galeano

Equality is one of the basic components of the normativity created by capitalism. A paradoxical reply to the struggles against the patrimonialism of feudal lords, churches and empires, equality is one of the basic supports of modernity. Equalization of men before the law, which leaves behind a wide range of human beings, maybe starting with the feminine, turned out to be one of the premises that permitted the establishment of *universal* parameters. From the moment in which equality among men is proclaimed, an absolutely excludent process of decantation begins, restoring the proliferation of othernesses; it is the time of the epistemological generation of Orientalism, in a generic sense. Easterns, Indians, Africans, wilds and savages, and whatever emerged in the historical way of the process of western capitalist expansion were registered as the *others* in Calibán, *others* from the western whites, *others* from modernity; with a special treatment in the case of women.

It is never enough to remember Marx's arguments about the existing contradiction between the ideological or legal equality as a means to cover up and even deepen structural inequality. That all men are equal means that they are recognized as equivalent private owners who will be able to relate among themselves through their exchange of merchandises of a similar value, though of a completely different nature one exchanges to accumulate and the other, to survive; one exchanges material life conditions, while the other delivers a part of his own life. All of Marx's work is a critique of social relationships established on such bases of 'equality', and the type of society therefrom derived, but it is not my intention to expand on this question. The importance of rediscussing it is that equality is not only a basic normative component, to a certain point perverse, but that it is still a longing for part of society.

Monsanto as a paradigm of capitalist equality (first dissident reading)

Monsanto is one of the biggest 500 most powerful enterprises of the planet. In the well-known annual list of *Fortune*, Monsanto occupies the 197th place in 2015, and it has been on that list ever since its beginning in 1955 (*Fortune*, 1955; 2015). Created in the United States, Monsanto is now displayed around the globe. It is not the largest food producing enterprise, but it is the largest seed producer. It currently produces seeds of the eight principal agricultural grains: alfalfa, canola, corn, cotton, sorghum, soybeans, sugar beets and wheat, besides 2000 vegetable seeds sold in 160 different countries (Monsanto, 2016).

Three companies control more than half of the seeds market in the world. This means that the reproduction of the world population, including that of animals raised as cattle, has an extremely high vulnerability. Monsanto (26%), DuPont (18%) and Syngenta (9%), the first two resident in the United States, have the key to put the world in crisis.[1]

According to the ETC researcher Phillips McDougall's (2013) data base, Monsanto owns 26% of the world's seed market, and leads the list of 10 which control 75% of the world seed market. We may well assume, according to its recent evolution, that its leadership position must have been strengthened in the past few years.

Monsanto marks territorialities in an extended zone of the world. Its infrastructure is located in 66 countries – besides those in US territory – and it has 32,000 employees, 21,183 of whom are outside the United States. Nonetheless, its strategic character does not come from its size in terms of production and market, though both are undoubtedly significant. Its major relevance lies in its capacity to define the conditions for reproduction – or not – of life.

The area cultivated with transgenics was raised from 2 million hectares in 1996 to 170 million in 2012 (Marshall, 2013). This represents a shift, both in material conditions of reproduction according to the type or quality of a product, and also in the way of using territories and relating to nature.

And it is precisely in this space of definition where one can identify the paradigmatic nature of Monsanto. Capitalism is a combination of greed and power: its profits guarantee a power position and this allows it to increase its profits. The difference between a common capitalist and a top capitalist is basically the way in which he is inscribed in competence and manages to handle it. This means, in the way in which he is successful in transforming a confrontation among equals (seed producers, for example) into an asymmetrical confrontation, in which one of the competitors is way more qualified than the rest. But even more than that, the advantage must imply submission, or leadership. And by controlling the essential part of a process, he establishes the conditions to create *general equivalents*, relatively unavoidable directions and normativities (Ceceña, 1998).

Monsanto transforms creole seeds into other types that substitute them, and imposes modes of use for them:

1. Regularized seeds, which allow a standardized production: corn ears, in the case of maize, will almost be of the same size and thickness, with aligned and regular seeds. In this way, they can be administered easily and more quickly (cut or kept mechanically, for example), and the returns will always be close to the average.
2. Patented seeds, whose use necessarily generates a rent.
3. Objectified seeds, suggestively called *Terminator*, without a capacity of reproduction, due to genetic transformations operated by Monsanto. Seeds no longer contain long life (transgenerational) and they cannot be kept from one crop to the next one. They are objects or merchandises, not seeds of life.
4. Dependent seeds, from a technological package that forces the use of agrochemicals to ensure a good performance. Natural interaction among species is cancelled, and so is the organic fertilization of peasant economy.

This supplanting of natural creole seeds by *Terminator* seeds – or genetically modified seeds – has completely modified the logics of agricultural production and the treatment of soil. Monsanto seeds are also invasive and tend to eliminate all the rest. By only watering their seeds using their patent, Monsanto[2] guarantees that, in a reasonable term, it will have control of all basic grains crops.

The question is in what sense is this Monsanto's behaviour, or this competitive strategy, a paradigmatical example of capitalism or, even more, of modernity, and how does it relate with the principle of equality? In regard to modernity, it is indispensable to define which are the elements or epistemological and organizational principles that characterize it. This is not an easy question to solve, given the different interpretative currents that exist on the matter. For an argumented approach I quote some of my previous texts. I will be here just referring to some questions that I consider essential.

1.   Modernity is built upon the basis of the superiority of men[3] over nature. It is mostly so because of the advance of technics (artistic, linguistic, mechanical or of any other kind), after which man perceived himself as the subject of history, over and separated from the rest of the alive species, thus establishing a relational dynamic objectifier of the non-human and even of what can be considered, in this hierarchical-lineal vision, semi-human.[4] A fundamental axis of modernity, built as contrary to the magical or mysterious forces of nature,[5] was the one of *subjectness*,[6] exclusive of humans – or of a certain kind of humans – when facing the correlative objectivation of all other living entities, assimilated to the inorganic or inanimated, according to geographical, cultural, phenotypical, economic and political criteria. With this desubstanciation, relationships and social hierarchies were lineally established as subject–object relations.

2.   The criteria of technical ordering the objectual took to a process of simplification and disciplining, in order to turn reality into comparable, measurable and easily administered dimensions. The chaotic forests were substituted by ordered woods, as James Scott's research (1998) proves. Not only were superfluous species (from the standpoint of profit) eliminated – or attempted to, at least – but also those which were kept had to be ordered. Among the *accepted* species, the extremes were also eliminated: a tree too high or too low, searching to keep the population in question centred around its mean. Equality of measures, the capacity to reduce everything to comparable terms, was – and permanently is – an unavoidable condition to concur to the ordaining space of social relations which is the market.

A voiding of concrete, distinct, incomparable substances is operated, in order to place everything in conditions of comparison and exchangeability. Universal, abstract and epistemologically commited to the modern vision, referents are built and they prevent the recognition of diversity, while tending to displace it to the level of abnormality or insufficiency. Thus, an impulse towards homogenization is generated, and it tends to confuse itself and be processed as an equivalent to equality. Specificities, differences or variations are considered accidents, abnormalities or roughnesses that have to be physically or symbolically remodeled, in order to guarantee a good performance of market or of the political arena where everyone comes to be a citizen. The way of ordering the infinite diversity is achieved through abstraction.

This homogenization, which does not consider real disparities and differences, is studied by Marx with respect to value. The abstraction of concrete conditions is what allows to establish the general comparability, the general equivalence, which makes the kingdom of merchandise, possible.

3.   The nature-object was considered not only unduly magical, but also imperfect, and the technical capacities developed by *man* were oriented towards its correction. Human beings were conceived as a model of perfection. That explains the cult exhibited in Renaissance arts, and this superior quality was sustained in man's ability to create the means or tools capable of controling, correcting and directing both the processes of life in the face of the forces of nature, as well as other phenomena concerning the material world. Either the elements considered inadequate were eliminated, or they had to be corrected. And what best than correcting once and for all the original matrix: the intervention in genetical definition to avoid the appearance of elements with an unadmissable degree of imperfection. The same happens in the case of molecular intervention. A kind of preventive war, applied to the reproduction of life. Not letting an imperfect element – or a noxious one to the standardization required by market – to be born. Instead or besides applying energies in the subsequent selection of adequate or inadequate elements, the idea of unique *subjectness* was taken to the manipulation of the objectual, to the point of wanting to correct the ways in which nature has chosen to give way to life. Imperfection justifies elimination.

Taking only these three founding traits of modernity, which gave way to capitalism, we can undoubtedly state that Monsanto is a faithful expression of its epistemological core, of its *way of being and doing*. As a buoyant company, in complete process of expansion, we may examine Monsanto in order to better understand our present capitalism.

We can say, without exaggeration, that Monsanto has proposed itself to direct nature: design it, correct it and even generate it. Maybe this was meant to establish, in a planetary dimension, what Scott observed in the European woods. All ordered by a qualifying entity, in its undisputed carrier of the idea of perfection: 'At Monsanto, we believe agriculture should be improved [...] because human innovation is at the center of human progress' (Monsanto, 2016).

And being true to that premise, Monsanto launches the total ordering of seeds and crops, convinced that ' ... the world [...] needs to find ways to make the process of growing food more efficient and aligned with our environmental needs ... ' (Monsanto, 2016). But 'our' environmental needs are not similar to those of nature. They are ruled by enslaving criteria, like that of producing more grains today, in the idea that grain equals food, even though that may imply levelling the planet.

In all senses, there is a tendency towards unilineality:

> The world population has to be fed as if it did not have the capacity of feeding itself. Human beings are denied its subjective capacity. It is mass.

> Grains are the best food and then everything else must be eliminated, because it does not possess the same levels of nutritional efficiency, thus impoverishing nutrition itself. There is a hierarchization of species according to Monsanto's evaluation of its efficacy and profit.

> To extend grain crops to their limit, contrary to any other plant growing in them. To clean the earth of everything that is not defined as productive from this perspective, which in this case is considered evil herb.

> Biological complexity is *individualized*, just as happens in human communities, and also stereotyped, and thus, enormous and growing cultivation camps[7] are implanted, with all plants of the same species nearly the same size and almost with the same aesthetic and nutritional characteristics.

> Traditional and communitarian knowledges are ousted by technical instructions – not even technical reasoning – and these, once again, impact the desubjectivization of direct producers, converting them, as Marx said, in a machine appendix.

> Impoverishment of biodiversity, elimination of the variety within each species, de-*subjectness* of producers and consumers, elimination or reduction of vital processes and of the versatility of nature. The zombies' army thus created can redress the image of immense cultivation camps aligned and in equivalent forms and sizes, with only one species and variant, to produce *objects* so similar that they will have a great degree of exchangeability. It can also look like the image of hungry, incapable or undefended human beings who cannot do anything but raise their arms to ask for food and accept, of course, anything that is given to them. It is not strange that Hollywood today insists in that image.

> Producing individuals, in any of these camps, depersonifies, desubjectivizes, devivifies ... and concentrates. Just the system that reproduces and deepens power relationships, but, also, generates a defenselessness propicious to manipulation, be it genetic, or social.

By the introduction of technological packages and seeds, Monsanto promotes credit packages that often come through the State, and that have been a powerful element for submission of peasants, who are thus obliged to depend on buying seeds or, so to speak, become completely incorporated in the market and subject to financial fluctuations that in India alone have already caused 300,000 suicides.

If creole seeds keep their diversity and furnish a large spectre of variations, Monsanto seeds are relatively equal, same and exchangeable, produce relatively equal plans, same and exchangeable, and result in eating objects devivified, relatively equal, same, and exchangeable. That equality does not serve for life.

Cherrapunji as a paradigm of diversity and disorder (second dissident reading)

In a hidden corner of India, called Cherrapunji – which we will consider as a paradigm of non-predatory civilization – the main protagonist is water. It rains so much that these rivers of Cherrapunji are always vigorous and abundant, and the population, instead of trying to control, dry, deviate them or anything of the sort, has learned to live with them and has organized its life, its knowledges and its activities in a permanent relationship with water.

At a time of generalized draughts, it is a privilege to have water in abundance, as the inhabitants of Cherrapunji have, but it can't stop being a problem when its presence is so overwhelming. It has required time, patience and wisdom to establish a convivial relationship in which both rivers and trees are as members of the community, as are the inhabitants of the place.[8]

The world visions that have been built in India are multiple and varied, and it would not be adequate to bring them in to this text. However, in order to understand Cherrapunji, from my own vision, I believe it worthwhile to rescue some of its elements of substantiation:

1. One of the most epistemologically transcendent elements is referred to as the idea of incompleteness, which holds that no one or no one thing can be explained by its own self, but in connection to its surroundings. A tree is the rain that wets it, the soil that feeds it, the sun, the air, the animals that inhabit or visit it, and of all the other elements or processes that fill it with substance.

The same happens to persons, who exist in interrelation with other persons, but also with plants, animals, the mountains, the weather, rivers or any other of their surrounding elements. In contrast with the Monsanto epistemology, in which it is the seed that makes the plant (and Monsanto, who plants the seed), the Cherrapunji epistemology supposes a relational and interdependent existence. The idea of incompleteness also has a sense of process, in which everything happens until the end of the time. Life processes or social processes do not end, they are constant. The movement of life is infinite. Life itself is understood as that process without limits that is not stopped with the singular existence, but refers to existence in a generic sense. Incompleteness is an essential principle that reappears in the conception of time, complementariness, permanency–impermanence, *subjectness* and proportion, guaranteeing a life organization intrinsically non-predatory.

2. Time conception as circular, present also in the pre-Columbian civilizations of the Americas, allows us to think of an individual person as part of the community. The permanency of the community, the integrated and moving totality is what gives sense to the contribution of the individual person, which is impermanent. Whoever lives in the community takes care of the good conditions of permanency of the totality (soil, *pacha mama* or whatever it is conceived as), which will be revisited with the return of time. Everything passes again through the same place, which is the place of everyone, where it must be preserved and enriched. In the lineal time of capitalism there is never a return, the construction is always ahead, and must abandon the past; it is a perpetual present. Here, the past lives with the present. And that conviviality between past and present determines that the intergenerational relationships have a great importance, as they constitute the space of transmission of the accumulated knowledges, and of the creation of the new knowledges. It is that conviviality that sustains the continuity of the community. And this supposes a constant presence of long circular time.

3. Complementariness is a construction. It is not *natural*, it requires an interaction in which terms of exchange are adjusted. Complementariness is deliberate and can also be broken, it can be out of joint. It appeals to a political action. The negotiation it supposes comes from an *agreement* among the concurrents, which in this case are humans, and with what is called nature in the West. It is a kind of negotiation that is set upon the wisdom emanating from a large and patient relationship of observation and experimentation in order to understand the ways of mutual coupling.

4. Placing oneself in the long time, in circularity, complementarity, intersubjectivity and intergenerationality implies a special care about proportions. There cannot be coupling or *agreement* based in disproportion. Disproportion is epistemologically absent, contrary to what happens in the case of Monsanto paradigm, in which disproportion is part of the success.

One of the main public works in Cherrapunji is the building of bridges, in order to coexist with the rivers. Many bridges are required because of the exuberance of rivers that, already being abundant, grow in more intense rain seasons. And that is where the experience of complementariness starts, because the bridges are made by weaving the roots of trees that grow to one and the other side of the river. Thanks to these tree roots, the community can move from one edge to another. And as there is so much water, trees and roots keep strengthening themselves. But being right on the edge of the river could cause the trees to be dragged by the water, if it were not for having their long roots interweaved. But time goes on and the live structures grow stronger because they are also constantly reinforced by the community, which has to guarantee that their bridges stand up.

Interweaving those roots requires long periods of time during which they grow until they reach the necessary length to get to the other edge. These are not the times of one generation, but the sequence of several generations. It is necessary that grandparents and grandchildren work together to extend human times and couple them with that of the trees. Intergenerational relationships thus established are not egalitarian, but neither are they hierarchical: they are communitarian. No one can do without the other and the agility of grandchildren is combined with the experience of grandparents.

Cherrapunji is a difficult place where it would be hard to say that there is equality, but there is not inequality. There is no disproportion, though there is a difference. There is diversity and complementariness. There is not an established order, but a complexity in movement being organized according to the demands of its relationship with nature. Community's wisdom, its capacity of coupling and its permanence are just the opposite to the Monsanto way of solving problems. Equalization, order, homogeneity, individualization, disproportion, de-subjectivization is what makes the Monsanto way exactly the contrary to difference, diversity, complexity, complementation, proportionality, subjectness, intersubjectivity and coupling in the Cherrapunji way.

In the case of Monsanto, the process has a beginning and also a precise order and end. It starts with the Terminator seed and ends with the crop sale. There is no continuity. There is no long time. Equality here is indispensable to achieve the highest levels of efficiency.

For Cherrapunji, the process has a life duration and, as such, it is complex, uncertain and disordered or driven towards the order of chaos. Equality here is unthinkable, unnecessary and even undesirable.

From paradigms to challenges

Ecological disaster, systemic crisis, climate change, desertification, unprecedented social exclusion, forced migration, focused wars, diffuse wars, accelerated extinction of species, generalized violence, impunity, permanent exception states, necropolitics, indiscriminate pillage, accelerated extinction of species, are only different names of the same tragedy. They are facets of a general collapse that lead to the total elimination of life if this does not have the capacity and strength enough to face it.

The crisis configured within the framework of all these dimensions and problematics comes from the conception of reality itself, as generated by capitalist modernity. It is the crisis of the world vision carrying progress, equality and market.

The life organizing system which grew during the last 500 years has come to the limit of its sustainable conditions of possibility. The snake has bitten its tail and its destructive capacity is faced by the strength of life struggling to find the remains of other life systems. The regards, the conceptions and the practices that correspond to them are spaces of challenge and of uncertain and varied construction, but all of them alive. To imagine, from the diverse experiences of life, non-predatory, non-capitalist paradigms, and make them walk or strengthen their steps is the only chance of breaking the perverse spiral of general desertification provoked by the Monsanto capitalist modernity.

L'armée la plus puissante dans les mains de l'oppresseur est l'esprit de l'oppressé.

Steve Biko, Black Consciousness

Notes

*   Translated by Raquel Sosa Elízaga.

1   At present, Monsanto is in a merger process with the German company Bayer. Bayer offered US$ 65 billion to guarantee the merger, which indicates the strategic importance of Monsanto. To finalize the agreement, they are only awaiting the approval of the corresponding authorities who are in the process of evaluating the merging based on two criteria: the impact on national security and Germany's antimonopoly policies. We must emphasize that just a little earlier, Chem China started a similar process in order to absorb Syngenta. This must have surely been considered among the reasons to accelerate the Bayer–Monsanto process. See: www.monsanto.com/global/es/noticias-y-opiniones/pages/bayer-y-monsanto-crear%C3%A1n-un-l%C3%ADder-mundial-en-agricultura.aspx.

2   I took Monsanto as a paradigmatic case, but in practice, agricultural control of basic grains could, as in fact happens, be in the hands of an oligopoly. This does not change anything in terms of the generated territoriality, nor in the implications in the discussion of the derivatives of the principle of equality.

3   Modernity is not announced as a human conquest over the other forms of life and subjectivity, but, significantly, as a conquest of man, though understood in a generic sense that rapidly acquired an exclusive specificity. This question has been dealt with by feminist thought, and in some other way, by all the expressions of anti-colonial thought. On one hand, the relation of gender is emphasized, while on the other hand, that of interculturalism of world visions is seen as determinant. See O´Gorman, Federici, Said, Mariátegui, Bonfil.

4   Such a conception not only establishes generalized subject–object relationships, recognizing thus a subjective exclusivity to the human species, but it also extends and is multiplied by the same by adopting criteria of geographical, cultural, phenotypical, economic and political criteria.

5   Magic was synonymous to the uncontrolled, of the limits of possibility of a way of life centered in man as a figure destined to supremacy. The vitality of nature was understood as a barrier or challenge to be beaten, and this explains in a great measure, the spectacular development of techniques. See Elías, Wallerstein, Ceceña.

6   By subjectness we understand the essence or active force that constitutes and embody the subject. Taking Castoriadis' words, subjectness can be considered as the magma which makes the emergence of the subject. There is not a passive subject (this would be a *contradictio in adjectio*), although the subject can opt for a way of low intervention or relative invisibilization in certain moments. Even so, and with varied modalities, this refers to a political act or a particular exercise of politicity.

7   Monsanto has a goal to duplicate the world's cultivated area in 2000, by 2030 (Monsanto, 2016).

8   A community is a space of contradictions and conflicts, as much as one of agreements. Communities are sewn and unsewn, break and rebuild. For the purposes of this text, we gather that community is a space of synthesis or confluence, as the result or political agreement of the conflicting encounters among its constituents.

References

Bonfil, Carlos (2005) *México profundo*. México. Grijalbo.

Ceceña, Ana Esther (1998) 'Proceso de automatization y creación de los equivalentes generales tecnológicos', in Ana Esther Ceceña, (ed.), *La tecnología como instrumento de poder*. México, El Caballito.

Ceceña, Ana Esther (2015) 'Ecology and the Geography of Capitalism', in I. Wallerstein (ed.) *The World is Out of Joint*. New York. Paradigm Publishers.

Elías, Norbert (1994) *Conocimiento y poder*. Madrid. La Piqueta.

Federici, Silvia (2011) *Calibán y la bruja. Mujeres, cuerpo y acumulación originaria*. Spain. Traficantes de sueños.

Fortune (1955) *Fortune 500*. Available at: http://archive.fortune.com/magazines/fortune/fortune500_archive/snapshots/1955/902.htm.

Fortune (2015) *Fortune 500*. Available at: http://fortune.com/global500/.

McDougall, Phillips (2013) El carro delante del caballo. Semillas, suelos y campesinos. ¿Quién controla los insumos agrícolas? Informe 2013, ETC Group Cuaderno No. 111, September.

Mariátegui, Carlos (1979) *7 Ensayos de interpretación de la realidad peruana*. Caracas. Biblioteca Ayacucho.

Marshall, Andrew (2013) 'Brazil, Canada and South Africa bullish on agbiotech', *Nature Biotechnology* 31. Available at: www.nature.com/nbt/journal/v31/n4/box/nbt.2552_BX4.html.

Monsanto (2016) *Monsanto Vegetable Seeds*. Available at: www.monsanto.com.

O'Gorman, Edmundo (1958) *La invención de América*. México. FCE-SEP.

Said, Edward W. (2002) *Orientalismo*. Barcelona. Debate.

Scott, James C. (1998) *Seeing like a State*. New Haven. Yale University Press.

Wallerstein, Immanuel (1995) *¿El fin de qué modernidad?* en www.elcorreo.eu.org/El-fin-de-que-modernidad-Immanuel.

14

Framing Arab Poverty Knowledge Production: A Socio-bibliometric Study

Sarah El Jamal and Sari Hanafi*

Introduction

Based on Mannheim's theory (1936) that knowledge is socially constructed, and its production process is influenced by the social context in which it occurs, this study seeks to identify and analyze the social influences and forces behind the knowledge produced and disseminated in the form of academic journal articles on the topic of poverty in the Arab World. Certain features and elements of the final body of knowledge (the articles) will be taken as telling indicators of the process in hindsight. These will be the basis of three kinds of analyses that will be carried out: content analysis, authorship analysis, and citation analysis. In content analysis, I will scrutinize the poverty concepts used, the methodologies applied, the use of theory, including theoretical frameworks of the studies, the prevailing political and epistemological paradigms, the structure of the articles, and the types of articles (critique, essay, fieldwork). In authorship analysis, I will survey the sociological markers pertaining to the authors and institutions producing the articles. In citation analysis, I will analyze the characteristics and trends of the references. Ultimately, I seek to answer the following: What are the social factors conditioning the production of academic articles on poverty in the Arab World, and what are the observed trends thereof?

Methodology

A sample of 201 articles was retrieved by running a keyword search in Arabic, English and French, for the period between 2000 and 2014, for (Poverty OR Destitution OR 'Social Exclusion' OR 'Social Class') AND ('Middle East' OR Arab OR [The name of every Arab country]), or their equivalent in Arabic or French. English references were primarily obtained from the Web of Science (WoS) and Scopus (136 articles), but Arabic references were scarcer, primarily due to the limited availability of Arabic databases. E-Marefa, the only reliable Arabic database, yielded 29 results, while the rest of the articles were retrieved from other online or print sources. The French articles were obtained from the CAIRN platform (9 articles). Only articles that explicitly tackle 'Poverty' in any Arab country were analyzed, including comparative studies of other countries or regions.

In a spreadsheet, coded information on each article's sociological markers was collected and imported into SPSS for analysis: title in English; title in original language; language; translation; date of publication; journal issue number; journal of publication; author; number of authors; institutional affiliation; country of institutional affiliation; region of institutional affiliation; discipline; diasporic status of author; geographical scope; keywords; and a list of cited authors. The spreadsheet was also uploaded to Cortext Manager, an online Network Analysis tool that produces network maps of cited authors. The top cited authors were identified, and a co-citation network map was created using a statistical semantic measure proposed by Weeds (2003). The network is also organized according to clusters of interconnected subgroups of authors distinguished by colored circles. This is done by applying the Louvain community detection algorithm based on the work of Blondel et al. (2008).

Qualitatively, an analysis of the most cited authors was first conducted to examine their discipline, institutional affiliation, connection to other cited authors, their most commonly cited contribution to the body of poverty knowledge, and how their influence prevails in the articles. Secondly, a qualitative analysis of a sample of knowledge produced from within the Arab world was conducted to scrutinize the following elements: dominant paradigms, the choice of the research question, and what was being actively left out or dismissed.

Table 14.1 Number and percentage of production by language

Language	No	%
Arabic	55	27.4
English	136	67.7
French	10	5
Total	201	100

Sociological markers of the articles

The first major insight from our study is that the Arab poverty knowledge network of producers and influencers is highly elitist in nature in that it is run by certain institutions and academics to the exclusion of other factions of both the knowledge society and society as a whole. According to O'Connor (2001), this echoes the politics of knowledge in broad terms; well-placed researchers act as advocates for certain theoretical frameworks and methodologies. On one hand, this has resulted in the professionalization of poverty knowledge and the adherence to established standards of scientific expertise. On the other hand, 'the claim to scientific objectivity rests on technical skills, methods, information, and professional networks that historically have excluded those groups most vulnerable to poverty ... putting poverty knowledge in a position not just to reflect but to replicate the social inequalities' (O'Connor, 2001: 11). Arab poverty knowledge appears to be a political act or an exercise of power, in which academic elite overwhelmingly affiliated with the UN System institutions (World Bank, Economic Research Forum, UNDP, ESCWA, etc.) determines how poverty is defined, measured, studied, and ultimately dealt with.

Authorship

The majority of the authors in our sample are university academics (73.2%) hence the university is numerically the biggest producer of knowledge on poverty, and more frequently from inside the Arab World than outside. The second greatest producer is international organizations (10.5%), namely the World Bank. It is noteworthy that the World Bank is also the most cited author in the 201 articles.

Granted that all 201 articles are academic journal articles, working papers, or conference papers, 28.9% of them are working or conference papers published by the Economic Research Forum (ERF). The publication of the remaining articles is more or less divided equally among 102 academic journals, each publishing no more than 3.5% of the articles. This indicates that there is no single dominant producer of Arab poverty knowledge, but the ERF is nevertheless an outstanding one.

All of the articles published by the ERF are written from an econometric approach, mostly by academic economists, and mostly in the English language. This reflects the fact that, of the entire sample of articles, 67.7% are in English, 27.4% in Arabic, and the remaining 5% in French. Although almost half of the articles (47.3%) are co-authored by two or more authors, one author emerges as the most prolific: Sami Bibi has written 7% of all articles and almost half of the English articles on Tunisia (Bibi, n.d.). It is noteworthy that he is also the seventh most cited author by the authors of the 201 articles.

Geography of production of articles

Approximately 65.2% of authors were located inside the Arab World at the time of writing their respective articles. This leaves over a third of them writing from outside the region. Narrowing down to country, we find that 12.4% of authors were located in Iraq, 11.9% in Egypt, 10.9% in the USA, 9% in Tunisia, 7.5% in Jordan, 7% in Lebanon, 6% in the UK, 5% in Canada, and the rest were distributed among numerous other Arab and non-Arab countries.

Content as captured by keywords

How has the ideological evolution of the global poverty discourse influenced Arab poverty studies? A quantitative study of recurring keywords across the articles reveals that State Policy and Intervention is the most prevalent one (64.65%). This is in line with the Post Washington Consensus paradigm that promotes state intervention. After that, by decreasing frequency, we find that Social Inequality, Poverty Measurement, Rural Poverty, Employment, Poverty Causes/Determinants, Education, Urban Poverty, and Spending Behavior are tackled. The prevalence of Social Inequality as another top keyword also points to the adoption of the pro-poor growth literature in the poverty discourse after decades of neglect.

Looking at articles written from inside the Arab World and the rest of the articles separately, we find that the three most frequently referenced keywords/themes are still State Policy and Intervention, Economic System, and Social Inequality. This means that writing the article from inside the Arab World does not isolate the author from the dominant paradigm in the West. However, Poverty Causes, Education, and Employment are much more prevalent in articles written in the Arab World while Rural Poverty is more frequent in articles from outside the Arab World.

Separating the articles by language shows that Arabic articles are the most likely to tackle Education or Poverty Causes/Determinants, the English ones are the most concerned with Social Inequality, Rural Poverty, Poverty Measurement, and Spending Behavior, whereas the French ones have the highest frequencies for State Policy and Intervention, Economic System, Employment, and Urban Poverty.

Content as captured by research topic

Analyzing the choice of research questions tackled in the articles reveals another prevalent paradigm that echoes that of the West: poverty research 'takes postindustrial capitalism as a given and focuses primarily on evaluating welfare programs, as well as on measuring and modeling the demographic and behavioral characteristics of the poor' (O'Connor, 2001: 16). The two most frequently chosen research topics in our sample are, by decreasing order of frequency: poverty alleviation methods – mostly subsidies and transfers with the present economic system taken as a given – at 18.4% and profiling/measuring poverty within a certain location and/or for a certain demographic at 15%. After that comes pro-poor growth at 9%, where the effect of economic growth – again with the present economic system taken for granted – on the poverty level is studied. Pro-poor growth is based on Dollar and Kraay's (2001) paper and is in line with the 'inclusive growth' rhetoric put forth by the World Bank.

At 8%, Income Inequality is the fourth most tackled research topic. Only 5% of articles tackle gender inequality, and only one article provides social class analysis. This not only emphasizes the prevalent tendency to reduce human welfare to a mathematical equation, but also reflects the struggle between the individualist and structuralist interpretations in Western poverty knowledge and has created 'tension within liberal thought', as explained by O'Connor (2001: 9).

The individualist interpretation has become the most prevalent one as there is a 'virtual absence of class as an analytic category, at least as compared with more individualized measures of status such as family background and human capital' (idem). Another sign of the domination of individualist rhetoric is 'the reduction of race and gender to little more than demographic, rather than structurally constituted categories' (idem). The present economic and social structures are taken as inevitable conditions rather than systems that are 'socially created and maintained' (idem). The discourse on poverty and reform has unnoticed ideological boundaries that 'eclipse an alternative, more institutionalist and social democratic research tradition' for the sake of 'remaining realistic or "relevant" for political purposes' (idem). This individualist rhetoric is also echoed in the articles tackling the determinants of poverty as the main topic and making up 7% of the sample. The determinants are identified using regression analysis, and the possible factors considered are most often characteristics specific to the poor people or the space they inhabit, thereby isolating them from the grander scheme of the social and/or economic structure they are bound to. Conspicuous by its absence is a discussion of the non-poor's role or impact on the poverty level. Another remarkable observation is that the determinants of poverty are tackled less frequently than poverty reduction strategies. The discourse focuses on solving the problem more often than it tries to uncover its causes.

Network and citation analysis

The citations used in the articles are indicative of the collective knowledge production process and the dynamics of the underlying discourse among authors on a global level.

The co-citation network

Figure 14.1 depicts a map of the co-citation[1] network connecting the top 100 cited authors, who are the major influencers of the authors of our study. Rather than focusing on the authors of our study, i.e. authors of Arab poverty articles, the map is a visualization and mathematization of the broader field of global poverty scholarship reflected in the citations of the sampled articles. This is based on the assumption that scholarship can be seen as discourse among agents engaging in a network. Authors that are co-cited are inserted into a discourse with one another, forming together a certain intellectual tradition, niche or another commonality amongst them.

As Figure 14.1. shows, the nodes of the network are heterogeneous: the triangles correspond to authors cited at least five times in our sample, and the dots correspond to languages of the articles – Arabic, English, or French. The size of the node is directly proportional to the total number of times the respective author is cited. Every incident of pairs of cited authors is taken into account to construct a co-occurrence matrix from which a proximity network is tracked using a statistical semantic measure proposed by Weeds (2003: 82). The grey lines linking the nodes indicate co-citations, with widths directly proportional to the number of co-citations. The circles depict clusters, or groups of highly interconnected nodes representing authors that are cited simultaneously in the entire set of articles.

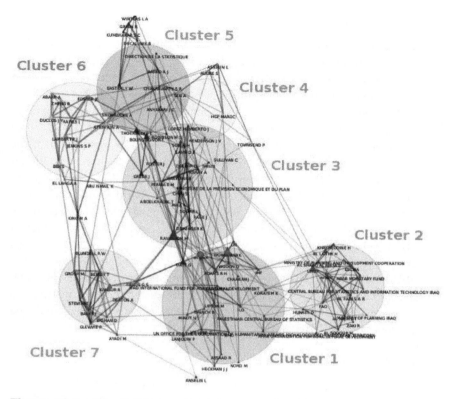

Figure 14.1 Co-citation map by language of article
Source: Author's own, created using the CorText platform

The network is also organized according to clusters of interconnected subgroups of authors represented by the circles labelled as Cluster 1 to 7. This is done by applying the Louvain community detection algorithm based on the work of Blondel et al. (2008). Each cluster is assigned a tag ('English', 'Arabic', 'French') indicating the most commonly used language in the publications citing the authors of the corresponding cluster (chi2 specificity score). The computation was performed using the CorText platform of IFRIS[2]. In order to analyze the network and understand the roles and relationships of its agents, we evaluate the position of the co-cited authors in the network map as a whole and in his or her respective cluster.

The map shows that the nodes representing the 100 top cited authors are well-connected across all three languages, yet each language belongs to a distinct cluster comprised of even tighter interconnections. The total number of clusters is seven and we describe them as the following:

The English language cluster

The English articles belong to Cluster 1, in which they are shown to frequently cite authors including, by decreasing order of citation frequency: The World Bank (WB), Richard H. McAdams, Karima Korayem, the International Labor Organization (ILO), the International Monetary Fund (IMF), Luc Anselin, and others. Although the WB is the top cited author in the network and the cluster, it is not uniformly co-cited with each of the agents of the English language cluster. As shown by the map, the darkest edges linked to it are linked to a few other authors, and lighter edges link it to the rest of the cluster members. It is most heavily co-cited with Quentin Wodon, an Adviser in the World Bank's Education Department, Richard H. McAdams, an economist who was part of the Economics Research team at the World Bank Group, the IMF, which is also highly affiliated with the WB, and the 'UN' as a generic author. This subcluster is highly redundant as all of the aforementioned are highly affiliated with the WB or the UN system institutions. This indicates that the authors who cite the WB tend to cite researchers and institutions highly affiliated with the Bank hence creating a discourse hegemonized by the narrative of the WB.

The Arabic language cluster

The Arabic articles belong to Cluster 2, in which they are shown to frequently cite authors including, by decreasing order of citation frequency: the UNDP, ESCWA, Heba El Laithy, Doukhi Hunaiti, and others. Similar to the English language cluster yet to a lesser extent, the discourse in this cluster is heavily influenced by UN agencies and economists affiliated therewith.

The French language cluster

The French language articles belong to Cluster 3, whose top co-cited authors are, by decreasing order: Martin Ravallion, Gaurav Datt, Nanak Kakwani, Shaohua Chen, Aart Kraay, and David Dollar, all of whom have worked at the WB as economists or statisticians. Hence the French-language poverty discourse is also heavily influenced by the WB narrative.

The Amartya Sen cluster

At the periphery of the network lies the smaller, singular Cluster 4 with fewer nodes and looser connections within itself and with other clusters. It is dominated by a singular yet highly influential author who holds a distinctive position in the poverty discourse. Amartya Sen is one of the few economists who are cited for their theories in addition to their econometric methods and poverty measurements. He is most frequently cited for his axiomatic framework (Sen, 1976) and theories on multidimensional poverty (Sen, 1987). He is one of the top cited authors who are not affiliated with the UN system institutions even though he has influenced the UNDP's Human Development Reports and the WB's poverty rhetoric with his capability approach to defining poverty.

The Foster-Greer-Thorbecke cluster

Cluster 5 has Francois Bourguignon, William Easterly, James Foster, Erik Thoerbecke, and Joel Greer as the main hubs. The most central node is Francois Bourguignon, Professor of Economics at the Paris School of Economics and former Chief Economist and Senior Vice President at the World Bank in Washington. He is most cited for his work on transfers and poverty targeting (Bourguignon and Fields, 1997).

The Atkison-Bibi-Duclos cluster

A sixth distinct cluster, Cluster 6 is centered around the economists Jeans-Yves Duclos, Anthony Atkinson, and Sami Bibi. Duclos is a researcher at CIRPÉE, an Inter-University Centre on Risk, Economic Policies, and Employment and a program coordinator at PEP, an international organization that links researchers globally. He is most cited for his work on measuring Horizontal Inequity (Duclos and Lambert, 1998).

The Kanbur-Deaton-Besley-Fields cluster

The last cluster in the co-citation network, Cluster 7, includes several mainstream economists, some of whom are highly affiliated with the World Bank. The core node is Ravi Kanbur, a British economist and university professor who worked at the WB for almost two decades and directed the World Development Report. He is most cited for his work with Tim Besley on food subsidies (Besley and Kanbur, 1988).

Top cited authors

Tracking down the institutional affiliations of major contributors to the discourse has shown, as depicted in Table 14.2, that the top 25 most cited authors on the topic of Arab Poverty are comprised of 19 central authors positioned at the cores of the co-citation clusters, three semi-peripheral authors positioned in between the core and the periphery of each cluster, and three peripheral authors positioned at the outer borders of the clusters. The central authors can be grouped into: authors who are directly affiliated with the UN system and its specialized agencies: The World Bank, UNDP, ESCWA, and their employees; two Arab economists affiliated

Table 14.2 Most Cited Authors

Cited Author; Network Position	No. of Citations	Most Commonly Cited for	Affiliation	Connection to Other Cited Authors
World Bank; Central	208	World Development Report data		Specialized agency of the United Nations
Martin Ravallion; Central	173	Poverty measurement steps (Ravallion, 1998)	As of 2013 he was the inaugural Edmond D. Villani Professor of Economics at Georgetown University, and previously had been director of the research department at the World Bank, Washington	Director of research department at WB from 1988 to 2013
UNDP; Central	119	The Human Development Reports		Specialized agency of the United Nations; Influenced by Sen's capability approach
Gaurav Datt; Central	66	Poverty targeting (Datt and Ravallion, 1995)	Monash University, Melbourne, Australia	Has worked in research positions at the WB and co-authored numerous publications with Martin Ravallion

Cited Author; Network Position	No. of Citations	Most Commonly Cited for	Affiliation	Connection to Other Cited Authors
Amartya Sen; Central	58	Multidimensional poverty (Sen, 1987) and the axiomatic framework (Sen, 1976)	Professor of Economics and Philosophy at Harvard University	Influenced UNDP's Human Development Reports
Heba El Laithy; Central	54	Poverty line studies (El Laithy, 1996)	Professor of Statistics, Cairo University	ERF Fellow, collaborates with Sami Bibi
Sami Bibi; Central	50	Methodology for studying pro-poorness of economic growth (Bibi, 2005)	Research Advisor, Human Resources and Skills Development Canada (HRSDC), Labour Program, Research and Data Development (RDD) Division	ERF Fellow, collaborates with Heba El Laithy, has provided training workshops on econometric software (STRATA) for poverty analysis at the World Bank Institute and UNDP Syria, is closely connected to Jean-Yves DUCLOS
Jean-Yves Duclos; Central	47	Measurement of Horizontal Inequity (Duclos and Lambert, 1998)	Researcher at CIRPÉE (Inter-University Centre on Risk, Economic Policies, and Employment) and Professor at University of Laval	Has collaborated with Sami Bibi
Nanak Kakwani; Central	47	Economic growth and inequality (Kakwani and Pernia, 2000)	Professor of Economics at University of South Wales, Australia	Consultant: World Bank, Washington DC and UNDP, Manila

(Continued)

Table 14.2 (Continued)

Cited Author; Network Position	No. of Citations	Most Commonly Cited for	Affiliation	Connection to Other Cited Authors
ESCWA; Central	47	Economic indicators from Technical Papers		Specialized agency of the United Nations; Collaborates with UNDP
Francois Bourguignon; Central	45	Transfers and poverty targeting (Bourguignon and Fields, 1997)	Professor of Economics, Paris School of Economics	Previously: Chief Economist and Senior Vice President, World Bank, Washington, Worked with Chakravarty and Atkinson
Erik Thoerbecke; Central	43	Foster-Greer-Thorbecke class of poverty measures (Foster et al., 1984)	Professor of Economics, Cornell University	FGT measure was developed by Professor Erik Thorbecke, his former student Professor Joel Greer, and another graduate student at Cornell University at the time, Professor James Foster
Ravi Kanbur; Central	43	Food Subsidies (Besley and Kanbur, 1988)	Professor of Economics, Cornell University	D. Phil. (Oxford). Thesis Advisers: Joseph Stiglitz, James Mirrlees and Amartya Sen, 1989-1997 World Bank
Anthony Atkinson (Sir); Central	42	Inequality measure (Atkinson, 1970)	Warden, Nuffield College, Oxford	Co-authored a book with Francois Bourguignon

Cited Author; Network Position	No. of Citations	Most Commonly Cited for	Affiliation	Connection to Other Cited Authors
Shaohua Chen; Central	41	Growth Incidence Curve (Ravallion and Chen, 2003)	Senior Statistician in the Development Economics Research Group of the World Bank	Senior Statistician in the Development Economics Research Group of the World Bank, Collaborated with Martin Ravallion and Gaurav Datt
Joel Greer; Central	38	Foster-Greer-Thorbecke class of poverty measures	US General Accounting Office, Washington, and previously with Cornell University	FGT measure was developed by Professor Erik Thorbecke, his former student Professor Joel Greer, and another graduate student at Cornell University at the time, Professor James Foster
Richard H. McAdams; Central	38	Measuring inequality and poverty (Adams and Page, 2003)	Professor of Law at the University of Chicago Law School	
William Easterly; Central	30	Economic growth	Professor of Economics, New York University	World Bank: 1985–2001
James Foster; Central	29	Foster-Greer-Thorbecke class of poverty measures	Professor of Economics and International Affairs at The Elliott School of International Affairs at The George Washington University	FGT measure was developed by Professor Erik Thorbecke, his former student Professor Joel Greer, and another graduate student at Cornell University at the time, Professor James Foster, co-authored a book and co-taught with Amartya Sen

(Continued)

Table 14.2 (Continued)

Cited Author; Network Position	No. of Citations	Most Commonly Cited for	Affiliation	Connection to Other Cited Authors
Doukhi Hunaiti; Peripheral	23	Rural Poverty (Hunaiti, 2005)	Professor of Rural Development and Agricultural Economics, University of Jordan	
Karima Korayem; Peripheral	21	Poverty measurement for Egypt	Professor of Economics, Faculty of Commerce (Girls), Al-Azhar University	Consultant to World Bank, UNDP, ESCWA, and ILO
Luc Anselin; Peripheral	21	Spatial Regression Analysis (Anselin, 2003)	Director of the School of Geographical Sciences and Urban Planning (ASU), Arizona State University	
Satya R. Chakravarty; Semi-peripheral	21	Poverty measurement (Chakravarty, 1983)	Professor of Economics at Indian Statistical Institute, Kolkata, India	Co-authored publications with Bourguignon, Ravi Kanbur
ILO; Semi-peripheral	21	Employment figures		Specialized agency of the United Nations
Angus Deaton; Semi-peripheral	20	The measurement of poverty in India and around the world (Deaton, 2005)	Professor of Economics and International Affairs at the Woodrow Wilson School of Public and International Affairs and the Economics Department at Princeton University	

Central Authors:: The United Nations System

with the ERF; and academics (mostly economists) who have influenced the work of the UN specialized agencies but are not directly affiliated with them. The semi-peripheral authors are the ILO, which is another UN specialized agency, and two academic economists unaffiliated with the UN and its agencies. The peripheral authors are two Arab economists unaffiliated with the ERF or the UN agencies and a niche economist who is specialized in spatial econometrics.

The most central authors who make up the cores of the co-citation clusters are the agencies and employees of the United Nations System consisting of: the World Bank, UNDP, ESCWA, and the authors who have worked for or collaborated significantly with these institutions: Martin Ravallion, Gaurav Datt, Nanak Kakwani, Francois Bourguignon, Ravi Kanbur, Shaohua Chen, and William Easterly.

The most cited author in our sample is the World Bank, a specialized agency of the United Nations System.

Central authors: Academics unaffiliated with the UN System

The top cited authors outside the UN System are mostly academic economists with long careers as university professors, who have influenced the work of the UN agencies in traceable ways, yet have never been employed by a UN agency. The top cited one in this category is Amartya Sen, Nobel Laureate and Professor of Economics at Harvard University. He contributed to formulating the United Nations' Human Development Index, which has become 'the most authoritative international source of welfare comparisons between countries' (Steele, 2001). He has also contributed the multi-dimensional definition of poverty, which examines the 'capability' to function in society and includes dimensions in addition to income, such as education, health, security, self-confidence, access to opportunities, facilities, resources, and human rights (Sen, 1987).

Central authors: Arab economists affiliated with the ERF

The only Arab authors with a central position in the co-citation network are Sami Bibi and Heba El Laithy, both academics and Research Fellows at the ERF. Heba El Laithy is an Egyptian statistics university professor, who is most cited for her poverty line studies (El Laithy, 1996). It is interesting to note that they are mainly cited by articles whose authors are affiliated to institutions within the region. This means that there is a local debate on poverty.

Semi-peripheral authors

The ILO is the only UN agency without a central position in the co-citation network. As an organization specialized in employment rights and data, its semi-peripheral position might be due to its less relevant role in the poverty discourse than, say, that of the WB's or UNDP's. It is most commonly cited for employment figures. Another semi-peripheral node is Satya Chakravarty, an Indian economist who has co-authored publications with central authors, such as Francois Bourguignon and Ravi Kanbur.

Peripheral authors

Three of the top 25 cited authors have a peripheral position in the co-citation network: Doukhi Hunaiti, Karima Korayem, and Luc Anselin. Hunaiti and Korayem are both Arab academic economists. While Korayem has worked as a consultant to the World Bank, UNDP, ESCWA, and ILO, Hunaiti is rather independent of the UN system. Korayem is most cited for figures on Egyptian poverty while Hunaiti is cited for his work on rural poverty (Hunaiti, 2005). Luc Anselin is also an academic economist specializing in spatial econometrics and is not affiliated with the UN system.

Qualitative analysis of Arab poverty knowledge production

Qualitative text analysis of the articles in our sample reveals that Arab poverty knowledge is of an overwhelming ideological nature, reflecting the evolution of the Washington Consensus in the US. Poverty knowledge is 'a project of twentieth-century liberalism ... deeply rooted in the rise of the "new liberalism" that emerged in late nineteenth-century Euro-American political culture as an alternative to the laissez-faire individualism of the industrial age' (O'Connor, 2001: 8).

The Western discourse on poverty in Third World Countries, led by the World Bank (WB) and academic economists, has gone through three distinct stages of ideological evolution and paradigm shifts. The major reference point in this historical evolution is the Washington Consensus (WC), a term that represents the near-consensus of the international financial institutions, the American government, the Federal Reserve Board, and the major think tanks in Washington to implement certain policy reforms in order to stimulate growth, decrease inflation, maintain a healthy balance of payments, and distribute income in an equitable manner in the developing world (Lora, 2009). Accordingly, the three phases are: the Pre-WC phase, the WC phase, and the post-WC phase (Saad-Filho, 2010).

There is a predominance of the rhetoric on the benefits of economic growth, economic reform/market liberalization, and subsidies and transfers as anti-poverty strategies then tested using policy simulation models. This, again, is in line with the 'trickle-down' paradigm that contends that poverty reduction is a by-product of economic growth and neoliberal policies. Again, inclusive growth is also present in the literature and represented by the term 'pro-poor growth'. As expected (because they are not in line with the dominant paradigm), the role of charity, income redistribution, the private sector, education, and health care receives little attention in the sampled articles. While microfinance, as a major anti-poverty strategy, has received remarkable attention worldwide, it was rarely referred to in our sample. Even in the least neoliberalist articles, the market and economic performance are still advocated for whatever they are worth. To quote one of the articles using this rhetoric: 'Despite the controversy about the causal link between openness and economic performance in the literature, the virtues of trade's contributions to faster growth and poverty alleviation are generally recognized' (Hassine and Kandil, 2008: 2).

In addition to the dominant neoliberal bias in the discourse, there is a less prevalent narrative that emerges in a minority of the articles. Its paradigms, frameworks, and talking points serve to point out the loopholes and omissions of the neoliberalist narrative while putting forth some alternative concepts, methodologies, and solutions pertaining to Arab poverty. The findings are based on qualitative text analysis of around 17 articles that comprise an alternative niche within the poverty discourse.

This anti-neoliberal discourse gives forth several arguments that challenge the benefits of globalization to alleviating poverty, criticize the effects of the Structural Adjustment Programs often prescribed for developing countries by the WB or IMF, and debate the validity of the 'trickle-down' argument. Besides explicitly contesting neoliberalism, some authors offer an alternative discourse by using qualitative methods to break away from the predominantly quantitative tradition in Arab poverty studies. Others refer to local faith-based concepts and solutions pertaining to poverty, revealing that, for the most part, they are in line with secular concepts and narratives yet offer untapped solutions designed to alleviate poverty and inequality. Only two articles study the historical context of Arab poverty by studying the history of colonialism, imperialism, war, and conflict.

One article does the exceptional by engaging the 'voices of the poor' in the study and comparing them with macro-level data.

Conclusion

The findings in this study indicate that the majority of academic knowledge on Arab Poverty is modelled after the typical empirical economics article, based on the norms of the UN Systems institution cluster, in its structure and methodologies. There is hegemony of the discipline of economics of this topic and not enough sociological, anthropological, historical, political, or interdisciplinary takes on the subject. The quantitative method is used enormously, and the qualitative one is almost completely neglected. The data source is predominantly secondary, and there is a lack of purpose-specific fieldwork. There is a lack of any study of social inequality or class analysis as a bigger picture in which poverty prevails. Fawaz Traboulsi (2005) criticizes poverty studies, as they replace studies on income distribution – the latter at best restricted to the global level (the rich billion and the rest) – as poverty begins to resemble a natural catastrophe or a contagious disease. Consequently, we study poverty without studying wealth. We define the 'poor' but not the 'rich.' As for the middle classes, they are either pictured as being reduced in size and effectiveness and consequently dying out or are assigned the role of repositories of the democratic mission. In both cases, very little in terms of socio-political effort is invested in studying their political behavior, assuming that they might tend toward a homogeneous and unidirectional political behavior (Traboulsi, 2005: 530). In the same line, Thomas Piketty (2014) sees the tax system as a chief reason of the social inequality and thus calls for taxing capital to redress wealth redistribution.

The vast majority of articles are concerned with poverty alleviation strategies, but significantly less so with determinants or causes of poverty. There is a prevalent neoliberal paradigm propagated by the Washington Consensus and observed in the text analysis of the articles, as most champion the free market, trade liberalization, and globalization and neglect the role of the grander economic structure, market failures, the non-poor class, income redistribution, charity, microfinance, etc. Most articles are produced in English although two thirds of them are written from inside the Arab region by non-diasporic writers. There is a prevalent Western hegemony of thought, structure, and language. In a nutshell, 'Globalization is now seen to be the only game in town: MENA had better learn the rules and start playing by them – or else' (Bush, 2004: 676).

Notes

* The authors would like to thank the Lebanese Council for Scientific Research for its grant.

1 Co-citation is the frequency with which two authors are cited together by the same article.

2 CorText is the digital platform of IFRIS (Institut Francilien Recherche, Innovation, Société) which includes a direct access to network computing tools named the CorText Manager.

References

Adams, R., and Page, J. (2003). Poverty, inequality and growth in selected Middle East and North Africa countries, 1980–2000. *World Development,* 31(12), 2027–48.

Anselin, L. (2003). *An Introduction to Spatial Regression Analysis in R* [PDF document]. Available at: http://geodacenter.asu.edu/drupal_files/spdepintro.pdf.

Atkinson, A.B. (1970). On the measurement of inequality. *Journal of Economic Theory,* 2(3), 244–63.

Besley, T. and Kanbur, R. (1988). Food subsidies and poverty alleviation. *The Economic Journal,* 98(392), 701–19. Available at: http://darp.lse.ac.uk/PapersDB/Besley-Kanbur_%28EJ_88%29.pdf.

Bibi, S. (n.d.). *Curriculum Vitae: Sami Bibi* [PDF document]. Available at: www.google.com/url?sa=t&rct=j&q=&esrc=s&source=web&cd=1&ved=0CB8QFjAA&url=http%3A%2F%2Fportal.pep- net.org%2Fdownload.php%3Ffile%3Duploads%2FCV%2FCV_3133.pdf&ei=-aiaVJ- oM8y3UZfxg7AL&usg=AFQjCNGEafReBJARxjm7bZl_G25efZ8YTA&sig2=-80xBlR3I9Tk7SDhOASo3g&bvm=bv.82001339,d.d24.

Bibi, S. (2005). *Measuring Poverty in a Multidimensional Perspective: A Review of Literature,* PMMA Working Paper No. 2005-07. Available at: www.gtap.agecon.purdue.edu/resources/download/2798.pdf.

Blondel, V.D., Guillaume, J.L., Lambiotte, R., and Lefebvre, E. (2008). Fast unfolding of communities in large networks. *Journal of Statistical Mechanics: Theory and Experiment,* 10(P10008), 1–12.

Bourguignon, F. and Fields, G. (1997). Discontinuous losses from poverty, generalized Pα curves, and optimal transfers to the poor. *Journal of Public Economics,* 63, 155–75.

Bush, R. (2004). Poverty and neo-liberal bias in the Middle East and North Africa. *Development and Change,* 35(4), 673–95.

Chakravarty, S. R. (1983). A new index of poverty. *Mathematical Social Sciences,* 6(3), 307–13.

Datt, G. and Ravallion, M. (1995). Is targeting through a work requirement efficient? Some evidence for rural India. In D. van de Walle and K. Nead (eds), *Public Spending and the Poor: Theory and Evidence* (pp. 413–44). Baltimore: Johns Hopkins University Press.

Deaton, A. (2005). Measuring poverty in a growing world (or measuring growth in a poor world). *Review of Economics and Statistics,* 87, 1–19.

Dollar, D. and Kraay, A. (2001). *Growth is Good for the Poor,* Policy Research Working Paper Series 2587. Available at: www- wds.worldbank.org/servlet/WDSContentServer/WDSP/IB/2001/05/11/000094946_01042806383524/Rendered/PDF/multi0page.pdf.

Duclos, J.Y., and Lambert, P.J. (1998). *A Normative Approach to Measuring Classical Horizontal Inequity*, Working Paper No. 9703. Available at: www.york.ac.uk/media/economics/documents/discussionpapers/1997/9703.pdf.

El-Laithy, H. (1996). *Structural Adjustment and Poverty*, paper presented at the International Conference on Structural Adjustment, UCLA, February.

Foster, J., Greer, J., and Thorbecke, E. (1984). A class of decomposable poverty measures. *Econometrica*, 52(3), 761–6.

Hassine, N.B., and Kandil, M. (2008). *Trade Liberalization, Agricultural Productivity and Poverty in the Mediterranean Region*, working papers 415. Available at: www.erf.org.eg/CMS/uploads/pdf/1215081639_415.pdf.

Hunaiti, D. (2005). Income distribution and expenditures of poor and non-poor families in remote communities: Field study in southern Jordan region. *King Saud University Journal*, 17(2).

Kakwani, N. and Pernia, E.M. (2000). What is pro-poor growth? *Asian Development Review*, 18(1).

Lora, E. (2009). *Washington Consensus*. Princeton: Princeton University Press. Available at: http://search.proquest.com/docview/189251596?accountid=8555.

Mannheim, K. (1936). *Ideology and Utopia.* London: Routledge & Kegan Paul Ltd.

O'Connor, A. (2001). *Poverty Knowledge.* New Jersey and Oxfordshire: Princeton University Press.

Piketty, T. (2014). *Capital in the Twenty-First Century*. Cambridge, MA: Belknap Press.

Ravallion, M. (1998). *Poverty Lines in Theory and* Practice, Living Standards Measurement Study Working Paper 133. Available at: www- wds.worldbank.org/servlet/WDS ContentServer/WDSP/IB/2000/02/24/000094946_99031911030079/Rendered/PDF/multi_page.pdf.

Ravallion, M., and Chen, S. (2003). Measuring pro-poor growth. *Economics Letters,* 78, 93–9.

Saad-Filho, A. (2010). *Growth, Poverty and Inequality: From Washington Consensus to Inclusive* Growth, DESA Working Paper No. 100. Available at: www.un.org/esa/desa/papers/2010/wp100_2010.pdf.

Sen, A. (1976). Poverty: An ordinal approach to measurement. *Econometrica*, 44(2), 219–31. Available at: http://links.jstor.org/sici?sici=0012-9682%28197603%2944%3A2%3C219%3APAOATM%3E2.0.CO%3B2-Z.

Sen, A. (1987). The standard of living. In A.K. Sen, J. Muellbauer, R. Kanbur, K. Hart, and B. Williams, *The Standard of Living: The Tanner Lectures on Human Values.* Cambridge: Cambridge University Press.

Steele, J. (2001). *The Guardian Profile: Amartya Sen.* Available at: www.theguardian.com/books/2001/mar/31/society.politics (accessed 3 September 2014).

Traboulsi, F. (2005). Public spheres and urban space: A critical comparative approach: Commentary. *New Political Science*, 27(4), 529–41.

Weeds, J. E. (2003). *Measures and applications of lexical distributional similarity* (Doctoral dissertation, University of Sussex).

Part Three

Reforms, Resistance and Alternatives: New Ways Towards Social Justice

15

The Limits of Reform in Liberal Democracies

Walden Bello

In much of the developing world, these are non-revolutionary times. Despite setbacks in terms of delivering on their promise of delivering prosperity, neoliberal policies continue to reign supreme, if only as default strategies that technocrats and elites resort to in the absence of a credible alternative paradigm for economic transformation.

Poverty and inequality are rife, but progressive movements remain marginalized in most countries. Whether reformist or revolutionary, these forces have failed to attain the critical mass that would propel them to hegemony in the political arena. There are exceptions, of course, mainly in Latin America, where Hugo Chavez in Venezuela, Evo Morales in Bolivia, and Rafael Correa in Ecuador were able to construct populist coalitions that propelled them to government, where they proceeded to successfully dismantle neoliberal economic regimes.

In most other countries, progressive parties active in the parliamentary arena have the choice of either remaining in permanent opposition or seeking alliances with liberal or traditional parties. Those choosing the latter option find that they need to place plans for comprehensive reform or strategic transformation on the backburner and settle for piecemeal reform, choosing carefully the issues for which they will stake their efforts in securing in the short or medium term. In the Philippines, for instance, my party, Akbayan or the Citizens' Action Party, of which I am one of the members sitting in parliament, is part of a mildly reformist coalition led by a traditional party.

In his *Political Order in Changing Societies*, Samuel P. Huntington asserted that reform is harder than revolution. After several years of serving as an elected official, I think that this is probably the only point on which I can agree with this neoconservative icon. Having said this, I would nevertheless like to say that there are real opportunities or spaces for achieving progressive reform in liberal democratic systems. The successful struggle for family planning in the Philippines against the cultural hegemony of the Catholic Church is an instance of this. But neither must the space for reform be exaggerated. Anti-corruption campaigns may boomerang and be transformed into movements against the empowerment of the poor and marginalized, as in Thailand, or, as the case of agrarian reform in the Philippines shows, there are limits that the prevailing class structure and political system impose on transformative initiatives.

Reproductive health as an opening

There are opportunities for building alliances that can achieve a critical mass to push through a progressive program in liberal democracies. In some countries where traditional institutions control the cultural discourse, reproductive health provides one such opportunity.

The Philippines offers an instructive example of the possibilities of fundamental reform at the cultural level. The struggle for a legislatively enshrined government-supported family planning program, to address both the issue of poverty and women's reproductive health, has been one of the central advocacies of the progressive movement since the late 1990s. The biggest block has been the powerful Church hierarchy in predominantly Roman Catholic Philippines.

The pro-reproductive health or pro-RH movement circumvented this block in two ways. First, it built a multiclass alliance for family planning, reaching out not only to the poor and middle class but to the elite as well. Undoubtedly, many in the elite that swung around to the family planning side did so out of enlightened self interest, meaning they saw a reduced birth rate among the lower classes as a way to ease popular pressures for redistribution. However, a not insignificant number, especially from the ranks of upper- and middle-class women, were won over by the argument that control over childbearing and family size would lead to greater women's control over their lives.

The second strategy deployed by the movement to circumvent the Church opposition was to 'change the discourse.' In the beginning of the parliamentary struggle over RH, the pro-family planning forces deployed the population control argument citing the Philippines' unsustainable 2.5 per cent annual population growth. Against this, the bishops deployed the argument that artificial contraception was immoral because the only purpose of sex was to have children. This had, however, limited appeal, so they enlisted another argument, this one from the extreme left: that family planning was a tool promoted by the United States to keep third world populations down. Thus, we had the incongruous spectacle of upper-class religious conservatives parading as anti-imperialists on the floor of the House of Representatives.

For a couple of years, armed with this bastard ideological formula of 'anti-imperialism' and anti-contraception, the alliance between the bishops, religious conservatives in the House, and presidents fearful of the Church blocked any movement on the legislative front, even as the rest of the country moved forward. Several factors, including the election of a president actively in support of the bill, broke the political stalemate beginning in 2010. But the decisive factor was the women's movement, which, in the 2000s, reframed the issue as one of women's reproductive rights and health. Women had the right to space their children and determine how many children they had. Women had the right to protect their family's quality of life by limiting their offspring. Women had the right to family planning to preserve their health. It was a winning argument, one that was deployed with skill not only at the rational level but symbolically, through the strategic dissemination of the image of an all-male hierarchy and a predominantly male Congress controlling women's choices.

By 2012, some 14 years after the RH bill was first introduced, the hierarchy and its allies in Congress were bereft of viable arguments and forced into pushing two related arguments that came across to the general public as outrageous or silly: that condoms and other contraceptives were 'abortifacients,' and that there was no conceptual or real difference between contraception and abortion. The Church's defeat was sealed, though the bishops chose to go down fighting during the congressional debates in 2012 and 2013. It was a spectacular end to a long cultural war.[1]

The key lesson that I have derived from this struggle is that even when pitted against hegemonic cultural institutions, progressives can register successes. In the RH battle, we witnessed the success of a strategy of constructing broad alliances across classes, with the end in view of driving a wedge between a conservative ideological institution and the ruling elites and the middle class normally under its sway. Central to this strategy was an attractive human rights or gender rights discourse that promoted a self-image of being 'enlightened' among elite and middle-class supporters of the bill.

Corruption as a double-edged sword

Another issue on which progressive forces can build broad alliances that can push through significant change is corruption. All sectors of society are bothered by the corruption of government officials and corrupt ties between government and business, often known as 'crony capitalism.' Corruption is often the main issue of opposition parties seeking to get into elected office in democracies; and, along with anger at dictatorial abuse, disgust with corruption has been one of the driving forces in the toppling of authoritarian regimes, this being particularly evident during the Arab Spring.

An alliance between civil society and reformist groups in government can be a potent force. This alliance can produce positive results; for instance, in the Philippines it played a central role in the historic abolition in 2013 of the 'pork barrel,' or unprogramed government funds given by the executive to members of the legislative branch in order to keep them on a short leash. The reformist thrust of the anti-pork barrel campaign has not yet been spent, resulting as it has in the high-profile prosecution of several senators who channeled public money into their personal accounts and the Supreme Court's placing severe limits on the executive's use of unprogramed funds.

Many countries can boast of such achievements in anti-corruption efforts. Probably even more exemplary than the Philippines in fighting corruption is Indonesia, where prosecution of corrupt officials by the Corruption Eradication Commission has achieved an astonishing 100 percent conviction rate, sending even high-profile politicians to jail for their misdeeds. As one account notes, the commission has enjoyed widespread popular support on account of its 'ability to prosecute those at the top of the food chain,' which has insulated it against reprisals from resentful elites.[2]

Reducing corruption undoubtedly contributes to reducing inequality, both directly and indirectly. Nevertheless, campaigning against corruption is not usually high up on the agenda of progressive groups. Prioritizing it is often mainly dictated by the popularity of the anti-corruption cause among the middle class, which is also the most articulate class in society whose discourse dominates public discussion.

The hesitation many progressives have with the corruption issue is that it is a double-edged sword. Multilateral agencies like the World Bank and Asian Development Bank have promoted the view that 'good governance' is the central problem in development, by which they mean that much corruption is brought about by government intervention in the economy, which creates opportunities for corruption. In other words, anti-corruption discourse is often tied to an ideologically motivated neoliberal agenda.

Also contributing to the discomfort of progressives is that elites jockeying against one another for political office have jumped on the anti-corruption bandwagon, and a key part of the reason is that it is a discourse that allows them to paint themselves as saints and their foes as devils while marginalizing the urgency for structural change like agrarian reform and income redistribution. In the Philippines, for instance, the Aquino administration has prided itself on its program of *Daang Matuwid*, or 'the Straight Path,' but as coalition partners, we have had a hell of a time placing agrarian reform and abandoning neoliberal policies as priorities on its political agenda.

For progressives, the greatest risk involved in the anti-corruption discourse is the way it can be manipulated by threatened elites to derail efforts at progressive transformation. The most recent case of this is in Thailand where the conservative royalist elites were able to mobilize the Bangkok middle class on an anti-corruption platform to create a political paralysis that provoked the military to launch the 22 May 2014 coup d'état against a populist government associated with the exiled former Prime Minister Thaksin Shinawatra. An earlier putsch in 2006 overthrew Thaksin, who is enormously popular with the rural lower classes.

It is worthwhile going into some detail here. There is no doubt that Thaksin bought many of his political alliances with elite politicians, but the main reason he was able to carve out such massive popularity among the rural and urban poor of Thailand was because he ended the enormously harmful policy straitjacket that the International Monetary Fund imposed on Thailand following the Asian financial crisis of 1997 and promoted programs that directly addressed the needs of the marginalized sectors. The most important of these were a universal health care program which gave people medical treatment for all diseases and ailments for the equivalent of 35 baht (slightly over a dollar at today's exchange rate), the so-called 'One Million Baht per Village Fund' that went to localities for them to invest in productive activities of their choice, and a moratorium on the debt of farmers. The Thai political and intellectual elites, resorting to corruption discourse, were able to define these programs as other forms of vote buying. The real issue, however, was the empowerment of the poor that Thaksin's programs brought about, which led to creation of a massive electoral majority that, in the eyes of the elite and the middle class, threatened a fundamental and permanent redistribution of political and economic power. With this perspective, it is not surprising that the struggle against corruption was turned in the middle-class mind into a struggle against democracy because the ballot allegedly enabled ignorant voters who did not know their real interests to bring corrupt politicians to power. The slogan 'reform before election' that mobilized the academics, professionals, white collar workers, and small business people was essentially a conservative call for constitutional measures that would keep electoral majorities based on the rural and urban poor from forming governments. The massive middle-class demonstrations were designed to bring about a military coup against the government of Thaksin's sister, Yingluck, to open the way for such anti-democratic innovations. And, indeed, the military junta that took power is now in the process of attempting to forge these constitutional mechanisms that would ensure continued rule by the royalist elite in alliance with the Bangkok middle classes.[3]

So the lesson for progressives is: take on corruption but don't be trapped by neoliberal and elitist anti-corruption discourses that undercut efforts at promoting an activist government role in development and transformative efforts to empower the poor and marginalized.

Agrarian reform: The hard realities of class

Let me now move to legislative initiatives that bear directly on class issues. The possibilities of and constraints on pushing issues that cut deeply into class interests are illustrated by the agrarian reform issue, one of the priorities of my party.

Asia has been the site of four major successes in agrarian reform. China experienced revolutionary land reform during the 1950s and 1960s. In Japan, the Allied Occupation Government under Gen Douglas MacArthur used land reform to destroy the landed elite that had served as the social base of militarism. South Korea and Taiwan saw reform from above carried out as a policy to preempt peasant insurgency.

In the 28 years since we overthrew the dictatorship of Ferdinand Marcos in 1986, I've been an active participant in the struggle for land reform in the Philippines – both as an activist and a legislator. This has taught me a lot about how democratic institutions can be used to promote deeply undemocratic interests.

Things appeared at first to be headed in the right direction. With the ousting of Marcos, not only was a constitutional democracy set up, but a sweeping land reform law – the Comprehensive Agrarian Reform Program, or CARP – was passed to give millions of peasants titles to their land. Redistribution would be accomplished peacefully under democratic governance, in contrast to the coercive programs in China, Vietnam, and Cuba.

Over the next few years, however, electoral competition – the key institution of liberal democracy – was reduced to a mechanism whereby members of the elite fought one another for the privilege of ruling while consolidating their control of the political system as a class. The vast majority of those elected to Congress came from either landlord or big capitalist families. One of the victims of this congealing of landed class power was CARP.

With a combination of coercion, legal obstructionism, and the conversion of land from agricultural to commercial and industrial purposes, the agrarian reform process stalled. Ultimately, less than half of the original 10 million hectares designated for redistribution was actually disbursed to peasants by 2008 – some 20 years after the beginning of the program. Indeed, with little support in terms of social services, many peasants ended up reselling their lands back to the landlords, while other beneficiaries lost their recently acquired lands to aggressive legal action by the targets of reform.

It was at this juncture that I and several other parliamentarians got together to sponsor the Comprehensive Agrarian Reform Program Extension with Reforms Law, or CARPER. We had a hell of a time getting this passed, but we did it in August 2009. What made the difference were peasant strikes and marches – including a 1700-kilometer march from the southern island of Mindanao to the presidential palace in Manila – and efforts by activists to disrupt congressional sessions.

CARPER plugged many of the loopholes of the original CARP, allocating some $3.3 billion to support land redistribution, subsidies for seed and fertilizer, and agricultural extension services. Most importantly, CARPER mandated that the distribution of all remaining land had to be completed by 30 June 2014.

My party – Akbayan, or the Citizens' Action Party – joined the Philippine government as a coalition partner after the elections of May 2010, partly because we felt that President Benigno Aquino III would put an emphasis on completing agrarian reform. Yet despite our monitoring and constant pushing, the process of land acquisition and distribution proceeded at a snail's pace. Thanks to landlord resistance, bureaucratic inertia, and nonchalance on the part of the president, over 550,000 hectares of land – including most of the best private land in the country – remained undistributed after the deadline of the five-year process on 30 June 2014.

I tried one last time late in 2014 to salvage CARPER by asking the president – a scion of one of the wealthiest landed clans in the country – to dismiss his timid secretary of agrarian reform. He refused – remarking sarcastically that I had too many complaints and I should run for president if I wanted to see comprehensive reform.

Today, even as the elites battle it out in the Philippines' thriving electoral politics, the rate of poverty – at nearly 28 percent – remains unchanged from the early 1990s. True, the economy has grown. But all studies show that the rate of inequality in the Philippines remains among the highest in Asia, underlining the fact that the fruits of growth continue to be appropriated by the top stratum of the population.

The limits of progressive reform in liberal democracies

Reforms, even significant ones, are definitely possible under liberal democracies. Skilled coalition building, command of the narrative or discourse, and timing are important ingredients, as we showed in the case of the battle for reproductive health in the Philippines. But there are limits to reform. One is the ambivalent nature of some issues. Eliminating corruption, a progressive demand under most circumstances, can be turned against social reform that would benefit the marginalized, as evidenced by recent events in Thailand. More important, there appears to be an iron limit to the kind of reforms that can be conceded by dominant economic elites. They can tolerate, indeed even support, a campaign for reproductive health against a hegemonic cultural institution like the Roman Catholic Church. But they draw the line at measures that directly cut into their class power, like agrarian reform.

What does this mean for the politics of reform?

I find it useful to turn to Thomas Piketty. In his celebrated book *Capital in the 21st Century*, which is now required reading for everyone, Thomas Piketty says that inequality both globally and locally is likely to become even worse. Let me quote from *Capital in the 21st Century*:

> [I]f the top thousandth enjoy a 6 per cent rate of return on their wealth, while average global wealth grows only at 2 per cent a year, then after thirty years the top thousandth's share of global capital will have more than tripled. The top thousandth would then own 60 per cent of global wealth …[4]

The dynamics of contemporary capital accumulation, he warns,

> can lead to excessive and lasting concentration of capital: no matter how justified inequalities of wealth may be initially, fortunes can grow and perpetuate themselves beyond all reasonable limits and beyond any possible rational justification in terms of social utility.[5]

Piketty's data show that since the eighteenth century, when capitalist growth took off, rising inequality has been the norm. This was broken only in the middle decades of the twentieth century. From what appeared to be the evidence of the first half of the twentieth century, the economist Simon Kuznets came out with the theory that as capitalism matured, inequalities would decrease, which he illustrated with the famous 'Kuznets Curve.'

Piketty says, however, that the Kuznets Curve is an invalid extrapolation of a theory beyond a period that was marked by exceptional circumstances: what he calls 'exogenous events' like two global wars and the domestic upheavals they produced led to political and social arrangements that temporarily reversed capitalism's natural dynamic towards inequality. As he writes,

> The sharp reduction in income inequality that we observe in almost all the rich countries between 1914 and 1945 was due above all to the world wars and the violent economic and political shocks they entailed. It had little to do with the tranquil process of intersectoral mobility described by Kuznets.[6]

As a member of parliament and long-time pro-democracy activist, I find Piketty's remarks unsettling, for what he seems to be saying is that democratic regimes, which are supposed to aim at promoting equality among citizens, don't really work when it comes to containing economic equality. They, of course, enshrine formal equality, run on the principles of one person, one vote and majority rule, but they are ineffective when it comes to bringing about greater economic equality.

Now my generation came of age in the Third World fighting to oust dictatorships and bringing about democracy. As one who participated in the anti-dictatorship struggles of the seventies, one of our potent arguments against authoritarianism was that it promoted concentration of income in dictatorial cliques allied with transnational capital. We said that democracy would reverse this process of impoverishment and inequality. From Chile to Brazil to South Korea to the Philippines, fighting against the dictatorship was a fight for both democratic choice and greater equality. When democracy was attained, some of us, like myself, decided to put our beliefs on the line, by running for political office.

Yet the evidence now seems clear that what Samuel Huntington called the 'Third Wave' of the spread of democracy in the South went hand in hand with the rise and consolidation of inequality.

Even more than dictatorships, Western-style democracies are, we are forced to conclude, the natural system of governance of neoliberal capitalism, for they promote rather than restrain the savage forces of capital accumulation that lead to ever greater levels of inequality and poverty. In fact, liberal democratic systems are ideal for the economic elites, for they are programed with periodic electoral exercises that promote the illusion of equality, thus granting the system an aura of legitimacy.

The old Marxist term 'bourgeois democracy' is still the best description for this kind of democratic regime.

To reverse the process requires not just an alternative economic program based on justice, equity, and ecological stability, but a new democratic regime to replace the liberal democratic regime that has become so vulnerable to elite and foreign capture.

What might be some of the features of this new democracy that must supersede liberal democracy?

First of all, representative institutions must be balanced by the formation of institutions of direct democracy.

Second, civil society must organize itself politically to act as a counterpoint and check to the dominant state institutions.

Third, citizens must keep in readiness a parliament of the streets, or 'people power,' that can be brought at critical points to bear on the decision-making process: a system, if you will, of parallel power. People power must be institutionalized for periodic intervention, not abandoned once the insurrection has banished the old regime.

Fourth, citizen socialization must move away from the idealization of liberal democratic forms and towards bringing people to participate in the formulation of new, more participatory democratic arrangements. Likewise, equality – in the radical French Revolution sense of the term, not simply the bourgeois notion of 'equality of opportunity' – must be brought back to center stage.

Finally, unlike in liberal democracy – when most people participate in decision-making only during elections – political participation must become a constant activity, with people evolving into active citizens instead of passive political actors.

Theorizing the features of the New Democracy is one thing. Bringing it about is another. What forms of struggle must we employ to leap from the old to the new regime? We must not give up the battle for reform via the mechanisms of representative, electoral democracy, but we should combine it with political mobilization outside the parameters of the liberal democratic regime. Insurrectionary methods, like the people's power uprisings in the Philippines, Middle East, and Eastern Europe, must be part of the repertoire of progressive groups.

Triggers of change

The question is, how do we bring such fundamental reforms about at a time when organized elites and disorganized, quiescent citizenries appear to be the norm in both the North and the South – when the conditions for insurrectionary change are not immediately evident?

Noting that 'the long term dynamics of the wealth distribution are potentially terrifying,'[7] Piketty asks whether the only solution might not lie in violent reactions or radical shocks, like the wars and the social revolutions they triggered during the first half of the twentieth century.

Perhaps we are now in for some of those radical shocks. Perhaps current developments in Iraq and Syria are not marginal events but explosions that will sooner or later also occur in other regions, including the North. When the political explosions occasioned by inequality and the search for identity are combined with what many foresee as the turbulent social consequences of the climate apocalypse, then perhaps we are not too far away from the volatile mixture of external and internal shocks that can trigger transformative change.

Will democracies survive and manage these transformative shocks as they did in the mid-twentieth century? Or will they be overcome by internal and external pressures, leaving future historians – as philosopher Richard Rorty puts it – to wonder why the golden age of democracy lasted only about 200 years?

Notes

1 For a more detailed analysis of the RH struggle, see Walden Bello (2014), 'Autopsy of a Debacle: Clerical Extremists, Timid Liberals, and the RH Debate', *Inquirer.net*, 13 April. Available at: http://opinion.inquirer.net/73562/autopsy-of-a-debate-clerical-extremists-timid-liberals-and-the-rh-debate.

2 Brendan McGloin (2013), 'Indonesia's Anti-Corruption Agency: A Model for other Asia-Pacific-Countries', *Business Intelligence,* 24 July. Available at: http://news.riskadvisory.net/index.php/2013/07/indonesias-anti-corruption-agency-a-model-for-other-asia-pacific-countries/.

3 For the role of the middle class in paving the way for the recent coup, see Marc Saxer (2014), 'Middle Class Rage Threatens Democracy', *New Mandala,* 21 January. Available at: http://asiapacific.anu.edu.au/newmandala/2014/01/21/middle-class-rage-threatens-democracy/; see also Walden Bello (2014), 'Class War: Thailand's Military Coup', *Foreign Policy in Focus,* 27 May. Available at: http://fpif.org/class-war-thailands-military-coup/.

4 Thomas Piketty (2014), *Capital in the Twentieth Century.* Cambridge, Harvard University Press, p. 439.

5 Ibid., p. 443.

6 Ibid., p. 15.

7 Ibid., p. 571.

16

Tensions Between Development, Public Policies to Confront Poverty/ Inequality and the Defense of Pluriculturality in South America

Edgardo Lander

Measured according to conventional criteria of income distribution Latin America is by far the most unequal continent.[1] Inequality is particularly extreme in some countries. In 2002 the ratio between the average income of the richest quintile and the poorest quintile was 44.2 to 1 in Bolivia and 34.4 to 1 in Brazil.[2]

In the last two or three decades there has been a clear tendency towards an increase of inequality in most of the world[3] as a result of neoliberal globalization and reductions in welfare policies. However, many countries in Latin America, particularly in South America have gone against these dominant trends. The governments of the diverse range of the so-called 'left turn' in the continent have defined the reduction of both inequality and poverty as one of their main goals and have carried out public policies aimed at reversing the devastating effects of neoliberal policies of previous decades. The main instruments used for this purpose have been social policies. According to the UN Economic Commission for Latin America and the Caribbean (ECLAC), between 1992–3 and 2010–11 in Latin America there was a significant increase in both public and social expenditure. The participation of social spending in relation to the total public budget increased from 50% to 65.9%, and social public expenditure increased from 12.5% to 19.2% of the GDP.[4] For the same period per capita social spending rose by 178%.[5]

The impact of these policies has been remarkable. In the last decade, there have been significant reductions in what official statistics define as poverty and extreme poverty.[6]

Inequality has also been reduced. According to ECLAC data, with the exception of Paraguay, between 2002 and 2012 in every other country in

South America there was an increase in the share of the poorest quintile in national income and a reduction in the share of richest quintile.[7] The Gini coefficient as well as the Theil and the Parkinson indexes indicate consistent reductions of inequalities in the continent between those years. These reductions were particularly significant in the cases of Uruguay, Bolivia, Argentina and Venezuela.[8]

These are important achievements. However, Latin America is still the most unequal continent. But even more important, there is much hidden behind these statistics, particularly a monocultural blindness to the reality of the profound historical and structural heterogeneity of these societies. The celebration of the advances expressed in the data mentioned above tend to ignore the fact that the current inequities in the continent are the result of five centuries of colonial racist history characterized by the systematic subjugation, extermination, exploitation and exclusion of indigenous peoples and Afro-descendants.[9] These are not inequalities that can be altered if their structural causes are not addressed.

As has been argued by Aníbal Quijano, Enrique Dussel, Walter Mignolo and others that have been working within the *modernity/coloniality perspective*, the experience of modernity has meant something radically different for the North and the South of the planet.[10]

What has been characterized as the luminous nature of modernity by the philosophers of the Enlightenment, by Kant, by Hegel, and more recently by Habermas, is only the most visible (for the North) side of a worldwide historical process that has its *dark underside* in the existence of colonies and imperial domination of others without which the 'bright side' would not have been possible. In the North, modernity led in time to material abundance, to liberal democracy and citizenship, to modern science and technology. For the majority of the planet's population living in the South, modernity has been an experience of imperial and colonial domination, genocide and slavery. This dark underside is as modern, as essential a component of the global modern experience as the historical processes of the North.

The three-century system of colonial subjugation of what was later called Latin America was structured around two main components. The first concerns the establishment of a power structure based on the hierarchical classification of the population based on an extremely potent political and epistemological construct, the idea of *race*. This was based on phenotypic characteristics of the population, especially skin color.[11] This device sought to naturalize the extraordinary hierarchical differences of the colonial order, characterizing indigenous people and enslaved Africans and their descents as biologically inferior. The White men of European origin occupied the apex of this hierarchical colonial order.

The second component concerns the role of the continent in the modern capitalist colonial world system. From the beginning of its colonial subjugation, the entire continent came to occupy the role of *exporter of nature*, especially precious metals (gold and silver) and precious plants (sugar, tobacco, cocoa). This form of participation in the international division of labor and of nature was closely intertwined with the regime of racial classification of the population. The export of nature was based on the relations of servitude imposed on indigenous peoples and the slave labor of Africans and their descendants.

With political independence in the early decades of the nineteenth century, not much changed regarding this racialized colonial order and the role of the continent in the international division of labor and nature. In Latin America struggles for political independence in the early 1800s operated within a liberal world view with both its emancipatory potentials and its Eurocentric racist baggage. In what Aníbal Quijano has characterized as *a process of political independence without a social revolution*, the basic patterns of the colonial racist power structure were preserved.[12] As can be clearly seen in the founding republican constitutions, the new independent states established a liberal grammar of politics that excluded the great majority of the population from citizenship. The imposition of a monocultural political system upon these very heterogeneous multicultural societies did not lead to democracy but to a systematic regime of exclusions. Liberal citizenship was the prerogative of the few. Varying between different countries, slavery continued for many years after independence. In Brazil, the reaction against the abolition of slavery (1888) contributed to the end of empire and the establishment of the republic. Across the continent, with independence, the colonial structure of power is transmuted into *internal colonialism*.[13]

From the mid-nineteenth century, under the influence of positivism, liberalism and social Darwinism, Latin American elites throughout the continent undertake an aggressive process of Westernization of their societies.

The dominant ideology, based on liberalism and positivism, considered that the Indian or native element had no place in the new national cultures. The state and the ruling classes used every possible means to eliminate such 'evils' that were considered to jeopardize their chances of becoming truly modern nations. In many countries violence and military expeditions 'cleared the field' for farmers and new agricultural pioneers and entrepreneurs, in a process that physically exterminated the indigenous peoples. This happened in Uruguay, Argentina and Chile, as well as in parts of Brazil and other countries. This model recalls the colonization process that worked so effectively in US history.[14]

Prototypical of this racist logic was the opposition between *civilization* and *barbarism* made by Sarmiento in Argentina, which resulted in the 'war of the desert' – a policy of extermination of indigenous peoples of Patagonia Argentina in order to create the conditions for the advance of 'civilization'.

Thus in societies with deep historical structural heterogeneities, societies with a rich diversity of peoples and cultures, a pattern of domination was imposed that denied this diversity and exterminated or subjected the 'others'. This racist colonial history (along with its basic continuity during two centuries of independent republics) is the fundamental basis of the structural inequalities and exclusions of contemporary Latin American societies.

Structural inequality, social policy and decolonization

In the last few decades indigenous peoples and Afro-descendants of the continent have carried out extraordinary organizational and political processes of cultural affirmation and construction of agendas that often come into direct conflict with the policies with which governments seek to address their condition of exclusion.

As a product of increasingly coordinated struggles and debates across the continent, common agendas have been systematized by organizations of both indigenous peoples and Afro-descendants. These have as a primary goal the achievement of equality, not in the terms defined by the dominant society, but through a process of decolonization that would make it possible for them to achieve their own alternative self-defined future. The aim of these decolonizing struggles is not just inclusion in the liberal state as citizens, but a profound transformation of these monocultural states into multinational plurinational states. This necessarily requires taking into account, in genuinely democratic terms, the diversity of the peoples and cultures present on those national territories. This implies the recognition of the multiplicity of languages, the diverse forms of property, juridical regimes, modalities of production, as well as the plurality of knowledges and forms of relating to the rest of the web of life.

The most important achievements of these struggles were the new constitutions of Ecuador and Bolivia. These texts, despite their profound internal contradictions, centrally incorporate notions of *plurinationalism* and *interculturalism*[15] and the notions of the good life of the Quechuas and the Aymara people (*Sumak Kawsay* and *Suma Qamaña*).

The political and organizational experience of Afro-descendants has been equally dynamic in the past two decades. Preparations for the United Nations' *World Conference against Racism, Racial Discrimination, Xenophobia and Related Intolerance*, held by the United Nations in Durban, South Africa in 2001, served as a trigger for organizations in different regions of the continent to advance in the creation of shared agendas.[16] As in the case of indigenous peoples, the aim of achieving the recognition of their traditional territories occupies a prominent place in these agendas. In the words of Venezuelan activist and intellectual Jesús 'Chucho' García:

> To prepare the agenda was to start with the self-recognition of the contributions of Africans and their descendants to the creation of cultural diversity as well as their political and religious contributions in this continent and the Caribbean.

This agenda was also linked to the territoriality that the Maroons (*cimarrones*) and their descendants had conquered for years in their struggles since colonial times. These territories were seen in a perspective that was quite different from Western approaches of conquering nature. In this alternative vision, man shares with nature, respects it and harmonizes it with their daily lives.[17]

The rights of Africans and peoples of African descent throughout the world were recognized in the following terms by the Durban Conference:

> We recognize that people of African descent have for centuries been victims of racism, racial discrimination and enslavement and of the denial by history of many of their rights, and assert that they should be treated with fairness and respect for their dignity and should not suffer discrimination of any kind.

> Recognition should therefore be given to their rights to culture and their own identity; to participate freely and in equal conditions in political, social, economic and cultural life; to development in the context of their own aspirations and customs; to keep, maintain and foster their own forms of organization, their mode of life, culture, traditions and religious expressions; to maintain and use their own languages; to the protection of their traditional knowledge and their cultural and artistic heritage; to the use, enjoyment and conservation

of the natural renewable resources of their habitat and to active participation in the design, implementation and development of educational systems and programmes, including those of a specific and characteristic nature; and where applicable to their ancestrally inhabited land.[18]

What is at stake in these platforms of both indigenous peoples and peoples of African descent, is the possibility of the preservation of different modes of living with different cultures in a world that is increasingly overwhelmed by the monoculture of the neoliberal market. *Equality in this context does not refer to equal access to one particular cultural tradition, but to equality of traditions.*

The lack of recognition of the multicultural significance of these demands has extraordinary implications. Even in countries with 'progressive' or left governments, and even in countries that are constitutionally defined as multinational, diverse mechanisms continue to block demands for decolonization. Eurocentric epistemological frameworks do not allow for an adequate historical-structural characterization of these societies. Framed in these perspectives, public policies tend to reproduce historical exclusions.

Views of inequality based basically on economic and quantitative criteria lead to considering the most excluded sectors of the population, particularly indigenous peoples and Afro-descendants as 'poor' or 'needy' and requiring state policies to 'elevate' their standards of living and consumption levels of urban middle classes. This monocultural conception assumes a particular cultural pattern (modern liberal society) as the universal template from which to compare and judge all of the society. This has become a standardized mandatory frame of reference of what it is to be 'modern' as the unavoidable destiny for every culture.

The recognition of cultural plurality in all its complex dimensions such as ancestral territorial rights usually remains in the discursive field.

These policies represent a fundamental continuity of the normalizing developmental policies that were promoted by multilateral financial agencies and the United Nations at the end of World War II. These policies have been described by Arturo Escobar in the following terms:

A type of development was promoted which conformed to the ideas and expectations of the affluent West, to what the Western countries judged to be a normal course of evolution and progress ... by conceptualizing progress in such terms, this development strategy became a powerful instrument for normalizing the world.[19]

Behind the humanitarian concern and the positive outlook of the new strategy, new forms of power and control, more subtle and refined, were put in operation. Poor people's ability to define and take care of their own lives was eroded in a deeper manner than perhaps ever before. The poor became the target of more sophisticated practices, of a variety of programs that seemed inescapable.[20]

In this sense, the recovery of the state and its ability to fund social welfare and redistributive policies have ambiguous and even contradictory consequences for indigenous peoples, Afro-descendants and peasants across the continent. On the one hand, it allows for the implementation of significant public programs to reduce hunger and improve access to education, and other public services. But simultaneously, these policies as a result both of their content and the top-down nature of their design and implementation, end up imposing external cultural logics upon traditional communities, weakening their identity and organizations, as well as the social fabric of peoples and communities as they become increasingly dependent on the transfer of resources from the state. Some of these policies have the implicit objective of weakening indigenous and Afro-descendant and peasant organizations, by undermining their own grassroots through direct cash transfers and other welfare programs. This is due to the recognition that the pluricultural claims made by these organizations, particularly their demands for recognition of their ancestral territories, are not compatible with the development plans formulated by national governments.

Inseparably associated with this mode of welfare expenditure is the continuation and even intensification of colonial forms of integration of South American economies in the international division of labor and nature. Across the continent, thanks to the extraordinary increase in both demand and prices of the commodities produced by these countries, there has been a sustained increase in the export of these primary goods with little or no processing, leading to the *reprimarization* of these economies. Even the historical deterioration of the terms of trade between the prices of exported commodities and imported industrial goods was largely reversed during the first decade of the century. In the last decade, the value of these commodities as a percentage of the total value of exports has increased in all of South America, in some cases quite significantly.[21]

This *neo-extractivism* has been characterized by increased state and national participation in the profits of the activity which in turn have made it possible to finance more expansive social welfare policies. However, due to its social and environmental consequences, in particular their territorial impact, extractivism has become a central focus of political debates, mobilizations and social resistance across the continent.

In what Maristella Svampa has called the *consensus of commodities*,[22] the left and progressive governments and the new integration organizations such as the Bolivarian Alliance for the Peoples of our America (ALBA)[23] and the Union of South American Nations (UNASUR)[24] consider extractivism as a unique opportunity which will supply the resources to respond both to the continent's accumulated social debt, through welfare policies, and to make the necessary investments in infrastructure, education, etc., which would make it possible to go beyond extractivism at a future stage of the society's transformation.[25]

This notion of extractivism as the first of a series of stages of the transformation process seems to ignore two issues that have been highlighted by Fernando Coronil. First is the fact that when countries decide to use their comparative advantages and specialize in the production and export of unprocessed primary goods, they are once again assuming their old colonial role in the international division of labor and nature, now in the context of neoliberal globalization. In addition to that, the production of commodities not only implies the production of goods, but also of social relations, subjects, subjectivities and institutions.[26] As evidenced by the Venezuelan experience, once the economic, political and cultural logic of an extractivist society (in this case oil-based) has been firmly established, it acquires a powerful dynamic of self-reproduction that becomes extremely difficult to reverse.

The critique and resistance to these policies come from many sources. Many critics have recalled the negative impacts of the specialization in the production of primary goods in the continent's history. These countries have been highly vulnerable to fluctuations in demand and prices for their exports in the international market. Moreover, recent data suggest that the favorable terms of trade of the last decade may have been a relatively transient phenomenon that is showing signs of abating. After years of trade surpluses, several countries in the continent begin again to present trade deficits.[27] Additionally, extractive activities tend to generate little employment and what employment is created tends to be low paying and unstable. The reprimarization of the economies can lead to *deindustrialization*, as has been pointed out by Pierre Salama for the case of Brazil.[28]

Of more immediate and direct consequences for indigenous peoples, Afro-descendants and peasants of the continent are the social and environmental impacts of these extractive activities: large-scale mining, exploitation of fossil fuels, extensive monoculture plantations (for example GMO soya beans), etc. As a consequence of both the high prices and an ever-increasing demand for commodities in the world market, and new technologies that have become available, the frontier of extractive activities has been rapidly expanding into areas that until recently were regarded as inaccessible or unprofitable. Regardless of the political leaning of governments, the logic of *accumulation by dispossession* is today systematically advancing over the traditional territories of indigenous peoples, Afro-descendants and peasants, displacing/destroying communities as well as devastating water sources, fertile land and forests.[29] These extractive activities are undermining the conditions of self production of life for millions of people.

This subordinate role in the international division of labor and nature is characterized by an *unequal ecological exchange*. There is a large deficit in the flow of materials in the continent's international trade. More tons of materials are exported than imported and the price of each ton exported is lower than the price of each ton imported. Given the environmental impact of extractive activities, 'an unfavorable structural environmental burden' is generated.[30]

As a result of the social metabolism of this unequal ecological exchange, industrial economies of the North are 'fed' by the imports of ecological flows extracted in the South to meet their needs of energy and primary goods for their productive systems. However, the countries of origin are left with a heavy burden, due to the ecological and social negative impacts arising from extractive processes.[31]

These processes are profoundly unequal in their impacts, primarily affecting indigenous peoples, Afro-descendants and peasants whose life depends on the preservation of their territories. None of this is reflected in national accounts, in indicators of GDP growth, or in the way official statistics define and measure 'poverty' and inequality.

Another way to look at (and to quantify) how this unequal ecological exchange operates is through the concepts of *biocapacity*[32] and *ecological footprint*.[33] According to successive Living Planet Reports, from the year 1970, humanity as a whole has been using the planet's biocapacity at a greater speed than the natural replacement rate.

The Ecological Footprint shows a consistent trend of overconsumption (...). In 2008, the most recent year for which data are available, the footprint exceeded the Earth's biocapacity – the area of land and productive oceans actually available to produce renewable resources and absorb CO2 emissions – by more than 50 per cent.[34]

As a result of this 'ecological overshoot', there has been a 30% overall decline in the planet's biodiversity health since 1970. This means that as humanity's ecological footprint increases the overall biocapacity is reduced and the gap between biocapacity and footprint widens.

Related to the issues of equality there are two trends that need to be highlighted. The first is the fact that ecological footprints vary enormously amongst different countries, regions and different groups of populations.

If all of humanity lived like an average Indonesian, for example, only two-thirds of the planet's biocapacity would be used; if everyone lived like an average Argentinean, humanity would demand more than half an additional planet; and if everyone lived like an average resident of the USA, a total of four Earths would be required to regenerate humanity's annual demand on nature.[35]

The second is that in the overall decline in biodiversity in the last four decades there have been some significant geographic differences, particularly between tropical and temperate regions. In spite of the fact that higher income countries have a much larger ecological footprint per capita than low-income countries, over the last four decades all of the worldwide decline in biodiversity has occurred in low-income and middle-income countries.

Between 1970 and 2008, there has been a 60% decline in the Living Planet Index of low income countries, while this index increased by 7% for high-income countries.[36]

This is likely to be due to a combination of factors, not the least being that these nations are able to purchase and import resources from lower-income countries, thereby simultaneously degrading the biodiversity in those countries while maintaining the remaining biodiversity and ecosystems in their own 'back yard' (...). The trend in low income countries is potentially catastrophic, not just for biodiversity but also for the people living there. While everyone depends ultimately on the biodiversity that provides ecosystem services and natural assets, the impact of environmental degradation is felt most directly by the world's poorest people, particularly by rural populations, and forest and coastal communities. Without access to land, clean water, adequate food, fuel and materials, vulnerable people cannot break out of the poverty trap and prosper.[37]

Thus, neo-extractive developmentalism that has as one of its main objectives the improvement of the living conditions of the population and the reduction of inequalities is actually producing a massive transfer of wealth to the major trading partners (United States, European Union and China). This implies that there is a widespread process of destruction of the material conditions that sustain life. This dynamic is not only made invisible by national accounts, but is celebrated as development. These impacts, as mentioned above, are profoundly unequal and with particularly negative impacts precisely on the people and communities that have been subjected to the worst forms of colonial domination.

In debates on equality/inequality it is essential to incorporate the dimension of intergenerational justice. The economic dynamics of extractivism implies the exchange of a short-term monetary benefit for the environmental devastation that future generations will inherit.

The most urgent global challenge that humanity faces today is the one represented by the limits of planet Earth and the predatory processes that are systematically destroying the conditions that make life possible. When the colonial and Eurocentric arrogance which is hegemonic in the current global order ignores the voices of the *suma qamaña*, the *sumak kawsay* and other conceptions of the good life of 'others', and insists on the path of overall cultural homogenization, of unlimited economic growth, and the destruction of the rest of 'nature' that development requires, when it denies and suppresses other forms of knowledge, of understanding life and well-being, other possible options in the face of the current crisis of modern industrial civilization, it is perhaps closing the door to the possibility of continuity of human life on Earth.

Notes

1   Fondo Monetario Internacional (2007), *Perspectivas de la Economía Mundial. Desarrollo y Desigualdad*, p. 159.

2   CEPAL (2013), *Panorama Social de América Latina*, p. 23, Santiago de Chile.

3   Oxfam (2014), *Working for the Few. Political Capture and Economic Inequality*, Oxfam Briefing Paper 178; OECD (2011), 'Growing Income Inequality in OECD Countries: What Drives it and How can Policy Tackle it?', p. 19. Available at: www.oecd.org/els/social/inequality.

4   CEPAL, *Panorama Social*, p. 40. The data refers to 21 countries in Latin America and the Caribbean.

5   Ibid., p. 200.

6   CEPAL, *Panorama Social*, pp. 17, 55.

7   Ibid., p. 80.

8   Ibid., p. 82.

9   This is not a small minority of the overall population. 'The indigenous population represents from 8% to 15% of the total population of the region while Afro-descendants,

including mulattos represent about 30%.' 'There are at least three countries in the region where the indigenous population accounts for more than 50% of the total (Peru, Bolivia and Guatemala), and at least a dozen countries where the Afro-descendants and mulattos represent more than 50%' (Álvaro Bello and Marta Rangel [2002], 'La equidad y la exclusión de los pueblos indígenas y afrodescendientes en América Latina y el Caribe', *Revista de la CEPAL*, 76). These demographic estimates depend on the source as well as on the criteria used to define ethnic groups (language, skin color, self-identification). Jhon Antón and Fabiana Del Popolo (2009), 'Visibilidad estadística de la población afrodescendiente de América Latina: Aspectos conceptuales y metodológicos', in *Afrodescendientes en América Latina y el Caribe: del reconocimiento estadístico a la realización de derechos*, Serie Población y Desarrollo, 87, CEPAL-Unión Europea, Santiago de Chile. According to the 2000 census, there were 75 million Afro-descendants in Brazil, accounting for 45% of the population. Ibid., p. 33.

10   See some of their essays in: Edgardo Lander (ed.) (2000), *La Colonialidad del Saber: Eurocentrismo y Ciencias Sociales. Perspectivas Latinoamericanas*, UNESCO, Universidad Central de Venezuela, Caracas.

11   Aníbal Quijano, 'Colonialidad del poder, eurocentrismo y América Latina', in Lander, *La Colonialidad del Saber.*

12   Aníbal Quijano (2000), 'Colonialidad del poder y clasificación social', *Journal of World-Systems Research*, 11(2).

13   Pablo González Casanova (2006), 'El colonialismo interno', in Pablo González Casanova, *Sociología de la explotación,* Consejo Latinoamericano de Ciencias Sociales, Buenos Aires.

14   Rodolfo Stavenhagen (1998), *Derecho Indígena y derechos humanos en América Latina*, Instituto Interamericano de Derechos Humanos, El Colegio de México, México, p. 24.

15   See Catherine Walsh (2008), *Interculturalidad y Plurinacionalidad: Elementos para el debate constituyente*, Universidad Andina Simón Bolívar, Sede Ecuador, Quito.

16   CEPAL (2009), *Afrodescendientes en América Latina y el Caribe: del reconocimiento estadístico a la realización de derechos*, series Población y Desarrollo, 87, Santiago de Chile, p. 17.

17   'Deconstrucción, transformación y construcción de nuevos escenarios de las prácticas de la Afroamericanidad', en Daniel Mato (ed.) (2001), *Estudios latinoamericanos sobre cultura y transformaciones sociales en tiempos de globalización 2*, CLACSO, Buenos Aires, p. 83. 'In Latin America, one of the most important cases related to land rights of Afro-descendants were the Quilombo or Afro-Brazilian rural communities, which were called "Quilombo". Quilombos emerged in the colonial period and were territories of refuge for slaves that had escaped from the plantations. These "liberated" areas were post traumatic spaces from which Afro-Brazilians sought to reconstitute autonomous forms of government and social organization, opposed to Portuguese slavery. In colonial Brazil, the Quilombos came to occupy enormous territorial sections of the country, being one of the most important Quilombo dos Palmares in Pernambuco, led by Zumbi, an icon of the black movement in Brazil today, that was defeated in 1695.' (CEPAL, *Afrodescendientes en América Latina y el Caribe*, p. 77).

18   United Nations (2001), World Conference against Racism, Racial Discrimination, Xenophobia and Related Intolerance, Durban, 2001, paragraph 34.

19   Ibid., p. 26.

20   Ibid., p. 85.

21   ECLAC (2012), 'Exports of primary products as percentage of total exports', in *Statistical Yearbook for Latin America and the Caribbean 2012,* Santiago de Chile, p. 101.

22   Maristella Svampa (2012), 'Consenso de los commodities, giro ecoterritorial y pensamiento crítico en América Latina', *OSAL*, año XIII, 32, Consejo Latinoamericano de Ciencias Sociales,.

23   *Declaración del ALBA desde el Pacífico*, XII Cumbre de Jefes de Estado y de Gobierno del ALBA-TCP, Guayaquil, 30 de julio de 2013.

24   Alí Rodríguez Araque (2014), 'Recursos naturales como eje dinámico de la estrategia de UNASUR', *ALAI, América Latina en Movimiento*, Quito. Available at: http://cancilleria.gob.ec/wp-content/uploads/2013/07/declaracion-alba-guayaquil-julio-2013.pdf.

25   Álvaro García Linera, Geopolítica de la Amazonía. Poder hacendal-patrimonial y acumulación capitalista, Vicepresidencia del Estado y Presidencia de la Asamblea Legislativa Plurinacional, La Paz, 2012; Las tensiones creativas de la revolución. La quinta fase del proceso de cambio. Vicepresidencia del Estado y Presidencia de la Asamblea Legislativa Plurinacional, La Paz, 2011; República del Ecuador, Consejo Nacional de Planificación, Plan Nacional para el Buen Vivir 2009–2013, Quito, 2009.

26   Fernando Coronil Ímber (2013), 'El Estado mágico. Naturaleza, dinero y modernidad en Venezuela', *Editorial Alfa*, Caracas, p. 82.

27   Pablo Samaniego, María Cristina Vallejo and Joan Martinez-Alier (n.d.), *Déficit Comercial y Déficit Físico en Sudamérica*. FLACSO, Ecuador e ICTA, Universitat Autònoma de Barcelona.

28   Pierre Salama (2012), 'China-Brasil: Industrialización y "Desindustrialización Temprana"', *Cuadernos de Conomía*, 31(56), Universidad Nacional de Colombia, Bogotá.

29   The displacement of communities from their territories in the name of 'progress' and 'development' is not of course just a rural phenomenon, as can be seen from the massive modernization projects carried out in Brazilian cities in preparation of the 2014 World Cup and the 2016 Olympics.

30   Samaniego et al., *Déficit Comercial*, p. 13.

31   Ibid., p. 16.

32   Biocapacity is '... the area of land and productive oceans actually available to produce renewable resources and absorb CO_2 emissions' (WWF [2012], *Living Planet Report 2012 Biodiversity, Biocapacity and Better Choices*. Zoological Society of London, Global Footprint Network and European Space Agency, p. 8).

33   'The Ecological Footprint tracks the area of biologically productive land and water required to provide the renewable resources people use, and includes the space needed for infrastructure and vegetation to absorb waste carbon dioxide (CO_2)' (Ibid., p. 36).

34   Ibid., p. 8.

35   Ibid., p. 43.

36   Ibid., p. 57. 'The Living Planet Index is a composite indicator that measures changes in the size of wildlife populations to indicate trends in the overall state of global biodiversity' (ibid., p. 20).

37   Ibid.

17

Inequitable Access to Citizenship in Democratic States: An Exploration of the Limits of Gendered Social Policies for the Attainment of Gender Equality

Grace Khunou

Although gender equality is central to the attainment of democratic states, its realization in conceptions of citizenship in democratic states has been marred with complications. Access to citizenship rights is most often unequally experienced due to unequal power dynamics emanating from racial, gendered and socio-economic factors. As a result of these factors women and men's experiences of democratic citizenship is a site of struggle and constant negotiation. Through a gendered analysis of social welfare policies and health policies in Southern Africa, this paper will illustrate how challenges with access to citizenship rights limits democratic governments' ability to attain gender equality.

Introduction

The interest of this paper is to illustrate how through normative universalizing notions of what it means to be a woman or man, the state shapes in limited ways what women and men need to experience democratic citizenship. The state has been conceived of in many contested ways. These conceptions vary and are influenced by the socio-economic and political context of the country in question. Among these conceptions are notions of the state as patriarchal, militaristic, welfaristic, developmental, bureaucratic, regulatory, democratic and as gendered (Manicom, 1992; Hassim, 2003; Khunou, 2007). These notions of the state are all played out in the regulatory function of the state (Manicom, 1992), which according to Mann (1984: 112) are contained in four main elements of the state:

1. Differentiated set of institutions and personnel; 2. Centrality, in the sense that political relations radiate outwards from a center; 3. Territorially demarcated area, over which it exercises; 4. A monopoly of authoritative binding rule-making, backed-up by a monopoly of the means of physical violence.

These elements speak to the fact that states hold power (Mann, 1984); this is true even though there is contestation with regards to how this power is used and conceived.

Mann's (1984) fourth element of binding rule-making is enacted through the making of policies and legislation (Khunou, 2007), which through an analysis of how they have been made, issues they signify and most importantly how they are implemented, illustrates a gendering of women and men. Manicom (1992: 450) suggests that, 'state practices and categorizations define, delimit and assign gender through constructions of "the domestic" – be it the household, the family, the tribe'; and through work, the provision of welfare and in how livelihoods are structured (Mosoetsa, 2011). Significantly, Manicom (1992: 450) illustrates that these practices and classifications, 'are ongoing and shifting constructions, varying between class, race, culture and state policy'. In the South African context, the varied experiences of state are intensified by the structural problems emanating from its apartheid history.

The notion of the state as gendered is widely held as true (Liddle, 1996; Khunou, 2007; Manicom, 1992). This gendering is reported to be in line with the institutionalization of what MacKinnon (1983) refers to as 'male power'. That is the use of law and state policies to institutionalize the ideals that signify 'masculine' thinking and ways of doing things. To indicate how this works Liddle (1996) indicates that 'the State coercively and authoritatively constitutes the social order in the interest of men as a gender, through its legitimizing norms, relations to society, and substantive policies'. Although this is somewhat true as shown in research (Liddle, 1996; Khunou, 2007; Manicom, 1992), it is not however, true for all men in similar ways. The gender question which accompanies state building also involves a differentiation of masculinities (Liddle, 1996). This acknowledgment of heterogeneity indicates the need to demonstrate how gender is a useful analytical tool in helping us understand the different life experiences of men rather than take it for granted that all men benefit equally from patriarchy because they are men (Khunou, 2007; Manicom, 1992).

To assume a fixed opposition between men and women suppresses the diversity within each of those binary categories, invariably allowing normative or essentialist gender definitions to infuse our understandings. (Manicom, 1992: 454)

Rather gender, because it is socially constructed, cannot behave in the same way across time and space (Oyewumi, 1997).

This chapter argues that South Africa's post-apartheid policies position women and men in both ways that continue and discontinue apartheid and colonial hegemonic gender ideals. More than 20 years after the first democratic elections in SA, we see discontinuities and continuities in how inequalities have been experienced in relation to access to citizenship rights. During apartheid, race was signified in how access to social being was defined; in post democratic SA, although there has been a shift towards inclusion of previously excluded racial groups through for example the growth of the black middle class (Khunou, 2015; Krige, 2012) and revisions of other social policies, these have however failed to provide full access to full citizenship as unemployment and underemployment continue to increase (Alexander and Wale, 2013). As a result, the attainment of democracy at an individual level continues to be a struggle. This I argue is true for particularly black men with regards to access to health as a democratic right. I argue elsewhere that men's health care needs are not signified (Khunou, 2014), illustrating how health policies are largely silent on men's needs or gendered and not useful where these needs are acknowledged.

Although gender inclusion in social policies is important and seen as such by policy makers where an attempt is made to acknowledge the impact of gender on social life and thus socio-economic needs, problematic gender assumptions still pervade such documents. However, because these inclusions happen in a context of continuing racial inequality and new class divisions especially among blacks, their reach is limited and thus making the attainment of democracy weak.

Democracy and access to citizenship

Democracy is ideally defined as, 'government by the people as a whole rather than by any section, class or interest within it' (Scruton, 1982). The idea of the people is problematic as it might mean the acts of particular interest groups. Still there are certain core distinctions that could be used or are used to identify democracies. Scruton (1982) identifies voting, representation, constitutionalism and in a more general sense, institutions of accountability that make such a system possible. Again, democracies promise its citizens a number of fundamental rights which includes freedom of speech, right to equal opportunity (Dahl, 1998) and what Marshall (1998) refers to as citizenship rights. Citizenship rights according to Marshall include political, economic and social rights, which are significant for access to freedom, that is, 'liberty of the person, freedom of speech, thought, and faith, the right to own property and to conclude valid contracts, and the right to justice' (Marshall, 1998: 94). Limitations with these rights are linked to whether the spaces to invoke them are available, for example if you can't afford an attorney there are limitations as to how far you can access your right to justice. Again, the exclusionary history of the development of these rights still lingers in how class, race and gender are signified in access to citizenship and thus democracy.

Shafir (1998) illustrates that the development of citizenship changes as social conditions change; so does the importance of different components of this concept. According to Lallo (1998: 440), 'citizenship is the set of practices that define membership in society and consequently shape the flow of resources to persons and groups. The political, civil and social components of citizenship are closely interwoven'. Marshall (1998) maintains that citizenship is more of a status than it is a value in itself; this is especially true with regards to access to formal political rights, like representation, freedom of expression and association. These rights, although vital to the survival of a democracy, fail to represent the totality of freedoms that are necessary for a true democracy to work. They should be accompanied by economic and social rights which citizens need if they are to exercise their political rights. Therefore, having the constitution that protects your rights is insignificant if you are unable to access these rights through employment and access to social services like health. The inequalities created by market capitalism as we are experiencing it now through increased unemployment and underemployment limits the democratic potential of a democracy (Dahl, 1998).

Masculinity and the state

Masculinity, since Connell's seminal publication *Masculinities* in 1995, has been widely studied. In South Africa, this is true in the works of Ratele (2008, 2009, 2013), Morrell (1998, 2001) and Khunou (2007, 2009, 2013, 2014) to name but a few. What is evident from these studies is an agreement that there isn't a single heterogeneous masculinity but multiple masculinities. Ratele (2009, 2013) takes the argument further to speak of the idea of ruling masculinities and subordinate men, which rightfully unpacks the varied positions men occupy. Ratele (2013: 253) specifically speaks to how young black men, 'generally do not have social power and wealth' and therefore they are, 'marginalized also because of, amongst others, skin colour, little or no income, level of education, nationality, and language'. This then importantly denotes that although their gender is significant in social positioning, it is not the only signifier of one's status and life experience.

Khunou (2007) in a study of the maintenance system and fatherhood indicates that the hegemonic ideal of masculinity is instituted in state policies and practices and this does not necessarily speak to all masculinities, but to a 'particular variety of masculinity to which others – among them young and effeminate as well as homosexual men – are subordinated' (Carrigan et al., 1985: 587). This then suggests that in its policies and programs on health the South African state caters to the needs of a few men – that which could be assumed to fall within hegemonic masculinity – which is a masculinity that, 'represents a set of cultural ideals that are constructed, defended and contested' (Morrell et al., 2012: 22). Therefore, the state should be understood as constituted and reconstituted in ways that ever-presently exclude and include (Liddle, 1996). Even though this is what is apparent from the analysis of SA health policies, one would be mistaken to assume a 'pre-existing, unitary category of "the state" with a coherent ruling project and essential functions and interests' (Manicom, 1992: 455). As Khunou (2014) indicates, the health context in SA is complex and undoubtedly not coherent in providing health for men. Khunou (2014) indicates that health inequalities between women and men and between those on private medical aid and those who depend on public health are stark. The unfulfilled health needs of men who are mostly unemployed and 'poor' goes against the normative conception of men as not in need of health and man as a homogenous group.

Following on from similar thinking, this chapter will illustrate, through a presentation of men's experiences of health practices and access challenges, that the state in its normative conception of man contributes to the problems with health and therefore fails to provide space for men to fully engage as citizens with regards to access to their health. This chapter will allow us to see that the state is 'incoherent in its practices' (Mitchell, 1999) and therefore confirm that it is multi-faceted, and therefore difficult to conceptualize as a single consistent entity with unquestionable autonomy. Hassim (2003, quoted in Khunou 2007) rightly shows that, 'the state does not simply reflect gender inequality but plays a decisive role through its practices in constituting them'.

Method

The data informing this chapter is drawn from a bigger study on men and health undertaken in Polokwane and Johannesburg. However, this chapter is based on six interviews with men from Johannesburg. Johannesburg is home to about 3 million people and is the industrial and commercial heartland of South Africa (Beall et al., 2000). Beall et al. (2000: 110) go on to indicate that, 'high unemployment and a declining manufacturing sector in Johannesburg have reduced the demand for unskilled and, to some extent, semi-skilled, labour, resulting in lower wages for those in unskilled work and 29 per cent unemployment in Gauteng province as a whole. Africans are the worst affected'. The most recent statistics for unemployment in Gauteng indicates very little progress of 26% (StatsSA, 2014).

The study utilized both qualitative and quantitative research approaches and was interested in giving critical attention to the notion that men engage in limited help-seeking behaviour (Galdas et al., 2005). Again, this study was influenced by research evidence that suggests that serious health hazards experienced in industrial societies are more pronounced for men (Khunou, 2014; Chopra and Sanders 2004). Ethical clearance for this study was obtained from the Wits Ethics Committee with human subjects.

The quantitative data was collected between July and September of 2011, and at the end of this period 300 surveys had been collected between Gauteng and Limpopo. The rationale for using mixed methods is drawn from the principle that there are strengths in the use of both qualitative and quantitative methods, and that they complement each other. Quantitative methods have been mostly used to examine this topic but because of the limitations associated with them such studies have led to limited insights. Galdas et al. (2005: 620) maintain that, 'the body of research comparing help-seeking behaviour between genders notably lacks any qualitative methods of inquiry'. Consequently, this study will create the much-needed balance by using both methods.

This chapter however draws its discussion from the qualitative data; interviews were conducted in 2012 in both Johannesburg and Polokwane. At the end of the fieldwork process, 21 interviews had been collected with men in Johannesburg and 22 in Polokwane. The interviews were conducted with men between the ages of 25 and 55 and included men from the Black African, White, Indian and Coloured race groups. Again, the sample of men included men with varied educational and employment statuses. The inclusion of men from all racial groups in the study was influenced by the question of, 'whether there are masculine commonalities between men and how these are played out under different social circumstances' (Galdas et al., 2005). This inclusion was also influenced by the idea of difference put forward by conceptualizations of masculinity as multiple and the significance of the socio-economic context in these understandings of difference; this is succinctly captured by Ratele (2013: 253) when he suggests that, 'gender is not the only factor constitutive of the form that (subordinate young Black) manhood assumes' as this is also true for other forms of masculinities as well.

The six interviews presented here were analysed using thematic content analysis. And the emergent themes are reported in the chapter in a way that, 'forms a coordinated picture or an explanatory model' (Bazeley, 2009) that is useful to build and support a coherent argument. The names of the participants whose data is used in this chapter have been changed, and pseudonyms are used to protect their identity.

Discussion and findings

The discussion that follows is based on men's experiences of the provision of health care. This is presented through the discussion of two important and interrelated themes – that is service delivery in its broadest sense and the treatment received from mostly public health facilities – and this speaks directly to nurses, and long queues. These themes are presented in a way that illustrates how the state is experienced by men and how this is not in line with the attainment of democracy which is envisioned in the constitution and the democratic state formation.

Service delivery challenges

One of the biggest challenges to the appreciation of SA democracy has been with multiple experiences of service delivery problems. This has been true with services ranging from water, electricity (Khunou, 2002), maternal and child health (Kerber et al., 2007) and social services (Mosoetsa, 2011) to name but a few. These have been followed by widespread service delivery protests which indicate a continuity in pre-1994 protests (Alexander, 2010). Again, research on service delivery challenges in the health sector address maternal and child health (Kerber et al., 2007), nurses and health policy making and implementation (Walker and Gilson, 2004); and most significantly to broader service delivery challenges in the sector that raises the question of upscaling treatment for HIV (Schneider et al., 2006) and improving the quality of public health delivery. All these indicate that the Department of Health could benefit from a much-needed improvement in the making of health policy and most importantly in provision of health care.

Therefore, the stories of access shared in this section echoes stories shared elsewhere, and are presented in this chapter to illustrate how when the state does not function in line with how it envisions itself in its policies and how it is expected to be by its citizens, there is misalignment which problematizes neutral ideas of citizenship. When asked what government could do to improve hospitals and clinic services, Oratile a young man from Soweto said:

> I think they need to invest more on health services because I think yesterday I read on *New Age* Newspaper so they are investing more money on infrastructure and business instead of investing on education and health care, they like invest less billions on health care and education rather investing on infrastructure which does not make sense to me. (Oratile, October 2012)

Although Oratile did not feel any encouragement from the state to use health facilities like awareness programs and adverts for problematic ailments like cancer, the following contradictory and yet interesting statement was made:

> I think they are doing sufficient because of people are not responding hence I have told you because of our believes and culture that is why most men do not respond to such things they find them nonsensical and demeaning to their culture but they are doing sufficient when it comes to I think let me see on television and adverts and everything that they are doing its more than enough but the response is poor because of what I have mentioned culture and tradition I think is a vast implication when it comes to that. (Oratile, October 2012)

This above quotation is contradictory in that Oratile indicates that *they –* meaning the state – are doing enough, but goes on to subtly question who they are doing enough for, since Oratile does not clearly see his needs catered for in the programs available. The reference to culture is an interesting one here since it denotes that treating men as a homogenous group (Khunou, 2007) is not useful when trying to provide useful health services for them. The question then is who the programs Oratile is referring to are enough for if they are not significant for him and other men who from their cultural perspective the messages provided might be seen as '*nonsensical*'. The concerns raised by Oratile speak to an inconsistency in service provision which is a result of aiming for a citizen that you have not adequately defined. This is particularly so for the homogenized conception of masculinities put forward in health policy (Khunou, 2014). These inconsistencies then lead to a lack of use of public services because according to Oratile, 'the whole aspect from our governing system, that is what discourages me from visiting these, places especially the public sector'.

Oratile's reference to the problematics of the private sector for the attainment of health for men as a citizenship right is interesting as it has implications for the private sector and conceptions of market-linked citizenship rights. The private–public sector debate in relation to health is a contentious one. The private health sector in SA was started by the mining houses and expanded in the 1980s (Coovadia et al., 2009). Although the private health sector is generally seen as better in comparison to the public health sector, 'there is no oversight of quality of care provided by the private sector' (Coovadia et al., 2009: 828). The biggest challenge though with the private vs public health sector conception and provision of health is the income inequality it is based on, where those with medical aids can decide what to access whereas those who might be unemployed and don't have medical aids have no choice; these differences also indicate the deep-seated inequalities that make up SA society. Table 17.1 indicates how the public/private health sector is constituted.

Table 17.1 provides a picture of how health is experienced by those with low income or no income as compared to mainly the employed. In 2011 the South African Gini-coefficient was 0.69 (StatsSA, 2014) and argued to be the highest in the world (International Bank for Reconstruction and Development, 2012). This situation has been exacerbated by the unequal

Table 17.1 South Africa's dual health system

Private Health	Public Health
Cares for 20% of the population	Cares for 82% of the population
Consumes 60% of health expenditure	Consumes 40% of health expenditure
Cost increases in Private Medical aids	Services free to individuals or low cost
Provides world-class facilities	Under resourced
Provides world-class care	Over used
Nurses' high satisfaction with work	Nurses dissatisfied, over worked, underpaid
Nurses adequately resourced to improve the lives of patients	Nurses working conditions unsuitable for adequate provision of health

Sources: Chopra (2004) and Coovadia (2009)

distribution of economic growth that has been the norm during apartheid and continues in democratic South Africa. Even though Oratile is unemployed his experiences illustrate how the market economy influences access to citizenship. His obvious preference for private health services should not be mistaken to illustrate his economic standing but rather his need for dignified access to health care service. He said:

> private practitioners I think private sector and public sector I prefer the private sector its more efficient than the public sector if it's something serious then I will go pay for it rather than go and wait in queues at the clinic. (Oratile, October 2012)

Oratile's response on why he prefers the private doctor compared to the clinic is, 'yes the queues, but it's not only that its more than that those things are the result of the problem' (Oratile, October 2012). However, what is striking with this response is an understanding that waiting in a queue when you know useful service is on its way is something as compared to when you are clear that the problem is deeper. The deeper problem here is articulated as government priorities. Oratile goes on to indicate that reorienting priorities towards human investment is the answer. He said:

> I think this is a national crisis as reiterating there needs to be more investment on health resources and stuff instead of investing on infrastructure and creating jobs whilst people are dying. (Oratile, October 2012)

Nurses and access: Implementation gone wrong

The implementation of policies is significant in how we understand the state as both coherent law and linked to society who participates in reshaping it (Mitchell, 1999). This we see in how implementers of policies are seen to be shaping how the state is conceived and how policies are interpreted (Khunou, 2007). This is true for how nurses as implementers of health policy are conceived. For Muhammed, a young Muslim man from Eldorado Park in Johannesburg, nurses as experienced in the public health sector represent a democratic state gone wrong. He articulated this when he spoke of some of the challenges experienced with treatment in public health facilities as one of the reasons why he does not use them. His view of public health as not working was used to define lack of 'allocative and integrative capacities' (Lallo, 1998) of the health system in his community. This dysfunction of health facilities can be understood as a symbol of his exclusion from citizenship.

This sense of exclusion shared by Muhammed is experienced in a broader context of a shortage of healthcare workers. In a study on the shortage of nurses in seven countries, SA was reported to have a shortage of 32,000 nurses (Oulton, 2006). A variety of old and new factors contribute to this challenge. A few of these factors are reported as: more complex diseases; new infectious diseases; globalization and growing private sector; an aging nursing workforce; and unfavorable work environments (Oulton, 2006). These then have negative effects on healthcare systems and negatively impact how the democratic state, as the Department of Health, is experienced and therefore conceived.

Because of how the nursing profession came about, especially the training of Black nurses as to 'moralise and save the sick and not simply to nurse them' (Coovadia et al., 2009), the relationship they have had with patients has, therefore, been complex as they have been labeled as cruel and their relationship to patients has been reported to be influenced by, 'rudeness, arbitrary acts of unkindness, physical assault and neglect' (Coovadia et al., 2009: 829). Having made a note of that it is important to now indicate how this perception of nurses as rude impacted Muhammed's use of clinics and hospitals in his community. He said:

> Let me be honest, the problem we have with clinics is the staff at the clinics, they are not as friendly as the staff you will get at a private doctor or private clinic. They always have issues, they always have problems helping a person, that is the main problem, we never go there. (Muhammed, March 2012)

He later articulated the main challenge with this staff in the following ways:

> The problem is they come in late, open (the clinic) late, they come in late, they come in 8:30, 9 o-clock then they go for tea whilst we have 20 000 people waiting for them to help them. They will come in help 4 to 5 people most of the time they walk around talking with each other having conversations with each other instead of helping the patients when they come again to help patients its 12 O Clock, its lunch time. They help another 5, 6, 8 people and from there they rush now to help people because its past 12 already ... . (Muhammed, March 2012)

Muhammed, like many other men, would not use a public hospital unless it is absolutely necessary, that is when they have no options. This is not necessarily linked to ideas of masculinities as indicated in other studies (Galdas et al., 2005); rather it is because it is seen as the last place to get decent health service. Muhammed illustrated his views in the following way:

let me be honest, the only time that I will go to a hospital it's when am seriously ill or involved in an accident other than that I will not go to hospital or
advice someone to go to a hospital. The reason why is the same problem – you
go to Baragwaneth for example you come there at 2 o clock in the morning or
let me say you come at this time of the afternoon 5 o clock in the afternoon
they only attend to you 10 o clock which I have experienced myself I was in an
accident around 10 o clock in the morning at night sorry when I woke up about
9, 10 in the morning I was attended then. (Muhammed, March 2012)

Why would one then go there? This is a question Muhammed later raises.
This experience is similar to experiences across the country; where not
only men but women and children face challenging health service situations which eventually discourage even the most ill to use public health
facilities. Will, a young man from Eldorado Park who had been in treatment for prostate cancer at the time of the interview, was happy with the
treatment he received for the cancer; however his general view of public
health was not that positive. He said:

You see you don't get better, you stay the same so when you really have to
go to the doctor and you know sometimes like to go and see a doctor I mean
you thinking of seating in a queue, Haai! Not it just turns you off the minute
you are really sick, but you don't have a choice you will seat there. (Will,
March 2012)

This reluctance to use health facilities because of long queues might explain
the reason why some of the men will self-medicate; for Muhammed when
he has something light like flu, he would 'take flu tablets'; Oratile on
the other hand, completely tries to avoid doctors and says: 'I don't visit
a doctor like often, I am not a doctor person'. He later indicates that he
prefers traditional healers and has a mistrust of doctors. For Will a visit to
a doctor or the clinic is the last resort, he prefers to wait, he, 'stays three to
four days and I would sometimes try to take medication, home medication
when I see it doesn't work I will go to the doctor'. These acts of avoidance
speak to how the health sector is seen and experienced by these men.

Conclusion

In an attempt to understand the intersection of masculinities and the state
from a health perspective, this chapter has addressed multiple themes
from in-depth interviews with men from Johannesburg. The South African
state continues to put forth an idea of a hegemonic and homogenous idea

of masculinity that is not necessarily maintained in how for example the unemployed and or underemployed black man in particular accesses health and thus experiences citizenship. Even though the state might not necessarily be able to provide everyone equal health it has failed to ensure potential for equal health among men and the different genders. Lack of a focus and broad-based transformation with regards to gender and racial equity in the wider economic and social policies leads to these continuities in exclusion.

The chapter argues that the state is never a complete coherent entity but is a constantly shifting and complex body which is both separate and merged with society. In illustrating the heterogeneous nature of masculinities, the chapter also attempted to illustrate that men, like women, experience multiple challenges in their everyday lives and do so also in their attempts to access health. In conclusion, the chapter maintains that the interface between how state policies conceive of men and how these policies are implemented should move from an understanding of the multiplicities of masculine experience and most importantly from the structural challenges that tend to exclude some men from their rights as citizens. Such continued inequality taints the constitutional democracy and its ability to see through redistribution.

Acknowledgements

Data collection for this study was made possible by support from the Carnegie and Mellon Grants. The qualitative data was collected by Paseka Kgolopane and the quantitative data was collected by Tshepo Masupye, Listen Yenge, Ochard Banda, Mike Mogaoswa and Musa Malebela. I would also like to thank all the participants who shared their stories and time for the benefit of this study.

References

Alexander, P. (2010) 'Rebellion of the Poor: South Africa's Service Delivery Protests – A Preliminary Analysis'. *Review of African Political Economy*, 37(123): 25–40.

Alexander, P. and Wale, K. (2013) 'Underemployment: Too Poor to be Unemployed', in P. Alexander, C. Ceruti, K. Motseke, M. Phadi, and K. Wale, *Class in Soweto*. Pietermaritzburg: University of KwaZulu Natal Press.

Bazeley, P. (2009) 'Analysing Qualitative Data: More than Identifying Themes'. *Malaysian Journal of Qualitative Research*, 2: 6–22.

Beall, J., Crankshaw, O. and Parnell, S. (2000) 'Local Government, Poverty Reduction and Inequality in Johannesburg'. *Environmental and Urbanization*, 12(1): 107–22.

Carrigan, T., Connell, B. and Lee, J. (1985) 'Toward a new sociology of masculinity'. *Theory and Society*, 14(5): 551–604.

Chopra, M. and Sanders, D. (2004) 'From Apartheid to globalisation: Health and social change in South Africa'. *Hygiene Internationalis* 4(1): 153–74.

Connell, R.W. (1995) *Masculinities*. Cambridge: Polity Press.

Coovadia, H., Jewkes, R., Barron, P., Sanders, D. and McIntyre, D. (2009) 'The Health and Health System of South Africa: Historical Roots of Current Public Health Challenges'. *Health in South Africa Series, The Lancet* (374): 817–34.

Dahl, R.A. (1998) *On Democracy*. London: Yale University Press.

Galdas, P.M., Cheater, F. and Marshall, P. (2005) 'Men and Health Help-seeking behavior'. *Literature Review*, in *Journal of Advanced Nursing*, 49(6): 616–23.

Hassim, S. (2003) 'The gender pact and democratic consolidation: Institutionalizing gender equality in the South African state'. *Feminist Studies*, 29(3): (Autumn) 504–28.

International Bank for Reconstruction and Development (2012) *South African Economic Update: Focus on Inequality of Opportunity*. Washington: The World Bank.

Kerber, J.K., de Graft-Johnson, E., Bhutta, A.Z., Okong, P., Starrs, A. and Lawn, E.J. (2007) 'Continuum of Care for Maternal, Newborn, and Child Health: From Slogan to Service Delivery'. Review. *The Lancet*, 370: 1358–69.

Khunou, G. (2002) 'Massive cut offs cost recovery and electricity service in Diepkloof, Soweto', in D.A. McDonald and J. Page (eds). *Cost Recovery and the Crisis of Service Delivery in South Africa*. Cape Town: Human Science Research Council.

Khunou, G. (2007) 'Maintenance and Changing Masculinities as Sources of Gender Conflict in Contemporary Johannesburg'. PhD thesis, University of the Witwatersrand.

Khunou, G. (2009) 'Paying your Way and Playing with the Girls: Township Men and Meaning of Manhood'. *South African Labour Bulletin*, 35: 48–50.

Khunou, G. (2013) 'Men's Health: An Analysis of Representations of Men's Health in the Sowetan Newspaper'. *Communicatio*, 38(2): 182–93.

Khunou, G. (2014) *Are Men's Health Care Needs Important? A Critical Analysis of the South African Health Policy*. HSRC Press.

Khunou, G. (2015) 'What Middle Class? The shifting and dynamic nature of class position'. *Development Southern Africa*, 32(1): 90–103.

Krige, D. (2012) 'Histories and Changing Dynamics of Housing, Social Class and Social Mobility in Black Johannesburg'. *Alternation*, 19(1): 19–45.

Lallo, K. (1998) 'Citizenship and Place: Spatial Definitions of Oppression and Agency in South Africa'. *Africa Today*. 45(3–4): 439–40.

Liddle, A.M. (1996) 'State, Masculinities and Law: Some Comments on Gender and English State Formaion'. *British Journal of Criminology*, 36(3): 361–79.

MacKinnon, C.A. (1983) 'Feminism, Marxism, method, and the state: Toward feminist jurisprudence'. *Signs*, 8(4) (Summer): 635–58.

Manicom, L. (1992) 'Ruling Relations: Rethinking State and Gender in South African History'. *The Journal of African History*, 33(3): 441–65.

Mann, M. (1984) 'The Autonomous Power of the State: Its Origins, Mechanisms and Results'. *European Journal of Sociology*, 28(2): 185–213.

Marshall, T.H. (1998) 'Citizenship and Social Class', in G. Shafir, *The Citizenship Debates*. London: University of Minnesota Press.

Mitchell, T. (1999) 'Society, Economy, and the State Effect', in G. Steinmetz, *State/Culture: State Formation after the Cultural Turn*. London: Cornell University Press.

Morrell, R. (1998) 'The New Man?', *Agenda*, 37: 7–12.

Morrell, R. (2001) 'The Times of Change: Men and Masculinity in South Africa', in R. Morrell (ed.), *Changing Men in Southern Africa*. Pietermaritzburg: University of Natal Press.

Morrell, R., Jewkes, R. and Lindegger, G. (2012) 'Hegemonic masculinity/masculinities in South Africa: Culture, power, and gender politics'. *Men and Masculinities*, 15(1): 11–30.

Mosoetsa, S. (2011) *Eating from One Pot: The Dynamics of Survival in Poor South African Households*. Johannesburg: Wits Press.

Oulton, A.J. (2006) 'The Global Nursing Shortage: An Overview of Issues and Actions'. *Policy, Politics & Nursing Practice*, 7(3): 34S–39S.

Oyewumi, O. (1997) *The Invention of Women: Making an African Sense of Western Gender Discourses*. United States: University of Minnesota Press.

Ratele, K. (2008) 'Analysing Males in Africa: Certain Useful Elements in Considering Ruling Masculinities'. *African and Asian Studies*, 7: 515–36.

Ratele, K. (2009) 'Sexuality as a Constitutive of Whiteness in South Africa'. *NORA – Nordic Journal of Feminist and Gender Research*, 17(3): 158–74.

Ratele, K. (2013) 'Subordinate Black South African Men without Fear'. *Cahiers d'Etudes africaines* LIII (1–2): 209–10, 247–68.

Schneider, H., Blaauw, D., Gilson, L., Chabikuli, C. and Goudge, J. (2006) 'Health Systems and Access to Antiretroviral Drugs for HIV in Southern Africa: Service Delivery and Human Resources Challenges'. *Reproductive Health Matters*, 14(27): 12–23.

Scruton, R. (1985) *A Dictionary of Political Thought*. London: Macmillan.

Shafir, G. (1998) 'Introduction: The Evolving Tradition of Citizenship', in G. Shafir, *The Citizenship Debates*. London: University of Minnesota Press.

StatsSA (2014) *Poverty Trends in South Africa: An Examination of Absolute Poverty between 2006 and 2011*. Government of South Africa.

Walker, L. and Gilson, L. (2004) '"We are Bitter but we are Satisfied": Nurses as street-level Bureaucrats in South Africa', *Social Science & Medicine*, 59: 1251–61.

18

Collective Rights to Life and New Social Justice: The Case of the Bolivian Indigenous Movement

Paulo Henrique Martins

Introduction: Limits of liberalism to create new rules to associational life

To explore current interest in new collective and community rights that emerged through collective struggles, stripping the limits of liberalism perspective to solve systemic imbalances as current violence and inequality, we suggest Bolivia's case of political pluralism and community rights. For us, this case is important as it reflects the emergence of new collective rights focusing on human aspects and inspired by the perspectives of good life and common goods based on social justice and egalitarianism. Bolivia's case helps us to reflect about the limits of capitalistic private rights to rule the current complexity of global societies.

In this sense, we must underline that the current utopia of modernization of many societies in the world, particularly in Latin America, is marked by the failure of capitalism and private power ideology to inspire new social and cultural institutions marked by complexity and pluralism.[1] As Walzer stresses, 'liberalism in its standard contemporary version is an inadequate theory and a disabled political practice' (Walzer, 2004: xi). It is inadequate because autonomous individuals can only ensure a part of the story of democratic politics and liberalism is unable to deal with struggles produced by involuntary association. The failure of liberalism to rule complex societies and individual survival that necessarily belongs to diverse and complex networks and cultural communities expresses the shortcomings of liberal institutions and the dogma of individualism.

Deepening the understanding of limits of capitalist private rights, it is important to stress that the difference between private and community rights are not simply dualistic (individual versus community), revealing, instead, diverse possibilities to rule human institutions out of capitalist doctrine. On the one hand, the ideology of liberalism was founded on the illusion of market personal interest and voluntary association to rule life. On the other hand, the recognition of collective and community rights requires some affective, moral and aesthetic preconditions produced by the necessary 'symbolic construction of community' in present days (Cohen, 1985).

Thus, as we move in this direction we realize the urgency to consider some successful experiences that succeeded in overcoming liberal doctrines and individualism to create new rules to associational life. This collective view, as we testify in present Bolivian experience, demonstrates the value of state and public policies aimed at recognizing individuals and groups from their cultural, religious, linguistic and ethnic particularities that cannot be reduced to one another.

This kind of recognition, based on collective rights, brings to mind Honneth's recent book on the right to democracy, where the author suggests that effective social justice must be founded on an ethic of democracy, that is, a social liberty mediated by mutual recognition inspiring intersubjective equality. Because, for him, individual autonomy only exists in social relationships (Sobottka, 2013: 165–6). This way, Honneth's new understanding of recognition is confirmed by Bolivia's social movements.

These new community rights help show that liberalism's opposition between interest and passion, particularly in the political field, is wrong because 'passionate intensity has its legitimate place in the social world, not only when we are getting money but also when we are choosing allies and engaging opponents' (Walzer, 2004: 126). These community rights are also important to demonstrate that trivialization of rituals by individual rationality and by consumerism do not help to strengthen social links. Instead, rituals are very strategic to deepen individual and group consciousness about alliances and to define collective goals (Cohen, 1985: 15).

Bolivia's case suggests a new hierarchy about social justice that underlines the priority given to collective and natural rights inspiring public policy management. To present this case we must establish some points: first, the importance of Bolivia's case to transform colonial peasant life to an original ethnic and social movement. Secondly, the reconstruction of territory meaning produced by a new grasp of political autonomy and legal pluralism. Thirdly, the contribution of the indigenous movement in enlarging the ecological understanding of right systems, releasing a postcolonial original criticism based on *Pacha Mama*

(Mother Earth) symbolism. Fourth, the renewal of politics and society from the symbolic approach. Fifth, some elements to think about modernity beyond market limits.

The importance of Bolivia's case to transform colonial peasant life to an original ethnic and social movement

The 1952 revolution in Bolivia produced the agrarian reform, nationalized mineral resources and extended the right to vote to peasants, contributing to progressively transforming the coloniality. Since then, the indigenous movement has advanced and, as Guimarães notes (2011: 39) ethnic identity, built by anti-colonial reaction, has overcome union class identity. In this context, attempts to integrate indigenous peoples as citizens in a homogeneous national state failed. Instead, we observed a political change founded on affirmation of ethnic identity resulting in a major state reform taking place over the following decades.

From the 1970s, these changes became more evident, particularly by the emergence of the Katarist movement,[2] reflecting new political mobilizations by nationalist movements that had emerged in the revolution from 1952. The Katarist movement contributed also to the emergence of a new generation of indigenous intellectuals who do not relate only to the workers movement but also to youth movements (Hashizume, 2010: 89).

Between 1980 and 1990, the social players enlarged the class identification to form new social movements organized from an ethnic and community identity. Manifestations such as 'Dignity, territory and life' (a 600km march toward La Paz in 1990) seriously questioned the Nation–State idea. The State was then obliged to consider, progressively, both the indigenous peoples' rights and a national multiculturalism program. Some people testify that the actions adopted by the State to solve these pressures had some unexpected consequences, helping political self-representation of indigenous communities. So, interethnic organizations managed to integrate State administration and the new local authorities imposed interethnic relationships as an objective condition of the Bolivian political system (Guimarães, 2011: 337). This change in the power system gave rise to important collective rights (*derechos colectivos*). These new claims differ from traditional citizenship rights because collective and community property have more value than private property. The refounding of the national state into a plurinational state resulted also from the rupture of traditional oligarchic power and considering indigenous 'altersystemic' reaction in favour of autonomy and differentiation. It is a novelty when we consider that struggles against colonial national systems failed in diverse countries before Bolivia because social movements did not clearly realize the role of collective rights in a new democratic order. This conclusion is offered by the reading of Stavenhagen's *Conflictos étnicos y estado nacional* (Stavenhagen, 2000).

In the past decades, particularly after Evo Morales' election in 2002, Bolivian interethnic movements advanced significant political and institutional reforms turning *de facto* autonomy into legal autonomy that was enshrined in the 2009 Bolivian Constitution. Nowadays, for example, when someone asks supporters of ethnic movements to clarify the meaning of Good Living (*Buen Vivir*), they answer that 'the constitution must be respected' (*hay que aplicar la constitución*) (Stefanoni, 2012: 16). This means that epistemological dispute over the collective meaning of 'development' must be shifted from the linguistic field to the political one.

Thus, Bolivia's experiences are the expression of a new postcolonial consciousness emerging on the borders of the world system, leading social movements to deal with modernization programs founded on the privatization of collective and natural resources and on the destruction of memories and traditional knowledge, a practice that Santos correctly defined as an epistemicide (Santos and Meneses, 2009).

Postcolonial Bolivian consciousness progressively took the form of a social and intellectual movement directed at new collective rights that legitimate State and Nation reforms. These changed the nature of modern republican institutions marked by coloniality that influenced the separation between private and public rights to prioritize the former. This duality between private and public was replaced by a legal system that favors collective rights and participation in political decisions, particularly the right to life that inspires other rights, such as: ethnic recognition, republican citizenship, self-management. This helped strengthen participation at some levels of decision-making in political power. Private rights were not prohibited but reshaped to suit the new legal system inspired by collective rights.[3]

The reconstruction of the meaning of territory produced by a new grasp of political autonomy and legal pluralism

In Aymara's philosophy two notions are worthy of attention: territory and autonomy. Both played important roles in the new indigenous utopia and to rethink the system of rights. Then, after the colonizer refused Amerindian identity for centuries, reducing them only to poor peasants, we saw a rebirth of old local memories that were updated through new tactics of struggles. The current requests for autonomy emerge as an anti-colonial reaction that underlines indigenous movements in their new political manifestation. Autonomy means demands from local communities for self-government and to express their rights to elect representatives that have legal powers and capabilities to legislate (Rivera, 2010: 59).

On the other hand, the notion of territory has also a special meaning for local communities, particularly with respect to the role of the colonial state that traditionally denied the indigenous the right to manage their own lands. So, the deconstruction of the Western notion of territory that inspired the formation of the Nation–State, helped indigenous communities to look for their archaic collective meanings to face new political challenges. This redefinition of territory is founded on an understanding of a space and time relationship anchored not on centralized colonial power, but, rather on social and local power which favors the strengthening of Aymara's autonomy. In parallel, there are also other definitions of territory helping to reinforce the invention of politics. We can stress the symbolic definition of territory based on the old meaning of the links between society and nature (that enlarge the meaning of society) and the animist one, from Andean tradition, that focuses on the Earth as a living being. Here, the Earth is known as '*Pacha Mama*', '*madre tierra*' or Mother Earth which is considered the only legitimate entity to create the collective belief of Good Living (*Buen Vivir*).

Yet there is a definition of territory that is related to the idea of control and power, according to which the indigenous organizations consider local assemblies to be the most important decision-making instance when it comes to common welfare (Rivera, 2010: 53–7). This last definition contributes to complexifying political decisions as central governments are obliged to lead negotiations at different levels of power, making it necessarily more difficult for central and local powers to reach agreements on public policies.

Deconstruction and reconstruction of territory meanings produced by a new grasp of political autonomy in Bolivia, led interethnic Bolivian movements to recognize the role of legal pluralism in ensuring the diversity of rationalities and knowledge. Some concepts such as interculturality, diversity, recognition and inclusion became central to ensure pluralism (Rivero, 2011: 372). Further, although power decisions became more complex and uncertain, it is true that the Bolivian political system had made progress in the last decades as confirmed by the moving from a monolithic State to an original pluralistic State, impacting on the management of territory. Consequently, the Constitution of 2009 recognizes Original Peasant Indigenous Autonomy (AIOC) as one of the four kinds of autonomy besides departmental, regional and municipal autonomies, helping to advance the debate in indigenous organization field (Rivero, 2011: 51).

It seems, then, that the changes in Bolivian political imaginary do not represent an isolated event, expressing, instead, a significant epistemological revision of postcolonial system built by the Westernization of the world. This way, it is possible to state that the reasons for this indigenous imaginary shift are anchored on theoretical and practical, moral, ecological, economic and political claims.

The Western anti-utilitarian approach to solidarity contributes, furthermore, to enlarging the debate about development models and categories used to define material and symbolic wealth. This approach emerges precisely at a moment when territorial monopoly of the colonial State to manage the violence is challenged. For example, the creation of plurinational State challenging homogeneous national identity, favors decentralization and local power authority. This change of the relationship between territory and power pose some difficulties to the central government, but it proves the role of political and social pressures in favor of a necessary power decentralization that ensures expanded participation. These pressures in favor of a new local and cosmopolitan power are spreading to other Latin American countries as we see currently in Brazil.[4]

An ecological understanding criticism based on *Pacha Mama* (Mother Earth) symbolism

Pacha Mama (Pacha = Earth; Mama = mother or Mother Earth) invites us to think about postcoloniality from two approaches: one is symbolic, the other is political. The symbolic one emerged from an image of the human and nature relationship that benefits the ritual interactivity between both elements. But, here, the archaic and mythical representation of nature was replaced by a new postmodern representation that stresses the role of politics in setting a plural epistemology. Moreover, contemporary indigenous representation of life manifests an important ecological reflection that must be seriously considered by social science to organize the moral and cultural criticism of capitalism.

The *Pacha Mama* symbolical approach lead us to rethink Nature not only as a physical element but as a symbolism filled of a pluralistic meaning whose ritualization is central to ensure the survival of community. Here, we could also define Nature as the practical and necessary condition to ensure the alliances between families and individuals. This Amerindian approach is far from the Cartesian representation of society founded on the ontological separation between Human and Nature. Colonization experience taught indigenous community about destructive effects of private property of natural resources and it must be considered an important aspect to anticapitalist criticism.

The anthropological and symbolic importance of *Pacha Mama* lays in the impact of ecological and social representation of Nature to new forms of political and social change, breaking the modern understanding of Nature traditionally marked by a mechanical representation of life. The ecological understanding of Nature pointed out by Bolivian movements updates another factor: the importance of the notion of Gift, an old system of human exchange observed by Marcel Mauss in old societies. Gift theory contributes to clarify Nature as a living being that is an active part together with human beings in the symbolical construction of community. Both Human Beings and Nature must play an equalitarian role to preserve by reciprocity the life and the environment.[5]

The *Pacha Mama* utopia is different from this one called 'living well' that marks the Western style of consumption and private appropriation of wealth. Rather, *Pacha Mama* points out a view of legitimating collective well-being not as an abstract belief, but as a political purpose founded on an anti-utilitarian community experience that denies the reduction of society to market interests. About this, Bolivian sociologists Farah and Gil say:

> The Good Living must be thought in a market society context that integrate an ethical principle structuring another modernity and pointing out the plurality of reality and deepening the renewal of economic, cultural and political thinking, that is, advancing a broader understanding of life. (2012: 105)

Further, the *Pacha Mama* movement is founded not only on a traditional myth. It seems preferable as an altersystemic reaction and a historical innovation from the border of the world system. This myth seems very appropriate as we engage in a reflection on the relationship between material and symbolical wealth that is central to the emergence of Good Living heterotopy. Moreover, it could be also interesting to deepen the comparison between the Aymara heterotopy and the Western one that stresses anti-utilitarian solidarity to postcapitalist possibilities known as 'convivialisme' in French thinking (Caillé et al., 2011).

The *Pacha Mama* symbolism does not represent a novelty because the idea of Mother Earth is shared by many ancient cultures. However, Bolivian symbolism is particularly expressive in underlining the importance that this cultural element had in Bolivia to support a radical criticism against the colonial model based on economic growth. *Pacha Mama* is also of political relevance because its community foundations question private appropriation of vital resources such as water, land and others. In fact, Bolivians consider that natural resources were there before human presence, before indigenous and colonizers, before corporations, and, therefore, these resources continue to be the basis of material and spiritual collective survival. Here, the novelty is the Bolivian ethnic consciousness about the urgency to rethink territory managing the reciprocity between Human Beings and Nature. The old myth is updated by politics and culture. Therefore, we can observe that this linguistic construction is not arbitrary but results from a postmodern and communitarian reaction against capitalist strategies of appropriation and privatization of natural wealth in this area.

Pacha Mama is a metaphor that holds many meanings: it is the living memory of the indigenous tradition; it is the symbolism that gives meaning to collective movement; it is the argument against private appropriation of collective resources; finally, it is the way that politically differentiates ethnic movements from the other social movements when the debate revolves around the National State reform. This image helps to clarify the role of ethnic movements in the dispute that transformed the Bolivian State from a centralized apparatus into a Plurinational State which was validated by the 2009 Constitution.

Pacha Mama is then the symbolism that links tradition and modernity, rural and urban, the colonizers and the old servants, having become a key element indigenous population rely on to rethink society.[6] Thus, Farah and Gil (2012: 105) suggest that 'the Good Living can be thought from the context of a market society that integrate an ethical principle structuring another modernity that values the plurality deepening the renewal of economic, cultural and political thinking'.

The renewal of politic and society from the symbolic approach

The political approach of indigenous postcolonial thinking updates historical memories to seriously challenge the neoliberal development model.

This approach invites us to understand the limits of a domination model based on a private logic, legitimating private appropriation of material wealth by a minority. Indigenous movements help enlarge the understanding of rights' systems, showing the limits of coloniality and the egoistic modern view of life. *Pacha Mama* releases a postcolonial original criticism that shifts the understanding of social struggles from a modern economic approach to a contemporary one that values ethnic community symbolism.

It must be also underlined that the current representation of *Pacha Mama* casts new light on the Bolivian archaic and spiritual representation of politics, contributing to problematizing the material and symbolical conditions of today's development models. In fact, the Good Living (*Buen Vivir*) idea systematized by Aymara's intellectuals of common wealth is different from the individualistic and ethnocentric capitalist view, the Living Well (Farah and Gil, 2012: 100). More precisely, indigenous reaction updates an old and complex community tradition to support an anticapitalist approach that does not deny the market system but claims the self-government right to construct a new common life. *Pacha Mama*'s political meaning, particularly Aymara's one (the more representative ethnic group in this area), focuses on the struggle against the privatization of natural resources that are key to collective survival. Current events have contributed to reinforce indigenous feelings mobilized to update cultural and mystic traditions thereby legitimating a new consensus to reconstruct the State and Nation. These movements do not claim a return to the past but, instead, seek to refresh the political system to face globalization struggles and to reorganize the relationship between local and global.[7]

It is worth stressing that the emergence of a particular conception of society as a 'symbolic economy of alterity' (2012: 335) updates this archaic relationship between human beings and ecosystem shifting the hegemonic role from economics to the organization of society. Because, in this particular model, the ideology of economic growth must subject its linguistic recognition to a general system of beliefs and actions that value the active role of politics to the promotion of economic, cultural and legal plurality. That means that economic growth does not work as an isolated and preferential category into society, but must be related to other systems of action, political, cultural and moral, whose importance remain current. The reactivation processes of Bolivian peasant imaginary shows, then, those traditional meanings are forever available to be used activating diverse identifications and models of political actions.

This awareness suggests the emergence of a universal right to life and to have access to natural resources, having become the reason for the emergence of new community praxis and of a more active citizenship. For example, this new practice can be observed in everyday life when an individual goes to a government agency to request an identity card. Sometimes, in order to overcome bureaucratic hurdles, individuals come in organized groups (family, friends, and community) because as clarified by a leader of a community of neighbors, the simplest way to ensure equality in public service is through group pressure (Wanderley, 2009).

In this context, we can witness the change in the old representation of wealth that was previously linked to the possession of land and natural resources.

Some elements to think there is another modernity beyond market limits

We have tried to demonstrate that Bolivia's political experience does not represent a pre-modern or anti-modern reaction to the postcolonial system. Instead, this experience is modern because ethnic movements deny neither republican rights nor civil and political rights, nor the State role as a development agent. The Bolivian experience is original because it reveals social movements that were born from a renewal of traditions, opening itself to a pluralism of identities.

The novelty here comes from the collective political decision to subject both modern rights – Liberal and Republican – to original human rights to life and survival. That is, the task is to review modern rights from a perspective offered by the symbolism of nature suggested by community traditions that highlight a larger understanding of collective rights as is illustrated by the idea of Good Living. This reflection is more significant when we grasp that behind the plurality of rights there is an ecosocial understanding and also a public right innovation founded on the strengthening of the bonds between humans and nature. Giving priority to the right to life innovates when we consider the following: a) that collective rights to life and to appropriate natural resources to human survival are universal and must be shared by everyone; b) that capitalist rights to accumulation and economic growth are private rights which are not universal and, therefore, less important when we consider the scope of the rights to life. Capitalist rights must be applied to regulate corporations and market activities but not general society.

Furthermore, private rights organized during modernity to enable appropriation of common goods are now required to be subjected to comprehensive universal rights emerging from a community view about public and private relationship. The deconstruction of market ideology by new collective rights favors the understanding that economic growth and accumulation impose a linear imaginary of time and space which is not natural, contributing solely to reinforce coloniality. This colonial imaginary contributed to releasing an illusion of national growth as a necessary step linking developed and underdeveloped countries, and that was clearly criticized by Grosfoguel (2013). This way, politics and democracy could be freed from economic constraints and thus open new horizons for debate over collective responsibilities and thereby reshape nationality and state apparatus. Only then, the legal form of colonial State and institutional regulation can be politically questioned.

Market economy was not rejected but reinserted into a broader legal system that subjected private rationale to community and collective rationale. Someone does not reject material wealth but it must be considered as part of the collective values organized by community laws. Bolivia's case is very interesting to reflect about the economic element within the whole of non-economic institutions when we consider that Bolivia is a poor country, depending considerably on gas production to guarantee the majority of its public and social policies. However, for Bolivians, the economic importance of gas does not justify the priority given to private appropriation rights over collective resources and the privilege enjoyed by corporations. For Bolivians, the most important thing is to ensure the collective rights to life and to preserve material and symbolic conditions of social life. The gas industry is seen as a priority to strengthen collective rights but it does not mean that national and international corporations can exist out of State control and, most importantly, of the social control.

These experiences, which are poetically expressed through the images of *Pacha Mama* and *Buen Vivir* favor, moreover, a fruitful criticism of capitalist hegemonic development models at a global level, helping to shift the idea of unlimited economic growth. Bolivia's experience helps in understanding that the Westernization of the world has become a chaotic project, mainly when large economic corporations tried to impose a system of market appropriation as a universal rights system that could be applied to all institutions and spheres of everyday life. Also, the Bolivian case favors the understanding that the solution to the crisis necessarily requires political mediation based on a new legal system capable of reorganizing individual rights in view of collective rights, particularly of community rights. This way, the State had to be redesigned so that it could play a more complex role balancing ethnic and cultural differences and social pressures, integrating the notion of social struggles as an important ritual favoring transparent alliances between the multiple social groups and the new public policies, leading popular claims that are undermined by concentration of power and wealth.

Finally, we acknowledge that the concrete answers suggested by Bolivians' reactions converge to Western critical and political reactions shown in the recent protests against finance policies and in favor of democracy in Europe, United States, Latin America, Africa and elsewhere. What is novel about these reactions is their transnational aspects simultaneously linking from different places, unique *intersubjectivities* renewing traditional political and social strategies, and drawing a post-geographic panorama.

Notes

1   For a long time, the basis of capitalist power legitimation was the private power ideology revealed by the rights of the elite to privatize collective and natural resources. However, the current social and political recognition of the exhaustibility of resources and the increase of inequality is generating important reactions that question the privilege of private rights and the undermining of collective and community ones.

2   The term Katarist is inspired by the indigenous martyr Tupac Katari, killed by the Spaniards in 1781.

3   The renewed interest in the relationship between human beings and nature curiously influences the idea of salary. While the *Buen Vivir* ideal helps to influence the reinsertion of economics into the community system, salary reacquires its old symbolic role as an important device to allow exchanges centred on value in use. Therefore, work and salary must be adapted to a heterotopic dynamic capable of ensuring individual and family access to vital resources such as water and land as well as to organic and mineral resources that are necessary to human life. In this logic, market interests remain important but they are not the number one priority.

4   In Recife, Brazil, Occupy Estelita is a local movement against irregular occupation of strategic areas of the city by private companies, which is directly linked to national and international networks contributing to a widespread dissemination of a movement that otherwise, could be restricted to a local event.

5   However, we must remark that this relational approach in the Aymara and Kechua cosmologies is not an anthropological novelty. Ethnography shows that this ecological understanding of life exists in all archaic societies and exists currently among the indigenous population in Amazonia, including the Tupi, Panos and Aruaques. For the Amazonian natives, the relationship between Human and Nature continues to lay on a reciprocity logic inspired on gift that reveals a very important ecological and cultural understanding, as the anthropologist Viveiros de Castro remarked (2002: 327).

6   *Pacha Mama* contributes to articulate both community and intellectual knowledge in a collective movement that progressively questioned the utilitarian philosophy

of economic progress founded over the market rationale. Thereby, social movements came to denounce colonial characteristics of the mercantile development model founded over private appropriation of life resources and of social production and reproduction. It generates permanent inequalities and social injustices. To organize their altersystemic movements, the indigenous managed to gather from their imaginary the basic elements to value a policy aimed at refunding territory and legal system.

7   A special moment of this neo-community awareness is demonstrated through struggles around water distribution policies that were well presented in a movie from 2010 named *Even the Rain* (Spanish: *También la lluvia*). This movie clearly shows the recent abuse of power in Bolivia and the popular reaction against government policies in favor of privatization to benefit multinational corporations.

References

Caillé, A., Humbert, M., Latouche, S. and Viveret, P. (2011), *De la convivialité: dialogue sur la société conviviale à venir*. Paris: La Découverte.

Cohen, A.P. (1985), *The symbolic construction of community*. London/New York: Routledge.

Farah, I. and Gil, M. (2012), 'Modernidades alternativas: Una discusión desde Bolívia', in P.H. Martins and C. Rodrigues (eds), *Fronteiras abertas da América Latina*. Recife: Editora da UFPE.

Grosfoguel, R. (2013), 'Desenvolvimentismo, Modernidade e Teoria da Dependência na América Latina', in *REALIS – Revista de Estudos Anti-Utilitaristas e Pos-Coloniais*, 3(2): 26–54

Guimarães, A. (2011), 'Pluralismo, cohésion social y ciudadanía en la modernidad: Uma réflexion desde la realidad boliviana', in F. Wanderley (ed.), *El desarrollo en cuestión. Reflexiones desde América Latina*. La Paz: CIDES-OXFAM.

Hashizume, M. (2010), 'A emergência do Katarismo. Tensões e combinações entre classe e cultura na Bolívia contemporânea', *Anais do IV Simpósio Lutas Sociais na América Latina*, 'Imperialismo, nacionalismo e militarismo no Século XXI', 14–17 September, UEL, Londrina.

Honneth, A. (2015), *Freedom's Right. The social foundation of democratic life*. Columbia: Columbia University Press.

Rivera, J.L.L. (2010), 'El paso de la autonomía de hecho a la autonomía de derecho. Reflexiones desde el caso boliviano', in A. Uzeda (ed.), *Cultura y sociedad en Bolivia.*, Cochabamba: CISO-FACSO-UMSS.

Rivero, M.R. (2011), 'El pluralismo jurídico em Bolívia: Derecho indígena e interlegali-dades', in F. Wanderley (ed.), *El desarrollo en cuestión. Reflexiones desde América Latina*. La Paz: CIDES-OXFAM.

Santos, B. and Meneses, M. (2009), *Epistemologias do sul*. Coimbra: Editora Almeidina.

Sobottka, E.A. (2013), 'Liberdade, reconhecimento e emancipação – raízes da teoria da justiça de Axel Honneth', *Sociologias*, 15(33): 142–68.

Stavenhagen, R. (2000), *Conflictos étnicos y estado nacional*. México: Siglo XXI.

Stefanoni, P. (2012), 'Y quién no querría "vivir bien"?', *Critique et emancipación: Revista latinoamericana de ciencias sociales*, 4(7).

Viveiros de Castro, E. (2002), *A inconstância da alma selvagem*. São Paulo: Cosac & Naify.

Walzer, M. (2004), *Politics and passion. Toward a more egalitarian liberalism.* Yale/ London: Yale University Press.

Wanderley, F. (2009), 'Las prácticas estatales y la ciudadania individual y colectiva. Una mirada etnográfica de los encuentros de la población con la burocracia estatal en Bolivia', *ICONOS Revista de Ciencias Sociales*, 34, FLACSO, Ecuador.

19

Demanding Justice: Popular Protests in China

Chih-Jou Jay Chen

Questions

This article identifies emerging trends of popular protests in China. It evaluates their potential impacts on China's state–society relations and regime transformation. As China develops into the world's premier manufacturer and trader, its decades-long transformation has manifested a disturbing series of social problems, including underpayment of wages and pensions, rampant corruption and government malpractices, unjust land seizures and displacement, surging living and housing costs, and deteriorating environmental conditions. These social problems have all fueled widespread resistance, and even turned into collective confrontational protests demanding immediate corresponding justice be placed on the agenda. More importantly, they have raised the political consciousness of urban residents and rural peasants whose expectations to redress their grievances through normal legal channels and governmental institutions have largely been disappointed. As a result, mass protests have been rapidly escalating across the country, becoming an inextricable part of daily life in China.

Mass protests manifest in various forms, including peaceful small-group petitions, sit-ins, marches, rallies, labor and merchant strikes, ethnic conflicts, and even violent confrontations and riots. The protesters' discontent, not only caused by 'a small pinch of black sheep' in the government, is, more significantly, due to fundamental flaws of institutional arrangements in the contradictory spheres of capital–labor relationship, judicial governance, and political reforms. In 2011, citizens' resistance had reached such an alarming degree of expression that the government's budget for maintaining socio-political stability for the first time surpassed the expenditures of the People's Liberation Army. This critical measure exposes the insurmountable civil unrest that China has been facing.

This article highlights the various sources of social protest, and the substantial changes emerging in the early 2010s. What becomes apparent in this analysis is not only the growth in frequency and scale of violence, but also the involvement of various social groups, old and new, which in turn signal the unleashing of new social forces and a new development in state–society relations. What are the various sources of social tensions and injustices that plague China? How has social discontent evolved while the country is enmeshed in the grip of rapid structural changes in a highly unstable global macroeconomic world order? Who indeed are those disgruntled groups and what constitutes the basis of their resistance? Who are the targets of popular protests and how have they responded to those confrontations? Finally, what are the implications of the various upswings in protests on state–society relations and regime transformation in China? Does the recent wave of mass protests carry the potential to pose a significant political challenge to the regime?

Scholarship on collective action and public resistance in contemporary China has burgeoned over the past few years (e.g., Cai 2010; Chan 2011; Chen 2012; Deng and O'Brien 2013, 2014; Lee and Zhang 2013; Liu 2006; O'Brien and Li 2006, O'Brien 2008; Su and He 2010; Sun and Zhao 2007; Zhao 2000, 2001; Zhou 1993). Most of this work, however, relies on anecdotal evidence or case studies. To address this gap in the literature, this article aims to promote empirical progress by integrating and assessing a dataset of popular protest events in the context of contemporary China.

Data and measurement

This study has constructed a dataset by collecting around 6690 press reports on China's mass protests from 2000 to 2013. While this dataset is not statistically representative of national conditions, it can be read as a symptomatic trend reflecting the types of social conflicts in China. While there are inherent limitations in using media data to study social protest, sporadic media reports with remarkable patterns of anecdotal evidence still provide useful information, especially considering the fact that so far there is no existing data on the frequency, intensity, or types of popular protests in China.

In order to collect data on these collective protest events, a group of research assistants (graduate students) collected protest news from various Chinese newspapers, news datasets, and Internet websites. They then screened and identified all collective action events that conformed to the following four criteria: it had to be collective (involving more than ten participants on site); it had to present a claim, either a grievance against some target or a demand directed at some institution; it had to contain practical confrontational forms; and it had to be located in the public sphere. The main variables used in this report include date and location, protest group (claimants), claims (issues), form (tactic), targets, sizes (number of participants), police responses and socioeconomic conditions of the protest locations.

The year in which a particular protest event occurred was categorized into one of three time periods: 2000–03, 2004–08, and 2009–13. Taking the years of 2004 and 2009 as cut-off points was intended to assess whether there was any significant change in protest forms and policing under different political leadership since 2000. For the measure of protest group, the most salient social/demographic characteristics of the group that initiated any given protest event were used. In most cases, these claimants were clearly identified in the news reports (e.g., state-firm workers, peasants, home owners, and so on), although some groups were not mutually exclusive. Claims and purposes of events provide key information for sources of discontent. In operation, coders identified a wide variety of claims made in each protest event which were grouped and reduced into the following four main categories: economic claims, administration claims, rights issues, and incidental events. As for protest forms, for the purposes of this analysis, three categories were grouped: (1) nonviolent forms (i.e., gatherings, strikes, hunger strikes, sit-ins, chanting slogans and/or holding posters, and walkouts and demonstrations); (2) blocking traffic or factories, and (3) violent forms (i.e., physical attacks, damaging property, looting, and burning). Policing reflects the state's response to social unrest. In the analysis below, I categorized policing into 'presence' and 'no show,' while presence includes three sub-categories of police actions: arrest, disperse, and stand guard.

Results: The changing features of initiating protest groups

Table 19.1 shows that mass protests in urban China have involved a wide range of social groups, including: 1) blue-collar workers, including state-owned enterprise (SOE) and collective-owned enterprise (COE) workers, private-sector workers, and foreign-direct-investment (FDI) workers, accounting for 36 percent of protest events in 2000–13; 2) white-collar workers, including teachers, demobilized soldiers, and so on, accounting for 12 percent of events; 3) rights protection groups, such as home own-ers, petitioners, displaced residents, and students, accounting for 38 percent of events; 4) masses, 10 percent; and 5) religious and minority groups, 4 percent.

Before the mid-2000s, workers of state-owned and collective-owned enterprises in the cities were both early participants and the most con-sistently present during protests; they were either laid off, retired, or were still employed and were engaged in protesting for outstanding (or underpaid) wages. Meanwhile, the other social protest groups included private-sector workers, drivers (mostly self-employed), displaced city dwellers, and students.

Table 19.1 Major mass protest groups in urban China, 2000–13

	2000–13	2000–03	2004–08	2009–13
	N = 5224	N = 346	N = 1410	N = 3468
	%	%	%	%
Blue-collar workers	36	54	41	32
Private-sector workers	11	9	11	11
Drivers	6	6	7	5
SOE/COE workers	11	35	14	8
FDI workers	8	4	9	8
White-collar workers	12	6	13	11
Laid-off community (*minban*) teachers	3	0	3	3
Public school teachers	2	2	3	1
Demobilized soldiers	3	0	3	3
Rights protection groups	38	27	31	42
Home owners	8	3	8	8
Petitioners (*fangmin*)	11	0	6	14
Displaced residents	5	6	4	5
Students	3	5	4	2
Masses	10	8	11	10
Religious and minority groups	4	5	3	4

Since the mid-2000s, several protest groups have been emerging and have gradually changed the composition of social protest in China. Of all protest events in urban China, the proportion of blue-collar workers' protests decreased from 54 percent in 2000–03 to 32 percent in 2009–13. On the other hand, the proportion of protests initiated by white-collar workers increased from 6 percent in 2000–03 to 11 percent in 2009–13; and for protests by rights protection groups, its proportion grew from 27 percent in 2000–03 to 42 percent in 2009–13. That is, disgruntled blue-collar workers were not alone in voicing their anger, more and more middle-class citizens, such as white-collar workers and home owners, had chosen to launch collective protests to protect their rights and demand returns. Among blue-collar workers, over the past decade, the number of traditional city SOE/COE workers has decreased, while the number of migrant peasant workers in FDI and in private sectors acting as significant protest groups has grown rapidly. Also, the collective protests of petitioners have been increasing dramatically, accounting for almost zero in 2000–03 but rising to 14 percent in 2009–13, indicating that more and more disgruntled marginal people saw no alternative but to take more radical measures to collectively take their grievances to higher-level governments.

Protest claims

In cities, the biggest protest claims focused on income-related issues, accounting for 48 percent of all claims (see Table 19.2). The other two major claims were administration issues (e.g., government misconduct, specific government policy or regulations) and rights issues (e.g., forced evictions, environmental issues, and student rights), with each accounting for about 20 percent of all protest events. There was a slight change in the trend of protest issues over the past 15 years: the main stream of protest events responding to general economic discontent had been declining, from 52 percent in 2000–03 to 46 percent in 2009–13. On the other hand, the percentage of protests triggered by government misconduct or government policies slightly grew upwards, from 19 percent to 22 percent in 2009–13. Apparently, people's grievances were not limited to monetary issues, but more and more discontent and grievances were caused by local government policies and officials' wrongdoings.

In rural areas, the most important protest issue that emerged in the early 2000s and accelerated after the mid-2000s was linked to land seizures in suburban agricultural villages, where local cadres underpaid or embezzled

Table 19.2 Mass protest issues in China, 2000–13

	Urban cities and towns				Rural villages			
		2000–03	2004–08	2009–13		2000–03	2004–08	2009–13
	N = 5177	N = 343	N = 1399	N = 3435	N = 1482	N = 86	N = 419	N = 977
	%	%	%	%	%	%	%	%
Economic claims	48	52	53	46	2	2	1	2
Rural land seizures	1	1	0	1	50	23	51	52
Administration claims								
Officials and regulations	20	19	17	22	20	62	23	15
Ethnic conflicts	1	1	0	2	0	0	0	0
Rights issues								
Political economy[1]	9	9	9	10	23	9	20	26
Individual citizenship[2]	12	12	13	12	4	3	4	4
Incidental Events								
Incidental conflicts	1	2	2	1	0	0	0	1
Multiple group petitions	3	0	3	4	0	0	0	0
Nationalist protests	2	4	3	2	0	0	0	0

Note: 1. 'Political economy' claims include city development, forced eviction, anti-privatization, pollution and environmental issues; 2. 'Individual citizenship' includes student and parents' rights, community safety, medical malpractice, occupational injury, etc.

compensations originally awarded to displaced peasants. The displaced villagers received minimal compensation for ceding their land-use rights and were often forcibly evicted from their land. As a result, peasant protests against such confiscations have emerged as the major cause of social unrest in rural China since the 2000s (also see Ong 2014). Another source reported that land disputes accounted for 65 percent of the 180,000 mass incidents in 2010 (Yu 2005). The second confrontational rural issue was rights issues, such as pollution and environmental protection, followed by local government misconduct and cadres' corruption. Issues of mass protests regarding taxes and fees mostly occurred in the late 1990s, but faded out in the mid-2000s, presumably due to China's decision to reduce and gradually cancel agricultural taxes.

Table 19.3 shows the forms of collective protest in urban and rural China. During 2000–13, violent actions accounted for 28 percent and 54 percent in urban cities and rural villages respectively. They included clashes with police, physical attacks, damaging property, looting, burning, rampage, and random violence. 'Blocking traffic or factories' – occupations and obstructions – making up 18 percent, were forms not violent but purposely placed the actors in a potentially conflictual relationship with protest targets or authorities. Comparing protest forms between urban cities and rural villages, violent tactics were more frequent in rural villages than in urban areas. In 2000–13, 54% of protests initiated by rural villagers adopted some kind of violent form; whereas 28% of protests by urban residents culminated in violence. Overall, non-violent protests slightly increased over the past decade. Specifically, in urban cities the proportion of non-violent events increased from 47 percent in 2000–03 to 55 percent in 2009–13, while those in rural areas increased from 26 percent in 2000–03 to 29 percent in 2009–13.

Table 19.4 examines the relationship between protest forms and the level of economic development of the protest location. It shows that social protests in areas of low-GDP per capita were more likely to turn violent than those in areas of high-GDP per capita. With regard to cities, in 2000–13, the average GDP per capita of localities of violent protests (39,198 RMB) was much lower than that of localities where non-violent protests dominated (44,609 RMB). In rural areas, the differences of average GDP per capita between localities of violent and non-violent protests were much larger (26,359 versus 32,591 RMB). This suggests that economic development is indeed associated with social protest in China.

Table 19.3 Forms of social protest in China, 2000–13

(Number of reported incidents; %)	Urban cities and towns					Rural villages			
	N = 5199	2000–03 N = 346	2004–08 N = 1400	2009–13 N = 3453	N = 1487	2000–03 N = 86	2004–08 N = 419	2009–13 N = 982	
	%	%	%	%	%	%	%	%	
Non-violent	54	47	52	55	29	26	31	29	
Block	18	25	19	17	17	9	16	18	
Violent	28	28	30	27	54	65	53	53	

Note: 'Non-violent' forms include strike, sit-in, walkout, demonstration, and hunger strike. 'Block' includes building blocks and road blocks.

Table 19.4   Forms of social protest and economic indicators of protest
localities, 2000–13

(Number of reported incidents; %)	Urban cities and towns			Rural villages		
	N	%	2007 GDP per capita (RMB)	N	%	2007 GDP per capita (RMB)
Total	4,929	100	42,955	1,411	100	30,009
Non-violent	2,637	53	44,609	421	30	32,591
Block	922	19	43,808	241	17	36.841
Violent	1,370	28	39,198	749	53	26,359

Note: 'Non-violent' forms include strike, sit-in, walkout, demonstration, and
hunger strike. 'Block' includes building blocks and road blocks.

Source: The author's database of mass protest news in China. GDP data
source: drawn from city statistics provided by China Data Online (http://chinadata
online.org).

A well-developed city is more likely to see non-violent popular protests,
and an underdeveloped locality is more likely to have violent social unrest,
both in urban and rural areas.

Police response to protests

Table 19.5 presents the distribution of different police approaches between
urban cities and rural villages. In urban cities and towns, in 2000–13, the
number of no-shows (i.e., events where no police attendance was reported)
predominated – 38 percent of reported protest events occurred without
police presence; the other three types of police responses were standing
guard (21 percent), dispersing protesters (18 percent), and using arrests
(23 percent). By comparison, in the same period of 2000–13, a relatively
lower 24 percent of reported protest events in rural areas occurred without
police presence. However, more importantly, the percentage of resorting
to arrests in rural villages was much higher – 37 percent of events saw
police arrest protesters, a much higher percentage than in urban cities,
where 23 percent of events ended up in a police arrest. In rural villages,
the approach of standing guard – officers showing up and taking only limited action (which excludes the use of arrests or physical coercion) – was
the least frequent response to protest, representing 15 percent of all of the
events. Whereas in urban cities the least frequent police response was to
disperse crowds, accounting for only 18 percent of all urban events.

Table 19.5 Police response to mass protests in China, 2000–13

	Urban cities and towns				Rural villages			
	N = 5192	2000–03 N = 346	2004–08 N = 1396	2009–13 N = 3450	N = 1486	2000–03 N = 86	2004–08 N = 419	2009–13 N = 981
	%	%	%	%	%	%	%	%
Presence	62	54	65	61	76	73	76	76
Arrest	23	22	23	23	37	43	33	38
Disperse	18	13	20	17	24	21	26	24
Stand guard	21	19	22	21	15	9	17	15
No Show	38	46	35	39	24	27	24	24

Although the percentages of non-violent protests have increased in urban and rural areas over the past decade, the police have not significantly reduced the use of force toward protesters, particularly for protests initiated by rural villagers/peasants. In 2009–13, for example, 62 percent of protests involved the use of police force, including arresting protesters and dispersing crowds. In the same period, 40 percent of protests in urban areas were met with police force. This suggests that the use of force was highly common in China, either to disperse crowds or to arrest protesters. In 2000–13, these two approaches together accounted for 41 percent of events in urban cities and towns, and 61 percent of events in rural villages, respectively. Despite this trend, an important urban–rural difference is that police in urban cities relied on preventive and tolerant approaches more than their counterparts in the countryside, where highly repressive police actions were exceedingly prevalent.

Remarks

This brief report aims to provide a preliminary evidence-based quantitative description on the trends and characteristics of popular protests demanding justice in China. Although news data on social protests in China are largely underreported and carry both selection and description bias, they are still the best available data for analysis and further examination in order to understand social discontent and social unrest in today's China. This study finds that there is an increasing diversity of forms, claims, and initiating groups of social protests in China. Their characteristics and development are related to the economic and social contexts in which they are situated. For example, the frequency and scale of migrant workers' protests in FDI and the private sector have accelerated. Since the late 2000s, deteriorating labor shortages combined with relentless international competition have shrunk the benefits of FDI firms and led to the creation of an unfavorable management environment for FDI owners. On the other hand, workers and citizens have become increasingly conscious of their rights and have learned to bargain and fight for their interests. At first, the Chinese government was partial to the foreign capitalists, but of late it has altered its position and now leans toward a middle of the road stance to ensure its legitimacy and secure its political stability (Chen 2009, 2013, 2015). I have shown elsewhere that Chinese protesters have confined their struggles mostly to localized and materialist contentions; the state responses to social protests were influenced first and foremost by who was protesting and not necessarily by the protest issues or targets (Chen, 2017).

Meanwhile, the division of rural villages and urban communities, and the gap between rural peasants and urban residents, has led to distinctive differences between rural protests and urban protests. The impression that most mass protests in China can be resolved by monetary rewards is incorrect and oversimplified. A substantial part of social protests is initiated by nonmonetary issues, including government misconduct and official wrongdoings. Also, although mass protests took place both in rich and poor areas, they are more likely to become militant in poorer areas.

Reflecting on day-by-day incidents, it is clear that each wave of social unrest can be traced to a particular government policy, economic or political context. The Chinese government's dilemma is that many of these protests emanate from high economic growth that China is keen to maintain. As the Chinese economy slows, the rise of social protest and consequently the confrontation between government and protestors seem inevitable. The fundamental problems underlying social unrest are mainly collective property rights involving rural land, the unchecked power of local authorities, corruption, and the weak rule of law. China's single authoritarian party regime is unable to resolve these problems without comprehensive political reforms.

China's current political system lacks effective channels for citizens to express genuine grievances and to seek redress for the misdemeanors of local officials, and therefore social unrest is on the rise. Without any alternative, discontented people across diverse sectors tend to resort to collective action and extra-legal means, such as demonstrations and violent mass protests. It appears that protesters resort to confrontation when alternative means of redress prove futile or unavailable. With some notable exceptions, most of the mass protests across China remain unreported, unknown, isolated, short-lived, and lack strong leadership. Once a protest's scale is large enough to attract media attention, it may put pressure on high-level government authorities to ensure that local governments implement laws and policies from above, and thus may help high-level governments to keep local governments in check. Nevertheless, the rights discourse of protesters might be better understood as an expression of 'politics as usual' than as a novel demand for democracy on the part of a nascent civil society claiming autonomy from the state. As such, at present they have not developed to a degree that will constitute an immediate threat to political stability and regime survival. In the long run, however, there may be more serious threats to the country's stability.

References

Cai, Yongshun (2010). *Collective Resistance in China: Why Popular Protests Succeed or Fail*. Stanford: Stanford University Press.

Chan, Anita (2011). 'Strikes in China's Export Industries in Comparative Perspective.' *China Journal* 65: 27–51.

Chen, Chih-Jou Jay (2009). 'Growing social unrest and emergent protest groups in China.' Pp. 87–105 in Hsin-Huang Michael Hsiao and Cheng-Yi Lin (eds), *Rise of China: Beijing's Strategies and Implications for the Asia-Pacific*. London; New York: Routledge.

Chen, Chih-Jou Jay (2013). 'Die zunahme von arbeitskonflikten in China: ein vergleich von arbeiterin-nenprotesten in verschiedenen sektoren (Growing labor disputes in China: a comparison of workers' protests in different sectors).' Pp. 78–105 in Daniel Fuchs Georg Egger, Thomas Immervoll, and Lydia Steinmassl (eds), *Arbeitskämpfe in China: Berichte von der werkbank der welt*. Wien: Promedia.

Chen, Chih-Jou Jay (2015). 'Popular Protest in an Authoritarian Regime: A Wildcat Strike in Southern China Popular.' *Taiwanese Sociology* 30: 43–91 (In Chinese).

Chen, Chih-Jou Jay (2017). 'Policing Protest in China: Findings from Newspaper Data.' *Taiwanese Sociology,* 33: 113–64 (In Chinese).

Chen, Xi (2012). *Social Protest and Contentious Authoritarianism in China*. Cambridge and New York: Cambridge University Press.

Deng, Yanhua and O'Brien, Kevin J. (2013). 'Relational Repression in China: Using Social Ties to Demobilize Protesters.' *China Quarterly* 215: 533–52.

Deng, Yanhua and O'Brien, Kevin J. (2014). 'Societies of Senior Citizens and Popular Protest in Rural Zhejiang.' *China Journal* 71:172–88.

Lam, Willy (2011). 'Beijing's "Wei-Wen" Imperative Steals the Thunder at NPC.' *China Brief* 11(4): 2–4.

Lee, Ching Kwan, and Zhang, Yonghong (2013). 'The Power of Instability: Unraveling the Microfoundations of Bargained Authoritarianism in China.' *American Journal of Sociology* 118(6): 1475–508.

Liu, Dongxiao (2006). 'When do National Movements Adopt or Reject International Agendas? A Comparative Analysis of the Chinese and Indian Women's Movements.' *American Sociological Review* 71: 921–42.

O'Brien, Kevin J. (ed.) (2008). *Popular Protest in China*. Cambridge: Harvard University Press.

O'Brien, Kevin J. and Li, Lianjiang (2006). *Rightful Resistance in Rural China*. Cambridge: Cambridge University Press.

Ong, Lynette H. (2014). 'State-Led Urbanization in China: Skyscrapers, Land Revenue and "Concentrated Villages".' *The China Quarterly* 217: 162–79.

Su, Yang and He, Xin (2010). 'Street as Courtroom: State Accommodation of Labor Protest in South China.' *Law and Society Review* 44: 157–84.

Sun, Yanfei, and Zhao, Dingxin (2007). 'Multifaceted State and Fragmented Society: The Dynamics of the Environmental Movement in China.' In Dali Yang (ed.), *Discontented Miracle: Growth, Conflict, and Institutional Adaptations in China*. World Scientific Publisher.

Yu, Jianrong (2005). 'Tudi wenti yu chengwei nongmin weiquan kangzheng de jiaodian (Land disputes: the focus of rights-defending activities of peasants).' *Diaoyan shijie* 3: 22–3.

Zhao, Dingxin (2000). 'State-Society Relations and the Discourses and Activities during the 1989 Beijing Student Movement.' *American Journal of Sociology* 105: 1592–663.

Zhao, Dingxin (2001). *The Power of Tiananmen: State-Society Relations and the 1989 Beijing Student Movement*. The University of Chicago Press.

Zhou, Xueguang (1993). 'Unorganized Interests and Collective Action in Communist China.' *American Sociological Review* 58: 54–73.

20

Thomas Piketty and the Marikana Massacre

Peter Alexander

On August 16, 2012, the South African police intervened in a labor conflict between workers at the Marikana platinum mine near Johannesburg and the mine's owners: the stockholders of Lonmin, Inc., based in London. Police fired on the strikers with live ammunition. Thirty-four miners were killed.

These lines may be familiar. They are the first ones in the first chapter of Thomas Piketty's bestselling book *Capital in the Twenty-first Century.*[1] Piketty (2014: 39–40, 571) refers to what happened at Marikana as a 'tragedy'. It was the outcome of – I will quote him – 'distributional conflict' between, on the one hand, workers living in 'wretched conditions' and, on the other, 'Lonmin's excessive profits' and 'the apparently fabulous salary awarded to the mine's manager'. It symbolised the inequalities that lie at the heart of his concerns, and it provided a glimpse of a 'spectre' (not his word), that of a threat to 'democratic societies' and 'values of social justice' posed by 'a market economy ... left to itself' (those are his words).[2]

He observes Marikana from afar, picking it out with the telescope of historically grounded economics. What can be added if we see it close up, with the microscope of forensic sociology?

Massacre and aftermath: Scene 1 and Scene 2

Let us begin with the killings. The message conveyed by TV coverage was ambiguous.

Cameras were positioned directly behind the main line of police, literally providing their point of view; creating the impression of self-defence against a marauding armed mob. Footage included in the documentary *Miners Shot Down* reveals a very different story.[3] It shows workers seated peacefully on and around a hill (what the workers called 'the mountain'); the police begin surrounding them with razor wire and a full panoply of armoured might; a large contingent of about one hundred workers including the strike's leaders, moves northwards, towards a settlement where many of them live; they are walking, not running; police block their advance with vehicles and a stun grenade; some scatter, away from the gunfire, 37 are forced forward by another stun grenade, tear gas, and volleys of rubber bullets and shotgun pellets; confused, they are pushed through a funnel formed by police vehicles towards a line of paramilitary police armed with automatic weapons.

It is then they are shot – by live rounds, and on TV cameras. They were not attacking; they were attempting to escape. Of the 34 dead workers, 17 were killed in this small area, which was known to the Marikana Commission of Inquiry as 'Scene One'.[4] My own research on Marikana began two days later, when, together with colleagues and students, I attended a 10,000-strong rally of the Lonmin strikers and their families. Leaders described what had happened, but this was not reported in the media. No newspaper carried even a tiny quote from a single worker offering a sliver of insight from the receiving end of this massacre. We were served a one-sided version of a two-sided event.[5]

On 20 August I returned to Marikana with two fieldworkers. We had a simple goal: to get the workers' version of the event. What we were told – and then saw for ourselves – was horrific. In response to the initial gunfire, some workers had fled westwards across open ground, joining others escaping from the hill in the same direction. Under fire, and with armoured personnel carriers and horses charging them down, many took cover in a rocky outcrop covered by densely packed shrubs. Now, guided by workers, and with heavily armed police patrolling close by, we headed uneasily towards this place.[6] Soon we found dried blood, lots of it, and blood-stained clothes, and letters about 30 cm high painted in yellow on rocks and on the ground. We surmised, correctly as it transpired, that the letters marked sites where bodies had fallen (Lekgowa et al. 2012). Seventeen workers, half those slaughtered, were killed here, a place we called 'Killing Koppie', and the Commission named 'Scene Two'. Well away from TV cameras, strikers had been surrounded and murdered. This was the most chilling research I have ever undertaken.[7]

Events leading to the massacre

What follows comes partly from interviews and other material that appeared in a book we produced, which was entitled *Marikana: A View from the Mountain and a Case to Answer* (Alexander et al., 2012).

Most of the rest comes from details that have emerged from the Commission of Inquiry, which has answered some, but not all, of our questions, which were principally about culpability.[8]

The main demand of the strike was for a salary of R12,500 per month (about $1,500 at the time). This was first raised by just one category of workers, rock drill operators (RDOs), at just one section of the mine, Karee. Karee's manager stated that when he first heard the figure – at a meeting with two RDO delegates held on 21 June 2012 – 'it stunned me a bit', because they were 'effectively seeking an increase of approximately 150%'. According to him, the workers did not base their claim on specific calculations, but they felt it was reasonable given the difficulty and physically demanding nature of their labour, the long hours they toiled, and the wet conditions where they worked. When he pointed out that R12,500 was more than their team leaders received, they responded, he recalled, by saying: 'team leaders do not work much anyway' (Marikana Commission 2014a).[9]

Lonmin decided to award the RDOs a special allowance, which, in the case of those at Karee, amounted to R750 per month. They did this partly because they were competing with the two bigger platinum companies for the services of RDOs, and these companies – Anglo American Platinum and Implats – paid higher salaries. But the company's decision had by-passed well-established collective bargaining procedures, so it set a precedent, and also damaged the prestige of the dominant union, the National Union of Mineworkers (NUM).[10]

The workers were still dissatisfied but had gained confidence. The claim for R12,500 was taken up by RDOs across the whole mine, and on 10 August they struck work and marched to Lonmin's Marikana headquarters. Inconsistently, management now refused to meet with workers' delegates, and said that demands had to be channeled through NUM. That night the strike spread throughout the mine, which employed a total of about 28,000 workers.

NUM had developed a cosy relationship with the employer and was already losing support, especially at Karee, where it had removed a popular local leader, and workers had joined a new union, the Association of Mineworkers' and Construction Union (AMCU). At Eastern and Western, the other main sections of the mine, NUM was still the dominant union. As a means of uniting workers across the union divide, the RDOs had organised their own committee, and this was now expanded to include other categories' of workers (Sinwell with Mbatha 2016).

On 11 August, the next day, 3000 workers marched to the NUM office, calling on the union to take up their demand. One of the local NUM leaders, possibly more, shot at the marchers, and workers told us that two of their number were killed. It transpired, much later, that the two men had been severely wounded but lived.[11] However, perception mattered. The shootings are widely regarded as a turning point in the lead-up to the massacre. Workers retreated to the mountain, where they armed themselves with 'traditional weapons', such as spears – and NUM's credibility collapsed.[12]

On 12 August, a Sunday, the Minister of Police, Nathi Mthethwa, took telephone calls from NUM's president Senzeni Zokwana and Lonmin director Cyril Ramaphosa. They expressed concern about violence in Marikana and appealed for police intervention. In response, Mthethwa contacted General Riah Phiyega, head of the South African Police Service (SAPS), and before the end of the day she had established a Joint Operation Centre (JOC) in Marikana (Marikana Commission 2014c). Zokwana was not a typical union leader and Ramaphosa was not an ordinary company director. The former was National Chairperson of the South African Communist Party, ally of the ruling African National Congress (ANC), and the latter was Chair of the ANC's powerful national disciplinary appeals committee.[13] Their positions within the governing party ensured that, at the very least, Mthethwa took their calls.

The level of collusion between Lonmin and SAPS was astounding. The Company was represented at JOC meetings, and it helped plan the operation that led to the massacre. It provided offices, intelligence, access to more than 200 CCTV cameras, accommodation, food, transport, a helicopter, ambulances, a temporary gaol, back-up from 500 security officials of its own, and a convention centre for post-massacre de-briefing. There is evidence that SAPS even loaned Lonmin a water cannon and a detachment of police horses.[14] A critical component of the company's culpability was its refusal to meet with strikers. According to Bishop Jo Seoka (2012), who attempted to broker negotiations, the confrontation could have been averted if Lonmin had been willing to simply listen, and this assessment was substantiated by what we heard from some of the strikers.

Complicity between the police and Lonmin is reflected in the minutes of a meeting, held on 14 August, between the SAPS commissioner responsible for Northwest Province, which included Marikana, and Lonmin's Executive Vice-President for Human Capital. The Lonmin executive, Barnard Mokoena, provides reasons for taking action: he wants to avoid similar militancy elsewhere, he wants existing labour relations practices reinforced, and, agreeing with the commissioner, he wants to undermine radical politicians advocating nationalisation.[15] He argues in favour of arresting strikers, and it was this objective, combined with 'disarming' – as distinct from a primary concern with 'dispersal' – which led to the massacre. The SAPS commissioner, Lt Gen Zukiswa Mbombo, says: 'we were there [at the "mountain"] today and they did not surrender, then it is blood … we need to act such that we kill this thing'. She adds: 'I do not want a situation where 20 people will be dead' (note: '20' not 'two' or 'none'). These minutes add credence to the conclusion reached by former Minister of Intelligence Ronnie Kasrils (2012) offered just after the massacre. 'Why risk the manoeuvre', he asked, 'other than to drive the strikers back to work to work at all costs on behalf of the bosses, who were anxious to resume profit making operations'.

The next day, 15 August, Phiyega met with her nine provincial commissioners and three head office generals, and it was agreed to provide Mbombo with any additional resources she needed to disarm the strikers (Nicolson 2013). The following morning, Mbombo ominously told the media that today, 16 August 2012, was 'D-Day'. She also made a comment that adds further weight to Kasils' claim – she said, 'today we end this strike' – so she was conscious of taking action on the side of the employer (Evidence Leaders 2014: 307).[16] Her police ordered four mortuary vans, each with space for four corpses (Nichol 2015). They would soon be needed. SAPS planned for deaths, and Lonmin participated in the planning.

Ramaphosa's role

But who was behind this action? The Minister of Police, Mthethwa, was not only in contact with Phiyega, the national commissioner, he was also talking to Mbombo, the provincial commissioner, implying that he was overstepping the boundary between political and operational responsibility. According to the minutes of her meeting with Mokoena, Mbombo says the minister told her the name of somebody who was calling him, who she describes as 'politically high'. The identity of this person is then revealed as 'Cyril', Cyril Ramaphosa, who had previously influenced the minister to ensure high-level police intervention.

Ramaphosa had been the first general secretary of NUM and was the secretary general of the African National Congress (ANC) when it negotiated the end of apartheid. This 'high' political figure now owned a very substantial portion of Lonmin and, as we have seen, was on its board of directors.[17]

Ramaphosa's influence on events is confirmed by an email he sent to fellow board members on 15 August, the day before the massacre. He writes: 'I have just had a meeting with [the Minister of Mineral Resources] she agrees that what we are going through is not a labour dispute, but a criminal act. She will correct her characterisation of what we are experiencing. Two, she is going into cabinet and will brief the President as well, and get the Minister of Police ... to act in a more pointed way'. There can be little doubt that the police acted in a 'pointed way'. At the Inquiry, representatives of the massacre victims' widows and of injured and arrested miners, argued that there was sufficient evidence for Ramaphosa to be charged with murder. While there are many facets to an explanation of the massacre, my own opinion is that Ramaphosa's contribution was critical.

The main detail of this email was published before the ANC had its elective congress at the end of 2012, but this did not prevent the organisation from choosing Ramaphosa as its Deputy President. After the 2014 general election, he became Deputy President of the Republic of South Africa. Despite his role in the massacre, the ruling party has made Ramaphosa the second most powerful individual in the land, and he is the obvious choice as next president.

Fight continues

There is another side to the Marikana story. According to research by my colleague Luke Sinwell (with Siphiwe Mbatha, 2013: 51), at approximately 7 pm on the night of the massacre, 10–20 workers met below the mountain and, in memory of those who died, they resolved to continue the strike. They did not want the public to think that it was only those who died who were organising it. I commented: 'this was one of the most remarkable acts of courage in labour history' (Alexander et al. 2013: 195).

After five weeks, the workers were able to negotiate an increase in pay. By then a massive wave of wild cat strikes was spreading across the whole of the South African mining industry, with workers everywhere calling for at least R12,500, and the following year workers on other platinum mines and some gold mines left NUM and joined AMCU. The Marikana effect spread elsewhere, to farm labourers, whose strike led to an increase in minimum pay of more than 50%, and to major official strikes in key industries, such as auto and gold mining in 2013, and engineering in 2014. It also led to the formation of a radical nationalist party, the Economic Freedom Fighters; to the decision of Africa's largest union, the National

Union of Metalworkers, to break with the ANC, initiate a United Front with community organisations, and take steps towards forming a new workers' party; and, in 2017, to the formation of a new leftwing union federation, the South African Federation of Trade Unions.

In 2014, AMCU led an official strike among workers employed by the three big platinum companies: Amplat, Implats and Lonmin (see Foudraine 2014). The union demanded a minimum salary of R12,500 for underground employees. In terms of days lost, this was probably the second largest strike in South African history (the biggest being the 2010 public sector workers' strike). After five months, at the end of which some miners' families were close to starving, the workers won a partial, but very significant, victory. The massacre was a major factor in maintaining the workers' solidarity. The deal, which covered three years from 2013, provided an immediate increase of R2,000 (an improvement of about 40% in most cases). A significant proportion of platinum workers will secure R12,500 by 2015, and AMCU is committed to taking further action, if necessary, to ensure that all of them reach this target by 2017 (Matunjwa 2014).

Marikana was not just about inequality and a massacre, it was also an 'egalitarian movement'.[18] Platinum workers fought for, and secured, a flat-rate increase, not a percentage adjustment, and this was consciously aimed at reducing income differences among workers, as well as closing the 'apartheid wage gap' more broadly. Moreover, the workers had made a 'claim to justice', and their bosses will doubtless treat them with greater respect in future (see also Alexander 2014; Ngwane 2017).

Piketty and diagnosis

The massacre marked a turning point in South African history. Police acted in the interests of a major mining corporation against strikers fighting for a living wage. Bloodshed exposed intimate relationships between government ministers and representatives of corporate capital, and between both of these and the established workers' union. But, the repression also inspired workers to extend their struggle, and it triggered the formation of new left-wing organisations.

Let us now return to Piketty. In doing so, we will raise six issues: distributional conflict, capital and wealth, capitalist crises, volition, social democracy, and forces for change. One could point to accidents of history in my account of Marikana – the significance of a single NUM member releasing a bullet, for instance – or one could treat it as a peculiarly South

African event, which in many respects it was. But Piketty pushes us in the other direction, towards the bigger picture, and this is part of his strength. Certainly, Lonmin is a sizeable corporation (a constituent of the FTSE-250 index) and South Africa is a G-20 country with a democratic and pro-capitalist government, so the massacre cannot be written off as an aberration.

For Piketty, Marikana is symptomatic of a global malaise; part of the sickness of Capital in the 21st century. But has he correctly diagnosed what's wrong? What happens if we factor in our microscope findings? First, we must challenge Piketty's view of Marikana as 'distributional conflict'. Of course, a fight over wages is necessarily a fight over distribution of the value added to a product in the course of its production – that is, how much goes to the workers and how much to the owners and their representatives.[19] But, as we have seen, in the Marikana case workers demanded just rewards for (1) quantity and quality of *work* performed and (2) rotten conditions under which they *laboured*. These issues were, in essence, about production. I am not arguing that the struggle should be characterised as being about 'production' *rather than* 'distribution' – after all, success was measured in monetary terms.

Emphasis on the production aspect is important though, and for two immediate reasons. First, when workers protested, they did so by striking – that is, by halting *production* – and it was this that eventually brought success. Secondly, to appreciate why workers regarded the outcome of the 2014 strike as a victory, it is necessary to look beyond wages. Economists do not understand this because they only deal with numbers; sociologists have the ability to consider imponderables as well. In this case, the workers returned to their jobs far more united than before the action began. They had learned the benefit of solidarity, found new leaders and built new organisations (most importantly, at the point of production).

In addition, they narrowed pay differentials, and gained some revenge for the massacre. After the strike, workers were more likely to be treated with dignity by their bosses, and they gained confidence to confront unsafe and unpleasant working conditions and to resist retrenchments. The strike improved wages, but it also shifted the balance of power over production in the workers' favour. Refocusing attention on production signals the importance of workers in effective struggles against inequality.

This first concern relates to a second, more theoretical, problem. Marxist writers have criticised Piketty for conflating capital and wealth (e.g. Callinicos 2014; Harvey 2014). Not all wealth is capital, it may just be a worker's house for instance. A benefit of Marx's approach is that it treats capital as a set of social relationships; not just a thing with a price. Private ownership is a critical relationship, one that gives shareholders control over production, allowing them to compel workers to create surplus value. This provides an important clue to understanding Marikana. Remember, Mokoena wanted SAPS to break the 2012 strike because of fear that a workers' victory would encourage support for nationalisation, thus loss of ownership. In reality, capitalists never have unbridled control. They operate within structures of laws, agreements and customs that reflect their common interests and assist them in managing workers' grievances. Mokoena is important here too. His support for potentially fatal repression was also conditioned by desire to protect existing labour practices, including sweetheart relationships with NUM. Marikana was not just a battle between rich and poor over the distribution of income; it was also a conflict over the right to determine the level and form of exploitation. That is, it threatened capital as a relationship.

This takes me to a third concern. The timing of the Lonmin conflict is significant. It did not occur when surplus extraction was at its height, but later. During the boom years from 2000 to 2008, Lonmin achieved a profit to labour ratio that averaged 62:38 (that is, after costs, 62% of income went to capital and only 38% went to labour, mainly through wages). In 2009, with the delayed impact of the crash at its worst, the company recorded a loss. In 2010–11 it recovered, but the ratio was only 42:58, much less than in earlier years.[20] Lonmin was still making a profit, but not enough to satisfy shareholders, and by 2012 its space to make significant concessions to workers was much reduced. While Marikana did, as Piketty argues, reflect problems with the 'market economy', it was linked specifically to the 2007/8 crash, that is, a specific economic crisis. For Marxists, a crash was predictable, and explicable as part of the dynamics of capitalism (that is, capital as a set of relationships). The Marikana uprising should be seen – along with the global wave of massive popular protests that occurred between 2010 and 2014 – as a symptom of capitalism in crisis, rather than simply a response to inequality.

The fourth concern takes a different tack. Piketty does not refer to Marikana as a 'massacre'; it was just a 'tragedy'. The same terminology was adopted by the South African government, which did so in a co-ordinated fashion. While 'tragedy' connotes things like accident, calamity, misfortune, affliction, and so forth; 'massacre' implies the killing of many people (or animals) at one time, in circumstances where there is an imbalance of forces. Marikana was indubitably a 'massacre' (even if 'tragedy' might be used as a synonym). It is unlikely that Piketty's selection of words was politically motivated, but nor, I think, was it accidental.

For him, conflict over inequality is 'inevitable' (Piketty 2014: 2). The detail of who did what to whom and with what intentions and effects is not interesting for him. Defining Marikana as a 'massacre' recognises that victims were killed by the police and poses questions about the culpability of Lonmin, the government, NUM and specifically, Ramaphosa. There was nothing inevitable about the massacre, it was the product of human volition.

This moves me on to a fifth matter. In some respects, the post-apartheid state has been quite progressive, and this is partly why the massacre was so shocking. The ANC has sought to build a new black bourgeoisie while sustaining a pact with trade unions. Although this has provided a base for social reforms, it also produced a tightly knit grouping with common interest in repressing the Lonmin strikers. I emphasise this point because, whereas, for Piketty, the inequality upturn was a product of a 1980s 'conservative revolution' led by Margaret Thatcher, neo-liberal policies were being implemented earlier – in the case of Britain, under a Labour government that had a social contract with union leaders (there were no massacres, but powerful sections of the working class were decisively weakened, partly through police action).[21] Social democracy was implicated in both neo-liberalism and the massacre.

And, thus, to my sixth and final concern. What are the practical consequences of all this? At the end of his penultimate chapter, Piketty (2014: 570) returns to Marikana to argue that 'for collective action, what would matter most would be the publication of detailed accounts of private corporations', adding, 'the published accounts of Lonmin Inc do not tell us precisely how much the wealth produced by the mine is divided between profits and wages'. Actually, accounts detailing this division were available at the time of the five-month strike, and their impact was marginal at most (Bowman & Isaacs 2014; also, Alexander 2013: 612).[22] From what I saw, things like injustice, duty, self-sacrifice, honest leadership, endurance, bravery and solidarity were rather more important. Piketty's failure to grasp this detail is part of a larger problem.

His 'major conclusion' is that 'the history of the distribution of wealth has always been deeply political' (Piketty 2014: 20), but his own proposals, for democratic control of capital and a new global tax regime, seem puny when set against the magnitude of the problem he describes. The last decline in global inequality, in the first half of the 20th century, was, he argues – and most people would agree – a consequence of two world wars, the Russian Revolution, the 1930s slump, etc. The conservative revolution at the end of the century rested on the collapse of the Soviet Union, the defeat of major workers' movements and the imposition of structural adjustment all over the world. Rather than follow his theory of big conflicts and massive processes marking shifts in the world history of inequality, he ends with a whimper of fabian-style intellectual persuasion.

Conclusion

Piketty has produced a seminal tome that greatly enhances our understanding of a critical problem facing humanity, and he has encouraged valuable debate. However, his treatment of Marikana reveals significant limitations. His telescope picks out killings on the horizon, and he misses vast plains of complexity and contradiction that lie between there and the mountain of inequality data on which he stands. This middle ground is filled with a series of relationships: production/distribution, ownership/wealth, crisis/resistance, structural change/human agency, capitalism/reformism, and outcomes/programmes. A great strength of the work by the authors of *Capital* (in the 19th century), Karl Marx and Fredrick Engels, is that, in contrast to Piketty, they explored this middle ground. They did so by drawing on a more varied and richer body of scholarship than that accessed by Piketty, but, also, through lifelong participation in struggles to change the world.

Practical engagement is generally frowned upon in the academy. In my view, this is a mistake. It provides knowledge that is otherwise hidden, releasing ideas that pierce accepted wisdom. Piketty made good use of Marikana to exemplify the horrors of capitalism, but the massacre epitomised much more, including collusion between corporate capital and a democratic state. Most importantly, Marikana showed the following: having been floored by vicious repression, ordinary working people were able to find the resources to continue their struggle, and, eventually, to win. It will be battles like this that halt the advancing juggernaut of inequality and injustice.

Notes

1   The book reached the top of the *New York Times* bestseller list on 18 May 2014.

2   Given my South African focus, it is worth pointing to Piketty's Figure 9.9 (Piketty 2014: 327), which shows share of income going to the top percentile and includes a line for South Africa (see also Alvaredo & Atkinson 2010, the source of the

information). The turning points occurred later than in most other countries, and his dates are highly significant. Inequality peaked just before 1948, when the new apartheid government began providing benefits for a larger proportion of whites. It started to rise sharply from 1994, the year apartheid came to an end and the ANC commenced its now 24 years in government. The main beneficiaries of democracy have been South Africa's very wealthy elite, most of whom are white, though an increasing proportion is black.

3   Directed by Rehad Desai, for Uhuru Productions, Johannesburg. All of the workers killed were men, but about 5% of Lonmin's workers in 'core mining occupations' was women. A group of about 50 women joined the men soon before the massacre, and women played a critical role in the solidarity that sustained union mobilisation and strike action from the massacre onwards. On women and Marikana see Asanda Benya (2013) and Bridget Ndibongo (2015).

4   The Marikana Commission of Inquiry, established by South Africa's President, was chaired by Judge Ian Farlam. Its report was presented in 2015 (Farlam et al. 2015). I have provided a substantial review of the report that re-works evidence, submissions and findings to offer alternative conclusions (Alexander 2016).

5   In an analysis of South African press coverage of Marikana/Lonmin in the period 13–22 August 2012, Jane Duncan (2014: 181) found that only 3% of sources cited were workers. This media bias was one of the issues raised by South Africa's social scientists in a statement on Marikana published on 16 September 2012, which was rapidly signed by more than 200 academics (http://marikanastatement.blogspot.co.uk; see also Van Driel 2012: 38).

6   A team from September National Imbizo also visited Marikana on 19 October and provided a similar report to ourselves at about the same time (Fogel 2012). There was widespread scepticism about our 'discovery', but opinion changed after Greg Marinovich (2012), a Pulitzer Prize winning photographer, investigated the site and confirmed our findings.

7   A revised version of this book was published in German (Alexander et al. 2013). For this I added a summary of South Africa's mining history and a chapter on what happened after the massacre. English versions of these chapters are available on my website. A reflection on the significance of Marikana as an historical event appeared as Alexander (2013).

8   Most of what we found was corroborated by Crispin Chinguno (2013) and Philip Frankel (2013). Farlam et al. (2015) confirmed nearly all our conclusions and added further damning evidence against the police, though, in my opinion, its recommendations were pusillanimous (see Alexander 2016).

9   The delegates were Messrs. Magqabine and Mofokeng. To the best of my knowledge, inequality between managers' and workers' pay was not raised until after the massacre, and then it came from outside the workers; profits came later still. Income differences and profits helped justify subsequent strikes, but the demands always focussed on pay.

10   The resolution to increase the RDOs' pay was taken by Lonmin's Exco (Executive Committee), which was also responsible for other key decisions in the unfolding dispute. The Exco comprised the chief executive officer and chief finance officer, both of whom were members of the company's board of directors, plus three executive vice-presidents and, at that stage, the chief commercial officer (Marikana Commission 2014a)

11   On 15 August 2014, Brig A.M. Calitz (2012), representing SAPS, made a sworn statement maintaining: 'Saturday 11 August 2012: Unions clashed and two supporters were killed'. At one point, NUM intended to sue me for claiming its members had killed the two workers (Aboobaker 2013). NUM was mistaken (unlike Calitz I was more careful), and I refused to make the public apology it demanded. The case has not been pursued. In my view, the matter was important because the union's stance threatened academic freedom (and, fortunately, because of this, my university funded my lawyer's response).

12   NUM revealed its hostility to the strikers in other ways. On the night of 10 August, local leaders of the union attempted to bus scabs into work. On 12 August NUM's general secretary, Frans Baleni, issued a statement appealing for 'the deployment of the Special Task Force or South African Defence Force ... before things get out of hand' (it was the task force which, four days later, carried out the massacre at Scene One). Eight of the men who died in the massacre were members of NUM (Marikana Commission 2014b), but the union did not condemn the police action, or visit the families of their deceased members.

13   Zokwana was also president of the International Federation of Industrial, Chemical, Energy, Mine and General Workers' Union and a vice president of IndustiALL Global Union, so he had considerable influence within the labour movement internationally. After the 2014 national elections, he was appointed Minister of Agriculture, Forestry and Fisheries. We return to Rampaphosa below.

14   Lonmin, 'Briefing with SAPS Commissioner', presented to Marikana Commission of Inquiry, 23 October 2013. Also, Marinovich & Nicolson (2013), McClenaghan & Smith (2013), and Nichol (2015).

15   Lonmin, ibid, pp. 2, 10, 12. The politician mentioned is Julius Malema, who had been removed as President of the ANC Youth League and expelled from the party earlier in the year. He is now leader of the Economic Freedom Fighters, which received the third most votes in the May 2014 general election. While the ANC's *Freedom Charter*, adopted in 1955, can be read as supporting nationalisation, ANC governments have, in practice, engaged in privatisation (including some mines), and have opposed nationalisation in the mining industry.

16   In South Africa, strikes are not illegal, and the right to strike is enshrined in the constitution.

17   His company, Shanduka, owned 9% of Lonmin (Davis 2012).

18   The notion of 'egalitarian movement' comes from Göran Therborn's introduction to the series of plenary addresses of which this address was one. See also Therborn (2014).

19   Actually, owners offset increased wages in various ways. Labour costs can be reduced by retrenching staff and increasing efficiency, and platinum companies have benefited greatly from the rising value of the dollar against the rand, about 50% in the three years since January 2012.

20   My calculations draw on data provided by Bowman & Isaacs (2014).

21   See also Michael Burawoy's presidential address to the ISA, a version of which was given at the University of Johannesburg (available on YouTube, and see Burawoy 2017).

22   I provided them for 2011 and a full set was included in Bowman and Isaacs (2014).

References

Aboobaker, Shanti (2013) 'Union guns for Prof over Marikana', *Sunday Independent* (Johannesburg), 21 May.

Alexander, Peter (2013) 'Marikana, turning point in South African history', *Review of African Political Economy* 123: 605–19.

Alexander, Peter (2014) 'Op-ed: AMCU victory is more than just about the figures', *Daily Maverick,* 29 June.

Alexander, Peter (2016) 'Marikana Commission on inquiry: From narratives towards history', *Journal of Southern African Studies* 42(5): 815–40.

Alexander, Peter, Thapelo Lekgowa, Botsang Mmope, Luke Sinwell and Bongani Xezwi (2012) *Marikana: A View from the Mountain and a Case to Answer.* Jacana Media, Johannesburg. Revised versions published in 2013 by Jacana, Bookmarks Publishing (London) and Ohio University Press (Athens).

Alexander, Peter, Thapelo Lekgowa, Botsang Mmope, Luke Sinwell and Bongani Xezwi (2013) *Das Massaker von Marikana*: Mandelbaum – Kritik and Utopie. Translated by Werner Gilts, edited by Jakob Krameritsch.

Alvaredo, Facundo and Anthony B. Atkinson (2010) *Colonial Rule, Apartheid and Natural Resources: Top Incomes in South Africa, 1903–2007.* Centre for Economic Policy Research, London.

Benya, Asanda (2013) 'Absent from the frontline but not absent from the struggle: Women in mining', *Femina Politica,* 1: 144–7.

Bowman, Andrew and Gilad Isaacs (2014) *Demanding the Impossible? Platinum Mining Profits and Wage Demands in Context.* Sociology, Work and Development Institute (SWOP), University of the Witwatersrand, Johannesburg.

Budlender, Geoff et al. (2014) 'Heads of Argument of Evidence Leaders' presented to Marikana Commission of Inquiry.

Burawoy, Michael (2017) 'Social movements in the neoliberal age'. In Marcel Paret, Carin Runciman and Luke Sinwell (eds), *Southern Resistance in Critical Perspective: the Politics of Protest in South Africa's Cotentious Democracy.* Routledge, London and New York.

Calitz, Adriaan (2012) Statement under oath, 16 August, presented in evidence to Marikana Commission of Inquiry.

Callinicos, Alex (2014) 'Piketty's theory of capital – strengths and weaknesses', *Socialist Worker,* 13 May.

Chinguno, Crispin (2013) *Marikana and the Post-Apartheid Workplace Order.* Sociology, Work and Development Institute (SWOP), University of the Witwatersrand, Johannesburg.

Davis, Gaye (2012) 'Ramaphosa under fire at Marikana', *IOL News,* 24 October.

Duncan, Jane (2014) *The Rise of the Securacrats.* Jacana Media, Johannesburg.

Farlam, I.G, P.D. Hemraj and B.R. Tokota (2015) *Marikana Commission of Inquiry. Report on Matters of Public, National and International Concern Arising out of the Tragic Incidents at the Lonmin Mine in Marikana.* Marikana Commission of Inquiry, Pretoria.

Fogel, Ben (2012) 'September National Imbizo Report on Marikana', *Amandla*, 21 August.

Foudraine, Julia (2014) 'Mortal Men: The rise of the Association of Mineworkers and Construction Union under the leadership of James Mathunjwa and the union's move to the political left, 1998–2014', MA dissertation, University of Leiden.

Frankel, Philip (2013) *Between the Rainbows and the Rain: Marikana, Migration, Mining and the Crisis of Modern South Africa.* Agency for Social Reconstruction, Johannesburg.

Harvey, David (2014) *Afterthoughts on Piketty's Capital*, 17 May. Available at: http://davidharvey.org/2014/05/afterthoughts-pikettys-capital/.

Kasrils, Ronnie (2012) 'It was like poking a hornet's nest', *Sunday Times*, 26 August.

Lekgowa, Thapelo, Botsang Mmope and Peter Alexander (2012) 'How police planned and carried out the massacre at Marikana', *Socialist Worker* (online), 21 August.

Marikana Commission of Inquiry (2014a) 'Da Costa's evidence to the Marikana Commission of Inquiry,' 3 June: 30025–30028 and 30052–30056, and Exhibit OO17, 'Witness Statement of Michael Gomas Da Costa': 6–7.

Marikana Commission of Inquiry (2014b) 'Phase 2: Preliminary Report, 15 August 2014'. (Phase 2 was aimed at understanding underlying causes, and its preliminary report was drafted by a sociologist, Kally Forrest.)

Marikana Commission of Inquiry (2014c): 'Written Submissions on Behalf of the Former Minister of Police, Minister E N Mthethwa'.

Marinovich, Greg (2012) 'The murder fields of Marikana. The cold murder fields of Marikana', *Daily Maverick*, 8 September.

Marinovich, Greg and Greg Nicolson (2013) 'Marikana massacre: SAPS, Lonmin, Ramaphosa & time for blood,' *Daily Maverick,* 24 October.

Matunjwa, Joseph (2014) Press conference statement, 24 June. Author's recording.

McClenaghan, Maeve and David Smith (2013) 'The British mine owners, the police and South Africa's day of blood'. *The Observer*, 24 November.

Ndibongo, Bridget (2015) 'Women of Marikana: Survival and Struggles', MA dissertation, University of Johannesburg.

Ngwane, Trevor (2017) 'Against all Odds', in Trevor Ngwane, Luke Sinwell and Immanuel Ness, *Urban Revolt: State Power and the Rise of People's Movements in the Global South.* Wits University Press, Johannesburg.

Nichol, James (2015) 'Can the Farlam Commission Deliver Justice for Slain Miners', interview, *Amandla*.

Nicolson, Greg (2013) 'Marikana massacre: More disturbing questions about police planning and objectives', *Daily Maverick,* 23 October.

Piketty, Thomas (2014) *Capital in the Twenty-First Century.* Harvard University Press, Cambridge, MA. Translated by Arthur Goldhammer.

Seoka, Jo (2012) 'Charges against miners raise questions', *Business Day,* 5 December.

Sinwell, Luke with Siphiwe Mbatha (2013) *The Spirit of Matikana: The Rise of Insurgent Trade Unionism in South Africa.* Wits University Press, Johannesburg.

Therborn, Göran (2014) *Killing Fields of Inequality.* Polity Press, Cambridge.

Van Driel, Maria (2012) *Documents of the Social Movements 2012, Special Edition: Marikana.* Khanya Publishing, Johannesburg.

21

From Tekel to Gezi Resistance in Turkey: Possibilities for a United Collective Social Rights Movement

Aylin Topal

Neoliberal market-oriented policies implemented since the beginning of the 1980s have transformed both class and property relations to a great extent all over the world. One of the defining characteristics of the neoliberal era could be pinpointed as legal and institutional restructuring to pacify the social opposition in general and in particular weakening trade unions which had been the main actors of collective movements through the 1960s and 1970s. The 1990s saw the rise of political positions that argued identity and recognition-based politics should take precedence over class-based politics for a more liberal social life to be attained. Proponents of this position hailed mushrooming of civil society organizations claiming that they would bring a variety of actors and demands to the fore. Meanwhile, public services such as education, health, and social security were abandoned to the incursion of free market mechanisms, natural resources left to intensified commodification, and the patenting of and dictates of intellectual property rights imposed on all living organisms. Such policies that have been imposed on every aspect of social life through coercive and disciplinary forms of state intervention, which might also be evaluated as crisis-delaying strategies, have led to resistances of various forms in different countries towards the late 2000s.

In the new millennium, different resistances from various regions of the world have emerged. Some of the first news of the century came from South America: in 2000 the Aymara communities in Bolivia launched their struggle against the privatization of water resources; in 2001 the Argentine economic crisis sparked protests and factory occupations; in 2003 landless rural workers started to occupy idle plots of land belonging to big landowners; in 2006 high school pupils in Chile protested and occupied schools to voice their demands for free and equal right to education.

Resistance was not restricted to South America. In 2007, rising food and grain prices ignited protests in Bangladesh, Haiti, and Egypt among others. In addition to the continuing effects of the food crisis, the financial crisis burst in 2008. Persistent economic stagnation paved the way for a widened geography of resistances. When, in December 2010 a Tunisian street vendor committed suicide by setting himself on fire in protest of bad living conditions and unemployment, this ignited the 'Arab Spring' movement of the North African and West Mediterranean countries. The advanced capitalisms, too, were not immune. In September 2011, hundreds of protesters occupied Zuccotti Park across from Wall Street to protest the US government bailouts of big finance. The occupy movement spread to other US states in a very short time. In many southern European countries the so-called 'reform packages', composed of austerity for the already poor, that governments implemented to overcome the crisis also triggered resistances. Across Europe, 14 November 2012 was declared a day of resistance. In tandem with these many 'national' struggles, the broader anti-globalization movements and World (and European) Social Forums have also left their mark on the 21st century.

Turkey has also seen an awakening of sorts. While protests related directly to the 2008 crisis did not appear, one can point to the Tekel workers' resistance against enforcement of precarious employment status in the public sector. The Justice and Development Party (hereafter with Turkish acronym AKP) accelerated the process of privatization in Turkey since it came to power in 2002. Although impact of these privatizations has been on the workers, there had been a certain inertia against the whole process on the part of the working class, until the winter of 2009–10 when the workers of Tekel company (the privatized state monopoly of tobacco and alcoholic beverages) decided to show their discontent against AKP's privatization and employment policies by setting a tent city in the middle of Ankara which lasted for nearly three months in freezing winter conditions. Tekel resistance could be seen as a reemergence of Turkish working-class militancy after more than three decades.

Nearly three years after the Tekel resistance, another resistance, this time with more widespread participation and scope took place in 2013, when the then Prime Minister Recep Tayyip Erdoğan revealed government's redevelopment plans for Taksim Square, the main square of İstanbul and Gezi Park, one of the few remaining green spots in the city center adjacent to the Square. The redevelopment plans included reconstruction of a mosque in Taksim Square and a historical military barrack in the Gezi Park. Progressive civil society led by the Union of Chambers of Turkish Engineers and Architects and the Union of Chambers of City Planners immediately reacted. These organizations along with environmental activists declared that they would block the construction vehicles from entering the Park. On 28 May, they pitched the first tents in the park. These protests quickly spread over the country after the police forces intervened by allegedly using excessive force on these protestors at Gezi Park at dawn of 31 May. In the following weeks, millions rushed to parks in many provinces to protest, chanting 'Everywhere is Taksim, everywhere is resistance.' These protests that lasted through the month of June 2013 are recorded in the history as *Gezi Resistance.*

This article aims to focus on the form of organization in these two resistances as well as the role and possible strategies for trade unions and traditional left organizations. The article draws upon interviews with Tekel workers who had actively participated in the resistance and members of the leading collectives in Gezi Resistance. The interviews with Tekel workers were conducted between March and December 2013 in five cities (Samsun, İzmir, Hatay, Diyarbakır, Batman). The interviews with the Gezi collectives in İstanbul were conducted between November 2013 and June 2014. The interview questions targeted to inquire how they interpret their respective resistances in terms of their weaknesses and strengths in the eye of its active participants.[1] These interviews also explored how and to what extent the Tekel workers and Gezi protestors have become aware of the common ground for struggle. The article is organized in three sections. The first section provides a brief historical account for neoliberalization in Turkey and its implication for class-based politics. This section also lays out the AKP rule and the policies that triggered these two waves of resistances. Second and third sections are analyses of the two resistances in terms of their potentials to pave the ground for development of a counter-hegemonic strategy. The last section discusses the possibilities for a radical conception of combined rights movement. Under the light shed by these two case studies of social resistances that took place in Turkey, the article explores the possibilities for a new and creative form of organization based on collective social rights.

Transition to neoliberalism with an authoritarian state form and the AKP era

Neoliberalism in Turkey was ushered by an authoritarian state form that effectively shifted the balance of class forces since 1980 in Turkey. During the late 1970s, Turkey faced a grave political and socio-economic crisis which was primarily a crisis of balance of payments but it had important impact on the relations between capital and labor as well. The bourgeoisie was alarmed by deepening social conflicts through the late 1960s and 1970s. Along with the bourgeoisie, military generals also perceived that the very social was under threat. As elsewhere the Turkish Trade Unions, in the post-war years, had developed a strong bargaining position vis-à-vis the employers as well as an increasing vocal presence in the formulations of economic policies. Not surprisingly, the working-class movement was made scapegoat for the period of relative stagnation and world economic recession of the late 1970s. Having identified the scapegoat for the crisis, the early 1980s witnessed a crucial turning point in the socio-economic and political development process. There are two important dates in 1980: 24 January, for the structural adjustment program and 12 September, for the military *coup d'état*. Although the former was hailed by the international financial community and domestic business circles as a turning point, the decisive change in the balance of class forces came with the latter. The military junta had two major aims in taking over the power: the first one was to tame the political left and trade unions by applying harsh measures; and the second was to implement the structural adjustment program that the civilian government had been rather reluctant to adopt. Therefore, the military *coup* signified not only a change in the political regime but also transition to the neoliberal form of state which has maintained itself despite the return to civilian government within the confines of an authoritarian constitution put into effect by a referendum in 1982 (Yalman 2009).

From its inception in 1967, particularly through the 1970s, Revolutionary Workers Union Confederation (hereafter with Turkish acronyms DİSK) had been the main actor leading the class-based politics. By the late 1970s, rather than the economic demands and collective bargaining capacity of the DİSK, political aspiration of the working-class movement towards socialism seemed to toll the alarm bells at least in the eye of the ruling elite. One of the key themes in the very first speech of General Kenan Evren, as the head of the military junta, in the first hours of the *coup* revealed the class nature of the *coup* and signaled the determination to initiate repression on the rights and freedoms.

> All the rights of hardworking and patriotic Turkish workers will be preserved within the confines of present economic conditions. However, those who endeavor to abuse the Turkish workers and their trade union rights and lead them in certain ideological directions will not be permitted to achieve their ends. (*Milliyet*, 12 September 1980)

Following this first public speech on 12 September, the activities of all three existing trade union confederations were suspended, and the leaders of many unions were put under custody. On 13 September, all strikes and lockouts were banned until further notice as the junta reiterated the same theme by stating 'faithful and devoted Turkish workers will continue their work in the feelings of patriotism, national solidarity and fraternity' (Soner, 1996: 455). The immediate Laws on Collective Bargaining (no. 2821) and Strikes and Lockouts (no. 2822) enacted by the Junta government have practically ended trade union activities causing a meltdown in the number of members of the unions (Özveri, 2006).

The military junta decided to rewrite the legal framework to strengthen the authoritarian state while curtailing the democratic rights and freedoms with the 1982 Constitution (Özbudun, 1991). The spirit of the Constitution generally, and in terms of syndical rights in particular, was a manifesto of prohibitions. When individual articles of the Constitution are considered collectively, it becomes clear that this framework had the political objective of reversing the political as well as economic gains of the labor movement achieved during the previous two decades much to the chagrin of the business community. The Constitution was approved by some 92 percent of the votes in the referendum that was also presented as the approval of people for the military coup. Although public criticism of the Constitution had been banned via total control of mass media and rigid censorship, such a high percentage would also refer to considerable consent of the masses.

The military rule played a significant role in the implementation of this hegemonic strategy not only by establishing an authoritarian regime, but more importantly, by gaining the 'consent' of the masses who were disenchanted by the repercussions of the political as well as the economic crisis on their daily lives during the pre-coup era. The 'law and order' rhetoric was particularly effective among the working-class neighborhoods that had particularly suffered from the civil strife during the 1970s. The 'chaotic situation' of the late 1970s has been used very effectively to rouse the fears of the Turkish people since they were reminded with flashbacks of the political polarization of the period each time in a more exaggerated fashion. Moreover, the scenes of the recent past have been created, formed, shaped and reshaped in the minds of the people by the great help of mainstream media. The rhetoric of the military regime as well as the first civilian government which came to power in 1983 were keen to consolidate the new order by portraying the previous one as a highly undesirable one characterized by civil strife and disorder as a result of class-based politics as well as an economic crisis caused by outdated policies.

The post-military regime era was very much in line with the New Right politics. The task of the trade unions would be confined to negotiating wages with the employers, but not to negotiate economic policy with the government. The working-class movement aimed to be discredited and 'politics of distribution' which had characterized the main axis of politics in the 1960s and 1970s was effectively undermined. Putting an end to class-based politics by appealing to virtues of depoliticized individuals can be described as the core of the hegemonic strategy of the new right (Yalman, 2009). As the Prime Minister of the first civilian government says 'political freedom is the end result of economic liberalism. The coming century is that of the individual and virtues of the individual is an extension of the virtues of the free market competition' (Özal, 1992: 11, 23). The task of the government, therefore, is set a framework (the law and order) within which individuals can successfully pursue their respective ends (cf. Hayek, 1979: 139).

The working class has become overwhelmingly disorganized throughout the 1980s and 1990s in counteracting the neoliberal transformation of the capital–labor relations and labor processes. Except for a brief period between 1988 and 1991 in which workers of state-owned Turkish Cellulose and Paper Factories, Steel and Iron Factories, Glass Factories, and last but not the least the Coal Mines have struggled against the worsening conditions, the trade unions have been overwhelmingly weak as they were practically dispossessed of their organizational capacities (Topal and Yalman, 2015).

Implementation of free trade principles and the establishment of dynamic capital markets were coupled with policies to provide attractive and promising environments for international investors through privatizations. Although the first legislative changes to eliminate legal barriers to privatization had been made in 1986 and 1994, the massive privatization program became a policy priority especially in the aftermath of the 1999 IMF stand-by agreement and the 2001 economic crisis. When the Justice and Development Party came to power in the elections held on 3 November 2002, both the Turkish bourgeoisie and international financial circles had their faith in this single party government. As an economic analysis released by Merrill Lynch clearly pointed out, 'the arrival of a single-party government would strengthen Turkey's economic balances.'[2] And the party did not disappoint these expectations. The AKP government proved to be the suitable actor that could actually put privatizations in action. Within the first months in office, the government declared that to help end the ongoing economic crisis, state involvement in economic activities would be minimized and the financial burden of SEEs on the national budget would be relieved. Deputy Prime Minister announced that Tekel along with other state assets would be sold in the first half of 2003. Since then, privatization of State Economic Enterprises has become a policy priority and even the main fiscal management strategy of AKP. These privatizations have been in tandem with an overall transformation in public sector employment relations towards insecurity. Therefore, insecure temporary employment has facilitated the government's policy of reducing public sector workforces. This whole process did not face challenging working-class resistance until the winter of discontent between 2009 and 2010.

Coming to grips of the common ground in Tekel resistance

Privatization of Tekel was the biggest sale in the privatization process. According to diplomatic correspondence of the US Embassy in Ankara, both European and US companies attempted in various ways to hasten its privatization and even determine its sale conditions.[3] Inevitably the actual damage of this privatization has been on workers of this privatized enterprise who faced losing their jobs, deprived of their social rights. The workers at Tekel showed the first significant sign of discontent with AKP's privatization policies when the Privatization Administration declared that all the leaf processing units of Tekel would be closed down and workers' existing contracts would be annulled. All the remaining Tekel workers who had survived the privatization process were given two choices: to either resign from their positions, receiving severance pay and unemployment benefits, or to continue to work in another public institution under 4/C status, a legal status created to employ temporary workers in government jobs. The privatization administration gave them 8 months to make their decisions. They reacted immediately to the government's offer of 4/C employment status.[4]

On 15 December 2009, workers from 11 cities arrived in Ankara in 106 buses. When their buses were not allowed to enter the city, the workers crashed the police barricades and walked to the party headquarters of the AKP where the police assaulted the workers. The first four days of the resistance saw continuous assaults from police which caused

an immediate reaction from various social actors upon which the government made relative improvements in the 4/C status – the contract terms
were rearranged as not less than 4 and more than 11 months. Earlier it
was not less than 2 and not more than 10 months. This improvement only
raised the hopes of the workers. They responded to government by claiming 'what we are struggling for is our right to work and rights cannot
be negotiated'.[5] On the fifth day of the resistance, the workers started
sit-in protests in front of the headquarters of their workers' confederation, Türk-İş. On the 38th day, workers pitched tents and set up a fully
fledged 'tent city' which lasted for 40 days. On 17 January, the 34th day
of resistance, 10,000 workers gathered in a solidarity manifestation and
chanted for a general strike which was the agenda of a meeting of all
the workers' confederations on 20 January. Instead of a general strike,
the confederations agreed on a one-hour-late-beginning-of-workday as
of 25 January until Tekel workers' demands were all met. The government demanded a meeting around a negotiation table with the workers on
28 January. The confederations conditionally accepted this offer by stressing that they would not negotiate their rights. In the meeting on 28 January,
the government offered further improvements in the 4/C status, such as
employment termination/redundancy benefits and 22-day paid annual
vacation. Together with this so-called compromise, the government also
shortened the timeframe to transfer to 4/C from eight months to one month
on 1 March. Following this unsatisfactory meeting with the government,
the confederations were forced to called for a one-day 'solidarity' strike on
4 February.[6] Although the confederation failed to organize the strike effectively, more than a hundred thousand workers came out on the streets in
support of the Tekel workers. As a diplomatic correspondence of the US
Embassy in Ankara written on the 58th day of the resistance notes, the
'Tekel strike is emerging as a defining moment for Turkey's labor movement and a significant political challenge for Prime Minister Erdoğan.'

On 1 March, the day before the term to transfer to 4/C recognized by
the government expired, the Turkish Council of State, the highest court in
Turkish judiciary granted a motion for stay of execution on the grounds
that the 30-day period given by the government to make the choice was
'unnecessarily restrictive.' Although this decision did not mean any change
in the 4/C employment conditions, it was also the product of the tremen-
dous popularity and legitimacy of the movement itself (Savran, 2010).
Following this final decision, the union leaders declared that the tents
would be unpitched by the afternoon and the buses would leave Ankara

in the evening. The union leaders were forced by the dissident workers to announce that they would be returning back to Ankara on 1 April. At the same time, Prime Minister Erdoğan was announcing, 'we shall not let the same thing happen again'. Both Tekel workers and Erdoğan kept their word, 4000 people gathered in Ankara on 1 April, yet they were faced with very harsh police assault. They could not even gather in front of their confederation to make a press release. Protesters were disbanded through taking into custody, physical assaults and excessive use of tear gas. Downtown Ankara was under the fog of infamous pepper gas for hours. Although the strong voice of Tekel workers were silenced by force and all the former Tekel workers have eventually transferred to 4/C status in the aftermath of the resistance, the specter of resistance and of resisting workers was haunting: Sakarya Square where the tent city was pitched was unofficially renamed as Resistance Square. One of the main streets of downtown Ankara is renamed after the name of a worker, Hamdullah Uysal, who was struck and killed by a drunken SUV driver during the resistance.

As Savran (2010) rightly observes, 'the tent city turned into a Mecca for all kinds of opposition movements ... Socialists, ostracised and marginalised by state and society alike since the military coup of 1980, moved like fish in the sea among the workers.' The tent city received a wide range of supporters every day from students to academics, from unions of chambers to LGBTQ activists. Tekel workers received active support from all over Turkey. Sakarya Square turned into an open concert hall at New Years' Eve. A big crowd including students, artists and musicians celebrated New Years' Eve with the Tekel workers in their tents. On the 68th day, 20 February, 20,000 people spent the night with the Tekel workers in Sakarya Square. The same day, 21 civil associations organized a solidarity manifestation in Northern Cyprus. The resistance also received significant international solidarity with over 4000 solidarity messages received from about 100 countries.[7] Solidarity protests were organized in Berlin, Paris, Vienna, Amsterdam and London.

It seems that obstacles and challenges that spring from the neoliberal labor process have also influenced the performance of unions in orchestrating workers effectively against this organized assault on their livelihood. After all they are also part of this social relationship that begins at the 'point of production' and extends throughout society influencing politics, culture and life in general. Trade unions, like workers, perceive the conditions and craft their strategies accordingly. Needless to say, the relationship between the rank and file of unions has always carried some tensions, but it has never been antagonistic. However, this tension has been intensified in the neoliberal era in Turkey. The union leaders increasingly became tied to their salary. Their role has transformed to providing labor peace. They were now expected to assure the management that the workers will show up and work the next day. Disoriented by the changing structure of economy, it is not surprising to come across unionism that internalized the ethos of management. Many commentators claimed that both the one-hour late beginning of workday and the one-day general strike were not as successful as they could have been due to organizational weaknesses of their union, Tek-Gıda İş and the Confederation, Türk-İş. Many former Tekel workers complained about the organization strategies of the Türk-İş confederation and their union Tek-Gıda İş. Their comments were even suggesting that these trade unions during and before the resistance often attempted to tame the resistance. The workers claimed that the trade union leaders tried to narrow the agenda to bread and butter issues resisting against expansion of the scope of the resistance.

To recuperate the weakness of the trade unions, the Tekel resistance was organized to a great extent through a bottom-up fashion. It could even be argued that relative organizational weaknesses of trade unions may have strengthened the Tekel workers' self-organizational capacities. An expansive solidarity network among workers was established and maintained throughout the resistance. When the Privatization Administration declared the closure of the leaf processing units and the choices of the workers, the immediate reaction of the workers was setting up a communication network, through the networks of the trade union and contacts and acquaintances that had been established in the earlier demonstrations. Militant workers (or the workers with class consciousness) from different cities in the absence of effective trade union leadership, collectively decided to go to Ankara. As one worker said, 'moles decided to emerge from the ground'. They pressured their trade union to support them with all means available. Workers with the forced support of their trade union decided to go to Ankara for an indefinite time to resist against these options that they were forced to choose. During the resistance, the coordination among the workers was democratic: each tent aimed to function as a workers' council. Resistance committees were established. These committees put continuous pressure on the leaders of the confederations to call for a general strike, and at times demanded the leader of their confederation to resign. The tent city was called 'Sakarya Commune' (Savran, 2010).

Despite governments' active campaign against the workers, Tekel resistance did lead to a re-awakening of the Turkish working class. Capitalist labor processes at Tekel had been making workers unaware of collective labor. A significant feature of the labor process at Tekel is the geographical constitution of the enterprise. Collective work had been carried out simultaneously in six factories and 50 leaf processing plants in 22 cities. Tekel workers were workers on the move: they had often been uprooted from their social environment and subjected to reorientation in another environment. In addition to geographical dispersion, the production process at Tekel was extremely fractured and subdivided into a number of positions in regard to technical and sexual division of labor. This much-fragmentized labor process has isolated individual workers, or small groups at best, rather than organic part of the collective labor that produces the whole commodity. What neoliberalism has added to this picture is different employment strategies causing further dehomogenizing, the workers diverging even short term economic interests of the workers. When they met with workers coming from 11 cities, they faced collective labor and came to grips with the total assault on Tekel's collective labor.

Tekel workers' objective relations to the means of production had certainly generated conflicts which shaped workers' *experience* in *class ways* (cf. E.P. Thompson, 1963). As E.P. Thompson suggests, at the moment of resistance as the instances of 'making of working class,' class may be present yet they do not express themselves in class consciousness (E.P. Thompson, 2001). Yet, particularly in the neoliberal era capitalism further created other equalities, injustices that people have been experiencing. The success of the New Right ideology in dismantling the older collective class solidarity has brought 'new-identities' to shape social processes in different ways rather than a 'class way'. Therefore, Tekel resistance provides some insights for how class operates in the neoliberal era in the relative absence of class consciousness and with the presence of multiple identities with different forms of exclusion and dispossession. Transformation of the labor process at Tekel during its piecemeal privatization had weakened the ground for collective will formation against privatizations. It is true that with the resistance, a significant number of workers woke up from the deep sleep and decided to rebel against perceived injustice rooted in the system. Yet, the discovery of consciousness grew out of the process of struggle as workers came to grips with the common ground for resistance. As workers handle their class situations, they saw the false antithesis constructed between identity and class. Living in the tent city for 78 days, sharing a tent with other fellow workers, neighboring with workers from 11 cities, workers saw the unifying collective labor behind Turk–Kurd, Alevi–Sunni, Man–Women, Secular–Religious fractures that had been reinstated since 1980s onwards, particularly by the AKP government in the last decade. Therefore, Tekel resistance proved that struggle can indeed bring peace and solidarity between constructed conflicts. This is particularly important since the class struggle was held responsible for social and political polarization of the late 1970s period which were manipulated as the source of fear, legitimating source of the launching of the neoliberal policies. Tekel resistance destroyed the fear from class politics and brought hope. As Bergson (2001: 9) puts it 'what makes hope such an intense pleasure is the fact that the future ... appears to us ... under a multitude of forms, equally attractive and equally possible'.

What really distinguished the Tekel resistance from earlier successful working-class uprisings was its potential to pave the ground for development of a counter-hegemonic strategy combining different rights' struggles under its tent city. The struggle around narrow economic interests and legal statuses transformed or at least presented the potentials to transform into a much larger struggle for the common interest of all humanity. As a Tekel worker excitingly notes:

> When we first came out, we came for bread and butter. We came for ourselves. Tekel workers came only for themselves. We were about to be deprived of our jobs. As we continued to struggle, we received more support. With the increased support, we realized that the cause is not only ours .... we realized that this is not only the problem of the Tekel workers, this is the problem of all workers, youth and students, everybody. At the moment, we are struggling for the labor of all humanity not for my own labor or job. (Interview with AT in Sayılan and Türkmen, 2010: 152)

To begin with, Tekel resistance had been a moment where the concept of citizenry was scrutinized. In response to the President Erdoğan's statement against the Tekel workers 'there are owners of this country', many Tekel workers frustratingly reacted 'this government is not seeing us as citizens' (Kaldıraç, 2010: 32). As Marx (1844) notes in the Jewish Question, the legal identity of citizenry is the highest point of the state for Hegel. The emancipation of the Jews from ghettoes meant ascribing them the status of citizen incorporated in the state. Indeed, status of citizenry is to create an image of free and equal legal subjects in the very sense, while they are subjected to class relations in their private life. Aroused feeling of injustice among workers was a moment of rupture in the image of legal subjects who are free and equal. The biggest organization for the right to water, 'Fraternity of Rivers' gave active support to Tekel Workers' resistance declaring, 'Right to work is as essential as right to water'.[8] Right to Shelter and Right to Transportation collectives also expressed their solidarity with the Tekel Workers declaring 'We are uniting to reclaim our rights'.[9] In a matter of weeks, the struggle was not simply confined to Tekel workers' employment rights, but showed the potentials to expand to other social collective rights.

Midwives of Gezi Resistance: Accumulation of collectives, issues and rights

Nearly three years after Tekel Resistance, another wave of protests shook the country. In May 2013, Prime Minister Erdoğan revealed his government's redevelopment plans for the Taksim Square area. Taksim Square is the central square of İstanbul that has been 'a monumental public space' expressing the state and nation building processes of the early Republican era and the venue for political protests of the left and labor movement since the late 1960s (Topal, 2016). Along with these plans concerning the Taksim Square area, the Prime Minister also informed the public about the government's mega-projects like a third airport and a third bridge over the Bosphorus. Indeed, the AKP had already partially revealed its plans to transform the Square with the Taksim Pedestrianization Project launched on 31 October 2012. While the purported aim of this project was to reserve more space for pedestrians, it became clearer that the pedestrianization project of the Square with large blocks of concrete was a symbolic attempt to pave the ground for the forthcoming regeneration projects concerning the area. Furthermore, the fully fledged regeneration plans included Gezi Park that is adjacent to the Square and is one of the few remaining green spots in central İstanbul. These plans like every single piece of legislation the AKP government had passed, were not brought to the parliament let alone in consultation with any civil society organization. When the representatives of civil society organizations, together with environmentalists, pitched their tents in Gezi Park on 27 May to prevent the launching of the regeneration project by cutting down the trees, the form of the protest must have reminded the Prime Minister of the Tekel Resistance. In one of his first speeches on the newly unraveling Gezi Resistance, he referred to Tekel Resistance: 'These groups when they establish themselves in a place, refuse to leave. They continuously terrorize the place. We experienced it with Tekel workers'. In the same speech, he also aimed to criminalize the protestors by saying 'Those protesters in the Park are extreme groups'.[10] He infamously called them *çapulcu* (looters or marauders).[11] This time, he warned, the protesters would not be tolerated; they would be ousted from the Park by any means necessary.

On the dawn of 31 May, police violently attacked the protestors, destroying the camp area by burning the tents and using excessive force, tear gas and water-cannon on even non-resisting protestors. The evening of the same day, in every major city, various collectives called for protests in solidarity with the protesters in İstanbul. Millions of people rushed to the major public parks in their cities to protest primarily against violent police crackdown on protestors in Gezi Park. Among the common chants of these solidarity protests were 'dictator resign!' and 'everywhere is Taksim, everywhere is resistance!' Meanwhile as elsewhere, thousands gathered in Taksim Square in the following days pressing the police forces to retreat from Gezi Park. By the afternoon of 1 June, the protesters were in Gezi Park once again, this time multiplied in number and organization.

The Gezi Resistance radically opened the space of polity to a multidimensional horizon of meanings with the promise of liberation. The texture of space redefined by the resistance was conducive to produce different but more or less coherent struggles that could co-exist together. The Resistance held the promise of liberation not only from AKP's rule. In a very short time, the Park was transformed into an emancipated common space to harbor an all-encompassing resistance against different forms of social exclusion, repression, exploitation and domination. Feminists collectives, LGBTQ groups, environmentalist, right to shelter collectives, the right to water organization 'Fraternity of Rivers', independent artists, vegetarian and vegan collectives, youth organizations, trade unions, Tekel workers and workers of other previously privatized state economic enterprises, extra-parliamentarian political parties and collectives set up their tents, opened their stands, distributed their flyers. During the Gezi Resistance, Taksim Square – except for the police attacks – was a trouble-free area peacefully and commonly occupied by many, none claiming to possess. The Gezi Resistance pushed forward the meaning of public space as an ongoing forum where everyone can speak and listen. Taksim during the Gezi Resistance became a truly open space to public speeches, lectures, concerts, rallying cries and all forms of theatrical utterances. Reminiscent of the Tekel Resistance, the Council of State granted a motion for stay of execution of the Regeneration Plans for Taksim Square.[12]

This reaction was not surprising to many, as tensions and discontent had been growing and issue-based struggles had been accumulating particularly through the 2000s. As one of the leading activists of a right to city collective, *İMECE*[13] noted that 2009 local elections have been a turning point in the form of the organization. The right to city collectives, the members of which were mostly young graduates from urban and city development departments of different universities, had previously been organized in the old working-class neighborhoods presently cornered in the high-rent city center areas thus subjected to the urban regeneration projects for gentrification purposes. Among them, some collectives can be traced back to the 1999 Solidarity Volunteers and Earthquake Survivors Associations which defended the right to decent shelter of the families that became homeless with the destruction of the 1999 Yalova (a nearby province to İstanbul) Earthquake that also destroyed some adjacent neighborhoods of İstanbul.[14] From 2009 onwards, the right to city and right to shelter collectives started to coordinate with the other collectives such as Social Rights Association (SRA) established in 2006 in İstanbul.[15] The 2009 local elections led to some small-scale improvements, in terms of change of the ruling party in the municipality or change of the composition of the municipality councils which made AKP take a step back in its aggressive urban regeneration projects. With the relative success in this struggle, the right to city and right to shelter collectives searched for some ways to channel the dynamism they created in that movement while the old working-class neighborhood committees were still engaged. The first strategy was to call for a platform to unite all the existing neighborhood collectives.

In that context, the October 2009 Annual Meeting of Boards of Governors of the World Bank Group and the IMF and the July 2010 European Social Forum (ESF) meeting in İstanbul turned into two timely opportunities for various collectives to unite. A group of activists founded a collective called *Direnistanbul* (Resistanbul) to organize workshops, exhibitions, movie screenings, conversations and activities against the WB and IMF. The meetings of Resistanbul joined many networks of activists particularly combining the old working-class neighborhood committees and the activist youth. One year later, calling for a 'socially and environmentally just transition in the economy', the ESF declaration underlined that 'against those who try to create divisions between social and ecological justice, we assert that they do not contradict each other. They are and have to be complementary. Our vision is of a good life for all, not a nightmare of authoritarian eco-austerity.'[16] During the days of the ESF, these different collectives founded a new umbrella organization called the Urban Movements whose 'aim is to struggle collectively against the neoliberal attacks on our living spaces and cities.'[17] This organization established the coordination network among various associations and collectives, which, according to one activist 'had been going through a survival crisis of their own.'

Another important step for the accumulation of collectives and issues was taken during the summer of 2012 when Resistanbul and the Urban Movements collectives started a search for a more inclusive form of organization. The aimed objective was to attend the International Workers Day celebrations under a combined banner. For that purpose, a series of meetings were organized gathering various groups including but not limited to the ecology collectives, animal rights collectives, LGBTQ groups, immigrant rights collectives. An activist from IMECE claimed 'the common concern expressed by various groups in these meetings was the lack of organizational capacity. There was a wall that each individual collective was failing to pass through. We had to formulate a union of forces, perhaps a common ground for praxis and discussion. There was a simultaneous endeavor in different collectives to gather with others.' As another activist said, 'each individual group was feeling that they had exhausted their internal discussions. They felt clogged.' It was also noted:

> each collective and group in those meetings were perhaps represented by 15 to 20 people, yet they had the capacity to mobilize large masses around their respective agenda. For instance, the ecology collective's rather small headquarters was in Ankara but they were in constant contact with the villagers in dozens of hydroelectric plant construction zones. Furthermore, each collective has brought a rich array of resistance repertoire and an issue-related hinterland collectively covering various different issues.

Finally, a shared platform for such a rich composition of these collectives was called *Müştereklerimiz* (Our Commons), initially referring to a shared political position as anti-capitalist stand, but sporadically turned to refer to urban and ecological commons. Therefore, 'Our Commons' was not simply a melting pot, but, on the contrary, was holding a variety of groups together providing a shared ground of struggle. A parallel process was the foundation of another platform called Taksim Solidarity Platform with the purpose of resisting the Pedestrianization Project of Taksim Square. Our Commons became one of the central constituents of the latter platform. Apart from Trade Union Confederations and occupational associations (remaining elements of the corporatist pattern of interest representation from the 1950s onwards), the rest of the constituents of the Taksim Solidarity Platform were relatively new organizations founded in the 1990s and 2000s around a single agenda. The activists in such organizations defined themselves and their fellows as the 'members of non-partisan youth most of which are anti-capitalists'. One activist distinguished his cohort from what he called 'traditional left', with the 'will to get-together with others on common platforms.'

Following such a networking of different groups, a wave of protests ushered the Gezi Resistance. They started against the Pedestrianization Project of Taksim Square on 6 June 2012. Soon after, the Pride March on 1 July 2012 and animal rights protests on 30 September 2012, were exceptional due to the active attendance of all the groups under the umbrella of Our Commons. In November 2012, Taksim Solidarity Platform called for solidarity from progressive civil society by organizing night shifts to protect Taksim Square from the ongoing Pedestrianization Project. But the first protest against the AKP rule that became vocal in the public agenda was to prevent the demolishing of a historic movie theatre to make room for an entertainment and shopping venue. The top-down decision to demolish the Emek Theatre generated widespread protests in April 2013. Peaceful demonstrations resisted against police despite intense deployment of water cannons and pepper gas.[18] 'The tension was increasing with each protest', noted the activists who attended all these events. The success of the united struggle was strongly felt on 1 May 2013. 'We heard the footsteps of the Gezi Resistance at the 2013 International Workers Day Protests', said another activist. It was the first time the infamous chant of the Gezi Resistance – 'everywhere is Taksim, everywhere is Resistance' – was cried.

Finally, the Gezi Resistance became the collective voice of alienation, anger and frustration against various forms of dispossession and marginalization. Through the weeks of June, 2.5 million people from 78 cities participated in the protests. It was a non-subjective resistance against an overt and subjective power demanding the resignation of Prime Minister Erdoğan and his government. This non-subjectiveness was reflected in a description that was commonly used to refer to the ideals that the Gezi Resistance was representing: 'the Specter of Gezi'.

Combined collective social rights movements and trade unions

The labor process has been transformed in the neoliberal era that effectively functioned to contain resistance and even produce consent. Workers have become more dehomogenized which made their even short-term interests diverging. Furthermore, dehomogeneity is accompanied by the deteriorating position of trade unions enacted by the limitations of the legal framework, the legacy of the military regime. Effectively, workers are also fragmented in different federations and confederations. Consequently, the trade unions have been unable and even unwilling to mobilize and initiate collective action on a united basis since the 1980s. Both Tekel and Gezi resistances sadly depicted the weakness of the labor movement on an organized basis. It would not be unfair to claim that in both instances, the trade unions failed to initiate general solidarity strikes to support the protest movement.

There is a need for new, creative forms of organization with an ability to initiate collective action on a long-lasting basis. In this endeavor, daily experiences of workers in earning their living should be brought into the fore of our analysis as central elements of class awareness as well as hegemony and counter-hegemony. Experiencing exploitation in the everyday lives of laboring classes could be concealed through different strategies yet the sense of injustice, humiliation and frustration would be stronger and would be felt by those 'common-people' who are subordinated to all sorts of unequal power relations, and all sorts of dispossession. Various forms of dispossession and various movements can gather around a homogenous ground. It would not be due to class consciousness but rather the consciousness of an opposition which expresses itself in new modes of action. The struggle for collective rights are tangible and empirical; and because their absence is felt strongly, it is about the livelihood of a human being. These resistances showed that a possible counter-hegemonic strategy for workers and their trade unions would be to struggle for collective rights, non-negotiable defense of collective rights. Otherwise these multiple movements tend to weaken collective social struggle by dividing it into single item agendas confined to the corporate interests of a small group of people. Tekel Resistance appears to be a foreteller of a possible bonding of all rights movements under an expansive struggle for collective social rights (Yalman and Topal, 2017). The significant success of the Gezi Resistance further reinstated this possibility. However, it has to be noted that although participants of both resistances have definitely changed their perspective or prejudice vis-à-vis what they had previously called radical groups, they are hardly radicalized themselves in terms of their political inclinations. That is to say, the war of position proceeds slowly in establishing the ground for counter-hegemonic strategy to take shape.

Conclusion

The current phase of capitalism appears to be pregnant with crises of privatizations as a result of increasing unemployment, job insecurity, and extensive commodification. As such policies would not appeal to the active consent of popular classes, exclusion and marginalization have become the main strategy of ruling parties. This whole process has led to a rise of authoritarianization of state power that the new wave of social struggles inevitably targets. First and foremost, both the Tekel and Gezi Resistances questioned the nature of the political authority and troubled the AKP rule creating large fissures in the legitimacy of the state authority.

If hegemony concerns transformation of the common sense of everyday life, then the resistance would put forward its own set of norms, values and customs rather than mobilizing solely against others. Examination of both the Tekel and Gezi Resistances suggest that what is needed is proactive resistance. Tekel workers in the middle of Ankara and the Gezi Resistance in Gezi Park created their own norms, values and customs during resistance days by practically transforming the space itself. Particularly in Gezi Park, as the issues and struggles united, the resistance that had started to protect a public space evolved towards a set of broader political demands for enhancing democratic rights and freedoms (Yalman, 2016). It turned into a protest against the government with a rich bundle of rights demands.

As Gramsci (1971) underlines 'the prince acts on a dispersed and shattered people to arouse and organize its shattered will.' Such a popular prince would bond all the social organizations committed to social change. The antagonism of class struggle can motivate all other forms of social struggle against dispossession. Strategically, trade unions could not be left outside this strategy because it is the point of production where workers have real power. For a long-lasting institutional formation of the resistance, labor movements should be the leading agent of a solid platform around tangible claims for decommodification of basic needs and violation of rights. As one Gezi activist noted 'we are indeed a generation in the process of proletarianization, we are indeed precariat, even if we don't admit it often'. Similarly, the Social Rights Association defines their movement 'as peoples' or citizens' movement on the labor axis'. The declaration also notes 'social rights refer to all the demands made by those masses who have been subjected to the transformations in the labor process. Social rights' struggle aims to bridge different trade unions and confederations with its expanded scope.' Therefore, intensified commodification and violation of basic rights have been part and parcel of the process of proletarianization and increasing precarity of professionals and public-sector employees. Such perspective would also provide a new unifying potential to class struggle resolving the crisis of trade unionism in the neoliberal era.

As capital accumulation through privatizations and commodifications is actively undertaken by an increasingly coercive and disciplinary state power, further struggles for collective social rights would inevitably be directed against the political power challenging the very ground of the reproduction of the state.

Notes

1   These interviews were conducted for two different research projects. The interviews with the Tekel workers were supported by Middle East Technical University, Scientific Research Fund (BAP: 04-01-2012-003). Many of these ideas regarding the Tekel Resistance have been developed in conversation with Dr Galip Yalman and Dr Sermin Sarıca. The interviews conducted with the Gezi collectives were part of a research on 'Financialisation, Economy, Society and Sustainable Development' that received funding from European Union's Seventh Framework Program (Grant Agreement No: 266800). I would like to thank Dr Özlem Çelik for arranging most of these interviews and for our post-interview discussions. Most of all, I would like to express my gratitude and appreciation for Tekel workers and Gezi protestors for writing their/our history with courage and determination and for sharing their point of view on their respective resistance. This article is dedicated to those who lost their lives in the protests.

2   Merrill Lynch (2002) 'Turkey's Single Party Government Will Lend Hope', *Hürriyet*, 7 November. Available at: www.hri.org/news/turkey/trkpr/2002/02-11-07.trkpr. html#11 (accessed 10 August 2014).

3   See https://wikileaks.org/cable/2003/03/03ANKARA1447.html (accessed 18 June 2015).

4   For a more detailed analysis see Topal and Yalman 2015; Yalman and Topal 2017.

5   Interview with a former Tekel worker, Ahmet Inan (Kaldiraç, 2010: 23)

6   It was indeed a call for a general strike, which is not a legally recognized right in the Constitution as the legislative legacy of the 1980 Military Coup.

7   German food workers' union, European Federation of Food, Agriculture and Tourism Trade Unions (EFFAT), International Union of Food Workers, German IG Metal Union and Forza Livorno accepted 29–31 January as 'everywhere Tekel is, everywhere resistance' days. A member of the European Parliament and the German Die Linke (the left) party, Jürgen Klute together with a representative of the Dortmund Food Workers' Union visited the tent city on 25 January. The leader of the Greek Coalition of the Left of Movements of Ecology (Synaspismos) sent his solidarity message to the Tekel workers on 17 February. In this message Panagiotis Lafazanis said, 'Tekel workers' resistance is an inspiration for workers and left in Greece' (*Hürriyet*, 17 February 2010). A team of mountain

climbers' banner attached at 5,173 meters on Mount Ararat read: 'If the Tekel workers can brave the cold, so can we' and exhibitions of supporting banners in the European football stadiums was an untraditional form of solidarity (cf. Yeldan, 2010).

8 www.toplumgazetesi.com/mobil/haber.php?id=1429
9 www.sendika.org/2009/12/tekel-iscilerinin-direnisi-12-gununde-dayanisma-buyuyor/
10 www.akparti.org.tr/site/haberler/taksimdeki-olaylarda-asiri-uclar-var/45448#1
11 *The Guardian* (2013) 'Turkish protesters embrace Erdoğan insult and start "capuling" craze', 10 July. Available at: www.theguardian.com/world/2013/jun/10/turkish-protesters-capuling-erdogan (accessed 10 August 2014).
12 Nevertheless, the regeneration of Taksim Square remains within the official plan for 2015–19 of the İstanbul Metropolitan Municipality. See *AKP'nin 'yeni' planı: 'Taksim Kışlası*. Available at: www.sendika.org/2014/11/akpnin-yeni-plani-taksim-kislasi/ (accessed 9 February 2015).
13 The name of the collective, IMECE, is the Turkish word for the traditional form of solidarity in the countryside in harvesting the crops of each household's farm collectively with the participation of all the villagers.
14 See: www.birumut.org
15 See: http://sosyalhaklar.biz/#
16 See: www.fse-esf.org/spip.php?article694
17 See: https://kenthareketleri.wordpress.com/hakkimizda/
18 See: www.theguardian.com/world/2013/apr/15/turkey-historic-emek-theatre-final-curtain

References

Bergson, H. (2001) *Time and Free Will*. Mineola, NY: Dover.
Gramsci, A. (1971) *Selections from the Prison Notebook*. New York: International Publisher.
Hayek, F. (1979) *Law, Legislation and Liberty, vol. III: The Political Order of a Free People*. London: Routledge and Kegan Paul.
Kaldıraç,Y. (2010) *Tekel Direnişi Dersleri*. İstanbul: Kaldıraç.
Marx, K. (1978) 'On the Jewish Question' [1843], in Tucker, R. (ed.) *The Marx-Engels Reader*. New York: Norton and Company.
Özal, T. (1992) 'Özal: "Türkiye'nin Önünde Hacet Kapıları Açılmıştır"', Interview by Mustafa Çalık, *Türkiye Günlüğü*, (19): 5–25.
Özbudun, E. (1991) 'The Post-1980 Legal Framework for Interest Group Associations' in Heper, M. (ed.) *Strong State and Economic Interest Groups: The Post-1980 Turkish Experience*. Berlin, New York: Walter de Gruyter.
Özveri, M. (2006) 'Sendikal Hareket, Sorunlar, Arayışlar', in Sazak, F. (ed.) *Türkiye'de Sendikal Kriz ve Sendikal Arayışlar*. Ankara: Epos.
Savran, S. (2010) The Tekel Strike in Turkey. Socialist Project (326) Available at: www.socialistproject.ca/bullet/326.php (accessed 19 April 2017).
Sayılan, F. and Türkmen, N. (2010) 'Tekel Direnişi: Ekmek ve Gül' in Bulut, G. (ed). *Tekel Direnişinin Işığında Gelenekselden Yenide İşçi Sınıfı Hareketi*, İstanbul: Notabene.

Soner, Ş. (1996) '12 Eylül Döneminde İşçi Hareketi' in *Türkiye Sendikacılık Ansiklopedisi*, İstanbul: Kültür Bakanlığı ve Tarih Vakfı Yayınları.

Thompson E.P. (1963) *The Making of the English Working Class*. London: Pelican.

Topal, A. (2016) 'Taksim Square from the Ottoman Reformation Era to Gezi Resistance' in Berntharth, C. (ed.) *Urban Public Spaces*. Leipzig: Spector Books.

Topal, A. and Yalman, G.L. (2015) '2009–2010 Tekel İşçileri Direniş Öncesi ve Sonrası: Toplumsal Farkındalıktan Özelleştirme Mağduriyetine' in Özçelik, E and Taymaz, E. (eds.) *Türkiye Ekonomisinin Dünü Bugünü Yarını*. İstanbul: İmge.

Yalman, G.L. (2009) *Transition to Neoliberalism: The Case of Turkey in the 1980s*. İstanbul: Bilgi University Press.

Yalman, G.L. (2016) 'Crises as Driving Forces of Neoliberal "Trasformismo": The Contours of the Turkish Political Economy since the 2000s' in Cafruny, A. et al. (eds.) *Palgrave Handbook of Critical International Political Economy*. London: Palgrave Macmillan.

Yalman, G.L. and Topal, A. (2017) 'Labour Containment Strategies and Working Class Struggles in the Neoliberal Era: The Case of TEKEL Workers in Turkey', *Critical Sociology*, DOI: 10.177/0896920517711489.

Yeldan, E. (2010) TEKEL Workers' Resistance: Re-Awakening of the Proletariat in Turkey Available at www.sendika.org/english/yazi.php?yazi_no=29021, 30 January (accessed 19 April 2017).

22

Socio-ecological Inequality and the Democratization Process

José Esteban Castro

Introduction

During the last few decades, but notoriously since the beginning of the twenty-first century, Latin America and the Caribbean entered an exceptional historical moment in relation to the processes of integration of its different countries and regions. These processes involved the consolidation of relations in a diversity of fields – economic–financial, commercial, cultural, territorial defence, transport infrastructure, energy, and more importantly, political. In many ways, despite the problems, contradictions, and failures of these integration processes*, the recent period has been exciting in terms of the speed, scope and nature of the transformations, particularly, though not exclusively, in South America. Among other examples, it is worth mentioning the consolidation and expansion of the Southern Common Market (MERCOSUR), the creation of the Bolivarian Alliance for the Peoples of the Americas (ALBA) in 2004, the creation of the Union of South American Nations (UNASUR) in 2007, the creation of the Community of Latin American and Caribbean States (CELAC) in 2010, with the inclusion of Cuba as a full member, and the creation of the Pacific Alliance between Chile, Colombia, Mexico and Peru in 2011, this latter conceived as a block aiming to counterbalance the influence of the other initiatives, particularly ALBA and MERCOSUR[1]. It can be argued that even the most sceptical observer would admit that important aspects of these processes of integration represent a significant advance in relation to the recent past. Particularly in South America, integration has been clearly associated with the return of electoral democracies after long decades of civil–military dictatorships.

In this chapter I adopt a positive, even celebratory approach to the ongoing integration processes, in so far as they represent an advance of substantive democratization processes in the region. However, and for the same reason, I focus my attention on what I consider are among the most significant obstacles and threats to substantive democratization and regional integration in Latin America and the Caribbean, which are the growing socio-ecological inequalities and injustices that have emerged in the whole region, particularly since the 1990s. I argue that the destruction of the material basis and the related conflicts and struggles flaring up as a result of increasing socio-ecological inequality and injustice in the region not only constitute an obstacle to the processes of democratic integration but also a threat to the progress and consolidation of substantive, not merely electoral democracy. Although there is a degree of convergence with ecologist arguments in the chapter, I draw my arguments from a sociology-grounded political ecology. In this perspective, I address here the socio-ecological dimension as a relatively neglected aspect in the analysis of democratization processes, and argue that this dimension constitutes a fundamental arena in the struggle for human emancipation, especially in relation to struggles for greater equality in the access to socio-ecological goods and services and in the protection from socio-environmental threats and dangers. I consider that socio-ecological problems are among the most difficult and thorny challenges facing the democratic integration processes taking place in Latin America and the Caribbean, at least when considered from the perspective of substantive, not merely electoral democracy.

The capitalist nature of the integration processes

Independently of the heterogeneous intellectual and political traditions and specific conditions and circumstances predominating in the different countries of the region, the central dynamic of the ongoing integration processes is marked by the advance and consolidation of capitalist social relations of production, distribution, and consumption and their interrelated socio-cultural and political expressions. As could be expected, this expansion and deepening of capitalist social relations has not been homogenous, and we have witnessed the consolidation of pre-existing heteronomies, as is the case of Mexico, most of Central America, and parts of South America, notoriously Colombia, as well as the emergence of capitalist autonomies, in particular Brazil. These processes have involved large-scale and profound transformations, which have been uneven, often conflictive, that have produced significant benefits but also have imposed high costs, if we adopt a multi-dimensional approach that goes beyond the conventional understanding that reduces the complexity of progressive social change to economic growth, measured by the increase of the Gross Domestic Product of countries and regions. In this regard, several questions arise when we examine the processes under discussion. What kind of integration has been taking place? What and who are being integrated? What is the purpose and who are the beneficiaries of these integration processes? What is the cost of the integration? Who pays this cost? This short chapter does not have the ambition of providing responses to all these questions, but the questions provide a framework for the discussion by highlighting key issues that cannot be side-lined, even when integration is accepted as a positive, desirable goal.

Let us return for a moment to the contradictory nature of the integration processes under discussion, which are characterized both by the high heterogeneity of countries and regions being integrated and the common impulse towards integration driven by the advance and consolidation of capitalist social relations. For example, mainstream debates have under-acknowledged or even derided the recent experience of the South American countries that radically abandoned the strict neoliberal model of the 1990s and adopted instead strong State intervention, such as Argentina, Brazil, Venezuela, and more recently Bolivia, which are also the countries that took the lead in the integration processes discussed here. However, these countries succeeded in rapidly reversing the conditions of extreme poverty affecting a large part of the population, a fact that has been sufficiently documented (ECLAC, 2009; Cornia, 2010; López-Calva and Lustig, 2010; OECD, 2015). Also, some of these rejuvenated electoral democracies, notoriously Argentina, have showed a strong international leadership in the development of solid institutions for the scrutiny and prosecution of crimes against humanity committed by Western-backed civil military dictatorships (Crenzel, 2011). This fact, in relation to the advancement of substantive democratization, is very significant, and yet is largely ignored or at best played down in mainstream debates about democracy and democratization. Despite the ebb and flow of electoral politics and the economic–financial ups and downs in the region, these and other progressive developments represent a consolidation of fundamental elements of substantive democratization.

However, a positive assessment of the situation in these terms should not lead us to underestimate the crucial fact that the most dynamic and decisive forces driving these transformations are those associated with the expansion and consolidation of capitalist relations. Beyond their anti-capitalist rhetoric and political stance, even in the case of the group of countries that compose the ALBA, the dynamic of regional integration is driven by the global process of capitalist accumulation, which poses strong restrictions to the capacity of these countries to advance their stated goal of developing a 'socialism for the twenty-first century'. It is apposite that the recent economic success of the Bolivian economy, one of the ALBA countries, has been greatly praised by capitalist markets, moving the *Financial Times* to call President Evo Morales, somewhat ironically, 'the world's most successful socialist' (*Financial Times*, 2015; see also O'Hagan, 2014; Moody's Global Credit Research, 2015). The grounds for this analysis may be obvious to acute observers; however, too often the implications of these issues are downplayed or ignored, not least because they lead us to discuss very difficult, thorny aspects about the meaning, scope, and nature of democratization. In this regard, we need to demystify the analysis and recognize that the integration processes under discussion are embedded in and largely determined by the global dynamics of capital accumulation. Recognizing and celebrating the great advances made in the democratization of the region, in relation to the recent past, should not lead us to ignore the significant risks and threats posed by the predominantly capitalistic logic that permeates the ongoing integration processes. These risks and threats have become very notorious in the deepening of socio-ecological inequality and injustice that is already leaving very ugly scars and constitute one of the most important areas of social and political conflict in the region.

The tension between agency and structure, between human will and action on the one hand, and social forces and structures that condition and determine their scope for success, on the other, punctuates the processes under discussion. In this connection, it is worth recalling Norbert Elias' reflection on this matter:

> many people today believe that it is possible to approach social problems from the standpoint of their own inborn 'rationality', quite independent of the current state of development of social knowledge and thought, yet with the same 'objective' approach that a physicist or engineer brings to scientific or technological problems. Thus, contemporary governments commonly assert – perhaps in good faith – that they can overcome the acute social problems of their country 'rationally' or 'realistically'. In fact, however, they usually fill the gaps in our still fairly rudimentary factual knowledge of the dynamics of social interweavings with dogmatic doctrines, handed-down nostrums, or considerations of short-term party interests. Taking measures mostly by chance, they remain at the mercy of events, the sequence of which governments understand as little as those they govern. (Elias, 1978: 31)

Following on from Elias' consideration, it can be argued that beyond the political or ideological commitment, or the intentions of political leaders, governments, and country alliances in relation to the processes of democratic integration, we must focus on the objective analysis of the structural forces and factors that condition and drive these processes with independence of human wills, intentions, and wishes. In this chapter, I focus particularly on how these tensions play in the interrelation between the processes of democratic integration and the socio-ecological dimension of democratization processes in the region.

Another important aspect that has already been mentioned is the highly heterogeneous character of the countries, regions, and peoples being 'integrated', which has important consequences for the relationship between socio-ecological politics and integration processes. This takes us back to the second question placed at the beginning: What and who are being integrated? In effect, there is a high heterogeneity of regions, actors, ethnic origins, cultural and political traditions, territorial scales, physical–natural conditions, state formation and related institutional processes, power configurations at the intra, inter and trans state level, among other issues. In particular, there are highly diverse historical traditions, cultural values and practices, and their manifestations in the relationships that human groups have established with the material basis of their societies over time in Latin America and the Caribbean. For instance, the integration processes include the Andean peoples and countries, some of which have experienced in recent decades a rapid process of democratization with the re-emergence of indigenous communities as political actors after centuries of external and internal colonialism and marginalization. In the Andean region, at least at the discursive level, much emphasis has been placed in recent years in the recovery of traditions and cultural values such as the *Buen Vivir* (Good Living) that has inspired important political movements and constitutional reforms in Bolivia and Ecuador (Farah and Vasapollo, 2011; Gudynas, 2011). For instance, in 2008 Ecuador approved a Constitutional Reform that enacted the 'Rights of Nature' alongside the rights of citizens. These Andean traditions have a weak correlate in most countries of South America, especially in the Southern Cone, and also contrast very strongly with the prevailing traditions of Central America, Mexico, or the Caribbean. This is a good example of the extremely complex diversity of the countries and regions being integrated, in this case in relation to the understanding of human–nature relationships and the resulting institutional frameworks. It must be said that there is a significant hiatus between discourse and practice in relation to this in Andean countries, but we come back later to this point.

From a different angle, as already stated, the fact that the integration processes are driven and structured around the expansion and consolidation of capitalist social relations has an impact on the international power configurations of the different countries being integrated. In particular, integration is taking place within the framework of emerging capitalist autonomies, and the consolidation of pre-existing heteronomies, which are interconnected. The rise of Brazil as a global economic power and its consolidation as the 'growth locomotive' of South America, also taking a leading role in the integration process, has been the clearest example of an emerging capitalist autonomy. The consolidation of pre-existing heteronomies can be exemplified with the case of Mexico and Central America, a region that since the 1990s has become much more dependent from the United States both economically and politically. This increased heteronomy has several sources, from the impact of the North American Free Trade Agreement started in 1994 through other processes such as the dependence of entire countries on the remittances sent by millions of migrants working in the US or the regional militarization under US control, which also affects some South American countries, particularly Colombia (Delgado Wise and Ortega Breña, 2006; Gammage, 2006; Suárez Salazar and Ortega Breña, 2007).

Finally, sharing the political project seeking to integrate the 'peoples' of Latin America and the Caribbean should not blur our analysis of the realities taking place in the ground. In this regard, the ongoing processes of integration have been largely driven by particular interests, often not representing the interests of the region's peoples, and have also been triggered by the interests of actors external to the region. All these interests that drive the integration processes under discussion are fundamentally capitalist interests, that is, interests that privilege private accumulation and not the social distribution of the region's wealth. We come back to this point later.

The historical conditions

Although human beings have always transformed their natural environment, often with negative results for the environment and for human societies (De Vries and Goudsblom, 2002), the relationship between the global expansion of the capitalist system and the quantitative and qualitative increases in the destruction of life's material basis and of life itself is well documented. In particular, the twentieth century brought about significant anthropogenic transformations of the environment with consequences for life on earth that we still do not fully understand and explain (McNeill, 2000; Fischer-Kowalski and Haberl, 2007). Yet, the relationship between capitalist expansion and environmental destruction continues to be the subject of much debate and often denial, even among progressive intellectual and political actors, if not discursively at least in practice. For example, technological determinists may even admit that capitalism brings about environmental destruction, but argue that the system itself can provide the solution, which can only be achieved through more technological development. As Hermínio Martins convincingly argued, this position is shared both by defenders and opponents of capitalism (Martins, 1996, 1998a, 1998b, 1998c). In this extreme of the debate, it does not matter if we run out of trees or if we make fresh water unusable for life on earth, because, the argument goes, technology will allow us to create artificial solutions to these problems, in this case artificial trees and water. The evidence of this technological potential is there, as the human body itself is already the object of artificial tissue or organ transplants. In the perspective of this tradition of thought, it is a matter of time and of promoting adequate policies that provide full freedom to capitalist innovators for recreating the universe. A consequence of this extreme position, as is now clear in the global debate, is the tendency to deny the significance of human influence in worsening environmental conditions or even the denial of environmental change and degradation altogether. As stated by the former Director of Natural Resource Studies at the ultraliberal Cato Institute in the United States:

> [t]he world today is not only sustainable, but is more sustainable than ever before in the sense that future generations will inherit more natural and man-made capital to meet their needs than any preceding generation. That will be the case, however, only as long as the global economy is left relatively unrestrained. (Taylor, 1994: 49)

For this author, the sustainable development debate is 'a solution in search of a problem' (1994: 49). In the other extreme, several intellectual and political traditions have insisted, at least since the nineteenth century, that capitalism is inherently characterized by the destruction of the material basis of societies, which James O'Connor conceptualized as the 'second contradiction of capitalism' (O'Connor, 1998; see also Schnaiberg, 1980; Schnaiberg and Gould, 1994). If the first contradiction confronts capitalists and the proletariat, in the second contradiction capital confronts the destruction of its own material basis on which its very existence depends. It is worth reminding ourselves that the awareness of this self-destructive characteristic of capitalism has not been a preserve of socialists and romantic environmentalists who do not have a good understanding of hard economic realities. At least since the 1960s, in the international debate about 'ecological limits' to capitalist development there have been capitalists and intellectuals committed to capitalism who have been actively involved in intensive research efforts to demonstrate not only the existence of such limits but also the fact that we have gone over these limits and that the human species has been living on an 'ecological credit card' for a long time already. One of the most notorious and best-known examples is of course the Club of Rome, which in 1972 published the now classical research report *The Limits to Growth* (Meadows et al., 1972; see also Club of Rome, 2012).

In relation to Latin America and the Caribbean, the region was one of the territories of primitive accumulation during the development of capitalism. The region has been historically, and still is, subject to unequal exchange relations in different dimensions, not just economic but also, of high relevance for this chapter, unequal ecological exchanges. This concept is not merely, as some would argue, a matter of anti-imperialist and anti-colonialist rhetoric. The study of the mechanisms and impacts of unequal ecological exchanges has already produced substantial evidence of the ecological debt acquired by industrialized countries with the Global South, including Latin America and the Caribbean. These mechanisms have not been limited to direct colonial pillage, but have included a range of more subtle forms of unequal ecological exchange (see, among other, Bunker, 1984; Guha and Martínez-Alier, 1997; Hornborg, 1998; Martinez-Alier, 2002; Martínez-Alier and Olivares, 2003; Rice, 2007a, 2007b, 2009; Roberts and Parks, 2007; Nelson and Robertson, 2008; Jorgenson and Clark, 2009; Simms, 2009).

In this connection, in recent times a range of mechanisms of socio-ecological inequality and injustice, some with a long history, have acquired renewed relevance as a result of technological advances in the process of capitalist globalization, for example toxic imperialism and biopiracy. Toxic imperialism refers to the transfer, imposed or negotiated, of toxic waste originated normally in an industrialized country to poorer countries whose governments either accept to receive the waste in exchange for a payment or simply do not have the means to stop the illegal discharge of toxic waste in their territories. An event that took place in 2009 in Brazil helped to uncover this type of mechanism. The Brazilian government detected over 1500 tonnes of toxic hospital waste, including used diapers, condoms, and syringes, illegally exported from the United Kingdom, disguised as 'plastic' (BBC, 2009). The Brazilian government protested and the UK made arrangements to send the cargo back to its territory. As one analyst put it, 'globally, [this Brazilian episode] is not even a scratch on the surface' (Fox, 2009). In fact, it is a small example of a well-documented and extended practice (Martinez-Alier, 2002). However, toxic imperialism also takes subtler forms, such as the transfer of pollutants incorporated in products exported to other countries (Muradian et al., 2002).

In turn, biopiracy, defined as the appropriation of biological material and knowledge without acknowledgement or compensation, is also an old practice constitutive of what Crosby termed 'ecological imperialism', a process in which Latin America and the Caribbean played a central role, unfortunately on the losing side of the exchange (Crosby, 2004). In recent times, this practice has reached high levels of sophistication thanks to the advances in biotechnology and genetic engineering, notably in the field of bioprospecting related to the industrial production of commercial drugs, genetically modified seeds, and other commodities (Shiva, 1997). Latin America and the Caribbean is one of the hot spots of biopiracy activities. In this regard, a news article published in the United States back in 2007 asked 'Who has rights to nature's cures?' (Vecchio, 2007). The article was referring to the fact that a private company had secured a patent granting them exclusive rights to commercialize products based on the medicinal properties of the *maca*, a tuber that grows in the Andean highlands and that has been used by local Quechua communities in Peru as a cure for high-altitude sickness and as an aphrodisiac. The Peruvian government took legal action against the private company, and the case was still in the courts at the time of writing this chapter. The situation by now has become even more complex, as apparently *maca* seeds have been illegally exported to China for commercial production (Collyns, 2015). This case is also a relatively small example of a global process, whereby Latin America and the Caribbean are at the centre of many disputes around bioprospection/ biopiracy activities given the rich biodiversity of the region (Peritore and Niles, 1992; Falcon and Fowler, 2002; Helfrich, 2002; Mgbeoji, 2006; Brailovsky and Foguelman, 2007; Robinson, 2010).

However, in the context of the ongoing regional integration processes these and other mechanisms of unequal ecological exchange have taken renewed significance, for a number of reasons that I consider next.

Integration and unequal ecological exchange

The ongoing integration processes in Latin America and the Caribbean have been characterized by a consolidation and rapid expansion of economic growth promoted and facilitated by an active role of the State, whether in supporting private national and transnational capitalist actors or through straightforward state capitalism. This includes the experiences of ALBA countries, like Bolivia, Nicaragua, or Venezuela. A positive outcome of this development has been the increased degree of autonomy vis-à-vis the core capitalist governments and international financial institutions achieved by some of the region's countries, notably Brazil but also Argentina and Bolivia among others. This increased autonomy, partly reinforced by the creation of the new institutions of political integration (i.e. ALBA, CELAC, UNASUR), helped to re-equilibrate to some extent the historical conditions of unequal economic exchange that had been much worsened by the neoliberal policies of the 1990s. However, the forms taken by the integration process in the economic-productive dimension have threatened to worsen the relations of unequal ecological exchange both between and within countries and regions.

The process of economic growth recorded particularly in South America since the beginning of the twenty-first century has been related to the increased political autonomy achieved by several countries within the context of the integration processes. The positive aspects of this process have been widely discussed in the literature, particularly though not only in the case of Brazil (e.g. OECD, 2010), and more recently Bolivia. However, there are three interconnected aspects that I wish to highlight here: firstly, the continuity and deepening of the long-standing conditions of North–South unequal ecological exchange, which now also increasingly encompass South–South inequalities. Secondly, the extreme dependence on extractivist activities and the export of raw materials that continue to characterize Latin American economies. Thirdly, the reluctance of the developmentalist productivism prevailing among the political and intellectual elites of Latin America to incorporate the socio-ecological dimension in the analysis, beyond paying lip service to the notion of 'sustainability' and, more recently in some countries, to the Andean traditions of *Buen Vivir*.

Regarding the first point, the continuity and even deepening of the historical North–South relations of unequal exchange and the expansion or emergence of similar inequalities in a South–South dynamic constitute a barrier to the democratic integration process, and to the consolidation of substantive democratic practices more generally. In addition to the example of the attempted dumping of toxic waste on Brazil by British companies, the historical North–South inequalities in ecological exchanges involve the transfer of dirty industrial activities, most of them either forbidden or strictly regulated in the 'North' (making these activities economically or legally unviable in these countries' territories), towards the 'South', including Latin America and the Caribbean. One of the most significant examples is the cultivation of genetically modified crops and their associated 'technological packs' involving intensive use of agrochemicals, or 'agro-toxics', as the campaigners against these activities would prefer to call them. The commercial cultivation of genetically modified (GM) crops or the sale of food containing them is formally forbidden in the European Union, where there is an ongoing debate about the topic given the widespread public opposition to GM crops. However, in Latin America GM crops have been widely adopted, in an almost, if not entirely, unregulated (in practice, owing to the difficulties of enforcing rules where they exist) fashion. In addition to the unpredictable potential dangers of GM crops that have been unwelcome in Europe until now, there is virtually uncontrolled use of agrochemical/agro-toxics across the region, from Mexico to Patagonia (Newell, 2009; Austin, 2010). Another significant example is the expansion of open-cast mining, involving the use of dangerous substances like cyanide and mercury. In May 2010, the European Parliament banned the use of cyanide in mining activities in the territories of the European Union, on the grounds of the need to apply the Precautionary Principle and the Biodiversity Convention adopted in the 1992 Earth Summit in Rio de Janeiro (European Parliament, 2010). However, cyanide, mercury, and other dangerous substances are used massively, also with little or no effective regulation, by mining companies most of which have their headquarters in the 'North' but also in the 'Global South', including countries like Argentina, Brazil or Mexico (Sibaud, 2012). The ecological and particularly human impacts of these activities have sparked bitter conflicts and pose a threat not just to the environment but also to the democratization process in the region, which we come back to in a later section.

As mentioned before, relations of unequal ecological exchange have been increasingly documented between countries in the South, and are not limited to the historical North–South dynamic. Similar to the historical relationship between North and South, these inequalities are often fostered by the uneven implementation of regulatory norms between countries, which favours the migration of polluting activities to territories with weaker or no controls. There is also a reproduction of the historical relations of inequality between producers of raw materials and producers of industrialized goods, which in the past mostly corresponded to North–South exchanges but that in the recent period has increasingly taken also a South–South dimension. A classic example in South America has been the historical relationship of inequality between Brazil and Paraguay over the energy generated in the binational Itaipú dam, which was partly addressed during the friendly negotiations between the Brazilian President Lula da Silva and President Fernando Lugo from Paraguay between 2008 and 2013, within the context of MERCOSUR. However, analysts have pointed out that a number of agreements between Brazil and neighbouring countries over the construction of hydroelectric dams could represent a consolidation of unequal ecological relations between the countries of the region. For instance, the Bank Information Centre (BIC), an organization based in Washington that monitors the activities of the World Bank, including the environmental impacts of the projects funded by the bank, has alerted of the potential negative impacts of these activities. The BIC referred to agreements between the governments of Brazil and Peru to build several hydroelectric dams in the Peruvian Amazon and argued that Peru was accepting to become a provider of energy to Brazil, while all the ecological impacts would remain in Peruvian territory (Bank Information Center, 2011). Others have pointed at the fact that the dams would displace indigenous communities from the Asháninka ethnic group in Peru, some of which had resisted all historical attempts to strip them from their lands since colonial times, but that now would be finally evicted as a result of a democratic agreement between two countries in the process of increasing economic integration (Torres Espinoza, 2012).

In relation to the second point, it is widely known that Latin American and Caribbean economies are extremely dependent on extractive activities, including non-renewable energy resources (oil and gas), raw materials, and food stuffs, which also applies even to the most industrialized economies like Brazil's. This continues to be a global pattern: while industrialized economies are mainly exporters of manufactures, 'less developed countries' are over dependent on exporting mostly raw materials, which in the case of Latin America and the Caribbean amount to around 70% of total exports (UNEP, 2011: 45–6). This is an old, well-documented and researched pattern, but I want to highlight an aspect that has been historically played down or even excluded from the classical analyses of Latin American and Caribbean dependent development, which place the emphasis on economic unequal exchanges but have neglected unequal ecological exchanges, or perhaps we could say, neglected the socio-ecological costs of dependency. A range of studies have contributed to make observable the ecological dimension of economic processes, from production to consumption, highlighting the hidden ecological dimension in the 'cost' of export products such as food stuffs but also industrialized products. One such hidden ecological component is what Tony Allan termed 'virtual water' in order to conceptualize the volumes of water incorporated in agricultural export products in the Middle East and North Africa (Allan, 1998, 1999, 2002). This concept triggered an important international debate which has showed that most water incorporated in commercial exchange flows is not accounted for as a cost, but in many cases takes the form of an unequal ecological exchange, a transfer of ecological goods (water resources) and bads (e.g. environmental degradation) that is not remunerated or compensated in the transactions (Chapagain and Hoekstra 2004a, 2004b; Hoekstra, 2006, 2007). Similarly, as mentioned before, pollution flows incorporated in commercial products are not 'costed in' in export exchanges (Muradian et al., 2002). It is also well-known that transfers of soil quality, that is, the consumption of soil fertility is not accounted for as such in commercial exchanges, which is also the subject of an ongoing debate owing to the massive expansion of 'fertility mining' agricultural production in the region. In this regard, in recent decades Latin America and the Caribbean has experienced a 'boom' of the region's economies thanks to the favourable market price of primary exports, effectively reversing to some extent the historical pattern of unequal economic exchange. However, the region has been through an escalation and intensification of its dependency on these primary exports in conditions of worsening unequal ecological exchange, whose negative consequences are already evident and long-lasting. In fact, the ongoing integration processes are heavily oriented at consolidating the region as an exporter of primary products, for example through the development of multi-modal transport systems across the whole continent with the Initiative for the Integration of the Regional Infrastructure of South America (IIRSA) (e.g. da Rocha, 2012; van Dijck, 2013) and the Mesoamerican Integration and Development Project that includes Mexico.

Finally, the third point is closely linked to the previous two and relates to the economic growth-centred developmental productivism prevailing among the intellectual and political elites in Latin America, which find it extremely difficult to incorporate the socio-ecological dimension in the analyses and practices. For example, in perspective, it seems understandable that for many politically progressive intellectuals the socio-ecological dimension is a low priority within a context of highly complex and urgent challenges that need to be tackled. I focus in this comment on progressive actors, because I assume that less progressive actors and defenders of the *status quo* would have a higher propensity to play down the significance of socio-ecological inequality and injustice resulting from democratic integration processes, while I would expect progressive ones in principle to be more concerned about these issues. Thus, many South-American countries emerged from long decades of bloody military dictatorships or civil wars only to fall into the destructive neoliberal reforms of the 1990s. The main priority of the progressive governments that took power since the late 1990s in Argentina, Bolivia, Brazil, Uruguay, and Venezuela, among others, has been the need to abate the conditions of extreme poverty and destitution affecting a large sector of the population and move forward the democratization process. In this context, tackling environmental problems, even when they are related to highly negative impacts on the population, seems to have been considered an unaffordable luxury at best or a distraction from the main priorities at worst. This may explain why for many progressive intellectuals it seems to be very difficult to adopt a critical position in relation to the socio-ecological impacts of democratic integration processes that are almost exclusively centred on the promotion of economic growth with disregard for the socio-ecological costs. However, it is not possible to postpone the much-needed critique of the dominant forms of economic growth that prevail in Latin America and the Caribbean, even when the actors in government are committed to progressive political agendas in other fundamental aspects. A progressive political agenda cannot be predicated on the production and reproduction of socio-ecological injustice and inequality or the worsening of unequal ecological exchanges. The evident urgency to promote the material improvement of the living conditions of large majorities in Latin America and the Caribbean is not incompatible with tackling socio-ecological injustice and inequality, as the latter is a pre-requisite for the former. In this regard, a crucial issue is to examine the overall direction of the ongoing democratic integration processes, which takes us back to some of the earlier questions: Integration and material progress, for whom (who is integrated and who benefits materially from the integration)? At what costs (economic, environmental, political, socio-cultural, etc.)? Who pays the costs? How are these costs paid? These and other questions point at the fundamental tensions that exists in the relationship between integration and substantive democratization processes in the region.

Socio-ecological injustice and inequality

The destruction of the material basis provoked by unequal ecological exchanges constitutes a doubled-edged threat to the democratic integration processes and for substantive democratization more generally. On the one hand, the destruction of the material basis in itself is an obstacle to the democratic integration processes under discussion, which are grounded on the deepening and expansion of capitalist economic development, given that it erodes the long-term sustainability of the production process. On the other hand, the production and reproduction of socio-ecological injustices and inequalities have become a fundamental obstacle to the process of substantive democratization. As discussed before, the notion of 'natural limits' to the production process, that is, the awareness that despite the scientific and technological capacities developed (and potentially developable) by humans there exist natural boundaries, has been long-recognised by enlightened capitalists, not just by environmentalists and critics of capitalism. Along these lines, a report from the International Resource Panel of the United Nations Environment Programme (UNEP) alerted:

> As earlier reports of the International Resource Panel (IRP) have concluded, overexploitation of resources, climate change, pollution, land-use change, and loss of biodiversity rose toward the top of the list of major international environmental concerns. One result is that 'sustainability' has become an overarching social and economic imperative among governments, international organizations, and businesses. Leaders in these sectors now understand that making progress towards a more sustainable economy requires an absolute reduction in resource use at a global level, while human wellbeing demands that economic activities should expand and environmental impacts diminish. The dilemma of expanding economic activities while reducing the rate of resource use and reducing the environmental impact of any such use poses a serious challenge to society. (UNEP, 2011: 7–8)

In relation to these conclusions, several questions arise concerning the discussion in this chapter. Is it possible to accept this notion of 'limits' in the context of the ongoing regional integration processes in Latin America and the Caribbean? Would not the acceptance of the existence of such 'limits' be a tacit recognition of the impossibility of development for the region? In other words, would not accepting the existence of such 'limits' be a recognition that the expansion of economic activities to meet 'human wellbeing demands' while at the same time reducing the environmental consequences of such expansion, would be unfeasible? In this regard, a crucial issue is to what extent government, international organizations, and business leaders of the integration processes under discussion, to use the language of the UNEP report, understand and accept that addressing the contradiction between guaranteeing the general wellbeing and protecting the material base of the region's societies must be given top priority. The fact is that a significant share of the social conflicts flaring up in the whole region is directly related to the perceived or real impact of the growing socio-ecological injustices and inequalities caused by the expansion of extractivist productive activities. Among other triggers of these inequalities, injustices, and related social conflicts and struggles, it must be mentioned the impacts of open cast mining with extensive use of dangerous substances such as cyanide, mercury, and other elements, the agrochemical/agrotoxic technological packages involving the expansion of transgenic crops, uncontrollable deforestation, biopiracy, whether tolerated or even promoted by the region's governments, massive infrastructure developments mostly enforced without democratic debate and consultation and imposed on populations with the consequent displacement of people, frequently involving the destruction of indigenous ancestral places and irreversible transformations of the ecosystems, or the pollution of air, water and soil through unregulated (or poorly regulated) economic activities, just to mention some of the most salient examples (e.g. Alimonda, 2002; Jasanoff, 2006; Brailovsky and Foguelman, 2007; Kuecker, 2007; van Dijck and den Haak, 2007; Carruthers, 2008; Newell, 2009; Svampa and Antonelli, 2009; Urkidi Azkarraga, 2010; Zhouri and Laschefski, 2010; Pieck, 2011; Latta and Ibarra, 2015; Ochoa, 2015; Valencio, 2015).

Even if we can find evidence of growing levels of awareness among the political and business elites in the region about these challenges, the evidence suggests that there is a huge gap between awareness of the problems and the capacity and willingness to take political decisions and implement practical actions to tackle the problems. A relatively humble example, in an international context, though not less significant because of that, is the failed attempt to pass a law to protect the native forests in the Province of Cordoba, Argentina, in 2010. It is estimated that during the course of the twentieth century the province lost about 95 percent of its native forest owing to the expansion of human, mostly productive, activities and urbanization. An alliance of different actors proposed a law to protect the remaining 5 percent of native forest from deforestation caused by the rapidly expanding soybean production and other activities (Barri and de Luca, 2009). The proposal was not accepted, and the provincial legislature passed instead another law that made viable the continued deforestation of the province, which prompted the intervention of the National Ombudsman (*La Voz del Interior*, 2012). The evidence suggests that deforestation is at the root of the chronic water crisis of this semi-arid province that continues to be aggravated by the expansion of extractivist activities and speculative housing schemes. In local and regional debates, these confrontations are often presented as a clash between environmentalists preoccupied primarily with nature's conservation set against political and business leaders committed to the creation of economic wealth on which the wellbeing of the population depends. The fact that the ecological crisis provoked by these activities is not only affecting the wellbeing of people but is also eroding the material basis of the production process seems to be simply ignored by these elites. In turn, the crisis and the related socio-ecological inequalities, injustice, and recurring conflicts compromise the advance of substantive democratization and pose a threat to the democratic achievements gained after the return of electoral democracy in the early 1980s. The example of Cordoba is significant but it is not exceptional, and instead reflects a regional pattern in Latin America and the Caribbean. In the whole region, socio-ecological conflicts and struggles have taken central stage. Too often, these confrontations are leading to the repression of communities and social movements mobilized against the impacts of these inequalities, even in the countries of the region governed by progressive governments (CLACSO, 2016). These confrontations constitute an expression of deep-rooted contradictions in the regional democratization process and are a major obstacle for the expansion and consolidation of substantive, not merely rhetorical democracy.

Conclusions: substantive democracy and socio-ecological struggle

The discussion in the previous sections lead to a few additional questions that must be addressed. To what extent does the ongoing integration processes in Latin America and the Caribbean presuppose the worsening of socio-ecological injustices and inequalities? Is it possible to have a model of democratic integration grounded on simultaneously abating social and ecological injustice and inequality? Would it be that, tacitly, Latin American and Caribbean elites agree with Inglehart's postmaterialist hypothesis that environmental concerns tend to be a preserve of rich countries while least developed societies cannot afford 'to be green' (Inglehart, 1971)? Although Inglehart's hypothesis has been consistently rejected (Brechin and Kempton, 1994, 1997; Dunlap and Mertig, 1997; Martinez-Alier, 2002), the political practices, including those of the progressive governments of the region, too often seem to draw their development and environmental policies from premises not dissimilar to Inglehart's hypothesis.

In this regard, would it be possible to reconcile the principles of social justice and equality with those of ecological justice and equality? What would be the acceptable limit or threshold of tolerance towards ecological injustice and inequality when it appears to be incompatible with social justice and inequality? In what kind of situations would it be legitimate to subordinate ecological justice and equality to social justice and equality? Is it possible to entertain such considerations from a position of substantive, nor merely formal democracy? These questions have enormous relevance, as manifested in the ethical and political dilemmas confronting progressive governments in Latin America and the Caribbean in relation to the contradictions between their agendas for economic development and environmental policy. These contradictions emerge in all the problematic areas mentioned earlier, in the impacts of extractivist economic growth and massive building of transport infrastructures required for the integration processes, to which we could add the re-emergence of privatization and mercantilization of public and common goods and resources, the co-production of socio-ecological disasters (draughts, floods, epidemics), the revival of nuclear energy development in the region despite the lessons of nuclear disasters like Fukushima's in 2011,[2] or the impacts of global climate changes for the region. The pattern seems to be an almost complete reliance on technological-determinist beliefs and the continued neglect of the socio-ecological dimension of substantive democratization.

In this concluding paragraph, I will focus on four main points. Firstly, I have discussed before that a major driver of the processes of democratic integration is the expansion and deepening of capitalist social relations in the whole region, which helps to focus on the most crucial mechanisms that may help to explain and tackle the challenges facing the region's societies. Secondly, from another angle, it is also important to focus on the production of knowledge about these processes. Taking an analytical perspective that places more emphasis on structural aspects than on the individual wills or choices of politicians, businessmen, scientists, and other powerholders, I argue that it is worth examining the influence of epistemological obstacles and the underdevelopment of knowledge that may explain the non-observability of the interrelations between social and ecological aspects under discussion, which has consequences both for understanding and tackling the problems. Specifically, it is important to review the presuppositions of the developmentalist traditions that prevail in the region in the light of current international debates about the unsustainability of the current model driven almost exclusively by the promotion of extractivist capitalism and the goal of economic growth. Thirdly, it is important to discuss the retreat of social and political thinking and action to the 'present', leading to the primacy of hodiecentric, a-historical analyses characteristic of neoclassical economics and the techno-sciences but that in recent decades have strongly permeated the production of knowledge in the social sciences and the political practices of progressive social sectors committed to the pursuit of social justice (Elias, 2009[1987]; see also Goudsblom, 1977). How would it be possible to recover the capacity for constructive criticism, with detachment from immediate realities, to develop with historical perspective analyses of and designs for the construction of desirable futures grounded on the political principle of equality? Fourthly, emphasis must be placed on the ethical dimension of the dilemmas and contradictions under discussion. This is particularly important in relation to the process of moral autonomization and the subordination of values to the instrumental dimension in the name of realism, efficiency, and pragmatism that characterizes theory and political practice in the interrelations between development and environmental policies (Sánchez Vázquez, 2003). Substantive democratic politics predicated on a comprehensive approach that address the high complexity of socio-ecological and political processes, in long-term perspective, require overcoming the apparently unsolvable contradictions between social and ecological equality. In turn, in the intellectual domain, meeting the challenge requires epistemological ruptures to achieve higher levels of inter- and transdisciplinary coordination in the production of knowledge about socio-natural interrelations. This is a process where the social sciences in Latin America and the Caribbean are summoned to play an urgent, crucial role for the future.

Notes

* Signs of potential regression in the process of regional integration can be dated back probably to 2012, with the start of the Venezuelan crisis, and the institutional coup d'état against President Fernando Lugo in Paraguay in the same year. However, the threat of regression was heightened with the political changes that affected Argentina and Brazil

since 2015, as these two countries are central to the process of regional integration. In Argentina, the election of President Mauricio Macri in October 2015 marks a clear departure with the past, as his government seems to favour the demise of political integration and the reduction of the process to mere economic integration. More significantly, the legal-institutional-mediatic *coup d'etat* that destituted Brazilian President Dilma Roussef in August 2016 delivered a momentary but potentially fatal blow to the processes of regional political integration, as the new government has swiftly acted to disengage from the process.

1   The Pacific Alliance openly promotes a market-oriented approach and rejects the emphasis on state intervention and the promotion of social policies that characterized MERCOSUR and ALBA countries during the recent period.
2   Serious public discussions of the implications of Fukushima's lessons for Latin America and the Caribbean are almost non-existent and limited to the campaigns of NGOs and groups of concerned scientists.

References

Alimonda, H. (ed.) (2002). *Ecología Política. Naturaleza, Sociedad y Utopía*. Buenos Aires: Consejo Latinoamericano de Ciencias Sociales (CLACSO).

Allan, J.A. (1998). 'Watersheds and problemsheds: Explaining the absence of armed conflict over water in the Middle East.' *Middle East Review of International Affairs* 2(1): 49–51.

Allan, J.A. (1999). *Israel and Water in the Framework of the Arab-Israeli conflict*. Occasional Paper N° 15. London: Water Issues Group, School of Oriental and African Studies (SOAS), University of London.

Allan, J.A. (2002). *The Middle East Water Question. Hydropolitics and the Global Economy*. London and New York: Tauris.

Austin, K.F. (2010). 'Soybean exports and deforestation from a world-systems perspective: A cross-national investigation of comparative disadvantage', *Sociological Quarterly* 51(3): 511–36.

Bank Information Center (2011). *Represa Hidroeléctrica Inambari*. Available at: www.bicusa.org/es/Project.10078.aspx (accessed October 2012).

Barri, F., and N. de Luca (2009). 'El valor de los servicios ambientales', *La Voz del Interior*, 15 May. Available at: http://archivo.lavoz.com.ar/nota.asp?nota_id=516571 (accessed August 2017).

BBC – British Broadcasting Corporation (2009). *UK set to take back Brazil Waste*, 19 July. Available at: http://news.bbc.co.uk/1/hi/8157745.stm (accessed February 2016).

Brailovsky, A.E. and Foguelman, D. (2007). *Memoria Verde. Historia Ecológica de la Argentina*. Buenos Aires: Editorial Sudamericana.

Brechin, S.R. and Kempton, W. (1994). 'Global environmentalism: A challenge to the postmaterialism thesis?' *Social Science Quarterly* 75(2): 245–69.

Brechin, S.R. and Kempton, W. (1997). 'Beyond postmaterialist values: National versus individual explanations of global environmentalism.' *Social Science Quarterly* 78(1): 16–20.

Bunker, S.G. (1984). 'Modes of extraction, unequal exchange, and the progressive under-development of an extreme periphery: The Brazilian Amazon, 1600–1980.' *American Journal of Sociology* 89(5): 1017–64.

Carruthers, D.V. (ed.) (2008). *Environmental Justice in Latin America. Problems, Promise and Practice.* Cambridge, MA, and London, UK: MIT Press.

Chapagain, A.K. and Hoekstra, A.Y. (2004a). *Water Footprints of Nations.* The Value of Water Research Report Series. Delft: UNESCO.

Chapagain, A.K. and Hoekstra, A.Y. (2004b). *Water Footprints of Nations.* Appendices. The Value of Water Research Report Series. Delft: UNESCO.

CLACSO – Consejo Latinoamericano de Ciencias Sociales (2016). *Portal of Observatories of Public Policies, Social Rights, and Citizenship in Latin America and the Caribbean.* Buenos Aires: CLACSO. Available at: www.clacso.net/portal_observatorios/institucional/institucional.asp (accessed February 2016).

Club of Rome (2012). *2012: 40 years Limits to Growth. What Was the Real Message of Limits to Growth?* Available at: www.clubofrome.org/ (accessed February 2016).

Collyns, D. (2015). 'Peru's maca boom could fall flat if China starts growing its own'. *The Guardian*, 9 February. Available at: www.theguardian.com/global-development/2015/feb/09/peru-maca-indigenous-root-china-biopiracy (accessed February 2016).

Cornia, G.A. (2010). 'Income distribution under Latin America's New Left regimes.' *Journal of Human Development and Capabilities* 11(1): 85–114.

Crenzel, E. (2011). *Memory of the Argentina Disappearances: The Political History of Nunca Más.* New York: Routledge.

Crosby, A.W. (2004). *Ecological Imperialism. The Biological Expansion of Europe, 900–1900.* Cambridge: Cambridge University Press.

da Rocha, H.J. (2012). 'Disintegrating integration: The trajectory of hydroelectric power projects from iirsa to local communities' (in Portuguese). *Revista Mural Internacional*, 3(1): 30–36. Available at: http://dx.doi.org/10.12957/rmi.2012.5910 (accessed February 2016).

De Vries, B. and Goudsblom, J. (2002). *Mappae Mundi. Humans and their Habitats in a Long-Term Socio-Ecological Perspective. Myths, Maps, and Models.* Amsterdam: Amsterdam University Press.

Delgado Wise, R.D. and Ortega Breña, M. (2006). 'Migration and imperialism: The Mexican workforce in the context of NAFTA.' *Latin American Perspectives* 33(2): 33–45.

Dunlap, R.E. and Mertig, A.G. (1997). 'Global environmental concern: An anomaly for postmaterialism.' *Social Science Quarterly* 78(1): 24–29.

ECLAC – Economic Commission for Latin America and the Caribbean (2009). *Social Panorama of Latin America 2008.* Santiago de Chile: Economic Commission for Latin America and the Caribbean.

Elias, N. (1978). *What is Sociology?* London: Hutchinson.

Elias, N. (2009 [1987]). 'The retreat of sociologists into the present', in *Essays III: On Sociology and the Humanities, Collected Works, Vol. 16.* Dublin: University College Dublin Press. pp. 107–26.

European Parliament (2010). *European Parliament Resolution of 5 May 2010 on a General Ban on the Use of Cyanide Mining Technologies in the European Union.* Luxembourg: European Parliament.

Falcon, W.P. and Fowler, C. (2002). 'Carving up the commons – emergence of a new international regime for germplasm development and transfer.' *Food Policy* 27(3): 197–222.

Farah, I. and Vasapollo, L. (eds) (2011). *Vivir Bien: ¿Paradigma no Capitalista?* La Paz, Bolivia: Higher University of San Andrés (CIDES-UMSA) and University of Rome 'La Sapienza'.

Financial Times (2015). 'Bolivia upgraded as economic growth quickens'. 15 July. Available at: www.ft.com/fastft/2015/07/15/fitch-upgrades-bolivia-economy-grows-under-morales/ (accessed February 2016).

Fischer-Kowalski, M. and Haberl, H. (eds) (2007). *Socioecological Transitions and Global Change. Trajectories of Social Metabolism and Land Use.* Cheltenham, Gloucestershire, UK: Edward Elgar Publishing.

Fox, M. (2009). *Following the Trail of Toxic Trash.* New York and Bonn: Global Policy Forum, 13 August 2013. Available at: www.globalpolicy.org/globalization/cases-of-globalization/48037-following-the-trail-of-toxic-trash.html (accessed February 2016).

Gammage, S. (2006). 'Exporting people and recruiting remittances: A development strategy for El Salvador?' *Latin American Perspectives* 33(6): 75–100.

Goudsblom, J. (1977). *Sociology in the Balance: A Critical Essay.* Oxford: Wiley-Blackwell.

Gudynas, E. (2011). 'Buen Vivir: Germinando alternativas al desarrollo.' *América Latina en Movimiento* 462: 1–20.

Guha, R. and Martínez-Alier, J. (1997). *Varieties of Environmentalism. Essays North and South.* London: Earthscan.

Helfrich, S. (ed.) (2002). *La Vida en Venta.* El Salvador: Fundación Heinrich Böll Editions.

Hoekstra, A.Y. (2006). *The Global Dimension of Water Governance: Nine Reasons for Global Arrangements in order to Cope with Local Water Problems*, The Value of Water Research Report Series. Delft: UNESCO.

Hoekstra, A.Y. (2007). *Human Appropriation of Natural Capital: Comparing Ecological Footprint and Water Footprint Analysis*, The Value of Water Research Report Series. Delft: UNESCO.

Hornborg, A. (1998). 'Towards an ecological theory of unequal exchange: Articulating world system theory and ecological economics.' *Ecological Economics* 25: 127–36.

Inglehart, R. (1971). 'The silent revolution in Europe: Intergenerational change in post-industrial societies.' *The American Political Science Review* 65(4): 991–1017.

Jasanoff, S. (2006). 'Biotechnology and Empire: The Global Power of Seeds and Science.' *Osiris* 21(1): 273–92.

Jorgenson, A.K. and Clark, B. (2009). 'The economy, military, and ecologically unequal exchange relationships in comparative perspective: A panel study of the ecological footprints of nations, 1975–2000.' *Social Problems* 56(4): 621–46.

Kuecker, G.D. (2007). 'Fighting for the Forests: Grassroots Resistance to Mining in Northern Ecuador.' *Latin American Perspectives* 34(2): 94–107.

La Voz del Interior (2012). 'La Defensoría le pide a Córdoba que cambie su ley de bosques'. *La Voz del Interior*, 14 January. Cordoba, Argentina.

Latta, A. and Ibarra, V. (eds.) (2015). *Water Megaprojects and Epistemological Violence* (in English and Spanish), WATERLAT-GOBACIT Working Papers 2(2). Newcastle upon Tyne, UK, Waterloo, ON, Canada, and Mexico City. Available at: http://waterlat.org/WPapers/WPSATAM22.pdf (accessed February 2016).

López-Calva, L.F. and Lustig, N.C. (eds) (2010). *Declining Inequality in Latin America. A Decade of Progress?* New York: Brookings Institution Press and PNUD.

Martinez-Alier, J. (2002). *The Environmentalism of the Poor. A Study of Ecological Conflicts and Valuation.* Cheltenham, UK, and Northampton, MA: Edward Elgar.

Martínez-Alier, J. and Olivares, A. (2003). *¿Quién debe a Quién? Deuda Externa y Deuda Ecológica.* Barcelona: Editorial Icaria.

Martins, H. (1996). *Hegel, Texas e outros Ensaios de Teoria Social.* Lisbon: Século XXI.

Martins, H. (1998a). 'O deus dos artefatos: Sua vida, sua morte', in H. Reis de Araújo (ed.), *Tecnociência e Cultura. Ensaios sobre o Tempo Presente.* Sao Paulo: Estação Liberdade. pp. 149–68.

Martins, H. (1998b). 'Risco, incerteza e escatologia. Reflexões sobre o experimentum mundi tecnológico em curso (I).' *Episteme* 1(1): 99–121.

Martins, H. (1998c). 'Risco, incerteza e escatologia. Reflexões sobre o experimentum mundi tecnológico em curso (II).' *Episteme* 1(2): 41–75.

McNeill, J. (2000). *Something New under the Sun. An Environmental History of the Twentieth Century.* London: Penguin.

Meadows, D.H., Meadows, D.L., Randers, J. and Behrens III, W.W. (1972). *The Limits to Growth.* Washington, DC: Potomac Associates, New American Library.

Mgbeoji, I. (2006). *Global Biopiracy: Patents, Plants, and Indigenous Knowledge.* Vancouver and Toronto: UCB Press.

Moody's Global Credit Research (2015) *Bolivia's Ba3 Rating Reflects Strong Growth and Gradual Adjustment to the Drop in Oil Prices.* Moody's, 28 October. Available at: www.moodys.com/research/Moodys-Bolivias-Ba3-rating-reflects-strong-growth-and-gradual-adjustment--PR_337563# (accessed February 2016).

Muradian, R., O'Connor, M. and Martínez-Alier, J. (2002). 'Embodied pollution in trade: Estimating the environmental load displacement of industrialized countries.' *Ecological Economics* 41(1): 51–67.

Nelson, G.C. and Robertson, R.D. (2008). 'Green gold or green wash: Environmental consequences of biofuels in the developing world.' *Review of Agricultural Economics* 30(3): 517–29.

Newell, P. (2009). 'Bio-hegemony: The political economy of agricultural biotechnology in Argentina.' *Journal of Latin American Studies* 41(1): 27–57.

O'Connor, J. (1998). *Natural Causes. Essays in Ecological Marxism.* New York: Guilford Press.

Ochoa, H. (ed.) (2015). *Imposition, Resistance, and Alternatives in the Face of an Inter-regional Water Crisis in Mexico: El Zapotillo Project* (in Spanish), WATERLAT-GOBACIT Working Papers 2(1). Newcastle upon Tyne, UK, and Guadalajara, Mexico. Available at: http://waterlat.org/WPapers/WPSATCTH21.pdf (accessed February 2016).

OECD – Organisation for Economic Co-operation and Development (2010). *Tackling Inequalities in Brazil, China, India and South Africa.* Paris: OECD Publishing.

O'Hagan, E.M. (2014). 'Evo Morales has proved that socialism doesn't damage economies'. *The Guardian*, 14 October. Available at: www.theguardian.com/commentisfree/2014/oct/14/evo-morales-reelected-socialism-doesnt-damage-economies-bolivia (accessed February 2016).

Peritore, N.P. and Niles, L.B. (1992). 'El surgimiento del cartel biotecnológico.' *Revista Mexicana de Sociología* 54(2): 101–31.

Pieck, S.K. (2011). 'Beyond postdevelopment: Civic responses to regional integration in the Amazon.' *Journal of Cultural Geography* 28(1): 179–202.

Rice, J. (2007a). 'Ecological unequal exchange: Consumption, equity, and unsustainable structural relationships within the global economy.' *International Journal of Comparative Sociology* 48(1): 43–72.

Rice, J. (2007b). 'Ecological unequal exchange: International trade and uneven utilization of environmental space in the world system.' *Social Forces* 85(3): 1369–92.

Rice, J. (2009). 'North-South relations and the ecological debt: Asserting a counter-hegemonic discourse.' *Critical Sociology* 35(2): 225–52.

Roberts, J.T. and Parks, B.C. (2007). 'Fueling injustice: Globalization, ecologically unequal exchange and climate change.' *Globalizations* 4(2): 193–210.

Robinson, D.F. (2010). *Confronting Biopiracy: Challenges, Cases and International Debates*. Abingdon, UK, and New York: Earthscan.

Sánchez Vázquez, A. (2003). *A Tiempo y Destiempo. Una Antología*. Mexico City: Fondo de Cultura Económica.

Schnaiberg, A. (1980). *The Environment: From Surplus to Scarcity*. New York: Oxford University Press.

Schnaiberg, A. and Gould, K.A. (1994). *Environment and Society: The Enduring Conflict*. New York: St. Martin's Press.

Shiva, V. (1997). *Biopiracy: The Plunder of Nature and Knowledge*. Boston, MA: South End Pres.

Sibaud, P. (2012). *Opening Pandora's Box. The New Wave of Land Grabbing by the Extracting Industries and the Devastating Impact on Earth*. London: The Gaia Foundation.

Simms, A. (2009). *Ecological Debt: Global Warming and the Wealth of Nations*. London: Pluto Press.

Suárez Salazar, L. and Ortega Breña, M. (2007). 'The new pan-American order: The crisis and reconstitution of the US system of global domination.' *Latin American Perspectives* 34(1): 102–11.

Svampa, M. and Antonelli, M.A. (eds) (2009). *Minería Transnacional, Narrativas del Desarrollo y Resistencias Sociales*. Buenos Aires: Biblos.

Taylor, J. (1994). 'The challenge of sustainable development.' *Regulation* 17(1): 35–50.

Torres Espinoza, L.F. (2012). 'Exploring environmental governance in the Peruvian Amazon: Development, environment and indigenous peoples in the case of the Pakitzapango dam project', MA dissertation in Interdisciplinary Latin American Studies, Newcastle University, UK. A version of this work was published in Spanish in 2013 as 'Estado, organizaciones indígenas y movimientos ambientalistas: Un estudio de la gobernanza ambiental en la Amazonía peruana desde el proyecto "Pakitzapango" en el Río Ene', available at the Food and Agriculture Organization (FAO)'s Knowledge Platform on Family Agriculture. Available at: www.fao.org/family-farming/detail/es/c/328638/ (accessed February 2016).

UNEP – United Nations Environment Programme (2011). *Decoupling Natural Resource Use and Environmental Impacts from Economic Growth*, A Report of the Working Group on Decoupling to the International Resource Panel. Paris: UNEP.

Urkidi Azkarraga, L. (2010). 'Environmental justice and the politics of scale in Latin American social movements against gold mining. The cases of Pascua-Lama in Chile and Marlin in Guatemala', PhD thesis in Environmental Sciences, Institute of Environmental Sciences and Technology, University of Barcelona.

Valencio, N. (ed.) (2015). *Water-related Disasters: From Trans-scale Challenges to Interpretative Multivocality* (in Portuguese and Spanish), WATERLAT-GOBACIT Working Papers 1(1). Newcastle upon Tyne and Sao Paulo, Brazil, September. Available at: http://waterlat.org/WPapers/WPSATADNo1.pdf (accessed February 2016).

Van Dijck, P. (2013). *The Impact of the IIRSA Road Infrastructure Programme on Amazonia*. London: Routledge.

Van Dijck, P. and den Haak, S. (2007). *Troublesome Construction. IIRSA and Public-Private Partnerships in Road Infrastructure*. Amsterdam: Center for Latin American Studies and Documentation (CEDLA).

Vecchio, R. (2007). 'Bioprospecting: Who has rights to nature's cures?', *The Seattle Times*, 12 January. Available at: www.seattletimes.com/nation-world/bioprospecting-who-has-rights-to-natures-cures/ (accessed February 2016).

Zhouri, A. and Laschefski, K. (eds) (2010). *Desenvolvimento e Conflitos Ambientais*. Belo Horizonte: Editora UFMG.

Index